Reading Science

'. . . puts down a marker for the debate in this field. It gathers up work done over the last two decades or so, in Australia, in the US and in the UK, and presents it in a generous, theoretically integrative framework. At the same time it pushes strongly into quite new areas; it will be a point of reference and become a point of departure.'

Gunther Kress, *Institute of Education, University of London*

Reading Science is a unique collection which brings together the most recent work of leading scholars in linguistics, rhetoric, critical theory and education. It looks at the distinctive language of science and tech-nology and the role it plays in building up scientific understandings of the world and explores this language in a range of contexts, from research and industry to education, popular science writing and science fiction.

This book is unique in its interdisciplinary approach; contributors examine science discourse from a number of differing perspectives, drawing on new rhetoric, functional linguistics and critical theory. This is the first time this range of perspectives has been brought together in a single volume and enables a more holistic perspective on the role of science discourse in our culture.

Reading Science is also the first book to include analysis of the role of images in science writing and to consider the importance of reading science discourse as multi-modal text.

The internationally renowned contributors include M.A.K. Halliday, Charles Bazerman, Jay Lemke and Frances Christie.

J.R. Martin is currently Associate Professor of Linguistics at the University of Sydney. His publications include *Writing Science* (with M.A.K. Halliday) and *Working with Functional Grammar* (with C. Matthiessen and C. Painter). **Robert Veel** is co-ordinator of Teacher Professional Development and Languages at the Centre for Continuing Education, University of Sydney.

Reading Science

Critical and functional perspectives on
discourses of science

Edited by J.R. Martin and Robert Veel

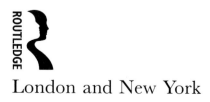

London and New York

First published 1998 by Routledge
11 New Fetter Lane, London EC4P 4EE

Simultaneously published in the USA and Canada
by Routledge
29 West 35th Street, New York, NY 10001

© 1998 J.R. Martin and Robert Veel

Typeset in Baskerville by
J&L Composition Ltd, Filey North Yorkshire
Printed and bound in Great Britain by
Biddles Ltd., Guildford and King's Lynn

British Library Cataloguing in Publication Data
A catalogue record for this book is available from the British Library

Library of Congress Cataloguing in Publication Data
Martin, J.R.
    Reading Science: critical and functional perspectives on
  discourses of science / J.R. Martin and Robert Veel.
        p.   cm.
    Includes bibliographical references.
    1. Science–Study and teaching–Methodology. 2. Technology–Study
and teaching–Methodology. 3. Discourse analysis. 4. Technical
writing. 5. Rhetoric. I. Veel, Robert, 1962– . II. Title.
Q181.M1777   1998
501'.4–dc21
                                                          97-21777
                                                               CIP

ISBN 0–415–16789–2 (hbk.)
ISBN 0–415–16790–6 (pbk.)

Contents

List of figures

List of tables

List of contributors

Charles Bazerman is Professor of English and Education at the University of California, Santa Barbara, USA.

Frances Christie is Research Professor at the Department of Language and Literacy Education, University of Melbourne, Australia.

Anne Cranny-Francis is Associate Professor of English at Macquarie University, New South Wales, Australia.

Gillian Fuller teaches semiotics and communication at the University of New South Wales, Australia.

M.A.K. Halliday is Emeritus Professor of Linguistics at the University of Sydney, Australia.

Jay Lemke is Professor of Science Education at Brooklyn College, New York, USA.

J.R. Martin is Associate Professor of Linguistics at the University of Sydney, Australia.

C.M.I.M. Matthiessen is Associate Professor of Linguistics at Macquarie University, New South Wales, Australia.

David Rose teaches and researches with TAFE in Adelaide, Australia.

Robert Veel is co-ordinator of Teacher Professional Development and Languages at the Centre for Continuing Education, University of Sydney, Australia.

P.R.R. White is a linguist working primarily in the areas of genre modelling, interpersonal semantics and functional varieties of language.

Peter Wignell is a lecturer in Education at the Northern Territory University, Australia.

Part I
Discourse on science

1 Discourses of science
Recontextualisation, genesis, intertextuality and hegemony

J.R. Martin

The impetus for this particular assembly of papers comes from research conducted by Halliday, Martin and their colleagues in and around the Department of Linguistics at the University of Sydney through the 1980s. During this period, Halliday focused his attention on the evolution of English science discourse in professional research contexts, while Martin was more concerned with the development of science literacy in primary and secondary schools. In 1993, the publication of a collection of this work in Europe and North America (Halliday and Martin's *Writing Science: Literacy and discursive power*) made their research available to a wider audience. In response to a range of feedback from colleagues in Australia and around the world it seemed appropriate in 1994 to take advantage of the visits of Charles Bazerman and Jay Lemke to Australia and organise a workshop focusing on issues arising from a range of contemporary readings of science discourse. Lemke, of course, had been collaborating with Halliday and Martin since the late 1970s – both with respect to science education and various questions having to do with semiotic theory and text semantics. Only a few Australian linguists on the other hand had an opportunity to work closely with Bazerman, inspiring though his complementary work on the social formation of Newton's discourse had been.

In the event a two-day invitational workshop was held in July 1994 when Bazerman, Halliday and Lemke were available. At that time Martin was involved in the supervision of a range of research into science discourse in secondary school, science-based industry and popular culture – and a number of the researchers involved in this work presented at the workshop. In addition, Frances Christie reported on her investigation of science pedagogy in primary school classrooms. Approximately fifty colleagues from across Australia participated in the discussions.

Obviously the richly textured dialogue that ensued was read and enjoyed in different ways by the various participants. By way of introducing the papers in this volume, I will focus on just four of the themes which have resonated through our networks since that time: recontextualisation, semogenesis, intertextuality and hegemony.

1   RECONTEXTUALISATION

Science discourse is one of those concerns which functional linguists find
interesting and which an unusually wide range of researchers finds
interesting too. Understandably then, one of the most common reactions
to presentations over the years has been, 'Yes, but what about "x" (where
"x" is something that hadn't been considered)?' Both Halliday and
Martin had encountered this reaction frequently in the 1980s. For Halliday it was received as, 'Yes, but what do we do with these ideas; what do
we actually do in the classroom?'; for Martin, it was, 'Yes, but what
actually happens outside the classroom; what do scientists really do?' At
least we had each other to relay the questions to. But beyond this it was
clear that the work of one school of functional linguistics on relatively
canonical science research and education was limited in significant ways.

For one thing, Halliday and Martin were linguists, albeit with wide-
ranging concerns. Their tools for analysis were for the most part based
on functional grammar (Halliday 1985/1994) and discourse analysis
(Martin 1992) – accompanied by excursions into mode (e.g. Halliday
1985/1989) and genre (e.g. Martin 1985/1989). This obviously foregrounds the linguistic over the social in the sense that the social practice
of science is interpreted through language – through grammar and text
structure in particular. The natural complement to a perspective of this
kind is an approach that begins with the social, especially where the
social is interpreted through discourse. In Australia, work on literacy in
schools and on language and gender had already opened up an important dialogue between functional linguistics and contemporary critical
theory (as exemplified in Cope and Kalantzis 1993; the Australian
journal *Social Semiotics* was founded to promote this negotiation). Rhetoric however, as practised in North America, is a voice less often heard in
Australia – and so Bazerman's perspective was an especially valuable
one. One of the important innovations in this book has been to recontextualise Halliday and Martin's linguistic perspective with respect to
work in rhetoric and critical theory (see especially Chapters 2, 3 and 4).

Another feature of Halliday and Martin's work which stood in need of
recontextualisation was their focus on canonical science discourse. For
Halliday this was the result of reconstructing an evolutionary trajectory
for science discourse in English. As chaos theory has taught us, a project
of this kind, however rewarding, tends to draw attention away from side
currents and dead ends, and thus tends to idealise certain kinds of
science discourse as mainstream. It seemed important to recontextualise
Halliday's 'grand narrative' with something of the mess and mush of
scientific goings-on. For Martin, the focus on the canonical had to do
with analysing science discourse in educational contexts where for the
most part canonical science discourse is what students are expected to
learn. This kind of focus, however rewarding, raises a question as to

whether other types of science discourse might be more accessible to students from other than mainstream backgrounds, and might thus provide a way into scientific practices that canonical science discourse precludes. And it raises a further question as to the nature of the relation between science discourse in the community and science discourse as it is deployed for pedagogic purposes in schools. Consequently, it was important in this volume to recontextualise Halliday and Martin's work by looking at science discourse across a broad range of social contexts, including popular science writing (Chapter 3) and science fiction (Chapter 4), its technological deployment in science industry (Chapters 9 and 10), and its influence on social science (Chapter 11) and cognitive science (Chapter 12); and to consider more carefully the recontextualisation of science as pedagogic discourse in primary (Chapter 7) and secondary (Chapter 6) schools.

Finally, while the role of images was addressed in passing here and there in Martin's work, the complementarity of verbiage and image in shaping science discourse was never properly developed. By the 1990s, Kress and van Leeuwen (1996/1990) had inspired some concern with the role of photographs in science texts, and their unpublished mimeo on diagrams was opening up work on figures in relation to text (van Leeuwen and Humphrey 1996, Chapter 6 this volume). Lemke's work on science discourse as multi-modal text thus represents a crucial recontextualisation of Halliday and Martin's language-focused account (see also Ochs *et al.* 1996 on language, image and activity in science discourse).

This book is by no means the last word as far as theoretical and descriptive recontextualisation is concerned. But it does demonstrate the productivity of opening up dialogue – across a range of socially and linguistically informed theoretical perspectives, across a range of institutional sites where science discourse is practiced, and across the language and image modalities through which science discourse is construed.

2 SEMOGENESIS

Another theme which the papers in this volume are designed to promote is that of language change – where this is interpreted broadly to encompass change at all levels of language, including the evolution of new forms of discourse. As a functional linguist, Halliday has been particularly concerned with semantic change (semogenesis as he terms it), and this is reflected in his description of the evolution of scientific English. Critically, his work demonstrates that changes in discourse function co-vary with changes in the grammatical resources a language makes available to construe discourse. Specifically, he outlined the ways in which nominalisation evolved as a resource for construing scientific reality as a world of logical relations among abstract entities.

In Halliday's theory, research into semogenesis is organised according to the time frame from which change is viewed. The smallest time frame orients to change in terms of the processes by which text unfolds (logogenesis). If we broaden this time frame to take the lifetime of individual members of the species into account we reorient to change in terms of language development (ontogenesis). Beyond this, if we take a multigenerational perspective, we reorient to change in terms of cultural evolution (phylogenesis). In these terms, the focus of Halliday's research into the evolution of scientific discourse was phylogenetic; the focus of Martin's work (also Lemke 1990) on learning science in schools was ontogenetic; and both these strands of research depended on close readings of individual science texts as they unfold (logogenesis). These three time frames are summarised in Table 1.1.

With respect to the development of resources for nominalised discourse, Halliday suggests an important homology across the time frames – namely, that nominalised discourse tends to develop out of more concrete discourse in the history of science, in the process of science education and in science texts themselves. Obviously, for linguists, the longer the time frame, the more daunting the research – so for the most part functional linguistic research has focused on text as process (e.g. Halliday and Hasan 1976, Martin 1992). Pioneering work on language development from a functional perspective is found in Halliday 1975 and Painter 1984. Aside from Halliday's work on scientific discourse, and some suggestive work by the Prague School on intellectualisation (cf. Gonzalez 1988), functional linguists have devoted little productive attention to phylogenesis.

Critical theory and rhetoric on the other hand are far more comfortable with longer time frames, since their tools of analysis facilitate analysis across large numbers of long texts. Where this work has been influenced by Bakhtin it is especially relevant to functional linguists' concerns. Critical feminist studies (e.g. Cranny-Francis 1990) of the evolution of genre fiction, for example, consider entire genres (such as science fiction, romance, fantasy) in relation to entire bodies of work by several authors. Similarly, the scope of Bazerman's 1988 study of Newton's discourse and its social context ranges well beyond that attempted by Halliday.

Table 1.1 Time frames for semogenesis

logogenesis	'instantiation of the text/process'	**unfolding**
ontogenesis	'development of the individual'	**growth**
phylogenesis	'expansion of the culture'	**evolution**

As Halliday and Matthiessen (in press) have commented, phylogenesis provides the environment for ontogenesis which in turn provides the environment for logogenesis; conversely, logogenesis provides the material for ontogenesis which in turn provides the material for phylogenesis. Thus shunting across time frames is the key to a richer interpretation of semantic change – and the papers in this volume range across time frames in ways that are suggestive of a richer interpretation of science discourse. Work by Rose and Veel in particular on the correlation between levels of achievement in science education and levels of employment in science industry in the context of the change from Fordist to post-Fordist industrial organisation are especially revealing as far as the interaction of ontogenetic and phylogenetic time frames are concerned. Christie explores in some detail the relation of logogenesis (her curriculum genre) to ontogenesis (learning science). And a range of papers look in one way or another at the negotiation among discourses within a text (logogenesis) that have given birth to new fields (science fiction – Cranny-Francis; popular science – Fuller; social science – Wignell; cognitive science – Matthiessen) in much the way that technology and mathematics gave birth to science discourse in Halliday's account. In this respect, White's accounts of technological discourse as a discourse in its own right is of special interest.

One of the outstanding issues that remains to be explored is Halliday's suggestion that as far as developing nominalising linguistic resources for abstract discourse is concerned (what he terms ideational metaphor; Halliday 1985/1994), for English science discourse has been the cutting edge. This implies that the abstract discourses of the humanities are in some sense derived from scientific discourses, in ways we do not yet understand, and that our abstract discourses for regulating populations through business and government (bureaucratic discourse) are similarly dependent on borrowed resources for abstraction. I suspect that contemporary critical and linguistic discourses need to evolve a little before we feel confident about an answer to these questions.

3 INTERTEXTUALITY

Of continuing interest in the context of this focus on language change has been the issue of what has come to be known as intertextuality and how it is modelled in functional linguistics and critical theory. The basic complementarity of approaches here has to do with reactions to Saussure's langue/parole opposition, along two main trajectories (which I will associate here with Halliday and Bakhtin respectively). Along one trajectory, Halliday and his colleagues have extended a tradition that reinterprets langue/parole as the relation between potential and actual (technically between system and text). In this tradition, which derives from Firth and Hjelmslev, parole is reread as the instantiation of language – the manifestation of a culture's linguistic meaning potential in text. Systemic functional linguists have been especially concerned with modelling this meaning potential as networks of choice that function as a kind of phylogenetic record of the meanings that are relevant to (or perhaps better, immanent in) any particular act of speaking or writing. Structural descriptions in the model are designed to relate, automatically and explicitly, specific texts to choices in the system which were not selected but might have been (for discussion see Halliday and Martin 1993, Eggins 1994). Important work on genre as system is reported in Chapter 9 (for further work on generic relations see the collection of papers in Christie and Martin 1997).

The manifestation of system in text in Halliday's model is referred to as instantiation – which has to be interpreted as a dialectical process, since instantiation continually manifests, construes and reconstrues the meaning potential of a culture. Following Matthiessen (mimeo) we can productively interpret instantiation as a cline – a gradual foreclosing of options until those selected for a particular text are specified. Register and genre theory, for example, (as outlined in Eggins and Martin in press) is designed to make predictions about which meanings of the total meaning potential of a language are at risk in particular contexts of situation. Narrowing this, we might consider the meanings taken up across a group of texts instantiating one or another register or genre (Firth's 'generalised actual'). Finally, there is what Matthiessen refers to as the instantial system – the set of meanings manifested in a specific text. The challenge is to build a model which reads instantiation as a two-way process, so that the system can be seen to rework itself (to evolve) as required through the momenta of innumerable instantiations. Research towards a model of this kind is reported in Halliday 1991, 1992 a, b, c, 1993a, b, Nesbitt and Plum 1988 (see also Lemke 1995 and the many references to his related work cited therein).

Along the other trajectory, Bakhtin, and the critical theorists influenced by this work, rejected the idealisation and formalism involved in Saussure's langue/parole distinction and developed models which focused on the heteroglossic nature of cultures and the dialogism inherent in texts. Kristeva (e.g. 1986) developed the term intertextuality by way of interpreting Bakhtin's insistence on the multivoiced nature of texts and the senses in which they must be read in relation to other texts. Within this tradition, approaches which outline explicit frameworks for tracking intertextual relations (e.g. Kress 1985/1989 on discourse, narrative and genre, Fairclough 1992 on inter- and intra-textual relations) have been particularly fertile as far as opening up dialogue between the two trajectories is concerned (see especially Chapters 3 and 4 this volume).

What these two trajectories share is a concern with textualisation as the site of semiotic and thus cultural change. At the level of discourse this foregrounds the question of mixed texts – of instances which manifest novel combinations of meanings (e.g. early science discourse in relation to the discourses of technology and mathematics). How is it, for example, that detective fiction (Poe) and science fiction (Shelley) grow out of Gothic – cf. Cranny-Francis 1990; does the 'western' derive from the detective fiction of Conan Doyle? And how is it that over time what once seemed a novel mix of voices (e.g. Conan Doyle's Pinkerton detectives sleuthing in America's Wild West) blends seamlessly into a canonical genre, effacing its own history to the point where deconstruction is required to uncover its phylogenetic lineage?

The main difference between the two trajectories has to do with formalisation. The functional linguistics tradition has been strongly influenced by European structuralism, and attempts to describe (some might argue, prescribe) the meaning potential of a culture as precisely as possible; for a useful discussion of the techniques deployed see Eggins 1994, Martin and Matthiessen 1991, Matthiessen 1995. At its worst, this perspective foregrounds the system over the instance to the extent that the processes whereby instantiation reconstrues the system are obscured. The critical perspective on the other hand has stronger roots in the humanities (so is less formal), and more experience in reading texts, especially longer texts at the cutting edge of a culture's meaning potential (Bakhtin himself worked in detail on the history of the novel). At its worst, this perspective foregrounds the instance and its relation to other extant instances, so much so that the relation of the instance to the meaning potential of the culture as a whole is obscured – keeping in mind that only a tiny fraction of the texts our culture could have manifested at any point in its genesis were ever manifested, and that of those manifested, the vast majority were spoken and have thus provided us with no tangible record. Dialogue across trajectories is the best insurance against these missteps, as is well exemplified in the chapters following (for exemplary negotiations see also Thibault 1991, Lemke 1995).

I should perhaps caution here that we need to take care how we position functional linguistic and critical trajectories as complementarities if we wish to encourage dialogue. The least helpful positioning of which I am aware is one which glosses functional linguists as concerned with the textual, and critical theorists as concerned with the social, cultural and political. I find this misleading, since the social, cultural and political can only be studied through their instantiation as texts, across a range of modalities, including language, image, music, activity, etc. and their multimodal assemblages. The gap between textual and social analysis is one that needs closing, as linguists get better at formalising readings of more and longer texts at deeper levels of abstraction and as critical theorists get better at focusing their readings on the details of instantiation (Fairclough 1992, 1995, Iedema *et al.* 1994, Iedema

1995, Lee 1996, Lemke 1995, Rose *et al.* 1992, Thibault 1991 exemplify the kind of bridging I have in mind here). Recently the transdisciplinary fields of social semiotics (in Australia) and critical discourse analysis (in Europe) have emerged to address these concerns.

4   HEGEMONY

The final theme I would like to consider briefly here is that of hegemony – in this context, the question of the role of science discourse as far as the distribution of discursive power in Western culture is concerned. There is no doubt that the place of science discourse is a privileged one, however stigmatised in specific contexts of resistance (e.g. certain feminist and post-colonial discourse or certain science teaching classrooms), and however uncertain the channels of funding for pure research in the future. What seems at times to be at issue (e.g. Lee 1993, 1996, Luke 1996) is a question as to whether this privileged position is based on power or status. In other words, is the prestige of science discourse like the prestige of a standard dialect – of say London and environs phonology, morphology and syntax in the history of British English? Is it like the question of accent and attitude, so that if we change the way in which people evaluate the accent its power recedes? Alternatively, is the prestige of science discourse based on the functions it serves, where the functionality can be measured in terms of economic and political parameters and the values attached to those parameters by mainstream groups in the culture? In this case, in order to change people's attitudes it is necessary to renovate the economic and political structure of a society as a whole; changing how people feel about the discourse will not, in itself, greatly diminish the discourse's power.

Considering the genesis of science discourse, Halliday addresses this issue of power and status as follows:

> A newly evolving register is always functional in its context (whether the context itself is one of consensus or conflict); the language may become ritualised, but it cannot start that way, because to become ritualised a feature must first acquire value, and it can acquire value only by being functional.

(Halliday and Martin 1993: 68)

Halliday, in other words, makes the strong claim that discourses do not arise for reasons of status (lawyers, for example, did not invent legal English in order to be associated with a privileged discourse). Rather, Halliday suggests, discourses evolve for functional reasons, having to do with what these can accomplish in newly emerging social contexts, which they take part in fashioning. The more functional the discourse in those contexts, the more status it will accrue – perhaps to the point where the discourse becomes ritualised, that is to say, used in contexts where it is not functional but used simply for reasons of status. In this form discourses may hang around in a culture long after the contexts motivating their genesis have disappeared (as happened, arguably, in the case of certain registers of Latin in the Roman Catholic church; and as happens, the Plain English movement would argue, with certain registers of administrative discourse in relation to consumers' needs).

The power of science discourse (and only secondarily its status) no doubt derives from the ever-growing control it affords over the material environment (over physical and biological resources) – through technology. This technological control of the environment lies at the heart of capitalism, in both its Fordist and post-Fordist manifestations (Harvey 1989, Rose *et al.* 1992), and thus at the heart of the distribution of power in western society – a commanding position to say the least. Beyond this, Halliday implies that the functionality of its discourse has spread across disciplines and on to the realms of government and administration where social in addition to material resources have to be controlled (see Martin 1993, Iedema 1995 for discussion). On my reading, the work of Bazerman on Newton's discourse confirms this picture; Newton's discourse emerged and evolved in response to the social conditions in which he attempted to communicate his research. By no means was it a discourse he assumed for reasons of status; rather it was a discourse he developed to get on with his work, communally, as one scientist among others.

Some of course would argue that the technology science has made possible and the use to which government and industry have put it have got out of hand – to the point where science-engendered technology has made the future of human and other forms of life on the planet quite uncertain (Halliday 1993b). Fortunately for the prestige of science, having gotten us into the mess it has an integral role to play in getting us back out.

If Halliday is correct, and I believe available evidence confirms his position, then the implications for science education and the role of 'other' seem clear. On the one hand, educational institutions have a responsibility for making available canonical science resources, preferably to a wider range of consumers than in the past, and preferably with explicit deconstruction of the nature of science discourse and critique of its circumscriptions (Veel 1997). On the other hand, challenging the power of science discourse is going to be a lot harder than challenging the status of standard accents and promoting non-standard ones. Challenging the power of science discourse is tantamount to challenging the distribution of economic and governmental power in the society as a whole, so woven is it into the fabric of western hegemony. If feminist renovations of genre fiction are any guide, than this challenge is better mounted from within science discourse than without, through subtle and not so subtle processes of subversion and opposition by non-male, non-Anglo, non-middle-class scientists who recontextualise science discourse by involving it in new social practices. In short, there is little point in dismissing science discourse as technicist and masculinist or whatever; it has to be engaged with and reworked, at least in part from the inside . . . much as this book has attempted to rework our understandings of science discourse and the role it plays and could play in our lives.

REFERENCES

Bazerman, C. 1988. *Shaping Written Knowledge: The genre and activity of the experimental article in science.* Madison, WI: University of Wisconsin Press (Rhetoric of the Human Sciences).

Christie, F. and J.R. Martin 1997. *Genres and Institutions: Social processes in the workplace and school.* London: Cassell (Open Linguistics Series).

Cope, W. and M. Kalantzis (eds) 1993. *The Powers of Literacy: A genre approach to teaching literacy.* London: Falmer (Critical Perspectives on Literacy and Education) and Pittsburgh, PA: University of Pittsburgh Press (Pittsburgh Series in Composition, Literacy, and Culture).

Cranny-Francis, A. 1990. *Feminist Fiction: Feminist uses of generic fiction.* Cambridge: Polity.

Cranny-Francis, A. and J.R. Martin 1991. Contratextuality: the poetics of subversion. F. Christie (ed.) *Social Processes in Education: Proceedings of the First Australian Systemic Network Conference, Deakin University, January 1990.* Darwin: Centre for Studies of Language in Education, Northern Territory University. 286–344.

Cranny-Francis, A. and J.R. Martin 1993. Making new meanings: Literary and linguistic perspectives on the function of genre in textual practice. *English in Australia* 105. 30–44.

Eggins, S. 1994. *An Introduction to Systemic Functional Linguistics.* London: Pinter.

Eggins, S. and J.R. Martin. forthcoming. Genres and registers of discourse. T.A. van Dijk (ed.) *Discourse as Structure and Process.* London: Sage (Discourse Studies: a multidisciplinary introduction. Vol I). 230–256.

Fairclough, N. 1992. *Discourse and Social Change.* Cambridge: Polity.

Fairclough, N. 1995. *Critical Discourse Analysis: The critical study of language.* London: Longman (Language in Social Life).

Gonzalez, A. 1988. The intellectualisation of Filipino – agendas for the twenty-first century. *Philippine Journal of Linguistics* 19.2 (Special Issue: setting a research agenda for the intellectualisation of Filipino – a theoretical base for teacher training). 3–6.

Halliday, M.A.K. 1975. *Learning How to Mean: Explorations in the development of language.* London: Edward Arnold (Explorations in Languuge Study).

Halliday, M.A.K. 1985. *Introduction to Functional Grammar.* London: Edward Arnold. (second edition, with annotated further readings, and an index, 1994).

Halliday, M.A.K. 1985. *Spoken and Written Language.* Geelong: Deakin University Press (republished by Oxford University Press 1989).

Halliday, M.A.K. 1991. Towards probabilistic interpretations. E. Ventola (ed.) *Functional and Systemic Linguistics: Approaches and uses.* Berlin: Mouton de Gruyter (Trends in Linguistics Studies and Monographs 55). 39–61.

Halliday, M.A.K. 1992a. How do you mean? M. Davies and L. Ravelli (eds) *Recent Advances in Systemic Linguistics.* London: Pinter (Open Linguistics Series). 20–35.

Halliday, M.A.K. 1992b. Language as system and language as instance: The corpus as a theoretical construct. J. Svartvik (ed.) *Directions in Corpus Linguistics: Proceedings of Nobel Symposium 82, Stockholm, 4–8 August 1991.* Berlin: De Gruyter (Trends in Linguistics Studies and Monographs 65). 61–77.

Halliday, M.A.K. 1992c. The act of meaning. J.E. Alatis (ed.) *Georgetown University Round Table on Languages and Linguistics 1992: Language, communication and social meaning.* Washington, DC: Georgetown University Press.

Halliday, M.A.K. 1992d. The history of a sentence: An essay in social semiotics. V. Fortunati (ed.) *Bologna, la cultura italiana e le letterature straniere moderne,* Volume terzo. Ravenna: Longo Editore (for University of Bologna). 29–45.

Halliday, M.A.K. 1993a. Quantitative studies and probabilities in grammar. M. Hoey (ed.) *Data, Description, Discourse: Papers on English language in honour of John McH. Sinclair (on his sixtieth birthday)* London: HarperCollins. 1–25.

Halliday, M.A.K. 1993b. *Language in a Changing World.* Canberra, ACT: Applied Linguistics Association of Australia (Occasional Paper 13).

Halliday, M.A.K. 1993c. Towards a language-based theory of learning. *Linguistics and Education* 5.2. 93–116.

Halliday, M.A.K. forthcoming. On language in relation to the evolution of human consciousness. (Paper prepared for Nobel Symposium 92 'The relation between langue and mind'. Stockholm, 8–12 August 1994.)

Halliday, M.A.K. and R. Hasan. 1976. *Cohesion in English.* London: Longman (English Langauge Series 9).

Halliday, M.A.K. and J.R. Martin 1993. *Writing Science: Literacy and discursive power.* London: Falmer (Critical Perspectives on Literacy and Education) and Pittsburgh, PA: University of Pittsburgh Press (Pittsburgh Series in Composition, Literacy, and Culture).

Halliday, M.A.K. and C.M.I.M. Matthiessen. forthcoming. *Construing Experience through Language: A language-based approach to cognition.*

Harvey, D. 1989. *The Condition of Postmodernity: An enquiry into the origins of cultural change.* Oxford: Blackwell.

Iedema, R. 1995. *Literacy of Administration (Write It Right Literacy in Industry Research Project – Stage 3).* Sydney: Metropolitan East Disadvantaged Schools Program.

Iedema, R., S. Feez and P. White 1994. *Media Literacy (Write It Right Literacy in Industry Research Project – Stage 2).* Sydney: Metropolitan East Disadvantaged Schools Program.

Kress, G. 1985. *Linguistic Processes in Socio-cultural Practice.* Geelong: Deakin University Press (republished by Oxford University Press 1989).

Kress, G. and T. van Leeuwen 1996. *Reading Images: The grammar of visual design.* London: Routledge. (An earlier version, *Reading Images,* was published by Deakin University Press 1990.)

Kristeva, J. 1986. Word, dialogue and novel. T. Moi (ed.) *The Kristeva Reader.* Oxford: Blackwell. 34–61.

Lee, A. 1993. Whose Geography? A feminist-poststructuralist critique of systemic 'genre'-based accounts of literacy and curriculum. *Social Semiotics* 3.1. 131–156.

Lee, A. 1996. *Gender, Literacy, Curriculum: Re-writing school geography.* London: Taylor & Francis (Culture and Society – Critical Perspectives on Literacy and Education).

Lemke, J.L. 1990. *Talking Science: Language, learning and values.* Norwood, NJ: Ablex (Language and Educational Processes).

Lemke, J.L. 1995. *Textual Politics: Discourse and social change.* London: Taylor & Francis (Culture and Society – Critical Perspectives on Literacy and Education).

Luke, A. 1996. Genres of power? Literacy education and the production of capital. R. Hasan and G. Williams (eds) *Literacy in Society*. London: Longman (Applied Linguistics and Language Study). 308–338.

Martin, J.R. 1985. *Factual Writing: Exploring and challenging social reality*. Geelong: Deakin University Press (republished by Oxford University Press 1989).

Martin, J.R. 1992. *English Text: System and structure*. Amsterdam: Benjamins.

Martin, J.R. 1993. Technology, bureaucracy and schooling: Discursive resources and control. *Cultural Dynamics* 6.1. 84–130.

Martin, J.R. in press. A context for genre: Modelling social processes in functional linguistics. R. Stainton and J. Devilliers (eds) *Communication in Linguistics*. Toronto: GREF (Collection Theoria).

Martin, J.R. and C.M.I.M. Matthiessen 1991. Systemic typology and topology. F. Christie (ed.) *Literacy in Social Processes: Papers from the inaugural Australian Systemic Linguistics Conference, held at Deakin University, January 1990*. Darwin: Centre for Studies in Language in Education, Northern Territory University. 345–383.

Matthiessen, C.M.I.M. mimeo. Instantial systems and logogenesis. (Paper presented at the Third Chinese Systemic-functional Linguistics Symposium, Hangzhou, June 17–20, 1993).

Matthiessen, C.M.I.M. 1995. *Lexicogrammatical Cartography: English Systems*. Tokyo: International Language Sciences Publishers.

Matthiessen, C.M.I.M. and M.A.K. Halliday in press. Systemic Functional Grammar: A first step into theory. J. Ney (eds) *Current Approaches to Syntax*. Tokyo: International Language Studies.

Nesbitt, C. and G. Plum 1988. Probabilities in a systemic-functional grammar: The clause complex in English. R.P. Fawcett and D. Young (eds) *New Developments in Systemic Linguistics vol. 2: theory and application*. London: Pinter (Open Linguistics Series). 6–38.

Ochs, E., P. Gonzales and S. Jacoby 1996. 'When I come down I'm in the domain state': grammar and graphic representation in the interpretive activity of physicists. E. Ochs, E. Schegloff and S.A. Thompson (eds) *Grammar and Interaction*. Cambridge: Cambridge University Press (Studies in Interactional Sociolinguistics 13). 328–369.

O'Donnell, M. 1990. A dynamic model of exchange. *Word* 41.3. 293–327.

Ogborn, J., G. Kress, I. Martins and K. McGillicuddy 1996. *Explaining Science in the Classroom*. Buckingham: Open University Press.

Painter, C. 1984. *Into the Mother Tongue: A case study of early language development*. London: Pinter.

Rose, D., D. McInnes and H. Korner. 1992. *Scientific Literacy (Write It Right Literacy in Industry Research Project – Stage 1)*. Sydney: Metropolitan East Disadvantaged Schools Program.

Thibault, P. 1991. *Social Semiotics as Praxis: Text, social meaning making and Nabakov's 'Ada'*. Minneapolis: University of Minnesota Press (Theory and History of Literature 74).

van Leeuwen, T. and S. Humphrey 1996. On learning to look through a geographer's eyes. R. Hasan and G. Williams (eds) *Literacy in Society*. London: Longman (Applied Linguistics and Language Study). 29–49.

Veel, R. 1992. Engaging with scientific language: A functional approach to the language of school science. *The Australian Science Teachers Journal*. 38.4. 31–35.

Veel, R. 1997. Learning how to mean – scientifically speaking: Apprenticeship into scientific discourse in the secondary school. F. Christie and J.R. Martin (eds) *Genre and Institutions: Social processes in the workplace and school*. London: Cassell (Open Linguistics Series). 161–195.

Ventola, E. 1987. *The Structure of Social Interaction: A systemic approach to the semiotics of service encounters*. London: Pinter (Open Linguistics Series).

2 Emerging perspectives on the many dimensions of scientific discourse[1]

Charles Bazerman

Over the past centuries, several forces have tended to suppress our consciousness of the rhetorical, communicative and symbolic character of scientific knowledge – thereby suppressing awareness of the role of language in the production of knowledge: the desire to get closer to the material object and the empirical experience of it; the warranting of representation through material practice; and the desire to remove misleading forms of representation. Perhaps the very success of scientific representations has suppressed awareness of language in the production of scientific knowledge, for scientific knowledge seems to be cast in naturally authoritative forms, unthinkable in any alternative representation.

But for whatever reasons, we are caught much in the dilemma of the inhabitants of the two-dimensional world described in the novel *Flatland*. These plane geometric creatures literally cannot rise above themselves to see their own world in the richer perspective of a third dimension, a perspective that would reveal to them their own shapes and the peculiarities of their own interactions.

Nonetheless, by the force of our own reflexive gyrations we have been gaining glimpses of a few dimensions in which the language of knowledge operates. These glimpses are starting to show us how much language is part of complex webs of human activity and meaning making.

The language of science has in recent decades interested researchers from different disciplines, including sociology, rhetoric, psychology, history, philosophy and linguistics. The reasons for the interest are varied, from social critique to epistemological concerns, from educational goals to specific disciplinary puzzles in linguistics, rhetoric or sociology, from practical advice and policy choice to theory building. The researchers have thus used a variety of disciplinary tools for making visible and analysing phenomena, and have been driven by different ranges of questions concerns, and intellectual and practical programmes.

A responsible synthesis would attempt a comprehensive search of literatures in a variety of fields, an archeology of each to identify the shape of each of the disciplinary projects and a principled account of the variety of sciences and technologies whose languages have been studied. Research is currently making incontrovertibly visible that scientific language is no unitary or stable thing, although certain tendencies or characteristics may be widespread. Scientific discourse is evolving and multiple, emerging in relation to the specialties, projects, methods, problems, social configurations, individual positionings and other dynamics that drive scientific activities. Further, as science studies have indicated, even all the sciences together form no essentially marked and bounded domain, although various enclosures (such as societies or journal readership or university departments) may partially direct the circulation of communication. These problems of identifying crisply bounded discourse domains become even more difficult if we extend our survey to technology, which itself is not clearly bounded from the sciences. I will consider none of these things here.

What I will consider are the accomplishments of a few of the more illuminating approaches to the discourse of science to see what kinds of things they have made visible and how their objects may be of interest to each other. Namely, I will be considering Latour's actant network theory as a semiotic and rhetorical account, Greg Myers' construction of scientific communication as a field of social negotiation, Halliday and Martin's semiotic representation of scientific language, and my own attempt to place scientific communication within a systematizing account of scientific activity.

All of these projects are social constructivist in a broad sense, in that they attempt to understand our accounts and knowledge labeled as science as the product of human social activity, although there are many varieties of social constructivism, varying both in their claims about how social activity is accomplished and in the relations between social accounting and material experience. The four projects I discuss have different positions on these issues, which I will not attend to either. However, for all four language is important. Language is part of human relations to material experience, to other humans, and to knowledge.

LATOUR'S POWER SEMANTICS

We will begin with the ostensibly most social of the accounts of scientific communication, actant network theory, most clearly articulated in Bruno Latour's *Science in Action*, a work which draws upon much of the work in social studies of science in the last two decades. Latour presents scientists and engineers – or purveyors of technoscience – as powerful rhetorical actors enlisting others in networks, to serve as resources in trials of strength with the critiques, claims, and projects of competing technoscientists. The end of this competitive enlistment is to create webs of relationships so strong that certain ideas, objects, facts become blackboxed, and are thereafter no longer seen as competitive sites of struggle.

Rather they are taken for granted as unproblematic, primarily because the cost of opening up the black box is too great – one can't find a place to insert the crowbar, or if even one could find some break in the seamless web of interacting support, one could not marshal the strength and resources to force open the now-unexamined to serious questioning. Consequently, while science-in-the-making is deeply competitive and contentious, science-once-made appears co-operative and harmonious, as traces of division are excised within a narrative of progress towards current belief, taken as true. Moreover, it is in the interest of the entrepreneurs of new technoscience to downplay the questionings and opposition of others, thereby increasing the appearance of strength of their projects to attract further allies and to encourage further use of their would-be black box, thereby making it increasingly indispensible in widening alliances of practice.

This is a deeply political and rhetorical view of science, where all is a matter of building alliances and then enacting the roles that maintain the political position, although the alliances may be as much with machines and microbes as with humans. Latour's account begins with the visible texts and the resources of citations, ideas, and experiments that are displayed there, but then moves backwards into the resources that stand behind the represented appearances in the text. In this light the citations become networks of social alliances and the labs become locales for producing inscriptions – turning mice into data and graphs that serve as resources and warrants for texts. As the alliances and rhetorical alignments become embodied in machines and funded laboratories, interests of various actors become committed in material and financial practice, establishing strongholds in the world that are not easily disassembled. Ultimately if the entrepreneur of knowledge is successful, labs become tribunals of reason and centers of calculation, thereby becoming compulsory passage points for subsidiary and related networks of knowledge production and maintenance, and they become the site of production of immutable mobiles that spread throughout society. So all activity becomes part of the extension of the rhetorical struggle, then transformed into centres of communication and rhetorical power. The rhetoric enters both into the representations that contend and pass for knowledge, and in the ways that actants position themselves with respect to potential allies in the network.

In this entrepreneurial game, communications are central to enlisting allies, largely by the ways specific allies are built into or represented in the texts, through such semantic elements as citation and reference to the literature; the inscription of phenomena; metrics that imply certain procedural, material, and intellectual commitments; and technicality of description that displays methodological and instrumental resources. The semantics of the article thereby locate the claim in networks of strengths that provide support and obduracy to the knowledge represented. This can be called a semantics of power.

Such an approach to semantics moves beyond semantics as a set of taxonomic relations of possible referents carved up into different conceptual objects. This approach to semantics examines the social and power implications of each term and concept – who has a stake in which term and how that stake brings power to bear in the deployment of a particular word or meaning. In a sense this can also be seen as a socially activated semantics, where each act of reference is also an act of affiliation, enlistment, or a display of allies to threaten those outside the web of alliances. Thus semantics becomes the visible mobilisation of resources that are drawn on and deployed in a text. A further extension of this research programme that would enter more fully into a discourse analysis, as suggested by the metaphor of deployment of resources, would be to examine the manner in which various resources are elaborated and linked within a cohesive text. What we would be looking at then are not only the forces gathered within a centre of strength, but the architectural, billeting and co-ordinated action plans.

MYERS' COOPERATIVE PRAGMATICS OF INTELLECTUAL AGONISM

Where Latour has seemed most interested in the aggregation and display of intellectual power, Myers has been most concerned with how people continue to talk to each other despite the arguments, differences, criticisms, and harsh evaluations that are part of scientific contention.

Myers has not pretended to a comprehensive account of the language of science nor of the social relations of science, but has rather investigated a variety of phenomena, largely defined in rhetorical and linguistic terms. He has been particularly concerned with the linguistic and rhetorical means by which disagreements are negotiated. His work on biology, gathered together in *Writing Biology*, examines the discursive back and forth by which researchers stake claims, attempt to advance them, and are restrained by gatekeepers and opponents, who attempt to restrict claims. Arguments move through various spheres, from the funding cycle, to publication, to the popular realm, each with characteristic methods of presentation and resistance, tropes and dynamics of knowledge negotiation. In short, Myers identifies interactive rhetorical processes that shape the communal production of knowledge among people largely in antagonistic positions.

More recently he has examined the management of conflictual discourse through techniques of irony and politeness, which allow one to oppose by indirection, avoiding the social ruptures of direct opposition (see, for examples, Myers 1989 and 1990a). He has also studied the deployment of various forms, such as narrative or dialogue, to advance arguments. As well he has looked at the verbs used to characterise the speech acts of claim-making in scientific articles to show how these may be adjusted to indicate the appropriate level of assertiveness given the nature of the disciplinary project, social relations, and individual claim and warrant (see Myers 1992b).

Another line of Myers' scientific discourse work is more semantically based, looking at how the recognition of coherence relations in texts is related to domain-specific, specialised knowledge (see Myers 1991). While this work might have implications for pragmatics through identifying insider–outsider boundaries and the modes of communicating that respect the audience's conditions of being either insiders or outsiders, it has much more in common with Hallidayan work of the sort described below.

If Latour may be said to concern himself with a rhetorical semantics, showing how resources can be effectively aligned and displayed, Myers may be said to be concerned primarily with a rhetorical pragmatics of sciences, demonstrating how personal relations and self-presentation of arguments and argumentative positions may be adjusted both to advance arguments and avoid rupture of co-operative principles. Interestingly, in his critical reviews and discussions of other works in rhetoric of science, he winds up evaluating the effectiveness, ethics and social interaction of those texts he criticizes, as in discussing an article by Howe and Lyne, where he concludes by commenting, 'There is no future in fighting dirty and trying to stay clean' (Myers 1992a: 201).

HALLIDAY'S GRAMMATICAL SEMANTICS

Halliday and Martin in *Writing and Science* pursue a kind of grammatical semantics. Embedded in the larger Hallidayan programme that connects linguistic observations with social, political, and psychological implications, this book most concretely provides an analysis of particular lexical items and semantic relations found in a variety of educational and research texts ranging over a number of fields and periods. By far the largest amount of analysis is devoted to nouns, both in relation to taxonomy and the nominalisation process, driven by grammatical metaphor – long an especial concern of Halliday. The most salient finding is that nominalisation has increased historically within science and other domains and that a similar process of nominal compacting occurs in individual texts. Historically this nominalisation has served to create higher and higher order abstractions which provide conceptual objects that populate the intellectual landscape of scientific specialities. These nominal abstractions are increasingly removed from concrete experience, and at each stage of the abstracting nominalisation process, concrete referential information is lost, so that the material meaning of higher order nominals becomes increasingly hard to follow and agree on. Within each individual text there is a similar process as earlier concrete reference is compacted and abstracted in the unfolding of the article's argument, where events turn into phenomena into conceptualised processes. Thus each article also projects a conceptual landscape populated by nominal objects constructed in the course of the text. Moreover, both historically and in individual texts, these objects become arrayed in taxonomies dividing up the conceptual landscape into discrete technical objects, whose definitions are linked through their abstract relations. The processes by which terms are made technical and are arrayed in taxonomies are also examined in some detail.

(Here we may also remember the comment from Latour and others in social studies of science that when arguments heat up, they become technical. This comment suggests that competitive struggle or agon makes distinctions useful and differences visible, if not indeed the sites of discussion. This further suggests that in the vocabulary of any technical field we have the fossils of earlier points of contention, with the surviving representation and its internal articulations drawn not only in contrast to suppressed losers, as deconstruction might point out, but also in relation to the resources by which the conquest was made – all the time remembering that the standing representation is likely to be a negotiated collaboration over a period of struggle, showing respect to all the powerful resources any of the contending sides may have brought to bear, rather than a simple choice of a primitive dichotomy. We might also remember that the agon is not only with intellectual opponents, but also possibly with practical problems that demand effective action and elusive phenomena that tease the imagination. But this set of speculations needs to be examined against historical evidence.)

In Halliday and Martin's analysis, the system of verbs in scientific writing relates those nouns to each other, either as descriptions of external events or internal logical operations. As actions are increasingly embedded in abstracted nouns, verbs also increasingly express abstracted relations. Typically the verbs are relational intensive, (such as *to be* and its equivalents – ranging from *signal* and *embody* to *confirm* and *prove*), or circumstantials (such as *cause* and its equivalents). Halliday gives particular attention to causal verb phrases and the syntactic relations they establish among nouns. Martin also begins to map causal implication sequences, where one state is described as being transformed into another. Thus again we have discrete objects that are acted upon to become new objects. This transformation is represented through typical syntactic relations among nominal objects. So the basic semantics is of conceptual objects deployed in nominalised grammatical forms, put in syntactic relations of coexistence, revelation or causation. One thing is another, or reveals another or causes another.

Similarly Halliday and Martin discuss conjunctions and prepositions that put nouns in elaborating, extending or enhancing relations.

SOME PERSPECTIVES ON THE HALLIDAYAN VIEW

The overall picture we obtain of scientific discourse from Halliday and Martin is of a process which is constantly creating new conceptual objects that populate its domain and can be arrayed in various syntactic relations, primarily of coexistence and causality with other states. (There may be processes other than discussed by Halliday and Martin by which the semantic/conceptual/ontological field of objects grows.) Difficulties students and others have with scientific language are in the recognition and appropriate manipulation of the verbal objects which correspond to conceptual objects. Myers would add to this that students have difficulty in recognising the semantic relations among different synonymous, antonymous, hyponymous or sequentially linked terms. We can see in this view of the creation of scientific lexical/conceptual objects some-thing like Latour's black-boxing – once the object is given a stable name, its details, problems and material particularities and relations to other objects in its network vanish in a higher level abstraction which becomes difficult to unpack once made. Moreover, certain of these objects get displayed as resources to be relied upon in articles. They form a ground of ontological certainty upon which one can construct new objects.

From a Vygotskian perspective we can also see these terms as tools for organising and manipulating perceptions of the world, so that these objects and their appropriate manipulations become the very means of thinking that are difficult to escape once engaged with, but difficult to engage with when approached from any other form of intellectual life. While this observation reverberates with both Wittgenstein's 'forms of life' and Kuhn's 'untranslatability', it points the way toward a more moderate and precise account of the mechanisms by which perceptual and accounting frames are formed, and of the difficulties in attempting to engage the perspective of those immersed in a different discoursal universe.

We may also see in this synthesis of Halliday and Martin with Myers, Latour and Vygotsky the beginning of a conjunction of the grammatical code with the intellectual code and the code of representation of nature. Thus the semantics become a kind of cognitive semantics, having from the Hallidayan perspective their origin in narrative descriptive processes and grammatical metaphor (see Halliday and Matthiessen in press) or from the Latourian perspective having their origin in agon and alliance building, but ultimately having their consequences in the cognitive structure and contents of scientific thought. The implications of this for educational projects are significant, both in identifying the difficulties of entering into scientific discourse and in identifying the kind of symbolic–cognitive practice one is trying to foster in science education.

When just looking at lexical and grammatical processes, we see a unified view of the sciences as uniformly engaged in precisely the same discursive practices of object creation, abstraction, and relation-building. It also presents the sciences much on the terms that science itself would like to consider itself, with attention to the cognitive objects it creates in representation of natural objects and processes. The fissure-laden and contentious social and material processes by which phenomena are construed into widely accepted symbolic form are hidden from Halliday and Martin's view. They represent the field as a series of textual objects – the field already filtered through the mode of textuality, and therefore seeming to have textualised homogeneity – that is the field is reduced to a semantic field which names the conceptual objects of study and analysis, to be syntactically manipulated according to a limited range of accepted symbolic procedures to make arguments in the symbolic domain. For this reason, Hallidayan grammatical and syntactic studies frequently move freely between analyses of classroom and research science, without noting differences in the language that may appear only at other levels. The typical move of research articles to pretend the truth and acceptance of their claims, even while wrestling uncertain phenomena into some stable-appearing symbolic form and arguing with competing views, results in the rhetorical and epistemic activity of the writing not being highly marked at the grammatical and syntactic level. The form of the argument is to black-box itself as much as possible and make itself look as much like accepted textbook knowledge as it can manage within the context of disciplinary discussion at the research front.

In a broader activity construal of field, the textual mode would be part of the social and material activity but would not encompass it. There are things that happen beyond the edge of the paper, some of which get represented in the text as textualised objects (as in Halliday's tenor, or interactional component of discourse), but others that never appear directly although they may have great influence on the things that do appear. It is in these realms that sciences may look most different from each other – as a physics laboratory and a physics seminar may look very different from an anthropological expedition and an anthropology seminar, although the textbooks and journals of both may have certain resemblances as they sit on the shelf. The texts only serve operationally as important parts of this larger range of activity of knowledge production, education, dissemination and application, although they may refer to various parts of the processes. Even more complexly, texts may be sensitive to or influenced by these larger social activities. Further, the texts' relations to these encompassing activities may be translated into textually displayed objects, as well as translated out into other forms of practice, in a variety of different ways.

We can see Halliday and Martin's focus on the textual representation from a different path. Although Halliday and Martin mention other dimensions of language as represented within the Hallidayan system, particularly tenor (which is the interpersonal element), the primary emphasis of their analysis is on the field and mode, or ideational and textual elements. Moreover field is given a particularly lexical, textual interpretation – the field being represented by the names of objects that populate the conceptual field. Thus chemistry is indicated by the names of chemical objects displayed within the texts from the names of chemicals such as acids, to methods and tools, such as litmus and test tubes, to chemical processes such as calcification. Chemistry is not considered to be the social and institutional and material configurations that stand behind the text but are not mentioned – such as disciplines, journals, collegial relations, reward systems, networks, and the test tube racks and sinks that do not get mentioned in the text – the kinds of things sociologists of science might associate with the field and its practices. To Latour these may include some of the black boxes so taken for granted that they are no longer seen, but they also might contain the many contingent relations and interests that one is attempting to draw under control by proposing the right objects that will tie those alliances, interests and contingencies together around a new black box.

That is, in Halliday and Martin science is much as it presents itself in its texts, only we have to find out how to read those difficult texts, and perhaps recover some of the concrete narrative that has been pressed out of the abstraction. So the dimension we recover here from the textual appearance is the process of textualisation which makes the text more compact and abstract – and therefore difficult. Myers would also point out that the compactness and abstraction are in part achieved through the web of semantic relations taught as part of specialised training, as in textbooks, but that are left implicit and invisible in texts that circulate only among the fully trained. As both Halliday and Martin repeatedly suggest, it is the difficulty and abstraction of the text that define the applied social problems that drive their analysis – how to make the textualised knowledge more accessible to students and adults and how to bring that knowledge more in line with the concrete transitive activity of the real world that is being covered by the nominalized abstraction.

BAZERMAN'S RHETORICAL FORMS FOR SYMBOLIC ACTION

My sets of problems and sites of observation cut across these other three lines of work. As a writing teacher, I have been most concerned with what one must attend to in order to write successful documents in scientific and other domains, and then how those forms of attention can be appropriately translated into successful textual choices. It is the textual relations with those encompassing activities and how one engages with the material and social through textual action that have held my attention most. Genre provided a grasp on this complex and inchoate activity, because it is through the typified utterances of genre that one interacts with others and encapsulates what one has to report on the material phenomena one has grasped through material experiences and inscriptive practices. By genre I do not just mean the formal character- istics that one must observe so as to be recognised as correctly following the visible rules and expectations. Genre more fundamentally is a kind of activity to be carried out in a recognisable textual space. That activity embodies relations with the readers and kinds of messages to be devel- oped in order to carry out generically appropriate intentions and inter- actions – to complete the rhetorical and social possibilities of the genre. Thus genre presents an opportunity space for realising certain kinds of activities, meanings, and relations. Genre exists only in the recognition and deployment of typicality by writers and readers – it is the recogni- sable shape by which participation is enacted and understood (see, for examples, Bazerman 1994b and 1997).

This conception of genre differs from the Hallidayan conception of genre, which places genre on an equal footing with register. Genre in Hallidayan and other functional linguistic formulations refers primarily to broad patterns of semantic organisation that may come to dominate passages of text longer than a sentence – such as narration, description, report, etc. Genre may be seen in these traditions either as a series of linguistic features that co-vary or as a locus of utterer's decisions that will influence the emergence of staged textual features.

My attention was drawn to the specific expected forms of discrete texts through which one's literate action is framed and recognised in relevant communities. That is, texts of recognised types, appearing in certain perceived circumstances, are perceived to have particular force. If a particular message does not fulfill all the expectations that usually attach to its type, or if it confuses its appearances among various possible actions, it may evoke various kinds of confusion and ineffectiveness or may be engaged in an intentional deception. Thus I have tried to understand textual appearances within the entire set of relations and transactions in which appearances are embedded, and I have attended largely to the framing devices and the shaping of actions – in this spirit I examined the emergence of the modern experimental report in sciences, its many transformations, its diffusion to the social sciences, the social structure that arose in conjunction with the textual structure, and the kinds of activities that are influenced by the regularised forms of literacy (Bazerman 1988). I also have examined how communicative forms and actions have been proposed in relation to specific social and epistemo- logical projects that are to be realised through communicative relations (see Bazerman 1994a and Bazerman and Paradis 1991).

In my recent work on Thomas Edison, some of those activities I have been exploring have been the gaining of value and meaning within structured discursive spaces. In order to create the technology of central power and light in the everyday life world, Edison must get various other people linked in various discursive networks to see the meaning of his project and to see the value in that meaning. Thus incandescent lighting must gain specific presence in the patent system through the approval of claims of novelty embedded in patent application and the assignment of patent numbers that give legal standing to the claims. The specific value and meaning created through the patent application/review process then gives particular standing in legal proceedings where the patent rights are defended and enforced. Each of these structured forums are constituted out of sequences of allowable and appropriate generic utterances distributed differentially to people with different institutional roles. Typified utterances embedded with these forums then create specific meanings and values in interaction with the particularities of each instance as represented within that forum. Late nineteenth-century newspapers, the financial markets, technical journals, the inner circles of industrial financiers and so on each identify specific discursive realms on which Edison had to represent himself and his project appropriately and successfully for all the parts of this large techno-socio-legal-financial-industrial-commercial undertaking to come together in the construction and use of the material system of electric power delivery – the wires, transformers, generators and light bulbs along with the buildings that house them and the workers that operate them (Bazerman forthcoming.)

The power semantics here are a bit different than in Latour's account. Rather than tying alliances together in a centre of calculation, which becomes in a sense a semantic gathering place of the interests and representations of all members of the network, here we look at the movement of representations outward across complexes of discursive networks, each having its own standing. Each, therefore, remoulds the project as part of its enlistment. We have a project that is representationally distributed in a kind of pragmatics of negotiation of the kind suggested by Myers. That is, we have adjustments among many centres of discourse, accommodated through the semantic flexibility and pragmatic distances negotiated by skilled language users who know how to maintain social networks despite differences among themselves and who know how to take meanings from one domain and transform them appropriately for another domain.

LOCATED ACTS OF MEANING

I am also beginning to explore another dimension of scientific discourse, a dimension suggested by Halliday and Martin's analysis: the operation of meaning within each discursive system. Once a representation gains place within a discursive system, is accepted as properly represented in it, and therefore becomes a valued discursive object, how is that meaning operative within that discursive system? How is it linked with and transformed into other meanings? What kinds of intellectual operations can be performed on it, and what kind of operations can it perform on other meanings? What kind of tools do these meanings or concepts or representations become for thinking? How are those tools used? And how do other tools get used on them? These might be said to be the formal operations or knowledge and intellectual procedures of the field. In some empirical fields there may be material, empirical procedures for identifying appropriate objects such as new chemical processes or species of plants and admitting them into the pantheon, and these procedures and instances of their application can be argued and contested in symbolic ways as in experimental reports and methodological arguments, but once in the pantheon they can be operated on in certain purely symbolic ways. These symbolic operations we might call chemical meaning and thinking, or botanic meaning and thinking. The kinds of grammatical semantics of nominalisation and causal relations that Halliday and Martin point to and the underweb of semantic cohesive relations within a knowledge representational field pointed to by Myers are clearly parts of that story.

From my first works in the rhetoric of science, I have given readings of the intellectual operations of texts, in large part to examine how those operations point outwards to contextual operations or draw on contextual resources, and in both instances actively engage with those contexts. However, this is always carried out in the local textual environment where there is a kind of local textual thinking which carries out the disciplinary project through the creation of an allowable and forceful textual object. For example, I have looked at how the introduction of quantum theory helped reconfigure the organisation and intellectual operations of articles in spectroscopy. I have also examined how Newton attempted to construct compulsive relations within a discursive space that eliminates external distractions – in part by using argumentative resources of mathematics, which was furthest along as a self-contained discursive system. Similarly, I also considered how Adam Smith in order to create a space for calculation and exchange through quantification – countable money – began to identify certain calculative operations that formed the grounds of economics, which now appears as an enclosed discourse even though Smith's own text constantly draws on much wider concerns to try to focus them on this space. McCloskey points out that modern quantitative-appearing economic argument has been able to suppress and make covert these wider discursive concerns, but has not been able to eliminate value and policy concerns that keep the discourse open, much as Newton's setting the terms of argument restricted allowable meanings in optics for a hundred years and in mechanics for two hundred.

Also most recently I have begun to give some thought to the nature and role of concepts as active operators in disciplinary discourses of different sorts. But these all represent pieces that I have barely begun to fit together – to try to understand meaning actions, in a sense which goes beyond Austin's reference acts and Searle's propositional acts. Austin and Searle's concern for states of affairs represented within speech acts considers isolated representations as contained acts of assertion, but what I have in mind is the working out of complex meanings in related representations – meaningful representations that can only become meaningful and persuasively forceful within a complex of related assertions and that are worked through in the course of building an allowable set of cohesive representations. It is one thing to consider the conditions under which we can appropriately assert 'the cat is on the mat', and quite another to consider the conditions appropriate to asserting an account of the influence of the increase of the price of crude oil on the gross world product in the previous quarter. Understanding the way concepts work within specialised discourses provide a way into understanding how meanings are organized and realized within those discourses.

The manipulation of symbols within generic disciplinary space to unfold meaning is also a cognitive activity, drawing together the understandings and interests of the writer and readers in joint projects, so that the readers must be engaged, influenced, and persuaded by the unfolding text, so that they give continuing meaning-constructing attention to the temporally and spatially unfolding text, without the alienation of alternative commitments and understandings that distance the reader from the representations of the text. The joint construction of meaning is more than simply a calculus of symbols, it is a rhetorical sharing of thought within a generically identifiable space using the accepted resources appropriate to be deployed in that space in ways that keep enlisting the meanings and understandings and procedures the readers will bring to that space.

All the projects I have described here remain sketchy glimpses of different spots on different kinds of maps, but they all form pieces of a complex n-dimensional puzzle. They start to reveal specialised and consequential linguistic practices in complicated systems. Years ago, I commented that some sample articles I examined from literary studies, sociology and biochemistry played different moves in different games, on different game boards. We still don't know what all the games are or what the full range of moves or game boards is, but are getting some better snapshots of moments of play. The richer the picture we develop, the better a mirror we will create for the reflective practice of language use, which I see as the end of rhetorical knowledge: to help a skilled behaviour become even more self-monitoring, self-knowing, precise and skilled.

NOTE

1 I would like to thank John Gumperz, Jenny Cook-Gumperz, Sandra Thompson, Greg Myers, Wendy Newstetter, Khavi Mahesh, Bill Evans and Bob Woods for their comments and discussion of earlier versions of this essay.

REFERENCES

Abbott, E. 1953. *Flatland*. New York: Dover.
Austin, J.L. 1975. *How To Do Things With Words*. Cambridge, MA: Harvard University Press.
Bazerman, C. 1988. *Shaping Written Knowledge: The genre and activity of the experimental article in science*. Madison: University of Wisconsin Press.
Bazerman, C. 1994a. *Constructing Experience*. Carbondale: Southern Illinois University Press.
Bazerman, C. 1994b. Systems of Genre and the Enactment of Social Intentions. In A. Freedman and P. Medway (eds) *Rethinking Genre*. London: Taylor & Francis: 79–101.
Bazerman, C. 1997. The Generic Performance of Ownership. In B. Gunnarsson (ed.) *The Construction of Professional Discourse*. London: Longman.
Bazerman, C. forthcoming. *The Languages of Edison's Light*. Cambridge, MA: MIT Press.
Bazerman, C. and J. Paradis (eds) 1991. *Textual Dynamics of the Professions*. Madison: University of Wisconsin Press.
Halliday, M.A.K. and J. Martin 1994. *Writing Science*. Pittsburgh: University of Pittsburgh Press.
Halliday, M.A.K. and C.M.I.M. Matthiessen. in press. *Construing Experience through Language: A language-based approach to cognition*. Berlin: De Gruyter (Foundations of Communication and Cognition).
Kuhn, T. 1970. *The Structure of Scientific Revolutions*. Chicago: Chicago University Press.
Latour, B. 1987. *Science in Action*. Cambridge, MA: Harvard University Press.
McCloskey, D. 1986. *The Rhetoric of Economics*. Madison: University of Wisconsin Press.
Myers, G. 1989. The Pragmatics of Politeness in Scientific Texts. *Applied Linguistics* 10 (1): 1–35.
Myers, G. 1990a. The Rhetoric of Irony in Academic Writing. *Written Communication* 7 (4): 419–455.
Myers, G. 1990b. *Writing Biology*. Madison: University of Wisconsin Press.
Myers, G. 1991. Lexical Cohesion and Specialized Knowledge in Science and Popular Science Texts. *Discourse Processes* 14 (1): 1–26.
Myers, G. 1992a. Clean Talk in Genetics. *Social Epistemology* 6 (2): 193–202.
Myers, G. 1992b. 'In this Paper We Report': Speech Acts and Scientific Claims. *Journal of Pragmatics* 17: 295–313.
Searle, J.R. 1969. *Speech Acts*. Cambridge: Cambridge University Press.
Wittgenstein, L. 1953. *Philosophical Investigations*. New York: Macmillan.

Part II
Popularising science

Introduction to part II

Over the years the question of 'exclusivity' in science language has been raised many times. The technicality and abstraction which characterises scientific language is a double-edged sword. Whilst it extends the meaning potential of language considerably, allowing for new kinds of relationships between grammar and semantics to construe new kinds of meanings, the very process of technicality and abstraction renders scientific language inaccessible to many (cf. the 'black-boxing' referred to by Bazerman in Chapter 2). The differential access to scientific meaning amongst individuals means that the meaning potential of scientific language can be easily translated into a tool for political and economic domination within and between societies. This phenomenon has been commented upon both by lay observers, who criticise the 'jargon' of science and technology, and by critical theorists, who express concerns that the users of scientific forms language (including linguists) employ scientific language purely to enhance their own power and prestige, and not for the construal of distinct kinds of knowledge.

What is to be done about this inequality, be it potential or actual? The most obvious response is to 'translate' scientific language into 'everyday language', to remove the technicality and abstraction so that all 'normal' users of language may have access to it. This response has been a popular one in a number of fields, from the 'plain English' movement (Solomon 1996) in law and business to attempts in the 1980s to introduce narrative texts and advertisements as a way of teaching science in the junior secondary school. Despite these attempts to translate the language of science, technicality and abstraction persists. Indeed, some areas of 'everyday' or popular culture seem not just to accept the technicality of science, but to celebrate it. The popularity of television series such as *Star Trek* and the *Star Wars* movie trilogy make it hard to ignore the apparent fascination with technicality of a significant proportion of the community.

The debate about the accessibility of scientific language to the non-specialist reader assumes, of course, that we have a clear understanding of the nature of both 'technical' scientific discourse and 'popular' forms.

Whilst we know a considerable amount about the former, how much do we know about the latter? What is the meaning of the term 'popularisation' when it comes to scientific discourse? Do 'popular science' and 'science fiction' construe meanings in the same way that research science construes meanings? The two chapters in this section look at the issue of the popularisation of scientific discourse in two different but complementary ways.

In examining the 'popular science' writings of American biologist Stephen Jay Gould, Fuller argues that 'popular' does not necessarily mean 'accessible to the general reader', nor 'open to a range of narrative voices'. Fuller suggests that, rather than translating scientific discourse into forms which make it more 'everyday', the popularising of scientific discourse for writers such as Gould involves the translation of the scientific into another uncommonsense discourse, that of the liberal humanities. Through a careful analysis of the generic structure of several of Gould's articles, Fuller shows how Gould places competing scientific theories and opinions side-by-side, presenting science as a set of contested ideas about the physical world, but couches them within a grand narrative, so that only one authoritative voice, Gould's own, emerges at the end of the text. The ideal reader constructed through Gould's texts, suggests Fuller, is not the general reader, but a middle-class, probably male reader with a liberal education. The 'popularisation' of science in Gould's writing does not make it any more accessible for the non-specialist reader, nor does it remove the potential for domination in scientific discourse. It simply makes it accessible to another dominant group, providing those educated in the liberal humanities with another set of discursive tools with which to exercise symbolic control.

Cranny-Francis, on the other hand, examines a field of language activity that is genuinely popular, that of science fiction. Even though she demonstrates that emergence of science fiction as a genre within fiction writing is intimately linked to the historical development of western science itself, Cranny-Francis suggests that it is the 'fiction' rather than the 'science' which drives science fiction. In presenting an historical overview of the development of science fiction she shows how the genre has exploited the potential of fiction to examine and challenge social realities. The use of technicality and scientific detail, argues Cranny-Francis, is not to construe meanings in the same way as the discourse of research science, but to draw attention to the very constructedness of our environment (especially in the late twentieth century) and therefore open it to challenge. For Cranny-Francis the challenge to the hegemony of scientific discourse in science fiction writing comes not from the demystification of technicality within narrative forms, but in the use of technicality as a vehicle for social critique.

Both Fuller and Cranny-Francis make use of a range of analytical techniques, drawing in particular on contemporary critical theory. Fuller shows how it is possible to address the kinds of concerns voiced by Bazerman, Latour and Myers about the invisibility of social processes in the construction of scientific discourse from the perspective of a socially situated linguistic theory. Cranny-Francis shows how a Bakhtinian conception of genre as a 'dialogic' social artefact (Bakhtin 1981) can be used to explore the location and function of texts in a social context, taking into account the ongoing evolution of science fiction genres across a range of media.

REFERENCE

Bakhtin, M. 1981. *The Dialogic Imagination: Four essays by M.M. Bakhtin* Austin, TX: University of Texas Press.

3 Cultivating science

Negotiating discourse in the popular texts of Stephen Jay Gould

Gillian Fuller

INTRODUCTION

The work of Stephen Jay Gould, Harvard Professor of Geology and prolific popular author, occupies a sanctified position within the realm of popular science writers. The way in which his popular texts negotiate relations of science and society fulfils the requirements of the socially responsible populariser for many readers. Academic critic Midgley places Gould on her 'honours list' of popularisers (1994: 225), while Masur states that '[no] one has been more visible, successful [and] influential' (1993: 114) in the task of 'translat[ing] internalist scientific developments into public questions of both philosophical and practical significance' (1993: 113).[1] A translator alters something that was previously uninterpretable into something 'we' can understand. Any translation is, according to Benjamin, a 'regulated transformation' (1969). The highly regarded status and popularity of Gould's writings provides insight into the claims and motivations of popular science writing as a whole, in that Gould's transformation of the technicalities of science is suitably regulated to the hegemonic ethos of popular science. That is, Gould manages convincingly to negotiate a relation between science and society that discharges his target audience's expectations.

The difficulty of popular science would seem to lie, for its authors, mainly in 'translating' technicality into 'everyday' terms. Many popular science authors point to the problems of relating the complexity of the ideational (or referential) content of science in texts that should display none of the characteristically forbidding forms of academic science, such as high degrees of nominalisation, embedded causality, technical lexis and mathematical equations.[2] Stephen Hawking notes that books on the early universe range from the 'very good' to the 'very bad' and discusses the difficulty of writing about cosmology without including equations (1990: vi). Richard Dawkins talks about deleting 'jargon' and writing for a layman who has no special knowledge, but who is not 'stupid' (1992: v). Stephen Jay Gould, whose work is the focus of this chapter, writes in the

Prologue to his 1992 collection of articles *Bully for Brontosaurus* (hence-forth referred to as *BfB*):

> I deeply deplore the equation of popular writing with pap and distortion . . . it denigrates the intelligence of millions of Americans eager for intellectual stimulation without patronization.
>
> (*BfB*: 11)

Here, the agenda of popular science is evoked in terms that are opposi-tional to an unspecified hegemony that would denigrate Gould's read-ership. This combative rhetoric coupled with the interpersonal insinuation that popular science readers are intelligent and indeed 'get-ting the full story' is a manoeuvre that is often employed in the *BfB* collection.[3] This inclusive rhetoric has been claimed as serving a demo-cratic socialist agenda,[4] however such anti-elitism is couched within terms which necessarily privilege those who would be eager for prestige forms of knowledge.

This chapter will examine how notions of the 'popular' or 'everyday' are constituted in the writings of Stephen Jay Gould. Within liberal discourses and 'plain English' movements the notion of 'everyday' language may seem unproblematic, however the process of 'translation' is a process of negotiating a bridge between distinct registers. Registers are contextually (socially, historically) specific ways of speaking. In the transformative act of making science accessible a process of recontex-tualisation occurs where science is repackaged to fit the discursive con-figurations of more overtly social and political texts. In this chapter, I will explore the rhetorical strategies and discursive interests that operate in Gould's popularising project.

HOW COMMON IS POPULAR?

Pierre Bourdieu's (1991) discussion of the social function of the epithet 'popular' reveals some of the ambivalence around the term 'popular' which is relevant to the analysis of popular science texts in general and to the texts of Stephen Jay Gould in particular.

> Sayings containing the magical epithet 'popular' are shielded from scrutiny by the fact that any critical analysis of a notion which bears closely or remotely on 'the people' is apt to be identified immediately as a symbolic aggression against the reality designated – and thus immediately castigated by all those who feel duty bound to defend the people, thereby enjoying the profits that the defense of 'good causes' can bring. Equally, the notion of 'popular speech', like all sayings from the same family ('popular culture', 'popular art', 'popular religion', etc.), is defined in relational terms, as the set of things which are excluded from the legitimate language by, among other things, the

durable effect of inculcation and imposition together with the sanc-
tions implemented by the educational system.

(Bourdieu 1991: 90)

If the epithet 'popular' is taken to designate discourses excluded from the
legitimated realms of state education then popular science in general and
that of Stephen Jay Gould in particular is deceptively named, yet there is
a preoccupation in the author's notes of Gould texts with the disdain in
which the popular science genre is supposedly held. From the Prologue
of *BfB* again:

> In France, they call this genre *Vulgarisation* – but the implications are
> entirely positive. In America, we call it 'popular (or pop) writing' and
> its practitioners are dubbed 'science writers' even if, like me, they are
> working scientists who love to share the power and beauty of their
> field with people in other professions.

(*BfB*: 11)

Gould goes on to say that popularising science is held in such disregard
in professional scientific circles that forays into the genre may damage
the research careers of budding young scientists. The criticisms from the
scientific community directed at popularising practices are that they are
'simplifications', 'adulterisations' and focus on the 'whiz bang' (*BfB*: 11).
While Gould admits that criticisms hold true for some popular texts, he
claims that 'accessible science' can be reclaimed as 'an honourable
intellectual tradition' and that 'any conceptual complexity can be con-
veyed in ordinary English' (*BfB*: 12). By defending the popular in such a
way Gould not only manages to claim a maverick position with regard to
science but also with regard to its popularisation. As suggested in the
Bourdieu quote above, by adopting a protective attitude to the 'illegiti-
macies' of popular science Gould reaps considerable moral reward from
defending the good causes of the 'people', he also importantly casts
himself as 'of the people' whose common sense is informed by an
enlightened science. In many ways, Gould's work ascribes to Enlight-
enment doctrines of 'equality, liberty, faith in human intelligence (once
allowed the benefits of education) and universal reason' (Harvey 1989:
13). In this way his work traces its geneaology to Victorian scientist
philosophers such as Darwin and Huxley but with the updated morals
and political sensitivities of an American scientist historian and baseball
fan.

Notions of democracy and empowerment proliferate in many popularising discourses. Therefore, in order for a popular text to be ranked as
successful, it must in some ways accede to the values of these and other
discourses that cluster around and intersect with popular science. Con-
cordant with notions of liberal democracy is a philanthropic ethos that
pervades discussions on the motivations for popularising science. For

example, Shortland and Gregory, authors of *Communicating Science: A handbook* (1991) which is designed for scientists who want to 'go public', argue that 'science is part of our culture and heritage and scientific knowledge ought therefore to be common property' (1991: 7). This argument, however, is followed with a hortatory rhetorical flourish that casts this 'egalitarian' rationale into a voice that expresses the poetic yearnings of humanist individuality. Shortland and Gregory borrow a quote from biologist Jean Rostard taken from a 1960 issue of *Science* to bring their point home:

> The true and specific function of popularisation is purely and simply to introduce the greatest number of people into the sovereign dignity of knowledge, to ensure that the great mass of people should receive something of which is the glory of the human mind . . . to struggle against mental starvation and the resulting underdevelopment by providing every individual with a minimum ration of spiritual calories.
>
> (Rostard cited in Shortland and Gregory 1991: 7)

The hyperbole of the above quote is underpinned by a liberal romanticism that highlights the discursive alignments of inclusive access and equity discourses with universalising statements about the edifying properties of knowledge. Such sentiments can be found in Gould's discussions of the 'true beauty of nature' (*BfB*: 16) and 'the intellectual delights that she offers [us]' (*BfB*: 13). Within such sentiments are notions that 'truth' releases one from the 'camera obscura' of ideology: a truth that is articulated through the registeral forms of historical privilege. In other words, my argument is that much popular science, even that of the highly regarded Gould, does not make the technicalities of science accessible to this problematic and normalised concept 'the people'; rather it is a discourse that enmeshes the 'facticities' of science with the master narratives of liberal bourgeois cultures.

CULTIVATING SCIENCE

Gould is not only a working scientist but also a historian of science and his popularising texts differ markedly from works of scientific journalism – exemplified by *New Scientist, Scientific American* and also in books written by John Gribbin and James Gleick.[5] Many of these texts fall into the category of what Jeanne Fahnestock, working from a rhetorical perspective, would call 'scientific accommodations'.[6] Using Aristotilean classifications she identifies the rhetorical mode of these texts as epideictic. She states of scientific accommodations that:

> [Their] main purpose is to celebrate rather than validate. And furthermore, they must usually be explicit in their claims about the value of the scientific discoveries they pass along. They cannot rely on

the audience to recognise the significance of the information. *Thus the work of epideictic rhetoric in science journalism requires adjustments of new information to an audience's already held values and assumptions* [my emphasis].
(Fahnestock in McRae 1993: 20)

Fahnestock identifies two major appeals that enable the epideictic argument. She labels these the 'wonder and the application appeals' (1993: 20). These appeals are clearly visible in any newspaper text, from the endless breakthroughs in new 'green' inventions to the array of diseases that will be exterminated through genetic biology. Science accommodations could be said to reinforce a technocratic ideology that science is good for us, that it improves our lives. As an essayist rather than a journalist, Gould's work does not sit comfortably in the category of science accommodator (although his work is ultimately redemptive of scientific models), nor is he really a writer who apprentices the lay reader into the technicalities of science; he is rather what I'd like to call a cultivator of science.[7] In *BfB*, the 'wonder and application' appeals are enunciated according to the values of a more cultivated literacy whose discursive antecedents in 'humanist natural history' (*BfB*: 12) motivate the forms of its accommodation. A prototypical discussion of the concerns of such a literacy project is flagged in C.P. Snow's *The Two Cultures* (1964), based on Snow's Rede Lecture at Cambridge in 1959.

Snow's lecture, which is often adduced in discussions on popularisation (Selzer 1993, McRae 1993), expressed alarm at the increasing mutual incomprehensibility between the disciplines. Prefiguring his discussion on the increasing inaccessibility of science and how these differing epistemic modes manifest in widely diverse cultural preoccupations, Snow provided an anecdote based on his fractured social life as indicative of the disciplinary divide. Discussing how he worked with scientists during the day and dined with literary colleagues at night, he says:

> For constantly I felt that I was moving among two groups – comparable in intelligence, identical in race, not grossly different in social origins, earning about the same incomes, who had almost ceased to communicate at all, who in intellectual, moral and psychological climate had so little in common that instead of going from Burlington House or South Kensington to Chelsea, one might have crossed an ocean.
>
> (Snow, 1964: 2)

This quote reveals quite clearly what has been a primary concern of much popular science, but has been buried under the rhetoric of knowledge dissemination and plain English. Much popular science has been foremost an attempt to construct dialogue between discursive elites, who for the main share cultural values. This point about shared discursive values is paramount to this discussion, for I intend to show that although

Stephen Jay Gould is often rightly singled out for particular praise as a
'bold and clear headed explainer' (Midgley, 1994: 2) his discourse nevertheless is primarily an exploration between two distinct modes of uncommonsense. Gould explicitly pitches his texts to what fellow humanist
Noam Chomsky refers to in his 1992 film *Manufacturing Consent* as the
'top ten percent'. Of his audience Gould himself says:

> The 'perceptive and intelligent' lay person is no myth. They exist in
> millions – a low percentage of America perhaps, but a high absolute
> with influence beyond their proportion in the population.
>
> (*BfB*:12)

Gould's notion of his readership is revealing in a number of respects.
First, it implicitly locates the highly rated qualities of perception and
intelligence to those with socio-economic power. Second, it explicitly
gestures towards a social agenda of popular science that extends beyond
'rationing spiritual calories'. Third, prefigured in the quote above is a
rhetorical ambit that is key to Gould's popularity, namely, the cultivation
of his readership.

The term 'cultivation' is used to suggest not only a process of textually
flattering this 'perceptive and intelligent' reader that is managed through
Gould's considerable rhetorical skill, but it also is an apt description for
the mode in which Gould socially contextualises scientific discourse.
Gould cultivates his readership through a rhetorical flattery that draws
them into a textual conspiracy by insinuating prestigious discursive positions as shared intersubjective values. He also realises his critical musings
on scientific theorising through a schema in which references to 'high or
hegemonic culture'[8] form both orientation and resolution. In a recent
panegyric to Gould, Louis Masur writes that 'Gould is chiefly concerned
with illuminating the interpenetrations between science and society, fact
and fiction, nature and history' (1993: 115). The interpenetrating points
of Gould's discourse, however, could be said to be remarkably restricted
to classically Victorian visions of society and history and hence necessarily
aligned to an exclusivist and universalising education tradition. Moreover, true to the grand preoccupations of the canonical literary tradition,
Gould resolves epistemic tensions through poetic visions and moral lessons endowed upon us through reflecting upon nature.

Clear examples of 'cultivation' can be seen in the introductions of texts
from the *BfB* collection. For instance, the text called *Of Kiwi Eggs and the
Liberty Bell*, which explains the anomalous size of kiwi eggs begins:

> Like Ozymandias, once kings of kings but now two legs of a broken
> statue in Percy Shelley's desert the grand facade of Union Station in
> Washington D.C. stands forlorn while Amtrak operates from a dingy
> outpost at the side.
>
> (*BfB*:109)

Or another *BfB* text called *To Be a Platypus* ostensively concerned with the functional delicacy of the Platypus's bill begins thus:

> Long ago, garrulous old Polonius exalted brevity as the soul of wit, but later technology, rather than sweet reason, won his day and established verbal condensation as a form of art in itself. The telegram, sent for cash on the line and by the word, made brevity both elegant and economical – and the word telegraphic entered our language for a style that conveys bare essentials and nothing else.
>
> (*BfB*:269)

The opening stage of a *BfB* text is the site of a richly intertextual and plurifunctional performance. Authorial *ethos* is established by enacting cultural solidarity rather than institutional expertise: thus a text that will deal with ideational issues in science commonly begins with a reference from high culture. The interpersonal and ideational work in the opening stages of a Gould text are part of a rhetorical enterprise that takes the reader on a journey with science in which not only do traditionally discrete discourses intersect to create agnations, alliances and disjunctions, but intersubjectively, the reader is cast in new relations to different knowledges.

In *English Text: System and Structure* (1992) Martin uses a journey metaphor to discuss the texturing principles of texts: 'A text is a trip: method of development is the route taken, while point is why you went there in the first place – what you've seen/learned/experienced/taken away' (1992: 493). In these texts the starting point is not common sense,[9] but rather 'a good humanities education'. This is not merely by dint of the literary references to Shakespeare and Shelley but it is also due to the indirect way that these texts wind across distinct textual surfaces in order to arrive at their scientific topics. In these texts the concerns of the 'social' inflect science. However, the 'social knowledge' that is positioned as familiar in terms of the essay's information structure (in that what 'we know' generally comes first) is articulated through the literary concerns of the canonical. This no doubt is due in some part to the mythologies that surround 'cultural knowledge'; one must be apprenticed into science, but be naturally sensitive in the humanities. In other words, a love of Shakespeare is acquired merely by exposure to it. This general acceptance that 'cultural' capital is more intuitively natural than technicality is a starting point that is (generally) unquestioned by science writers and fully exploited by Gould.

Gould's textual beginnings are striking not only because they counter one's expectations of how a text on science begins, but they also construe somebody else's text as their starting points (in the cases above Shelley's and Shakespeare's). In beginning his texts by negotiating texts from non-scientific traditions Gould reconfigures the intertextual history against which his essay will be read. In a discussion of a technical review text, *Spandrels of San Marco and the Panglossian Paradigm* by Gould and Richard

Lewontin, which shows similar generic tendencies to the *BfB* texts, Bazerman writes:

> Especially if we are to convince readers of fundamentally new positions, at odds with existing thought, we must somehow uproot the intertext upon which the current audience perceptions rest. It is not sufficient for readers to integrate a finding into their existing mental framework: we must engage them in a radically new line of discussion by discrediting the former discussion with all its implied dynamics and intellectual freight.
>
> (Bazerman 1993: 21)

In this respect Gould's work attempts to construe a discursive space where new relations between science and society can be imagined. As a critical scientist Gould invests as much in the social contingency of scientific knowledge as he does in the historical contingency of biological evolution. Thus his sense of epistemic evolution then falls in line with his pluralistic and historical sense of evolutionary biology. Consequently, in many ways Gould's 'popular' discourse is in some ways exemplary of a critical pedagogy, despite its proliferation of canonical resonances. That is to say, his texts foreground scientific knowledge as partial and contingent on social, historical ideologies. In this way Gould's writing counters much of the popular science tradition by constructing a critical multi-voiced 'narrative of science' rather than a seamless and monologic 'narrative of nature'. This bifurcation of science narrative structure identified by Myers (1990) describes the fundamentally distinct constructions of technical and popular science. According to Myers:

> The professional articles create what I call a *narrative of science*; they follow the argument of the scientist, arrange time into a parallel series of simultaneous events all supporting their claim, and emphasising in their syntax and vocabulary the conceptual nature of the discipline. The popularising articles on the other hand, present a sequential *narrative of nature* in which the plant or animal, not the scientific activity is the subject, the narrative is chronological, and the syntax and vocabulary emphasise the externality of nature to scientific practices.
>
> (Myers 1990: 142)

Gould's focus on the social construction of scientific knowledge is achieved by bringing together a plurality of voices to comment, critique or support the subject matter to hand. In this sense Gould's texts are exemplary of the dialogic process of meaning making discussed by Bakhtin.

> Our speech, that is all our utterances (including creative works) is filled with others' words, varying degrees of 'our-own-ness', varying degrees of awareness and detachment. These words carry with them

their own expression, their own evaluative tone, which we assimilate, rework and accentuate.

(Bakhtin 1986: 89)

Gould's texts overtly bring together distinct discourses, with all their disparate contextual resonances, to negotiate meanings in a manner that is analogous to a dialogue where both writer and reader are 'democratically' and manifestly involved in the production of meaning. However, the paradox of such inclusiveness is that in order for 'all' to be involved, 'each' must exclude their particularities of class, race, ethnicity and gender in order to be participants in such a textual democracy – in which only readers who are willing and able to align themselves with Gould's reworkings and assimilations (rather than their own) are included.

AN OVERVIEW OF 'LIFE'S LITTLE JOKE'

The analysis in this chapter will focus specifically on one text from *BfB*, 'Life's Little Joke'. This text has as its ostensive field focus the evolution of horses. It begins thus: 'I still don't understand why a raven is like a writing desk, but I do know what binds Hernando Cortes and Thomas Henry Huxley together.' This text follows a recognisable Gould pattern – there is an oblique literary reference (Lewis Carroll's *Alice's Adventure in Wonderland*) enticing the reader with the apparent incongruity of such a reference in a piece of science writing. (Why does he begin an essay on kiwi eggs with a reference to Ozymandias, or an essay on the platypus with Polonius?) Rhetorically, these types of beginnings function as general part of what is an 'ethical appeal', they flatter the reader and insinuate cultural solidarity. The ethical appeal is often bound up with an 'insinuatio', in which an author must establish their credentials and counteract prejudices which may be brought against them, thus in many popular science texts (not just Gould's), literary and biblical references abound. These function, on one level to counteract prevailing notions that scientists are 'dry' and single-mindedly technical, and on another level by establishing these literary references as 'commonplaces' an intersubjective *ethos* forms an orientational stance to the text as a whole: a moral seed is sown at the very outset.

The essay's opening ambit of comparing two unlikely historical figures is familiar. In the *BfB* collection of 32 essays he uses it four times.[10] Although most of Gould's *Natural History* essays could be characterised as an historical narrative of science which comprises historical recounts interspersed with taxonomic reports and scientific explanations, this description does not really capture the complexities of the genre, which is better described by focusing on the sequencing of meaning as it unfolds in different phases of the text.

In 'Life's Little Joke' once the seemingly incongruent and mystifying literary reference has been adduced, the text begins in an elliptical fashion to construct a bridge from this to the field focus. The first step in this process is to relate Lewis Carroll's literary riddle to two historical figures – Hernando Cortes and Thomas Henry Huxley. Cortes is represented, after the fashion of traditional historiography, as a figure within the discourse of great men and wars: 'On February 18, 1519, Cortes set sail for Mexico with about 600 men and, more importantly, 16 horses. Two years later, the Aztec capital of Tenochtitlan lay in ruins, and one of the world's greatest civilisations had perished' (*BfB*: 168). This paragraph is then followed by an interpretation of the victory by nineteenth-century historian William H. Prescott, who explains amongst other things why a 'mere handful of horses and their riders [could] cause terror and despair for the Aztecs' (*BfB*: 168). It seems that '[the Aztecs] had no large domesticated animals, and were unfamiliar with any beast of burden' (*BfB*: 168).

After establishing the identity of Cortes (Huxley's is assumed), Gould then asserts a commonality between these unlikely matched figures and their discursive domains. By foregrounding the importance of horses to Cortes' colonial exploits Gould constructs a topical bridge across disciplinary borders to link Cortes and Huxley together. Temporal coincidence adds extra cohesiveness to such a link. Thus after discussing Cortes, Gould moves onto Huxley in the fifth paragraph: 'On the same date, February 18, in 1870, Thomas Henry Huxley gave his annual address as president of the Geological Society of London and staked his claim that Darwin's ideal evidence for evolution had finally been uncovered in the fossil record of horses – a sequence of continuous transformation, properly arrayed in temporal order' (*BfB*: 169). A portion of Huxley's speech is duly quoted and Gould then informs his readership that Huxley viewed the lineage of horses as 'a strictly European affair' (*BfB*: 169). Thus the reader is presented with a classic Gould ambit which constructs connections between figures across worlds, centuries and epistemological domains that in his words 'are so strange they must be meaningful'. (*BfB*: 169).

The resolution to the unlikely coupling of Cortes and Huxley is made in the eight-paragraph through a short (and uncharacteristic) narrative of nature with an interpretive closure full of pathos.

> Horses evolved in America, through a continuity that extends unbroken across 60 million years. Several times during this history, different branches migrated to Europe, where Huxley arranged three (and later four) separate incursions as a false continuity. But horses then died in America at the dawn of human history in our hemisphere, leaving the last European migration as a source of recolonisation by conquest. Huxley's error became Montezuma's sorrow, as an animal more American than Babe Ruth or apple pie came home to destroy her greatest civilisation. (Montezuma's revenge would come later, and by another route.)
>
> (*BfB*: 169–70)

The essay then devotes the next six pages of a fourteen-page article to a historical debate that occurred between Othniel C. Marsh and Thomas Henry Huxley in the 1870s which eventually convinced Huxley that he was wrong about the European location of horse evolution and that they did indeed evolve in America. Then a diagram drawn by Marsh for Huxley as the result of the previous debate, which shows the evolution of horses as a neat progression from three toes to one, from shorter to taller and so on, is used as a focal point for a series of indirect critiques on evolutionary theory projected through the locutions of scientists who have studied the evolution of horses since Marsh and Huxley.

It is the function of these historical debates, voiced through the projected locutions and ideas of others that will be the focus of analysis in this chapter, because the representation of historical scientific debates does not end in this text with Huxley's capitulation to Marsh but it continues right through to the end of the text. In particular, this text shows quite clearly a common Gould strategy of critiquing scientific notions of the past, showing how they were misguided by the conceptual paradigms of the time and then providing the 'correct' interpretation afforded by more data and modern theory.

In 'Life's Little Joke' the idealised reader is lead through the field by following and eventually become textually involved in the scientific debates. The accretion of technical knowledge occurs as textual participants (who are in the main scientists) take up each other's points and support, expand or contradict them. The reader is this case is not being apprenticed into the semantic configurations and formulaic structures of a scientific text. Rather they are being engaged in an intersubjective negotiation with distinct discourses by being positioned as occupying varying 'reader positions' that either concur or disagree with propositional meanings as the text unfolds. In addition to the writer/reader negotiation being enacted around propositional meanings, there is also the interwoven negotiations that occur between the propositions projected by the historical/scientific textual participants of the text. There are two semantically distinct but interdependent types of negotiations occurring in Gould's texts: negotiation construed in the form of the competing voices of scientists, and negotiation enacted between the shifting voices of the addressor and the addressee of the text.

DISCOURSE NEGOTIATION

A word, discourse, language or culture undergoes 'dialogization' when it becomes deprivileged, aware of competing definitions for the same things. Undialogized language is authoritative and absolute.

(Bakhtin 1981: 427)

Systemic functional grammar theorises the dispersal of grammatical resources across a range of qualitatively different kinds of meaning. Different regions of the grammar contribute to making up these meanings: these regions are called metafunctions. Halliday (1979, 1994) has theorised that language comprises three major functional elements: the *interpersonal* metafunction is a resource which enacts social relations and attitudes between discourse interactants; the *ideational* metafunction (comprising two sub-regions – *logical* and *experiential*) is a representational resource that construes phenomena into different configurations; the *textual* metafunction is the organisational resource of language that enables the textualisation of ideational and interpersonal meanings in context. Metafunctional theory makes explicit that each utterance makes different kinds of meanings concurrently and interdependently. Each clause is doing something both interpersonally and ideationally. Consider the example in Figure 3.1.

In the example below, two levels of content are realised textually. First, there is the content projected by the authorial persona of Gould which construes certain participants (here Huxley and Marsh) as 'Sayers' and enacts certain modalities around the propositions that are projected by the 'Sayers'. Second, there are the wordings themselves that are bound by the first order meanings in the text. Thus through interpersonal resources which enact degrees of certainty, probability and judgements around propositions (*perhaps, rightly, wrongly, cleverly*) and ideational resources of *projection* (resources for reporting and quoting speech) the reader is being positioned around the locutions of scientists who are construed as debating with each other's locutions. In this example, there is a dialogue being constructed between the locutions of Huxley and Marsh and interpersonal judgement ('rightly') guiding the reader's evaluation of Marsh's locution.

In Gould's work distinct discourses (different modes of construing the world) are negotiated within the discursive hierarchy enacted in textual practice. This negotiation is both enacted interpersonally, in the changing intersubjective stances around propositions. It is also construed

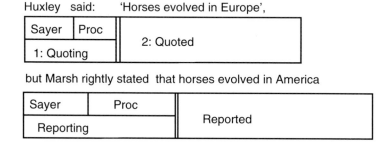

Figure 3.1

ideationally, most obviously in the way that the texts of others support or contradict each other via the resources of projection.

Heavy use of projection[11] is one of the most salient features of the Gould *Natural History* genre, as is his extensive use of first and second person direct reference. This constructs a dialogue between 'his' text and the text of others and also signals an overt dialogue between the reader and the rich intertextuality that he is building.

Masur (1993) stated above that Gould's work is concerned with the relations between science and society and fact and fiction. These concepts are realised through quite distinct semantics and yet there is a seamlessness in the way in which Gould moves from taxonomy to politics from quoting Shakespeare to referencing his own work on punctuated equilibrium. A superficial gloss on the semantic tendencies of those discourses which realise 'science' and those which realise 'society' is provided below, although it should be said that these categorisations are not 'pure': those texts which do not conform to such semantic generalities are not 'hybrids'. These glosses are provided as makeshift handrails to guide through the complex and heteroglot domain of disciplinary textuality.

In the Gould popular genre the reconstruing of the commonsense world into a world of science – turning processes into things or a general concept into a technical one – does not just occur through the monologic principle of reformulation; it occurs through negotiation. That is to say, many differently contextualised social voices discuss the issues at hand rather than just the one voice that constructs increasing technicality. Thus Gould's texts highlight the dialogic impulses of language, they weave not only recognisably distinct semantic configurations together, but they also explicitly raid, appropriate, incorporate and colonise specific texts from seemingly incongruous discursive domains.

In *Discourse and Social Change* (1992), Norman Fairclough located the

Table 3.1 Semantic tendencies in science and the humanities (based on Wignell 1992)

Science	Humanities
Turning commonsense understandings into technical understandings	Using abstraction to understand and interpret the world
Creating a technical language through setting up technical terms, arranging those terms taxonomically and then using that framework to explain how the world came to be as it is.	Abstraction involves moving from an instance or collection of instances, through generalisation to abstract interpretation
Move to increasing specificity	Specific to interpretive

intrinsically intertextual notion of register into a dynamic analytical framework which explicitly highlights the heterogeneity of texts. Fairclough notes, however, that texts vary a great deal in their degrees of heterogeneity and also to the extent to which their disparate discursive elements are evident on the surface of the text.

The notion of a semantics of 'discourse negotiation' as it is expressed here has much in common with what Fairclough has called 'manifest intertextuality'. Manifest intertextuality is categorised as other texts that 'are "manifestly" cued by features on the surface of the text, such as quotation marks' (1992: 104). The grammatical resources for marking another text on the surface of a text are extensive,[12] but they do not exhaust the terrain of intertextuality intrinsic in all text which is not always grammaticalised.

Technical texts resonate with the history of a scientific tradition in society. They are expected to be 'objective' and interpersonally 'neutral', realising affectual semantics of validity rather than morality. However, in the Gould texts technicality is interrogated by other texts ideationally and interpersonally through inferred judgements and multiple first and second person references. This process of negotiation itself enacts the pluralistic agenda that is intrinsic to Gould's ideational message. In other words, science is a social phenomena that occurs in context. In this way the authority of science undergoes a process of what Bakhtin has called 'dialogization', enabled by Gould's extensive exploitation of the semantic resources of discourse negotiation.

Negotiatory systems enable an intersubjective distance to be constructed around propositional meanings in text. They realise distinct levels of meanings in text. There are three major modes of discourse negotiation which form a functional cline from ideational meaning to interpersonal meaning.

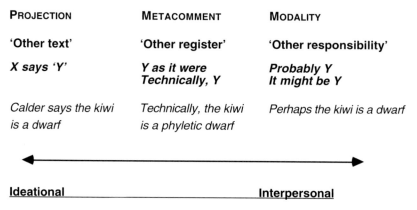

Figure 3.2 Overview of the functional resources of discourse negotiation

In the case of projection, another text is explicitly cued in the textual instance and as such creates ideational orders of discourse. In the case of metacomment, the motivation for using metacomments is not just phenomenological but interpersonal. A metacomment signals the awareness of other ways of construing propositions, hence the intersubjective assessment ranges over the appropriateness of the *term* rather than the *proposition*. Metacomment is a primarily interpersonal resource that has functional parallels with certain ideational resources, such as circumstantial elements of angle (*According to Science* . . .) and location (*In biology* . . .). Modality enacts levels of distance and engagement around propositional meanings and is functionally distinct from the other negotiatory resources because of the inherently meta-functionality of interpersonal meanings over others. This was shown in the example above – 'but Marsh rightly stated that horses evolved in America', where the comment adjunct *rightly* enacts an intersubjective orientation around the ideational meanings of the utterance.

A form of metafunctional complementarity between the interpersonal and ideational metafunctions becomes apparent when one considers the semantics of projection and modality from an intertextually motivated theorisation of discourse negotiation. This relationship becomes clearer if one thinks about these resources as organising a semantics of 'source', in which propositional meaning can be sourced specifically to an individual or institution through forms of projection (*Calder says X is Y*), less specifically to a register through forms of metacomment (*Technically, X is Y*) or to addressor or addressee of the text the resources of modality (*Perhaps X is Y*).

The forms of discourse negotiation of primary concern here are those of discourse representation (projection), metacomment and modality. The main issues are similar to those flagged by Fairclough in his discussion of discourse representation: '(i) to what extent [are] the boundaries between representing and represented discourse clearly marked, (ii) to what extent is represented discourse translated into the voice of the representing discourse' (Fairclough 1992: 119). In other words how does Gould in his role of science populariser make the texts of 'others' (scientific experts) ours? Crucial also to this discussion is at what point, if ever, does this dissolution between represented and representing or 'others' and 'ours' occur.

As stated earlier Gould manoeuvres his readers around the projections of others which are schematically arranged in the form of a historicized debate. This ambit performs multiple functions but will be considered here from a perspective which privileges interpersonal meaning rather than focusing on the disciplinary pluralism of his texts which highlights his ideational agenda.[13] An interpersonal reading is a revealing clue into Gould's success as entertaining populariser but which also marks his deficiencies as a 'popular' pedagogue.

'LIFE'S LITTLE JOKE'

In the initial stages of 'Life's Little Joke', Gould represents the debate that occurred between Marsh and Huxley through a series of direct speech projections in which these two participants are tracked arguing over the evolution of horses. Gould has already informed his readers that Huxley was wrong, that horses did indeed evolve in America, so there is an implication that Marsh (who championed this view) would be right, thus the conclusion of the debate is not surprising. The function of this debate is not to lead the reader to some kind of new thesis, namely, that horses evolved in America: rather it is to supply information about the motivations and methods of evolutionary reasoning at the time. The technical specificities of Huxley's and Marsh's disagreement are not elaborated on. In the early stages of the text technical discussion is wrapped up using a quote a Huxley biography from his son.

> At each inquiry, whether he had a specimen to illustrate *such and such a point* or to exemplify a transition from earlier and less specialised forms to later and more specialised ones, Professor March would simply turn to an assistant and bid him fetch *box number so and so*, until Huxley turned upon him and said, 'I believe you are magician; whatever I want, you just conjure it up' [my emphasis].
>
> (*BfB*: 170–1)

In the early stages of the article, narrativistic overdetermination, rather than field apprenticing scientific overdetermination, rhetorically carries the argument. The technicality of the argument at this stage is glossed as 'such and such a point' proved by 'box number so and so'.

Table 3.2 represents a summary of discourse negotiation in the early stages (paragraphs 5 through 14) of 'Life's Little Joke'. The first two columns represent the two content levels created in the text which demarcates 'our text' and 'others' texts' into representing and represented discourse. The third column tracks the interaction of meanings that occur between propositional meanings in the first two columns. The fourth column tracks in very broad terms the shifts in experiential meaning that occur during the text, focusing on how the text construes historical time and identifying the shifts in field focus (i.e., the moves from the applied field to a more theoretical field). The table takes up after Gould's discussion of Cortes and the Aztecs, and begins at his first mention of Huxley:

> On the same date, February 18, in 1870, Thomas Henry Huxley gave his annual address as president of the Geological Society of London and staked his celebrated claim that Darwin's ideal evidence for evolution had finally been uncovered in the fossil record of horses – a sequence of continuous transformation, properly arrayed in temporal order:

It is easy to accumulate probabilities – hard to make out some particular case, in such a way that will stand rigorous criticism. After much search however, I think that such a case is to be made out in favour of the pedigree of horses.

(*BfB*: 169)

There are actually two forms of projection in the above citation. The first is a form of indirect speech in which the proposition 'Darwin's ideal evidence had been found' is actually a qualification of the nominalised projection 'claim'. The second is direct speech projected from the paragraph as a whole. In Table 3.2, the arrow pointing to the first instance of represented discourse signifies that it is an embedded form of projection that creates a ambiguous tension between represented and representing discourse.

The text has been severely truncated in the tables for ease of reading, but each instance of projection and its variants has been included. Table 3.2 deals with paragraphs 5 through to 14.

Looking at the table it can be seen that at the end of paragraph 14, Huxley and Marsh have reached agreement without the reader really being informed of any field detail that would justify such agreement. What has occurred is basically an establishment of what is construed as a scientific commonplace – an intersubjective starting point that the reader is assumed to occupy. This has been supported by prosody of familiarity that has been amplified throughout this phase of the text (in italics) and is merged with a new ideational element (the scientific commonplace) in the concluding sentence: 'Marsh responded with one of *the most famous illustrations* in the history of palaeontology – the first pictorial pedigree of the horse' [my emphasis].

The next phase of the text has no overt representation of other's discourse and a great deal of interpersonal loading. At this phase the reader learns why the text is titled 'Life's Little Joke' but are kept in suspense as to what the joke actually is. Below is a truncated version of this next phase which spans paragraphs 15 to 21. Italics indicate those sections that evoke either directly or indirectly interpersonalised (you/I) involvement or familiarity with the text's message.

15 The evolution of horse – both in textbook charts and museum exhibits – has a standard iconography . . . (Marsh) also initiated an error that captures pictorially *the most common error of all misconceptions* about the shape and pattern of evolutionary change.

16 Errors in science are diverse enough to demand a taxonomy of categories. Some *make me angry,* particularly those that arise from social prejudice, masquerade as objectively determined truth, and directly limit the lives of those caught in their thrall (scientific justifications for racism and sexism, as obvious examples). *Others make me sad . . .* But *I*

Table 3.2 Overview of discourse negotiation in 'Life's Little Joke', paragraphs 5–14

para.	Representing	Represented	Exchange	Summary
5	Huxley staked his *celebrated* claim that →	Darwin's ideal evidence had been found. Such a case . . . is the pedigree of horses.		1860s
6	Huxley delineated the *famous* trend *that we all recognise.*	'3 toed *Anchitherium* . . . to modern *Equus*'	Thesis – horses evolved in Europe	Applied Field
7	Kurt Vonnegut →	strange ties . . . karass		(present time) linking Cortes and Huxley
8	Horses evolved in America		Gould–contradict	1870s
			Marsh–contradict	
9	Huxley visited Marsh at Yale Huxley said to Marsh	'Show me what you've got inside them, I can see bricks and mortar at home'		
10	Marsh (veiled criticism)	'the line was *probably* direct and American'	support	
11	Marsh (later)	'remains supply every intermediate form'	support	
12	Leonard Huxley describes the meeting	'Huxley said I believe you are a magician. . .'	(enhance)	
13	Huxley Marsh	'sit down before a fact' 'Huxley took my conclusions'		
14	Huxley Marsh responded with *one of the most famous illustrations.*	'your work settles it'	agreement reached	

reserve a special place in perverse affection for a small class of precious ironies – errors that pass nature through a filter of expectation and reach a particular conclusion only because nature really works in precisely the opposite way. This result, *I know,* sounds peculiar and unlikely, but *bear with me* for the premier example of life's little joke – as displayed in conventional iconography (and interpretation) for the most famous case study of all, the evolution of the horse.

17 *Marsh's famous chart,* drawn for Huxley, depicts these trends as an ascending series – a ladder of uninterrupted progress toward one toe and tall, corrugated teeth (by scaling all his specimens to the same size, Marsh does not show the third 'classic' trend toward increasing bulk).

21 *But what is so wrong with these evolutionary ladders? Surely we can* trace an unbroken continuity from Hyracotherium to modern horses. *Yes,* but continuity comes in many more potential modes than the lock step of the ladder. Evolutionary genealogies are copiously branching bushes – and the history of horses is more lush and labyrinthine than most. *To be sure* Hyracotherium is the base of the trunk (as now known), and Equus is the surviving twig. *We can,* therefore, draw a pathway of connection from a common beginning to a lone result. But the lineage of modern horses is a twisted and tortuous excursion from one branch to another, *a path more devious than the road marked by Ariadne's thread from the Minotaur at the centre to the edge of our culture's most famous labyrinth* [my emphasis].

(*BfB*:171–3)

This is a phase of strong interpersonal inducement; it explicitly engages the reader and marks intersubjective interaction through the resources of direct address, first person (singular and plural) references and presumptive comment adjunct such as *surely, to be sure,* etc. These resources enact an engaged and equal intersubjectivity between the personae of writer and reader. The textual interactant is constructed as though they are aware of the issues but just not quite aware of Gould's reading of the 'familiar picture'. Threaded through this rhetoric of cultivated engagement is a form of intersubjective relevance marking that highlights the significance of the scientific issues at hand in the language of 'cultural values'. In a method analogous to the previous section's (paragraphs 5–14) ideational negotiations, where the projected voices of scientists and their biographers constructed the field issues, in this section the field emerges through questions and answers flagged by the interpersonally enacted idealised reader.

After this period of interpersonal inducement the text pushes on into new experiential areas. In the next phase of the genre (paragraphs 23–30, summarised in Table 3.3) an interesting development occurs in the

Table 3.3 Overview of discourse negotiation in 'Life's Little Joke', paragraphs 22–27

para.	Representing	Represented	Exchange	Summary
22	Huxley extended the metaphor to all vertebrates	'teleost fishes are off the main line'	Debate between historical figures and 'Gould'	Theoretical thesis
			Huxley	
	How can we call them 'off the main line' just because we have common ancestors?		contradict	
			Gould	1920s
24	Matthews designated his ladder	'a direct line of succession'	Matthews	
			concessive	
	but acknowledged	'a number of branches'	Matthews	
			critique	
	Matthews adds indecency to charge of mere laterality	'side branches – aberrant – extinct. . .'	Matthews	
	But in what way are extinct lineages more specialised than a modern horse? . . .		contradict	
			Gould	
25	Yet we have recognised the bushiness of horse evolution from the beginning. . . .		Thesis – Evolution is a bush not a ladder	

				1950s
26	Simpson (1951) redrew the genealogy of horses as a modest bush . . . He also criticised the . . . bias of the ladder when he noted →	that the modern one toed horse is a side-branch – 3 toes the mainline.	Simpson	support
		'the sidebranch outlasted the mainline'	Simpson	
			(critique-refine)	
27	Yet Simpson could not let go of ladder biases	'Miohippus intergraded with several descendant groups . . . and confuses the story . . . . foolish to ignore the complications . . .'	Simpson	
	But these 'complications' are the stuff of evolution		contradict	
			Gould	

relationship between the represented and representing discourse. Prior to this stage there was a quite clearly delineated divide between the voice of Gould, who functioned as a discourse moderator, providing interpersonal orientations in representing discourse around the projected locutions of others who actually propelled the applied aspects of field. In this section Gould inserts himself (and the synthesised reader) into the exchanges being construed through projection; that is he inserts himself into the role of a textual participant.

There is a great deal of represented discourse in the section represented by the table above. The point to be made here is that the field of this text is expanded through exchanges between text participants. The reader follows the scientific debate through time and is apprenticed into the technicalities of the issues by a means of textual negotiation in which the dialogic resources of the interpersonal and the ideational are fully exploited. The text swings between negotiating the texts of others (ideational negotiation) to insinuating interpersonal judgments and interrogations around the ideational meanings that come out of such negotiations (interpersonal negotiation). For example, one strategy used by Gould is to pick up an element projected by a textual participant and provide a new interpersonal angle on it.

> 22 Speaking of teleost fishes, Huxley wrote (1880, p. 661) 'They appear to me to be *off the main line* of evolution – to represent, as it were, side tracks starting from certain points of that late line'. But teleost (modern bony fishes) are an enormously successful group. They stock the world's oceans, lakes and rivers and maintain nearly 100 times as many species as primates (and more than all mammals combined). How can we call them '*off the main line*' just because we can trace our own pathway back to a common ancestry with theirs more than 300 million years ago?

In the example above the represented discourse of Huxley is interrogated by 'us' in the form of question that is actually an embedded form of projection. 'How can we call them "off the main line"?' is actually a form of projecting assignment in which the projected content remains within the clause. While grammatically it constitutes representing discourse, it is semantically ambiguous.

The field is being propelled through exchanges between voices of representing and represented discourse. In this way Gould constructs a 'pluralistic' text in which dialogues occur across distinct orders of discourse and in which the authority of scientific projections is challenged by the intersubjectively enacted space of representing discourse.

As the text has unfolded it has followed a temporal linear sequence beginning in the 1860s with the Huxley/Marsh debate through the 1920s with discussion of Mathew's diagram into the 1950s with Simpson and discussions of bushes. The next section sees the arrival of the present time with the discoveries of paleontologists Don Prothero and Dan Shubin.

This near-final phase (paragraphs 30–35, summarised in Table 3.4) presents 'real science' in the light of modernity. The language becomes more technical, discoveries are listed in point form and there is a striking lack of modality and affectual lexis in a text that has been so inter-personally engaging. Gould becomes an assimilator in this stage; the boundary between represented and representing discourse becomes ambiguous. The 'discoveries' of Prothero and Shubin are assimilated via paraphrase into the voice of Gould, which is now located and affiliated with the institution of modern research science who redeems the errors of the past armed with the superior knowledge and empirical data of the present day.

Before moving on to the conclusion of the text and the punchline of 'Life's Little Joke', I would like first to review quickly the process of negotiation that has occurred in the text so far. There has been negotia-tion from two functional perspectives. First, there has been the construal of a negotiatory process in the ideational metafunction, witnessed most clearly by the exchanges that occurred between represented discourses. Second, there has been an enactment of negotiation occurring through interpersonal resources seen most clearly in the shifting intersubjective orientations around the text's propositions.

'Life's Little Joke' like many of the texts in *BfB* initially construes a great deal of textual heterogeneity by incorporating the texts of others. These intertexts then are challenged by and eventually exceeded by the enactment of textual heterogeneity, in which the interactants of the text are inserted as participants and comment upon the text at hand. In this sense ideational modes of discourse negotiation are overtly appropriated and given value within interpersonal modes of meaning.

It was stated at the beginning of this chapter that popular science is a dialogue across discursive domains, which does not necessarily appren-tice readers but cultivates them and exploits the interconnection that it construes between many fields. The audience of the popular science text is not expert and is not apprenticed to become such through the text; therefore the author must invoke a variety of authorities in order to convince. Readers must negotiate authorities beyond that of their own, in ways that will be accepted and flattering to their target audience. However, it was also claimed that popular science explores the relation-ship between registers of discursive elites. This claim was initially sup-ported mainly by reference to lexical tokens and concepts that are in many ways metonymic for 'high culture' such as literary jokes ('Why is a raven like a writing desk?') and Greek mythology (Ariadne's thread) but is further supported in the way that the text also enacts an interpersonal relationship indicative of those between discursive elites.

In the third phase of the text (paragraphs 23–29) a discursive incursion

Table 3.4 Assimilation phase of 'Life's Little Joke'

para.	Representing	Represented	Exchange	Summary
30	The enormous expansion of collections has permitted a test by Prothero and Shubin, which falsify Simpson's hypothesis . . .		The modern thesis – upturn	present
31	Prothero and Shubin have made 4 discoveries	paraphrase (?)		
32	1 They have cleanly distinguished the two genera			
33	2 Mesohippus does not turn into Miohippus . . . The 2 genera overlap by 4 million years			
34	3 Each genius is itself a bush of several related species, not a rung on a ladder of progress.			
35	4 The species arise with geological suddenness. Evolutionary changes occurs at the branch points . . . Of this Prothero and Shubin note	the gradualistic picture of horse evolution becomes a complex bush of overlapping closely related species.	support	
	Bushiness now pervades the entire phylogeny of horses.			

from representing discourse which enacts the interpersonal frame of the text into the represented field, projected by historically located scientists became salient. During this phase the reader becomes, like Gould, meta to the field of science and is construed as able to interrogate its reasoning. Side by side, Gould and his reader engage with the errors of the past. In this way, the Gould genre offers discursive power in lieu of technical knowledge. But only up to a point, for the primacy of science as a social discourse is ultimately restored as evident in the last section where the discourse became its most monologic.

THE LAST LAUGH IN 'LIFE'S LITTLE JOKE'

In the final stages of the text the previous negotiation across the vast traverse of textual domains has narrowed down to the intersubjective negotiation over the text at hand. The following is a truncated version of the concluding paragraphs.

> 36 We can appreciate the shift in iconography . . . but what is 'life's little joke'? Simply this. The ladder model is more than wrong. It could never provide the progressive, triumphant evolution, for *it can only be applied to unsuccessful lineages* [his emphasis].

> 37 Bushes represent the proper topology of evolution . . . The greatest successes (rodents, bats) do not become the classic illustrations . . .

> 38 But consider the poor horse, theirs was once a luxuriant bush, yet they barely survive today . . .

> 39 This is life's little joke. The ladder model guarantees that our classic examples of evolutionary progress can only apply to lineages on the brink of extermination. . . I need hardly remind everybody that at least one other mammalian lineage. . . shares with horses. . .a single surviving twig. . . we build a ladder reaching only to the heart of our own folly and hubris.

> (*BfB*: 180–1)

In the early stages of his text Gould mentions a term, 'karass', used by Kurt Vonnegut in *Cat's Cradle* which refers to 'the subtle ties that can bind people across worlds and centuries into aggregations forged by commonalities so strange that they must be meaningful'. Gould then goes on to locate Huxley and Cortes as members of the same 'karass'. By referencing this fictional notion of karass, Gould in fact signals early a desire for the teleological orientation of traditional historigraphical discourse which is at odds with his rhizomatic theories of evolution.

Hadyn White argues that the difference between mere succession and narrative is that the conflict that narrative resolves arises from and is a function of the 'impulse to moralise reality, that is, to identify it with the social system that is the source of any morality we can imagine' (1980: 18). This narrativisation is, in a sense, Gould's generic resolution of the recasting of theoretical issues in science into moral political issues. The paradox of a text that is so openly dialogic, which foregrounds scientific meanings as partial and intrinsically constituted in discourse, is that the plethora of conflicting arguments and contradictory impulses are assimilated into the one imperialising narrative voice in which 'continuity rather than discontinuity governs the articulation of discourse' (White 1980: 14).

So the punchline of this essay is actually my little joke on 'Life's Little Joke'. Gould identifies anthropocentrism epitomised by Huxley as the authorising principle of the traditional evolutionary narrative, but he does not consider the joke in his own discourse. Despite the 'pluralism' of his evolutionary theories and textual rhetoric Gould ultimately prunes the bush of conflicting voices into a single narrative ladder to arrive at a closure which must be moral, in order to show that a discursive purpose was there all along.

NOTES

1 The accolades for Gould are extensive. In 1990 he won the Science Book Prize for *Wonderful Life*; Stone (1993) singles Gould out for praise as a scientist/populariser, as does Lovejoy, who claims that Gould's work 'stands as a model for all aspiring popularisers of the scientific enterprise' (1991: 208).
2 See M.A.K. Halliday and J.R. Martin 1993 for a survey of the grammatical/semantic feature of scientific discourses.
3 *Bully for Brontosaurus* is the fifth in a series of books comprising articles written for Gould's monthly column in *Natural History* called 'This view of Life'.
4 Louis Masur in *The Literature of Science: Perspectives on popular scientific writing*, W.M. McCrae (ed.) argues that Gould's 'ideological perspective . . . is not so much traditional liberalism as democratic socialism' (1993: 119).
5 Glieck's *Chaos* and Gribbin's *In Search of the Double Helix*.
6 Fahnestock states: 'If a scientific subject cannot be recast under these appeals (wonder and application), it is not likely to make its way to a wider audience' (1993a: 21).
7 Thanks to Jim Martin who first suggested this term to me during our discussions on Gould's interpersonal ambits.
8 Gould's well-known preoccupation with baseball does not counteract this argument. Baseball occupies a privileged position in the public mythologies of 'America'.
9 'Common sense' is used here to refer to a mode of language that realises grammatical congruence. This is generally glossed as the grammar of the spoken language of a pre-pubescent child (Halliday and Martin 1993).
10 In Essays 1: 'George Canning's Left Buttock and The Origin of the Species'; parodically in Essay 5: 'Bully for Brontosaurus'; Essay 11: 'Life's Little Joke' and Essay 24: 'The Passion of Antoine Lavoisier'.
11 In 'Life's Little Joke' just over one-fifth of the article comprises direct speech.
12 A more complete consideration of the semantics of discourse negotiation

can be found in 'Engaging Cultures: Negotiating discourse in popular science', G. Fuller, PhD, Sydney University, 1995.

13 Several excellent readings of Gould's 'Spandrels of San Marco and the Panglossian Paradigm: a critique of the adaptionist programme' can be found in Selzer 1993. All these readings tend to focus on ideational meaning.

REFERENCES

Bakhtin, M.M. 1981. *The Dialogic Imagination*. M. Holquist (ed.) M. Holquist and C. Emerson (trans.) Austin: University of Texas Press.

—— 1986. *Speech Genres and Other Late Essays*. V.W. McGee (trans.) Austin: University of Texas Press.

Bazerman, C. 1993. 'Intertextual Self-Fashioning: Gould and Lewontin's representations of the literature' in J. Selzer (ed.) *Understanding Scientific Prose*. Madison: University of Wisconsin Press.

Benjamin, W. 1969. 'The Task of the Translator' in H. Arendt (ed.) H. Zohn (trans.) *Illuminations*. New York: Schocken Books.

Bourdieu, P. 1991. *Language and Symbolic Power*. London: Polity Press.

Dawkins, S. 1992. *The Selfish Gene*. Oxford: Oxford University Press.

Eger, M. 1993. 'Hermeneutics and the New Epic of Science' in M.W. McRae (ed.) *The Literature of Science: Perspectives on popular scientific writing*. Athens: University of Georgia Press.

Fahnestock, J. 1993a. 'Accommodating Science – The Rhetorical Life of Scientific Facts' in M.W. McRae (ed.) *The Literature of Science: perspectives on popular scientific writing*. Athens: University of Georgia Press.

—— 1993b. 'Tactics of Evaluation in Gould and Lewontin's 'The Spandrels of San Marco' in J. Selzer (ed.) *Understanding Scientific Prose*. Madison: University of Wisconsin Press.

Fuller, G. 1995. 'Engaging Cultures: Negotiating discourse in popular science', unpublished PhD thesis. Sydney University.

Fairclough, N. 1992. *Discourse and Social Change*. London: Polity Press.

Gould, S.J. 1992. *Bully for Brontosaurus*. Harmondsworth: Penguin.

Halliday, M.A.K. 1979. *Language As a Social Semiotic* London: Edward Arnold.

—— 1994. *An Introduction to Systemic Functional Grammar* (second edition). London: Edward Arnold.

Halliday, M.A.K. and Hasan, R. 1985. *Language, Text and Context*. Geelong, Victoria: Deakin University Press.

Halliday, M.A.K. and Martin, J.R. 1993. *Writing Science: Literacy and discursive power*. London: The Falmer Press.

Harvey, D. 1989. *The Condition of Post-Modernity*. Oxford: Basil Blackwell.

Hawking, S. 1990. *A Brief History of Time*. New York: Bantam.

Kelley, R.T. 1993. 'Order out of Chaos: The Writerly Discourse of Semi-popular Scientific Texts' in M.W. McRae (ed.) *The Literature of Science: Perspectives on popular scientific writing*. Athens: University of Georgia Press.

Lovejoy, D. 1991. 'The Dialectical Palaeontologist: popular writings of Stephen Jay Gould', review article in *Science and Society*, 55. (2) 197–208.

Martin, J.R. 1992. *English Text: System and structure*. Amsterdam: Benjamins.

Masur, L. 1993. 'Stephen Jay Gould's Vision of History' in M.W. McRae (ed.) *The Literature of Science: Perspectives on popular scientific writing*. Athens: University of Georgia Press.

Matthiessen, C. 1992. 'Language on language: the grammar of semiosis' *Social Semiotics* 1(2) 69–111.

Midgley, M. 1994. *Science as Salvation: A modern myth and its meaning.* London: Routledge.

Myers, G. 1990. *Writing Biology: The social construction of popular science.* Madison: University of Wisconsin Press.

—— 1991. 'Lexical Cohesion and Specialised Knowledge in Science and Popular Science Texts'. *Discourse Processes: A multidisciplinary journal* vol. 14, 1–26. Ablex Publishing Co.

Prigogine, I. and Stengers, I. 1985. *Order out of Chaos – Man's New Dialogue with Nature* London: Flamingo.

Selzer, J. (ed.). 1993. *Understanding Scientific Prose.* Madison: University of Wisconsin Press.

Shortland, J. and Gregory, M. 1991. *Communicating Science: A handbook.* London: Longman.

Snow, C.P. 1964. *The Two Cultures: And a second look.* Cambridge: Cambridge University Press.

White, H. 1980. 'The Value of Narrativity in The Representation of Reality' *Critical Inquiry* Autumn 5–27.

Wignell, P. 1992. 'Technicality and Abstraction in Sociology', paper presented to the International Systemic Functional Conference, Macquarie University, Australia, July 1992.

4 The 'science' of science fiction

A sociocultural analysis

Anne Cranny-Francis

In its evolution the fictional genre of science fiction traces the anxiety and excitement raised by the development of (primarily) western technology and science. This chapter examines that evolution by reference to the social context in which this fiction was and is produced. In order to identify these relationships between the discursive and textual I am working with a Bakhtinian conceptualisation of genre such as that elaborated by Fredric Jameson when he noted that:

> The strategic value of generic concepts . . . clearly lies in the mediatory function of the notion of genre, which allows the coordination of immanent formal analysis of the individual text with the twin diachronic perspective of the history of forms and the evolution of social life.
>
> (Jameson 1981: 105)

For Jameson the useful characteristic of genre as a critical concept is that the critic/reader is able to bring together for consideration a number of different textual properties and meanings: the way in which the individual text exhibits the characteristics of a genre ('immanent formal analysis'); the way in which that text has modified or transformed the genre ('the history of forms'); and the material and discursive practices which characterise the society in which the text was produced ('evolution of social life').

With science fiction this means examining how an individual text works as science fiction – the conventions of science fiction it uses. Its use of science fiction conventions is also considered in relation to other contemporary science fiction. Does it transform the genre? If so, how and why might this have happened? In looking for the answers to those questions the meanings generated by the text are considered in relation to contemporary social change. As Todorov notes of the Bakhtinian understanding of genre, 'Genre is a sociohistorical as well as a formal entity. Transformations in genre must be considered in relation to social changes' (Todorov 1984: 80). This analysis leads the critic to question how this particular text articulates the fears and desires which characterise the society which produced it.

In so doing the critic must address the particular role of science fiction as a voice of social change. What kinds of fears and desires does science fiction express? How do they differ from those articulated by other fictional genres? A comprehensive answer to that question requires a detailed historical examination of the genre, a simplified version of which follows (see also Scholes and Rabkin 1977; Parrinder 1980; Cranny-Francis 1990a). However, a broad starting point might be that in science fiction the events of the story must seem scientifically plausible. Of course, this might describe several other genres including detective fiction and realist fiction. Anne McCaffrey, writer of the 'Dragonriders of Pern' series, argues that her books are science fiction on the grounds that she provides a plausible scientific explanation for the evolution of the dragons: they were genetically engineered from large lizards and they breathe fire because of the phosphorous-rich rock they chew which results in the ignition of their expelled breath. Samuel Delany makes a similar point by reference to the phrase, 'the winged dog'. In fantasy, he notes, the idea of a winged dog is simply proposed and then accepted as part of the fictional world of the text; in science fiction the evolution of this creature would have to be explained. So science fiction stories have to be scientifically plausible – or appear to be so, which is not quite the same thing; the possibility of breeding dragons from lizards seems rather remote. Again we need to look to the sociocultural context of science fiction to understand the reason for this fetishisation of science.

MOTHERING THE GENRE: SHELLEY'S *FRANKENSTEIN*

Mary Shelley's *Frankenstein* told of more than one birth. As well as Victor Frankenstein's creature – the uncongenial pastiche of disinterred and stolen body parts – the novel was the genesis of a new fictional genre, science fiction. It, too, is a pastiche, formed of parts of older genres, primarily the Gothic.

From the Gothic *Frankenstein* retains the frame narrative, the story-within-the-story technique which is used to distance the reader and induce a critical perspective. From the Gothic also are the 'exotic' European setting of the tale and its references to alchemy and magic. For English Gothicists these distancing features enabled the writer to 'speak the socially unspeakable' (Punter 1980: 417), to raise concerns about the nature of the everyday, about accepted beliefs and values, and about the nature of knowledge which would have been too confronting in a familiar setting. Yet once raised such concerns were liable to reverberate even more acutely with social and individual anxieties. This interrogation of knowledge, of belief and of what we accept as the everyday real is at the very heart of Gothic, the genre from which science fiction evolved.

Shelley's genius was to direct this interrogative genre to a new and different area of contemporary interest and concern, science and technology which she embodies in the creature and his maker, Victor Frankenstein. There have been many different readings of the story. For example, it has been read as a critique of contemporary gender relations as realised in issues surrounding maternity, the feckless father, Frankenstein signifying the patriarchal appropriation of maternity and its negative consequences (Moers 1978: 93). For contemporary readers the development of new reproductive technologies lends this reading a new poignancy and relevance. Another, more popular reading understands the story as a reflection on the inability of humanity to deal with the social products and consequences of bourgeois science and technology; hence the novel's subtitle, 'the modern Prometheus'.

Bourgeois science and technology challenged the divine by assigning rational explanations to previously inexplicable phenomena and so caused great crises in faith for many people. It also enabled the development of new kinds of machines which not only revolutionised the domestic environment of the country, but also transformed England into an imperialistic world power. The nature of knowledge, of belief and of the everyday real were under challenge and this new genre evolved to meet that challenge: as both interrogator and apologist. The 'science' in this earliest science fiction was a focus or reference point for the social critique.

In the story Victor Frankenstein actually does not use conventional scientific procedures. He disappoints his university teachers by turning to alchemical studies and arcane technologies. Most readings – and certainly most re-readings such as movies – do not acknowledge this. Instead they depict Frankenstein as a scientist who has pushed scientific knowledge to higher levels, harnessing the force of nature in the great lightning-conductor scenes. This confusion about the nature and status of Frankenstein's 'science' suggests that the science itself is not what motivates the narrative or readers' responses to it. Instead the concern is the social consequence of that science, signified by the production of a being who is rejected by his creator, who is monstrous in the eyes of those he encounters, and who eventually turns to violence as a result of his personal and social rejection. He is an embodiment of social pathology.

Written early in the nineteenth century the social pathology, or pathologies, articulated in *Frankenstein* are most obviously those prompted by a time of rapid technological, social and political change. The French Revolution was a recent and frightening memory, the steam engine a disturbing reality. Land enclosures for large-scale farming facilitated by the developments in technology forced many country workers to the cities, which were themselves changing from semi-rural to mechanised, industrial centres – the 'dark, Satanic mills' of Blake's 'Jerusalem'. Gender-based and class-based inequality came increasingly under scrutiny with the aggregation of people and the increasing political freedom of middle-class women. At the base of many of these changes was the technology which enabled and necessitated them. Not only did it change the lived environment, but it also changed the ways people thought about themselves and their society. The Luddites set about smashing the machines which they saw as both material cause and signifier of the social transformation they were suffering; Mary Shelley developed a new literary genre, science fiction, from the interrogative genre of Gothic to explore those changes and articulate the anxiety and suffering they were causing.

THE FIRST CENTURY A.F.

Scholes and Rabkin write that 'in the first century A.F. [after *Frankenstein*] the as yet unbaptized genre of science fiction explored its potential in a range of different directions', among which they include 'Poe's metaphysical speculation, Verne's romance of hardware, Bellamy's social criticism, and ERB's [Edgar Rice Burrough's] tales of exotic adventure' (Scholes and Rabkin 1977: 14). Again the Gothic roots of the genre are visible, particularly in the work of Poe whose principal interest always is an interrogation of the rational – or what society decides to nominate as 'the rational'. With Burroughs and Verne the other side of the Gothic, its ability to facilitate the 'unlivable' (the flip-side of its power to speak the unsayable) is evident. As Punter notes:

> Gothic enacts psychological and social dilemmas: in so doing, it both confronts the bourgeoisie with its limitations and offers it modes of imaginary transcendence, which is after all the dialectical role of most art. Gothic fiction demonstrates the potential of revolution by daring to speak the socially unspeakable; but the very act of speaking it is an ambiguous gesture.
>
> (Punter 1980: 417)

In other words, Gothic – the genre transformed by Mary Shelley into the new genre of science fiction – is fundamentally ambiguous. Its otherworldly stories, frame narrative, and references to magic and the supernatural enable the expression of fears and desires which are commonly suppressed by rationalistic thought and practice. At the same time allowing that expression means that individuals living with those fears and desires are provided with an outlet for them, and do not have to address either them or the ideology and social structure which both produces and represses them.

For Burroughs and Verne the negative everyday consequences of technological change were sublimated in an exaltation of the possibilities it raised – travel to new worlds, conquest of new frontiers. In their work the power of the technology is the focus, rather than issues of access or consequence. This strand has remained very powerful within science fiction – ambiguous, politically conservative, socially pacificatory.

For many contemporary socialists Bellamy's work also falls into this category. His catalytic utopian romance *Looking Backward* is often categorised as science fiction (the generic boundaries between these genres needs careful exploration) because it uses a number of conventions associated with the genre such as time travel and high technology. For the English socialist, William Morris, Bellamy's use of high technology to produce a 'brave, new world' was a propitiatory gesture which avoided addressing the real social problems of his day (Morris, 1889). So science and technology in science fiction can also be seen as participating in the progressive rhetoric of bourgeois science and technology, which claimed it as the means of overcoming social pathology, rather than its cause.

H.G. WELLS

Writing at the very end of the nineteenth century was the writer who next took up the mantle of Mary Shelley, H.G. Wells. Wells studied biology under Thomas Henry Huxley and spent some time as a science journalist, so he had some professional understanding of contemporary scientific development. He was also a Fabian socialist and associated with some of the leading socialists of his time, such as Beatrice and Stanley Webb. His science fiction brings these two sets of knowledges and opinions, these two discourses, together. In books such as *The Time Machine* and *The Island of Doctor Moreau* Wells speculates on the nature of contemporary society and the effects on it of not only science and technology, but also the technological and scientific imaginaries it generates, particularly the notion that technology and science can 'improve' humanity. In *The Island of Doctor Moreau* the human–animal hybrids who are the wretched results of Moreau's experiments are the Darwinian successors to Frankenstein's creature.

Wells covered a range of scientific and technological possibilities in his work – time travel, biotechnology, space travel. However, in his stories they are not sources of personal, social or imperial power, but are used to explore the problems generated by technological and social changes – for society as a whole and for the individual caught up in those changes; the degenerate society of the Morlocks and Eloi as a graphic representation of late nineteenth-century social inequity, the monsters created by Doctor Moreau signifying the failure of contemporary scientists and technologists to understand the impact of their work on everyday life, the dehumanising effect on the individual of 'pure' or socially decontextualised science in *The Invisible Man*. Fundamental to Wells's work is an interrogation of the nature of the rational, of the real, and of the everyday which problematises the rhetoric of progress employed by bourgeois science and technology.

By the end of the nineteenth century, then, the new genre of science fiction was characterised as a fiction which 1) referred the reader to specific scientific theories and/or technologies; and, 2) in so doing, articulated contemporary hopes and fears about the impact on everyday life of science and technology, about the kinds of society they produced, and about its consequences for the individual subject. Science fiction thereby reflected its basis in Gothic fiction which was fundamentally concerned with the nature of the real and the limitations of the rational (rationalism being fundamental to the development of bourgeois science and technology). It also signalled contemporary awareness of the radical change to the industrial base of nineteenth-century society, figured in the science and technology described in the text. This reference to science and/or technology is a key textual referent which marked the text as science fiction rather than Gothic.

THE TWENTIETH CENTURY

A great deal has been written about the science fiction of the twentieth century: the utopian and dystopian adventures of the first thirty years, tracing the late Victorian period, World War I, the decadent twenties and the rise of fascism in the thirties; the pulp science fiction which followed World War II and the development of atomic power; the social science fiction of the sixties and seventies; and the information-based technology of contemporary science fiction. In each of these successive evolutions of the genre science and technology have continued to play a pivotal role, though the nature of the role differs radically from one period to the next.

Dystopia was far more common than utopia in the early decades of the twentieth century and this is commonly seen as reflecting the rise of fascist ideologies. Science and technology are often the villains in these fictions, serving the state and suppressing individual freedom; hence, the bureaucratically regulated assembly lines of Zamyatin's *We* (1972), in the 1930s, the genetically engineered, drug-controlled masses of Huxley's *Brave New World* (1955) and, in the 1940s, the ceaseless surveillance of Orwell's *Nineteen Eighty-Four* (1954).

After World War II this situation changed, with science and technology again taking a heroic role. The atomic weaponry of the forties and fifties was seen not as escalating world tensions but as saving the world for peace – an extraordinary rhetoric from this perspective, but believable at the time. So the science fiction of the time showed high technology – often atomic weaponry – saving the world against alien invasion (for which read the Eastern Bloc if in the West), against monsters produced by its own technology (irony often lost in the course of the battle!), against monsters from the Deep (usually the Eastern Bloc in another guise), against its own political divisions (irony seldom addressed!). The rhetoric of scientific 'progress' was once again in place and much science fiction dramatised and narrativised this discourse. But not all.

While the world was saved from alien invasion in the 1950s film, *Earth v. the Flying Saucers* (Fred F. Sears 1956) by the former's superior firepower, movies such as *The Thing* (Christian Nyby/Howard Hawks 1951), *Forbidden Planet* (Fred Wilcox 1956), *The Day the Earth Stood Still* (Robert Wise 1951) and *I Married a Monster from Outer Space* (Gene Fowler, Jr 1958) are far more ambiguous in their treatment of science and technology. In the Nyby/Hawks version of *The Thing*, the alien is dispatched by a group of 'good all-round American guys' (and one woman) working together, hindered rather than assisted by the scientists in their midst. If anything, this film dramatises a split between science and technology. The scientists try to communicate with the alien, which is clearly reminiscent of movie versions of Frankenstein's creature, and its only response is to murder most of them and drink their blood; the multiple Gothic signifiers again drawing attention to the role of this genre in interrogating the everyday and the rational, especially as it is now constituted via a scientific imaginary. The world is saved because the non-scientists use basic technical knowledge to rig a primitive technological trap for the creature and burn it to death. Science, it seems, can be dangerously out of touch with everyday life and its needs.

In *Forbidden Planet* the scientific genius Dr Morbius is revealed as a sociopath whose unconscious (the id) has been given a material form – an invincible monster capable of destroying anything in its path. Morbius underwent this transformation when using the intellect-enhancing technology of an alien life-form, the Krel, which he discovered on a remote planet, Altair 4. This side-effect of Krel technology led to the downfall of their entire civilisation; for Morbius the only solution is suicide. Once again there is a team of 'all-round Earth guys' and one woman who survive the encounter, and end by destroying the planet and its treacherous technology. As they leave, the commander of the Earth expedition to Altair 4 notes: 'Let's hope when the human race reaches the same level of development as the Krel it will be better equipped to handle it.' This summarises many of the concerns articulated in these movies and again harkens directly back to *Frankenstein*. The separation of science and technology in some of the science fiction of this period signifies this anxiety: on the one hand, the social problems which accompany a technological transformation, even when the technology itself offers greater luxury or intellectual stimulation; on the other hand, the antisocial nature of 'pure' scientific research which refuses to accept responsibility for its possible applications (such as nuclear weaponry).

RE-ENTER THE CYBORG

In the last few decades of the twentieth century science fiction has continued its role as social interrogator and/or conciliator. The 1960s television series *Star Trek* (Paramount 1967–69) proved to be the most popular television series of all time, with an ongoing fan audience in the millions. *Star Trek* demonstrated both capacities of science fiction: to explore the anxieties prompted by technological and social change, and to exalt in science and technology for its own sake (Punter 1980: 417). As an anthology series some episodes take one line, some another, but the overall framework for the series demonstrates the dual potential: a highly technologised society which sets out to explore the universe, along the way learning a great deal about its own nature, not least its capacity for injustice and savagery.

The technology of *Star Trek* now looks laughably primitive, but in its time was very convincing. Its function was not so much as focus for the action, as in *Frankenstein*, but as general context: this is a society which assumes a particular level of technological and scientific knowledge and use, and its way of thinking and acting is formulated in those terms. David Gerrold, in his account of the production of the series, *The Making of Star Trek*, discusses the science and technology of *Star Trek* in some detail. He quotes Gene Coon, a *Star Trek* producer, on the achievement of *Star Trek*'s creator, Gene Roddenberry:

> Gene created a totally new universe. He invented a starship, which works, by the way, and is a logical progression from what we know today. He created customs, morals, modes of speaking, a complete technology. We have a very rigid technology on the show. We know how fast we can go. We know what we use for fuel. We know what our weapons will do. And Gene invented all these things. He did a monumental job of creation. He created an entire galaxy, and an entire rule book for operating within that galaxy, with very specific laws governing behavior, manners, customs, as well as science and technology.
>
> (Whitfield and Roddenberry 1968: 74)

Coon's analysis of Roddenberry's success traces the critical link between the science and technology of a society and its social and political practice. As a storyteller Roddenberry utilises this relationship to produce a fictional universe in which contemporary social issues can be discussed from a radically new perspective. Sometimes *Star Trek* achieved this kind of radicalism; other times it did not. As an anthology the series featured many different writers, some of whom were less able than others to rise to the challenge offered by Roddenberry's universe. The science and technology of *Star Trek* operated as a signifier of difference – of the possibility of new perspectives and new ways of thought. That it was also the context for very conservative practices and stories is not surprising, since this conservative trend has always been one element of science fiction; the 'hard' science fiction in which science and technology operate as a backdrop for adventure stories based on very conservative ideas and practices (e.g. xenophobia, fears of miscegenation, colonialism). Perhaps more fundamentally it underlines the point that science fiction is an articulation both of other possibilities, and of its own time – with all its attitudes/prejudices, beliefs, and social practices.

The same ambiguity is evident in one of the most striking recent science fiction films, *Blade Runner* (Ridley Scott 1982). Based on a Philip K. Dick novel, the movie tells the story of renegade androids designed for off-world (off-Earth) duty who return to Earth in order to find a solution to their own in-built obsolescence. Rick Deckard is a retired blade runner (android hunter/killer), forced back into service to track down these renegades. In this and most other science fiction films science and technology have a disturbingly ambiguous role. How do you make a film about the dangers of high technology without making a film which relies for its visual impact on high technology? This central problematic is indicative of the interpellation of Western society by the very discourse under interrogation: we have to 'see' high tech in order to understand the question. Yet often that high tech is itself fabulous. For example, when asked why his spaceships rumble through the soundless vacuum of space, George Lucas explained that that's what people want to experience; the actual science is not the issue. In other words, the scientific imaginary at work here has no grounding in the material real.

Nevertheless *Blade Runner* does ask these questions: who is more human, the android fighting for life or the blade runner whose occupation is killing them? Who defines what it is to be human? What right has humanity to turn its back on the consequences of its own technology and its own scientific research? These questions again reiterate Mary Shelley's concerns in *Frankenstein*, a reference acknowledged in the movie as one of the androids, Roy Batty says to the genetic engineer, Dr Chew, maker of eyes: 'If only you could see what I've seen with your eyes.' The science and technology of *Blade Runner* is not simply an interesting *mise-en-scène*, though it is also that. It is the context within which such questions become imperative. As David Lange (Prime Minister of New Zealand when that country refused harbour entry to any ship not prepared to declare itself nuclear-free) argued against the development of nuclear weapons, the problem is not simply the weapons themselves but the kind of state they necessitate – one based on secrecy, on 'protecting' the public through the suppression of truth.

Late twentieth-century science fiction is centrally concerned with the nature of the State necessitated by its own science and technology. The social science fiction of the 1960s and 1970s – the work of writers such as Dick, Samuel Delany, Ursula LeGuin, Stanislaw Lem – decisively returned science fiction to its socially interrogative mode. Lem's *Solaris* (1971) interrogated the nature of not only science and technology but knowledge itself; making the (postmodern) point that all knowledge is situated and context-dependent. The ideal of 'pure' science and 'value-free' technology is a rhetoric of the bourgeois state within which that science and technology is practised, rather than an objective aim. The fiction of Delany and LeGuin narrativises that view, in the process deconstructing contemporary western society and its views on and uses of science and technology.

Yet familiar problems return. The successor to *Star Trek*, *Star Trek: The Next Generation* (Paramount 1987–94) features an on-going play on the notion of the android, the man-made creature, in the character of the android first officer, Mr Data. Dr Noonian Singh's Data is more life-like than Dr Frankenstein's creature, but he suffers a similar set of problems in trying to fit into human society – including rejection of his right to autonomous existence and to respect as an equal, but different, life-form. In a memorable episode from the second season of *Star Trek: The Next Generation*, 'The Measure of a Man', a research scientist demands the right to disassemble Data in order to discover how he works and so build more like him. The ship's captain, Picard, is forced to defend in court Data's rights to freedom and respect, which he does by reference to humanity's less than worthy record on 'disposable people' – a socio-cultural argument suggested to Picard by unofficial counsellor, Guinan, played by African–American actor Whoopi Goldberg. The android or cyborg remains a powerful figure in science fiction where, like the alien, it becomes a site for the expression of a wide range of fears and desires: about the way in which bourgeois science and technology – and the ideology they generate – affects our construction as individuals; about the ways in which human capabilities might be augmented by the technological; about the infiltration of the human by the technological.

The most recent developments within science fiction include the evolution of cyberpunk, a fictional genre primarily concerned with the effects on individuals of information technologies (Bukatman 1993; Cranny-Francis 1994, 1995). The best-known text in this genre is William Gibson's *Neuromancer*, though Dick's *Do Androids Dream of Electric Sheep?* (the basis of the film *Blade Runner*) is often seen as a precursor. Again the actual science and technology described are not the central issue, and the stories of Gibson's own computer illiteracy are legion: he wrote the book on a portable typewriter; he bought his first Apple Mac after he wrote *Neuromancer* (1986) but returned it to the store because it was making noises, not realising it actually didn't run on something like 'liquid crystal'. Yet Gibson has since been employed by US Government agencies such as NASA as a creative consultant; Gibson's grasp of the facts may be minimal, but his understanding of the contemporary technological imaginary is impressive.

With *Neuromancer* Gibson focused on a technology which is a source of contemporary fear and desire, the combination which imparts to the cyborg its particular *frisson*. Information technology is widely advertised as a source of unimaginably rapid information access; as a potential mode of democratic government; as a method of interpersonal relationship. Yet it is also feared as a violator of privacy, the contemporary panopticon. More critically there is widespread concern about who controls such a technology – government? Large business corporations? In *Neuromancer* the power of multinational business corporations is dramatised by their control of the individuals who rely on their information networks. The operators themselves are so interpellated with the ideology of their technology that they refer to their own bodies as 'meat' and they live for the times they are plugged literally into the machine – the late twentieth-century cyborg.

Generically *Neuromancer* combines characteristics of science fiction with others drawn from detective fiction, such as the tough guy narration. In detective fiction this narration signifies the struggle of the 'little guy', typically the ethical lower-middle-class man (Philip Marlowe, Sam Spade), to deal with the corruption within his society which is situated primarily in government and big business. This character dramatises the impact of that corruption on everyday life via a 'common man' character. Science fiction has not often dealt with the lives of individuals, conducting its analysis usually at the level of the social. By using this characteristic from hard-boiled detective fiction Gibson constructs a new pastiche or mixed genre, prefigured in *Blade Runner* with its Marlowe-like Deckard – cyberpunk.

Other cyberpunk novels such as Joan Vinge's Cat novels, *Psion* (1982) and *Catspaw* (1988) are similarly concerned with the world created by an information-rich but socially stratified society. The impact of this society on the individual is demonstrated in the life of an individual who is not from the privileged class which controls access to information. C.J. Cherryh deals with a similar problem in her space-rat novels, stories of asteroid miners and others whose lives are controlled by companies and governments who have no interest in and take no responsibility for their safety. The transnational, transworld companies in these stories are like the company with which Ripley battles in the *Alien* movies; they are willing to sacrifice the lives of thousands to make an extra bit of profit. And they have the power to force their operatives (like Ripley in *Aliens*, like Case of *Neuromancer* and Cat of *Psion* and *Catspaw*) to perform procedures to which they object ethically. All of these novels articulate the late-twentieth-century concern with the power of information technology, and perhaps more fundamentally with concerns about access to the technology and the nature of those who control the technology.

With *Frankenstein* Mary Shelley created a fiction which addressed the society of the industrial revolution. Her concern was not only the potential of the technology itself to change the material conditions of life, but also the social implications of the state constituted by this new industrial base; the kinds of thought processes it favoured, the imaginary it produced and which produced it. Her originary cyborg, Frankenstein's creature, signified the nature of the 'man' created by this new state – a sociopathic individual, a horrific travesty of a human being. One hundred and fifty years later the cyborgs are less horrific, but they still articulate a deep concern with the interface between humanity and technology. The questions they provoke are indicative of the Gothic roots of the science fiction genre. How do we define the rational and the real? Who has the right to define the real and the normal? What is knowledge? How do we understand our responsibility for the technology we use? And in the most recent science fiction, the fiction of information-based technology: who controls access to that technology? What effect does that control have on the lives of individuals? How can individuals escape domination by the information-rich, whether corporations or governments?

In each case the science and technology described in the text is highly sophisticated. Yet that technology and science is seldom the focus of the narrative, though science fiction does sometimes (often?) articulate a bourgeois rhetoric of 'progress'. Instead the technology and science draw attention to the nature of the state engendered by that particular industrial system, which often sacrifices individual human needs and desires to the demands of 'pure' science or a dehumanising technology. The nineteenth-century socialist William Morris lamented the reduction of workers from full human beings to factory 'hands', appendages to machines. In the late twentieth century the human being is no longer even a hand, but simply the 'meat', the 'wet-ware' which supports the machine.

THE 'SCIENCE' OF SCIENCE FICTION

This abbreviated historical account of science fiction suggests the ways in which the genre of science fiction articulates concerns raised by the nature of the science and technology used by the West; about the kind of state it generates, about problems of access to technology, about the ways in which the ideologies of science and technology determine our definitions of the 'human', about the mode of thought – rationalism – it demands from social subjects, about the reality it creates. It also suggests a striking feature about the science of science fiction, which is that it is primarily fiction rather than science.

This survey also touches briefly on the distinction between science and technology – science as pure research conducted with an inhuman and antisocial intensity, technology as humanity interfacing with the environment – which is addressed in some science fiction texts (see the earlier discussion of *The Thing*). The etymology of the name 'science fiction' is interesting in this respect. Nineteenth-century texts of the genre were often classified as 'scientific romance', the term 'science fiction' becoming the generic label in the twentieth century. Both labels, however, contain a reference to science, not technology. This is doubtless related to contemporary understandings of the relationship between science and technology, with science prioritised as the theoretical underpinning of technology. Currently there is a great deal of interest in the philosophy of technology, which reconsiders this relationship (see, for example, Ihde 1990, 1993a, 1993b). The focus here, however, is on the fiction which has responded to these two – somehow related – practices; debate about their relationship being one of the many concerns of science fiction *because* of the way it impacts on society. In considering the science of science fiction, then, I am not reflecting on the validity of that science or even how it reflects the scientific discourse of its day; rather I am considering science as a textual referent related to, but not identical with, contemporary scientific discourse.

Science takes a number of different identities within individual science fiction texts. It is sometimes signified by the presence of androids, cyborgs, clones or other man-made creatures. Commonly these creatures signify a range of concerns about the interface between the human and the mechanical, technological or biological. In the terms proposed by anthropologist Mary Douglas they are concerned with boundary definition – with what differentiates the human from the non-human. The disturbing feature of contemporary science and technology is that, at a range of sites, from scientific research into genetic manipulation to the development of cochlear implants for the hearing impaired, the boundaries blur. This blurring then operates as a focus for all kinds of social fears about boundaries and limits: are women human? Are people from a different racial or ethnic background human? Are children human? Or are there degrees of humanness (of which the boundary-maker represents the highest)?

Furthermore, the rejection of man-made beings by their makers and the society in which they find themselves recalls Mary Shelley's fundamental questioning of the social responsibility of the scientist and technologist. This leads to an interrogation of the rhetoric of bourgeois science with its constructions of 'pure' science and 'neutral' technology. Science and technology are shown in this argument to be, like any form of knowledge, context-dependent and socioculturally specific.

This point is the principal argument of Stanislaw Lem's novel *Solaris* (1971), where the scientific study of the alien planet, Solaris, is shown to be a fantasy. Solaristics, the body of research material collected, is shown to be an artefact of the science itself, a point demonstrated by the planet itself as it reads the minds of the scientists and depicts the images it finds back to them. They see only what their science, their mode of knowledge construction, allows them to see. In this novel and in the work of other writers of the 1960s and 1970s science is revealed as a mode of knowledge construction with its own ideology, rhetoric, boundaries and limitations. In these stories 'science' is less a specific set of theories than a name for a specific mode of thought which the texts deconstruct not as neutral but sociocultural.

Another science fiction convention used to make a similar point is the character of the alien. The alien is related to the android in that she or he is positioned to interrogate human values and beliefs through interactions with humans. Data of *Star Trek: The Next Generation* often fills this role, occupied in the original series by the Vulcan–Human officer, Mr Spock. These aliens either demonstrate or imply a different science and technology and a different mode of thought and practice which is often turned with devastating clarity on the society of the reader:

> the strange system of human society was explained to me . . . . I learned that the possessions most esteemed by your fellow-creatures were high and unsullied descent united with riches. A man might be respected with only one of those advantages; but without either, he was considered . . . as a vagabond and a slave, doomed to waste his powers for the profits of the chosen few!
>
> (Shelley 1968: 124)

These are not the words of one of *Star Trek*'s aliens or James Cameron's Terminators, though they might be, but of the creature of Mary Shelley's *Frankenstein*. So this convention, the character of the alien, which arises from the need to indicate the possibility of other kinds of science and different technologies – such as the flying saucer – functions within these stories as an interrogative voice, questioning human (Western) society and its values. Occasionally the purpose of the alien is simply to demonstrate bigger, faster, better technology – as in the *Star Wars* movies – but even then dramatic convention demands that the earth people win. In other words, the demands of fiction supersede the fascination with technology.

Well, almost always. In the iconoclastic fiction of James Tiptree Jr (Alice Sheldon) the aliens sometimes do win. For example, in the horrific story 'The Screwfly Solution', aliens have seeded the earth with chemicals which drive men to kill all women in a sexualised killing orgy. The murder is given moral authority by a 'Pauline Purification Cult' within the Catholic Church. At the end of the story a lone female survivor, knowing her time is limited, leaves a note for the one man who has helped her escape the purge:

> Let me repeat – it was *there*. Barney, if you're reading this, *there are things here*. And I think they've done whatever it is to us. Made us kill ourselves off.

Why? Well, it's a nice place, if it wasn't for people. How do you get rid of people? Bombs, death rays – all very primitive. Leave a big mess. Destroy everything, craters, radioactivity, ruin the place.

This way there's no mess, no fuss. Just like what we did to the screwfly. Pinpoint the weak link, wait a bit while we do it for them. Only a few bones around; make good fertilizer.

Barney dear, good-bye. I saw it. It was there.

But it wasn't an angel.

I think I saw a real estate agent.

(Tiptree 1981: 75)

Tiptree has the aliens win – and in the process she not only questions the uses of contemporary science, but also the nature of male–female gender relations, the constitution of male sexuality, and the role of the institutionalised church in lending moral authority to social practices which are inequitable and even genocidal. Again, science is there but its major function is to focus readers' attention around a set of issues to which it may be only marginally related.

The science of science fiction, therefore, has one major function: it establishes the constructed nature of knowledge by drawing attention to the ways in which science and/or technology determine and/or reflect the dominant rhetoric and ideology of a society. That is, by fetishising science and technology science fiction makes the point that the nature of a society – its values, beliefs, attitudes – is a function of its industry, the way it organises labour and the people who perform it. Furthermore, science and technology are themselves limited and defined by the dominant mode of thought of a particular society, such as rationalism. In other words, what is identified as science and technology in a rationalist society is a research practice and material application of abstract principle which corresponds to rationalist thought; anything else is superstition or magic and not authorised. This function of science fiction refers back to Gothic in its interrogation of the nature of knowledge, but focuses that interrogation specifically around issues to do with the industrial composition of a society and its sociocultural ramifications.

Textually, the science is construed either by reference to known science and technology or to common fantasies of science or technology which might be described as the technological or scientific imaginary. Textual features such as high tech practices (time travel, space travel, warp drive, embedded jacks for computer connection) and alien characters (aliens, cyborgs, androids, clones) signify the text's engagement with this imaginary. And each textual feature can be read in terms of the sociocultural context in which it evolved, as Jameson notes in his analysis of genre. Certainly some writers, such as Jules Verne, argued that their science was accurate and took care to make it so. However, while plausibility remains an important characteristic – distinguishing science fiction from genres such as fantasy and maintaining the reader's engagement with contemporary science and technology – accuracy is not necessary.

Detective fiction is fiction which deals with issues of concern raised by contemporary views on the nature of causality, criminality, the definition of normality, and the nature of social and individual pathology (Cawelti, 1976; Knight, 1980; Cranny-Francis, 1990b); it is not (necessarily) fiction about real-life detectives. Science fiction is fiction which uses science and/or technology to focus on issues of concern raised by the changing nature of a society's industrial base and by the ideological and discursive influences on and results of those changes; it is not (necessarily) fiction about actual science and technology.

REFERENCES

Bakhtin, Mikhail. 1981. *The Dialogic Imagination: Four Essays.* Trans. C. Emerson and M. Holquist. Ed. M. Holquist. Austin: University of Texas Press.
—— 1986. *Speech Genres and Other Late Essays.* Trans. Vern McGee. Eds C. Emerson and M. Holquist. Austin: University of Texas Press.
Bellamy, Edward. 1977. 'How I Came to Write *Looking Backward.' Science-Fiction Studies,* vol. 4 194–95.
—— [n.d.] *Looking Backward (2000–1987) or, Life in the Year 2000 A.D.* Reprinted London: William Reeves.
Brosnan, John. 1978. *Future Tense: The Cinema of Science Fiction.* New York: St Martin's Press.
Bukatman, Scott. 1993. *Terminal Identity: The Virtual Subject in Postmodern Science Fiction.* Durham and London: Duke University Press.
Cawelti, J.G. 1976. *Adventury, Mystery, and Romance: Formula Stories As Art and Popular Culture.* Chicago and London: University of Chicago Press.
Cranny-Francis, Anne. 1988a. 'Gender and Genre: Feminist Rewritings of Detective Fiction.' *Women's Studies International Forum,* vol. 11, no. 1, 69–84.
—— 1988b. 'Out Among the Stars in a Red Shift: Women and Science Fiction.' *Australian Feminist Studies,* no. 6, 71–86.
—— 1988c. 'Sexual Politics and Political Repression in Bram Stoker's Dracula.' *Nineteenth-Century Suspense: From Poe to Conan Doyle* ed. C.S. Bloom. London: Macmillan, pp. 64–79.
—— 1990a. *Feminist Fiction: Feminist Revisions of Generic Fiction.* Cambridge: Polity Press; New York: St Martin's Press.
—— 1990b. 'De-fanging the vampire: S.M. Charnas' *The Vampire Tapestry* as subversive horror fiction' in *American Horror Fiction.* Ed. Brian Docherty. London: Macmillan, pp. 155–175.
—— 1990c. 'Feminist Futures: A Generic Study' in *Alien Zone: Critical Theory and Contemporary Science Fiction Cinema.* Ed. Annette Kuhn. London: Verso, pp. 219–227.
—— 1990d. 'Man-made Monsters: the dystopian feminist science fiction of Suzy McKee Charnas' in *Science Fiction Roots and Branches: Contemporary Critical Approaches.* Eds R.J. Ellis and Rhys Garnett. London: Macmillan, pp. 183–206.
—— 1994. *Popular Culture.* Geelong: Deakin University Press.
—— 1995. *The Body in the Text.* Melbourne: Melbourne University Press.
Crary, Jonathan and Sanford Kwinter, eds. 1992. *Zone 6: Incorporations,* New York: Zone.

Day, Wiliam Patrick. 1985. *In the Circles of Fear and Desire: A Study of Gothic Fantasy.* Chicago and London: University of Chicago Press.

Delany, Samuel. 1978. *The Jewel-Hinged Jaw: Notes on the Language of Science Fiction.* New York: Berkley Windhover.

Deleuze, Gilles and Félix Guattari. 1983a. 'Rhizome'. In *On the Line.* Trans. John Johnston. New York: Semiotext(e).

—— 1983b. *Anti-Oedipus: Capitalism and Schizophrenia.* Trans. R. Hurley, M. Steen and H. R. Lane. Minneapolis: University of Minnesota Press [original French publication 1972].

Dick, Philip K. 1972. *Do Androids Dream of Electric Sheep?* London: Granada.

Douglas, Mary. 1966. *Purity and Danger.* London: Routledge and Kegan Paul.

Gibson, William. 1986. *Neuromancer.* London: HarperCollins.

Haraway, Donna. 1991. 'A Cyborg Manifesto: Science, Technology, and Socialist-Feminism in the Late Twentieth Century'. In *Simians, Cyborgs and Women: The Reinvention of Nature.* New York: Routledge, pp. 149–81.

Huxley, Aldous. 1955. *Brave New World: A Novel.* Harmondsworth: Penguin. [First published 1932].

Idhe, Don. 1990. *Technology and the Lifeworld: From Garden to Earth.* Bloomington: Indiana University Press.

—— 1993a. *Philosophy of Technology: An Introduction.* New York: Paragon House.

—— 1993b. *Postphenomenology: Essays in the Postmodern Context.* Evanston, Ill.: Northwestern University Press.

Jackson, Rosemary. 1981. *Fantasy: the Literature of Subversion.* London and New York: Methuen.

Jameson, Fredric. 1981. *The Political Unconscious: Narrative as A Socially Symbolic Act.* London: Methuen.

Knight, Stephen. 1980. *Form and Ideology in Crime Fiction.* London: Macmillan.

Le Guin, Ursula K. 1979. *The Language of the Night: Essays on Fantasy and Science Fiction.* Ed. Susan Wood. New York: Perigee.

—— 1980. *The Word for World Is Forest.* London: Granada.

—— 1981. *The Left Hand of Darkness.* London: Futura.

Lem, Stanislaw. 1971. *Solaris.* Trans. Joanna Kilmartin and Steve Cox. New York.: Berkeley.

Levy, Steven. 1992. *Artificial Life: A Report from the Frontier Where Computers Meet Biology,* New York: Vintage.

McCaffrey, Anne. 1978. *Dragonsinger.* London: Corgi.

Moers, Ellen. 1978. *Literary Women.* London: Women's Press.

Morris, William. 1889. 'Looking Backward.' *Commonweal,* 22 June, p. 194 col. 1–p. 195 col. 1.

—— 1970. *News from Nowhere, or, an epoch of rest, being some chapters from a utopian romance.* Ed. James Redmond. London: Routledge and Kegan Paul.

Orwell, George. 1954. *Nineteen Eighty-Four: A Novel.* Harmondsworth: Penguin. [first published 1949]

Parrinder, Patrick, ed. 1979. *Science Fiction: A Critical Guide.* London and New York: Longman.

—— 1980. *Science Fiction: Its Criticism and Teaching.* London and New York: Methuen.

Penley, Constance and Andrew Ross, eds. 1991. *Technoculture.* Minneapolis: University of Minnesota Press.

Piercy, Marge. 1991. *Body of Glass.* London: Penguin.

Punter, David. 1980. *The Literature of Terror: A History of Gothic Fictions from 1765 to the Present Day.* London: Longman.

Rose, Mark, ed. 1976. *Science Fiction: A Collection of Critical Essays.* Englewood Cliffs, NJ: Prentice-Hall.

Scholes, Robert and Eric S. Rabkin. 1977. *Science Fiction: History, Science, Vision.* London: Oxford University Press.

Shelley, Mary W. 1968. *Frankenstein.* In *Three Gothic Novels.* Ed. Peter Fairclough. Harmondsworth: Penguin.

Sobchak, Vivian. 1987. *Screening Space: The American Science Fiction Film.* New York: Ungar.

Suvin, Darko. 1979. *Metamorphoses of Science Fiction: On the Poetics and History of a Literary Genre.* New Haven and London: Yale University Press.

Tiptree Jr, James. 1975. *Warm Worlds and Otherwise.* Ed. and Intro. Robert Silverberg. New York: Ballantine.

—— 1981. *Out of the Everywhere, And Other Extraordinary Visions.* New York: Ballantine.

Todorov, Tzevetan. 1984. *Mikhail Bakhtin: The Dialogical Principle.* Trans. Wlad Godzich. Manchester: Manchester University Press.

Vinge, Joan D. 1982. *Psion.* New York: Bantam.

—— 1988. *Catspaw.* New York: Warner.

Wells, H.G. [n.d.] *The Island of Doctor Moreau.* London: The Readers Library Publishing Co. [first published 1896].

—— 1953. *The Time Machine.* London: Pan.

Whitfield, Stephen E. and Gene Roddenberry. 1968. *The Making of Star Trek.* New York: Ballantine Books.

Zamyatin, Y. 1972. *We.* Trans. B.G. Guerney. Harmondsworth: Penguin. [first published in English 1924].

FILM AND TELEVISION

Cameron, James (dir.) 1984. *The Terminator,* Orion/Hemdale/Pacific Western.

—— (dir.) 1986. *Aliens,* TCF/Brandywine.

—— (dir.) 1990. *Terminator 2: Judgment Day,* Pacific Western.

Fincher, David (dir.) 1992. *Alien,* Twentieth Century Fox/Brandywine.

Fowler, Gene, Jr (dir.) 1958. *I Married a Monster from Outer Space,* Paramount.

Nyby, Christian and Howard Hawks (dirs) 1951 *The Thing,* RKO/Winchester.

Scott, Ridley (dir.) 1979. *Alien,* TCF/Brandywine.

—— (dir.) 1982 *Blade Runner,* Warner/Ladd/Blade Runner Partnership.

Sears, Fred F. (dir.) 1956. *Earth v. the Flying Saucers,* Columbia.

Star Trek. 1967–69. Paramount Pictures Corporation.

Star Trek: the Next Generation. 1987–94 Paramount Pictures Corporation.

Wilcox, Fred (dir.) 1956. *Forbidden Planet,* MGM.

Wise, Robert (dir.) 1951. *The Day the Earth Stood Still,* TCF.

Part III
Recontextualising science

Introduction to part III

One of the main reasons science has remained a dominant discourse in western society is its ability to reformulate itself for new purposes and contexts. Indeed, one of the inherent characteristics of scientific discourse is its malleability – it is difficult to identify any 'pure' or 'original' form of science, from which 'applications' arise. 'Research science' cannot be easily distinguished from 'applied science' in the way that 'philosophy' or 'ethics' can be distinguished from 'law', because empirical methods of investigation require that even the 'research science' be about something. There is little room for speculative philosophy of the type seen in the humanities. Scientific discourse has always evolved in specific contexts and to meet specific needs. As Halliday has observed (1993), whenever new contexts for scientific activity emerge there is a tendency to borrow meanings from existing contexts, to reconfigure and reorder them according to the principles of the new contexts. This reconfiguration and reordering of knowledge has been referred to as 'recontextualisation' by Bernstein (1977, 1990, 1996). The term was first developed in this way to describe the reformulation of meanings that occurs in educational contexts when a field of activity is recontextualised in order to allow it to exist within the power, time and space relations of the educational system.

The reasons why scientific discourse recontextualises itself are many, as the three chapters in this section demonstrate. The first, and most obvious, is the emergence of *new fields of scientific activity*, or the specialisation of an existing field. This aspect is taken up in the chapter by Veel. There are many instances of this kind of recontextualisation in the areas of technology and medicine. The arrival of the technology of optical fibres, for example, required that meanings which had evolved in the study of light, electronics and chemistry coalesced and entered into new sets of relationships in order to construct a new field of activity, one concerned with the transmission of electronic signals through light and the use of chemicals to control the way the signals are transmitted. The result is a whole new body of knowledge, one with its own hierarchies of knowledge and its own specialists at various levels with access to this knowledge.

Another reason why scientific discourse recontextualises itself is in order to make itself meaningful to non-specialist groups of people. This kind of recontextualisation is not so much concerned with new fields of enquiry as it is with *new sets of social relations for users of scientific discourse*. The classic instance of this kind of recontextualisation is, of course, in schooling, and is explored by Christie in her chapter. Systems of knowledge developed in the 'field of production', as Bernstein calls them (1996: 112–5), are systematically reshaped according to the power, time and space relationships of the school system, the 'recontextualising field'. In order to exist within the school system knowledge must be in a form that allows the roles of the 'teacher' and the 'taught' to emerge. It must be divisible into the time units allocated (lessons, weeks, terms, years, primary, junior secondary, senior secondary, etc.). It must be able to exist within the physical resources of the school (classrooms, laboratories, textbooks, libraries, etc.). Most importantly, it must exist in a form that can be assessed, so that students can be distributed across a spectrum from 'successful' to 'unsuccessful'. In the end, the science we see in a recontextualising field such as schooling is often very different from the science we see in a field of production such as the research laboratory.

A third kind of recontextualisation occurs as *new modes of representing and (re)producing knowledge* emerge, as Lemke explores in his chapter. Scientific discourse, together with its related technological fields (see White, this volume), has always led the way in this kind of recontextualisation. Scientific diagrams, for example, have for a long time been just as valid a mode of representing scientific knowledge as written language. The history of scientific diagrams goes back as far as the history of modern science itself. Since the very earliest days scientific texts have been at the very least 'bi-modal', comprising written language and diagrams. As new technologies have developed modes of representation of scientific knowledge have proliferated. Nowadays a scientific text may consist of almost infinite combinations of written language, diagrams, images, tables, graphs, mathematical symbols, sound and moving images. Each mode of representation is a semiotic system unto itself, with its own 'grammar' or patterns of relationships between elements. Whilst the grammar of non-linguistic semiotic systems such as visual images has been explored by a few researchers (e.g. Kress and Van Leeuwen 1996), little is known of the meanings created through combinations of semiotic systems.

This process of reformulation, or 'recontextualisation', places pressure on the semiotic resources used to construe scientific meanings. As new fields of activity, new sets of social relationships and new modes of expression emerge, new forms of language develop. Thus the written language of 'school science' – its genres and lexico-grammatical patterns – is different from the written language of 'industry science'; and both are different from the written language of 'university science'.

In discussing three very different kinds of recontextualisation of scientific discourse, the three chapters in this section are concerned to show the kinds of shifts in language which enable recontextualisation to occur and the semantic implications of these shifts. In his chapter, Lemke is concerned with the recontextualisation of scientific knowledge which arises from interaction of different semiotic systems in modern scientific texts. He argues that complementary semiotic systems, including language, tables, graphs, images and diagrams do not just 'add-on' meaning to a text but actually create new orders of meaning – hence the title 'multiplying meaning'. Lemke's claim represents a significant new dimension to work already undertaken in the semiotics of non-linguistic systems, which have tended to treat each semiotic system as discrete (no doubt for the valid purposes of concentrating and simplifying analysis).

Veel is interested in the question of 'field-oriented' recontextualisation, in this case looking at the pressures placed on written language by the emergence of ecological science as a way of looking at the world. Whilst ecological science borrows the texts and grammatical configurations of 'traditional science' in order to gain recognition and acceptance as a viable discipline, it is at the same time trying to reconfigure the relationship between humans and the natural world in scientific discourse. This overtly social objective places great pressure on the language, resulting in a semiotic environment that is part humanities 'rhetoric' and part 'objective' science. Following the work of Kress and Van Leeuwen, Veel also argues that visual images in eco-scientific texts provide a major resource for reconfiguring the relationship between humans and the natural world.

In the third chapter in this section, Christie is concerned with the reformulation of scientific knowledge for pedagogic purposes, in this case a teaching sequence for primary school children. She explores the tension between the pressures for organising or 'framing' scientific knowledge into a pedagogical sequence with clear and identifiable roles for the teacher and the taught on the one hand and the desire to produce students who are independent producers of scientific knowledge on the other. In particular Christie argues the need for different linguistic patterns of interaction between teacher and student at different points in the pedagogic cycle, challenging many assumptions about the nature of 'desirable' interaction between teacher and taught.

REFERENCES

Bernstein, B. 1977. *Class, Codes and Control* (Volume 3) London: Routledge and Kegan Paul.

Bernstein, B. 1990. *The Structuring of Pedagogic Discourse* London: Routledge.

Bernstein, B. 1996. *Pedagogy, Symbolic Control and Identity: Theory, research, critique* London: Taylor & Francis.

Kress, G. and T. Van Leeuwen 1996. *Reading Images: The grammar of visual design* London: Routledge.

5 Multiplying meaning
Visual and verbal semiotics in scientific text

Jay Lemke

MULTIMEDIA GENRES IN SCIENCE

Science is not done, is not communicated, through verbal language alone. It *cannot* be. The 'concepts' of science are not solely verbal concepts, though they have verbal components. They are semiotic *hybrids*, simultaneously and essentially verbal, mathematical, visual–graphical, and actional–operational. The actional, conversational, and written textual genres of science are historically and presently, fundamentally and irreducibly, *multimedia genres*. To do science, to talk science, to read and write science it is necessary to juggle and combine in various canonical ways verbal discourse, mathematical expression, graphical–visual representation, and motor operations in the world.

In its efforts to describe the material interactions of people and things, natural science has been led away from an exclusive reliance on verbal language. It has tried to find ways to describe *continuous* change and co-variation, in addition to categorial difference and co-distribution. It has tried to describe what we know through our perceptual Gestalts and motor activities, to construct representations of the *topological* as well as the *typological* aspects of our being-in-the-world. Language, as a typologically oriented semiotic resource is unsurpassed as a tool for the formulation of difference and relationship, for the making of categorical distinctions. It is much poorer (though hardly bankrupt) in resources for formulating degree, quantity, gradation, continuous change, continuous co-variation, non-integer ratios, varying proportionality, complex topological relations of relative nearness or connectedness, or nonlinear relationships and dynamical emergence (which I refer to collectively as the *topological* dimensions of meaning; see Lemke in press, a).

These topological meanings can be enacted operationally through many forms of human motor activity other than speech, in the laboratory or just in our normal biological interactions with the world (cf. Lemke 1996). We can indicate modulation of speed or size, or complex relations of shape or relative position far better with a gesture than we can with words, and we can let that gesture leave a trace and become a

visual–graphical representation that will sit still and let us re-examine it
at our leisure. The dynamical aspect lost in the static graph is recovered
in the video simulation or animation, which we can repeat at will, speed
up or slow down and freeze in time.

When scientists think, talk, write, work and teach (cf. Lemke 1987,
1990; Ochs *et al.* 1994, 1996; Latour 1987; Lynch and Woolgar 1990) they
do not just use words; they gesture and move in imaginary visual spaces
defined by graphical representations and simulations, which in turn have
mathematical expressions that can also be integrated into speech. When
scientists communicate in print they do not produce linear verbal text;
they do not even limit visual forms to the typographical. They do not
present and organise information only verbally; they do not construct
logical arguments in purely verbal form. They combine, interconnect,
and integrate verbal text with mathematical expressions, quantitative
graphs, information tables, abstract diagrams, maps, drawings, photographs and a host of unique specialised visual genres seen nowhere else.

I have recently made some preliminary surveys of professional scientific
print publications to sample the relative frequency and common types of
non-verbal–textual semiotic expression. Here are some of the results:

Survey I

23 articles and chapters (341 pages in total):

- All feature articles from *Bulletin of the New York Academy of Medicine*,
  68(3), 1992. (4 articles on biomedicine, 1 on urban language diversity)
- 1 research offprint on cellular development
- All chapters from a conference proceedings on applications of
  chaos theory in ecology, medicine, astronomy, physics
- 1 book chapter on ecological succession (advanced treatise)
- 1 lengthy journal review article on thermodynamics
- 1 advanced-textbook chapter on nonlinear dynamics

Average length	14.8 pp.
Average graphics per article	16.2
Average graphics per page	1.1
Maximum per page	4.3
Articles with equations	17.
Average length	14.9 pp.
Average equations per article	20.8
Average per page	1.4
Maximum per page	3–4

Counted as *graphics* were all figures, tables, charts, graphs, photographs, drawings, maps and specialised visual presentations. Mathematical equations were *not* counted in this total and are reported separately

in these statistics. Only mathematical expressions set off typographically from running text were counted. Mathematical expressions are also often directly integrated into a line of running verbal text, and into its syntax, extending grammatical resources in register-specific ways.

The clear finding here is that there is typically at least one and often more than one graphical display *and* one mathematical expression per page of running text in typical scientific print genres. There can easily be three to four each of graphics displays and mathematical expressions separate from verbal text *per page*. (It is actually unusual to find high concentrations of both equations and graphics in the same article or on the same page. Experimental–empirical reports tend to have more graphics, theoretical analyses more equations.)

Survey II

Part A   All 20 articles from 2 issues of *Physical Review Letters* (62 pages   total)

Average length	3.1 pp.
Total graphics	76
Average per article	3.8
Average per page	1.2
Maximum per page	2–3
Total equations	169
Average per article	8.5
Average per page	2.7
Maximum per page	6–7

Part B   All 31 technical reports from 2 issues of *Science* (74 pages total)

Average length	2.4 pp.
Total graphics	187
Average per article	6.0
Average per page	2.5
Total equations	13
[only 3 articles used equations, 4.3 per article, 1.9 per page]	
Total tables	39
Average per article	1.2
Total graphs	30
Average per article	1.0

All visuals (excluding equations and tables)

Average per article	4.7
Average per page	2.0

Physical Review Letters is probably the single most prestigious journal in the physical sciences. It accepts only brief reports of major new findings (experimental or theoretical) for rapid publication. Each typical three-page article integrated four graphical displays and eight set-off mathematical expressions. Some had as many as three graphical displays per page of double-column text, or as many as seven equations per page.

Science is, alongside its British counterpart *Nature*, the corresponding journal for the biological and earth and space sciences. Each of these publishes longer feature articles as well as news items, all of which were excluded to achieve comparability to *PRL*. Mathematical expressions were less frequent in *Science* (only 10 per cent of articles, all of them in non-biological subjects, included any equations), but visual presentations other than tables, such as photographs, molecular diagrams, etc. were more common. A typical page has two non-tabular visual–graphical representations integrated with the verbal text. Each short (2.4-page) article typically has six graphics, including at least one table and one quantitative graph.

These were very preliminary surveys. There are considerable difficulties in deciding in practice how to count visual and mathematical presentations (count all lines of mathematics, or only separately numbered equations? Count all graph lines in the same figure or only the figure as a whole? Count combined tables separately or as a unit?). In all cases the statistical estimates given are conservative in the sense that almost any other counting choices would *increase* the frequency of mathematical and visual–graphical elements per article and per page.

To appreciate the absolutely central role of these non-verbal textual elements in the genres being characterised, it may help to ponder a few revealing phenomena:

- In one advanced textbook chapter, a diagram was included in a *footnote* printed at the bottom of the page (Berge *et al.* 1984: 84). It was necessary for even the minor point being made there (see Figure 5.4 below).
- In one seven-page research report in *Nature*, 90 per cent of a page (all but five lines of main text at the top) was taken up by a complex diagram (see Figure 5.5 below, from Svoboda *et al.* 1993) and its extensive figure caption.
- The main experimental results of a 2.5-page report in *Nature* were presented in a set of graphs occupying one-half page and a table occupying three-fourths of another (see Figure 5.2 below, from Martikainen *et al.* 1993). The main verbal text did not repeat this information but only referred to it and commented on it.
- In most of the theoretical physics articles, the running verbal text would make no sense without the integrated mathematical equations, which could not in most cases be effectively paraphrased in natural

language, even though they can be, and are normally meant to be read as if part of the verbal text (in terms of semantics, cohesion and frequently grammar).

PRESENTATIONAL, ORIENTATIONAL, AND ORGANIZATIONAL MEANING

How are we to analyse the ways in which verbal text and mathematical and visual–graphical media combine in scientific genres? Within what theoretical framework can we examine how people make meaning by linking text and figure, sentence and equation, caption and photo? I believe that the possibility of functionally integrating language, drawing, diagrams, pictures and mathematics arises from their common phyloge-netic origins and individual ontogenesis in material human communica-tion processes and their long co-evolution with one another in the uses we have historically made of them (Lemke 1987, 1993a, 1994, 1995a).

More specifically, I believe that all meaning-making, whatever semiotic resource systems are deployed, singly or jointly, has become organised around three generalised semiotic functions (Lemke 1989a, 1990, 1992, 1995a). When we make meaning we always simultaneously construct a 'presentation' of some state-of-affairs, orient to this presentation and orient it to others and in doing so create an organised structure of related elements. (For more detailed discussion of these *presentational*, *orientational*, and *organizational* functions, see below.) When we do this with the resources of language, then these functions correspond to the *ideational*, *interpersonal*, and *textual* linguistic 'metafunctions' of Halliday (1978). When we do it while 'talking science' (Lemke 1990) or in any other specialised linguistic *register* (Gregory 1967, Halliday 1978), we deploy some resources for each function with greater and others with lesser frequency (Halliday 1991). Moreover, as Martin (1991, 1992) has emphasised, we form particular, culturally typical combinations of meanings about things, attitudes toward them and our addressees and ways of organising our language, which in effect constitute the *genres* of a discourse community (see also Hasan 1995; Lemke 1988b, in press, b; Bazerman 1988).

Let's consider just a bit more of what we know about functional integration in linguistic meaning as a background for the more general case of multimedia semiotics. Linguistically we have evolved more than just functional combinations, we have evolved typical discourse forma-tions and stylistic strategies, which give these combinations a sense of familiarity even when their content is novel (cf. Kress and Threadgold 1988; Lemke 1988a, 1991, 1995a, in press, b). We use texts already in circulation, and discourse resources of the order of text (typical stories, typical patterns of scientific explanation, typical progressions of meta-phors) as resources for making meaning, every bit as much as we use more formal, paradigmatic, system-like resources such as lexicogrammar or the semantic options for speech acts.

 A clause or sentence means not just through the selections it makes in these systems, but through its place in a larger text organisation and its intertextual relations to other texts (Lemke 1985, 1988a, 1988b, 1995a, 1995b). It means something not just through its own selections, but through how those selections continue or develop the selections of prior clauses (and may be reread in light of subsequent ones; cf. Halliday 1982, Lemke 1991). Moreover, ideational–thematic (presentational) meanings contribute to organizational–textual ones (e.g. through cohesion and cohesive harmony, cf. Halliday and Hasan 1976, 1989; Hasan 1984; Lemke 1988b, 1995b) and so do intepersonal–attitudinal ones (cf. Lemke 1992). Likewise, organisational meanings contribute to ideational ones by defining clauses, clause-complexes, rhetorical structure units (e.g. Lemke 1988b, 1990, in press, b; Mann and Thompson 1986) and larger units of intratextual relationship, and in similar ways to the interpersonal and attitudinal texture of a text. Ideational choices of lexis, in turn, inevitably contribute to the attitudinal stance of a text to its audience, to its content, and to other text-embodied viewpoints. Conversely, we read the ideational meaning of a text differently depending on our interpretation of its ironies and other attitudinal features.

 In these ways and many others, the meaning of the linguistic text is the product of the subtle, conventional and creative interplay of presentational, orientational and organisational aspects of meaning-making. How much more so is this true when we take into account the co-deployment of visual, gestural, graphical, mathematical and other resource systems! Each of these semiotic systems provides resources specialised for each of the three generalised semiotic functions. When the resources of multiple semiotic systems are codeployed: 1) each semiotic can contribute componentially to each each functional aspect of meaning (e.g. lexical name and figural image to a presentational construct): 2) each can internally cross-modulate meanings across functional aspects (e.g. alternating point-of-view shots helping to construct a visual–organisational sequence); and 3) functionally specialised meaning resources in one semiotic combine with those for a different function in another semiotic to modulate any aspect of the meaning of the joint construct (e.g. the visual juxtaposition of verbal captions can allow their thematic meanings to interact with the different sizes of two graphs to determine their relative importance).

 In multimedia genres, meanings made with each functional resource in each semiotic modality can modulate meanings of each kind in each other semiotic modality, thus *multiplying* the set of possible meanings that can be made (and so also the specificity of any particular meaning made against the background of this larger set of possibilities).

 This combinatorial semiotic principle provides not just a theoretical framework, but an analytical engine for investigating multimedia semiotics. It poses for us the possibilities and the questions, what to look for and where to look. We will find some of the possibilities realized in some genres and not in others, in some texts perhaps and not in others. Just as the notion of *grammatical metaphor* (Halliday 1985, this volume) shows us how our meaning-making potential is enlarged when verbal resources normally used for one function (e.g. nouns for things) are deployed also for another (nouns for processes, which thereby become semiotically both in some ways thing-like while in others still process-like, a new semiotic hybrid reality), so the principle of functional cross-multiplication in multimedia genres shows us how we can mean more, mean new kinds of meanings never before meant and not otherwise mean-able, when this process occurs both within and across different semiotic modalities (i.e., language, visual representation, mathematics, etc.).

Because of their importance to the analysis, let me specify the three generalised semiotic functions a little further:

Every meaning-making act constructs a *presentational* 'state-of-affairs' that construes relations among semiotic participants and processes as if they were being observed, objectively and synoptically, from some outside vantage point. In language, this is the so-called *representational* or *propositional* function (Halliday's 'ideational' or 'experiential' metafunction, for which I also use the term *thematic*). It defines the sense in which we speak 'about' something, construct a theme or topic, make predications and arguments. In less philosophical and more linguistic terms, this means that we deploy the resources of grammar and lexis to specify some process or relationship and its semantic participants (agents, patients, instruments, etc.) and circumstances (when, where, why, how, under what conditions, etc.). In visual depiction, this is the *figural* or *representational* function that presents to us a scene whose elements we can recognise and which have comprehensible relations to one another in terms of the typical scripts of that scene. This is what tells us what we are being shown, what is supposed to be 'there', to be happening, or what relations are being constructed among the elements presented.

At the same time every meaning-making act constructs an *orientational* 'stance' toward that state-of-affairs, often to indicate how true or certain the producer wishes the interpreter to take it as being, or to indicate an evaluation of it as good or bad, ordinary or suprising, necessary or obligatory, in the perspective the producer is creating for the interpreter. But orientational meaning goes naturally beyond this to include also the construction of a social relationship between producer and interpreters (present or imagined), and more generally a relative positioning of the producer and 'text' (i.e., semiotic production or multimedia object) in the whole social space of possible discourses and viewpoints on the state-of-affairs. In language, this is the *pragmatic* or *interactional* function (Halliday's 'interpersonal' metafunction, including 'attitudinal' meanings), through which we take a role in the communication event and construct the nature of the 'speech act' we are performing (informing, querying, commanding) and the social relationship to the addressee we are enacting (bullying, beseeching, promising, threatening). This is always done in the context of larger social relations and groupings that transcend any particular communicative event or text, and against the background of the various other texts in the community constructed from other possible points of view (cf. Lemke 1985, 1993c; Bakhtin 1935/1981 on heteroglossia, and commentary in Lemke 1988a, 1995a).

In depiction, every image takes an orientational stance (O'Toole's 1994 term is 'modal') which positions the viewer in relation to the scene (e.g. intimate, distant; superior, subordinate), establishes some sort of evaluative orientation of the producer/interpreter toward the scene itself (tragic, comic; normal, surprising), and does so against the background of other possible viewpoints and depictions of similar scenes.

Finally, every meaning-making act constructs a system of *organisational* relations defining wholes and parts of those wholes, both in the semiotic space of the text and in the (ecosocial) interactional space of the meaning-making act itself. Language creates words-in-phrases, phrases-in-clauses, chains of reference and cohesion, and larger and subtler structures and textures of the verbal text (Halliday's 'textual' metafunction, cf. Halliday and Hasan 1976, 1989; Lemke 1988b, 1995a; Matthiessen 1992). Conversation as an activity creates in-groups and out-groups, and shifting dyads within larger groups. Depiction deploys *compositional* (O'Toole 1994) resources to organise the visual text into elements and regions, and to link disjoint regions by such features as colour and texture. As material objects, depictions participate in interactions that define parts and unite them into wholes in the ecosystem networks where objects are viewed and used.

In recent work, Michael O'Toole (1994) and, independently, Gunther Kress and Theo van Leeuwen (1990) have demonstrated these homologous dimensions of meaning in visual semiotic productions of many kinds: paintings, sculpture and architecture; photographs, advertisements and cinema. Their work clearly shows the usefulness of taking a 'tri-functional' perspective such as that sketched here in visual semiotics, and the interesting similarities and differences between these specialised semiotic resource systems and the genres we produce by deploying them.

In an early effort (Lemke 1987) I analysed how science teachers and students made sense with each other by codeploying verbal, gestural, and pictorial resources. I found that if we regard each of these as constituting a separate 'channel' of communication, then sometimes the same or equivalent information passes nearly simultaneously in more than one channel, sometimes the information in the two channels is complementary, and sometimes information comes first in one channel, and later in another. It became very clear to me that the meanings that were being constructed were joint meanings produced in the intersection of different semiotic systems. While it was useful to separate these analytically into different 'channels,' there was also an underlying unity to the meanings produced. Their separation neglects this fundamental unity of communicative meaning-making which makes the co-ordination among channels not only possible, but normal.

GENRES WITHIN SCIENTIFIC TEXT

How can we read scientific media that combine verbal text with mathematical expressions and various visual–graphical presentations? What are the component sub-genres within such scientific texts? How are they typically integrated with one another? How, across semiotic modalities, are resources for presentational, orientational, and organisational meaning combined? Here I can only begin to point at some interesting phenomena that warrant further investigation and study.

The medium of printed scientific texts is first of all a visual one. Even the linguistic meanings are presented through the visual semiotics of orthography and typography, including all matters of page layout as well as choices of font style and typeface sizes, the use of headings and footers, etc. It is precisely because language here is present through a visual semiotic that it is so readily integrated with other systems of visual meaning. (In face-to-face communication, where language is present in a motor-acoustic medium, it is our 'vocal gestures' that are integrated with other motor gestures, some being more perceptible auditorily, others more so visually. Cf. Scheflen 1975.)

Typography is quite conventionally used as an orientational as well as an organisational resource in printed text. Orientationally, the use of italic and boldface types signals emphasis or importance, as does the relative point size of type in titles, headings, abstracts, footnotes, captions, labels, etc. Organisationally, paragraphing and sectioning of text, and geometric relations of figure space to caption space indicate to us which elements are to be preferentially read in relation to which other elements; what goes with what.

Scientific text is not primarily linear, it is not meant to be read according to a unique implied sequence and represents a primitive form of *hypertext* (cf. Lemke 1993d). Footnotes represent an optional branch for readers, so do figures and their captions, and the parenthetic or main-text expressions such as '(Table 3)' or 'as seen in the first table' which point to them. Spoken language is linear in this respect, but no visual semiotic can be, for all are at least two-dimensional and any one-dimensional sequence represented in two-dimensions can be accessed at any point at any time. Many scientists, after reading the title and abstract, may skip to the end to see an endnote telling who supported the research or to skim the references for familiar or unfamiliar citations.

They may well read the tables or graphs first, and then their captions, and only then the main text. Some may pay more attention to the equations than to the words in which they are embedded. These are the habits of expert readers, those who could themselves have written this text or one very like it.

The constituent mini-genres of the scientific research article, in addition to its main text, include title, author list, author affiliations or addresses, abstract, section headings (which may be considered part of the main text), figures, figure captions, tables, table captions, priority dates, reference list, footnotes/endnotes, and acknowledgements. Figures, as a typographical component, are regions of the page which are not set in type but produced by some more photographic or direct image-printing process. They include photographs, drawings, diagrams, graphs, and maps. Tables, by contrast, are set in type, and are the most text-like of the non-textual visual presentations. Almost all figures have *labels* as well as captions, and often also brief textual notes printed as part of the figure proper (*legends*).

Tables as textualisable visual displays

Tables have their most direct origin in normal written text. They carry textual ellipsis to its greatest extreme, using visual organisational resources to enable meaning relations to be recovered from bare thematic items in the absence of grammatical constructions. There is always, however, an implied grammar, and a recoverable textual sentence or paragraph for every table. In my work on intertextual thematic formations (Lemke 1983, 1985, 1988a, 1990, 1995b), originally for scientific discourse, I noted that listeners and readers are expected to be able to supply the canonical semantic relations of thematic terms, which are often underspecified or omitted. This is done by familiarity with a canonical pattern of semantic relations (the *thematic formation*), either from another text or discourse, or from an earlier section of the present one.

Scientific tables most often have numerical entries, though not always, and the grammar of the numerical entries is generally that of the normal nominal group, with the Head constant through a row or column of the table and written at its end, and the table entry functioning as numerative of that Head. Table 5.1, however, shows a purely verbal table, with a brief introductory text, serving as a summary conclusion of a conference paper (Percival 1987). In the conference presentation it would almost certainly have been projected as a slide. Having read the text of the paper (excepts below), the reader would be in possession of a thematic formation whose slots could be readily filled by the pairs of entries in this two-column table. If it were glossed as full text, it might read something like this:

'In the old view of Hamiltonian dynamics [lefthand entry] was a key concept, but in the new view it has been replaced by the idea of [right-hand entry].'

As is typical with thematic formations, there are many possible tex-tualisations, but the underlying semantic relations among thematic items remain the same. Here is one instance of the formation from the text of the article which is being summarised in the table:

> According to one point of view, expressed by Laplace, dynamical systems are completely deterministic, so probability theory can have no relevance. But this point of view requires [an impossibility]. . . . For . . . [certain] systems [modern] theorists have introduced symbolic dynamics, which shows precisely how probabilities enter into deter-ministic dynamics.
>
> (Percival 1987, pp. 139–140)

It corresponds to the last pair of entries in the table.

When numerical values are placed in a table, it is still meant to be read, at least in principle, as full verbal text. While this convention today is so well-established that it is not in evidence in the surface forms of most tables, a historical example shows the textual nature of tables more clearly.

In a 1734 edition of an early treatise by Johan Bernoulli (*De motu musculorum*, p. 464), a table is set out giving the values of various lengths and angles resulting from a calculation of the movement of an animal's jointed appendages subject to a certain weight, set at a certain angle (see Figure 5.1). There is an accompanying figure of course whose labels identify these parameters. In the table, we find (left-to-right) first a thin vertical column with the word 'Positis' written vertically, then two col-umns of numbers headed 'Arcu' and 'Longitudine' and written in the usual horizontal way, followed by another very thin vertically ruled column containing the single word 'erit' (lower case) written vertically

Table 5.1 Changing viewpoints in Hamiltonian dynamics

old view	new view
integrability	invariant sets
stability and instability of orbits	regular and chaotic motion
variational principles for orbits	variational principles for invariant sets
convergence of perturbation series	K.A.M. theorem and analyticity in complex domains
continuity	fractals and renormalisation
analysis	geometry, computers and number theory
determinism	probability

Source: from Percival 1987: 142, reproduced by permission

Positis	Arcu EA, vel ãg. EAR, qui est semiff. EAD.	Longitu-dine ar-cus AE, & resi-stentia z in part. æqu.	erit	Radius AC,vel EC.	Sinus rectus AR.	Eleva-tio re-sisten-tiæ.	Vis susti-nens, seu requisitæ firmita-tis fibræ muscu-laris.	Vis absolu-ta elasticita-tis auræ mo-tivæ quam-proximè.	Vis ela-sticitatis auræ mo-tivæ,qua premitur semilatus machinu-læ AE.
	gr. m								
	0 0	100000		infinit.	100000	0	50000	0	0
	0. 30	100000		11454546	99958	84	50002	$\frac{1}{229}$ pau.min.	435
	1. 0	100000		5727273	99954	92	50007	$\frac{1}{114}$ p. m.	873
	1. 30	100000		3818182	99948	104	50017	$\frac{1}{76}$ p. m.	1309
	2. 0	100000		2863636	99939	122	50030	$\frac{1}{57}$ p. m.	1747
	3. 0	100000		1909091	99914	162	50068	$\frac{1}{38}$ p. m.	2622
	5. 0	100000		1145454	99832	336	50191	$\frac{1}{22}$ p. m.	4281
	10. 0	100000		572727	99454	1192	50774	$\frac{1}{11}$ p. m.	8865
	15. 0	100000		381818	98822	2356	51764	$\frac{1}{7}$ p. m.	13557
	20. 0	100000		286363	97942	4116	53209	$\frac{1}{4}$ p. m.	18582
	30. 0	100000		190909	95454	9092	57735	$\frac{1}{2}$ p. m.	30242
	45. 0	100000		127272	89994	20012	70710	$\frac{1}{2}$ pau. pl.	57145
	60. 0	100000		95454	81665	34670	100000	1 p. p.	104708
	70. 0	100000		81818	76883	46234	146191	2 p. m.	178678
	80. 0	100000		71590	70492	59016	287968	4 p. p.	403785
	85. 0	100000		67379	67122	65756	573709	9 p. m.	851465
	90. 0	100000		63636	63636	72728	infinit.	infinit.	infinit.

Figure 5.1 Table from Bernoulli (1734: 464). Reproduced courtesy of the New York Academy of Medicine Library

again, and then a series of further columns of numbers headed 'Radius', 'Sinus', etc. Here we have the grammatical elements of the complete Latin sentence which can be constructed for any row of the Table: given [*Positis*] arc . . ., longitude . . ., [then] radius, sine, etc. will be [*erit*] . . ., etc. Latin is already more sparing lexically than modern English, and there may certainly still be some ellipsis (of *aequale* and perhaps of *et* for 'equal to' and 'and'), but the table has been set with the most necessary words, especially the future tense of the copula *erit*, to make the table a representation of verbal text. (The inflections on *Positis, arcu, longitudine* are all ablative case, appropriate to textual grammar, as opposed to the nominatives usual for isolated headings.)

In a modern table (Figure 5.2, from Martikainen *et al.* 1993), we find a mixture of textual entries and numerical ones, including the 'Tree Stand' entries which preserve the nominal group form. Nowhere in the main text of this article do we find a sentence that textualises any row of this table, but no competent reader of the text would be unable to do so. What is important to notice here is that the table makes sense precisely because it is textualisable, i.e. because there is a thematic formation in this community, intertextually available, which enables readers to make specific semantic relations between '4.3' and 'pH', 'Drained' and 'Virgin', 'Tall Sedge Fen' and 'Total N in peat'.

The important *visual* resources here, apart from the orthography of words, numbers, special symbols and abbreviations, are *organisational* ones, arranging in vertical columns the semantically homogeneous (and therefore comparable, contrastable) items, and in horizontal rows the semantically heterogeneous (and therefore combinable, presentationally interdependent) items, respectively. We can read the table either for information about a site or for comparison of sites, to see the range of variation in a site-feature across sites, or to look for co-patternings. The topological meanings represented by decimal fractions and percentages as measurements of continuously varying physical quantities have been integrated *visually* as well as implicitly linguistically with the typological categories of this register. (Note, by the way, how the semantics of standard grammar is extended in delicacy by such quantitative expressions as 'a tree stand of 50 cubic metres of wood per hectare' or 'a rate of emission of nitrogen oxide of 0.143 grams of nitrogen per square metre per year.')

A relevant bit of the main text reads: 'the higher tree growth in the minerotrophic sites [fn8] (Table 1) had increased evapotranspiration and contributed to the lower water table (Fig. 1a-c).' In this one compound clause we are referred to a citation for the published details on the sites, to the table for the 'higher tree growth' at the 'minerotrophic sites', and to the figure for graphs of water table levels over time. Even when we refer to Table 1, we need to look to a footnote within the table caption, hung on the header text 'Site number and type [*]', to identify which sites are 'minerotrophic,' and recognise this as a classifier in contrast with 'ombrotrophic.' The visual organisational conventions here are critical to following the verbal presentational argument. We could even pick up the *-trophic* contrast by noting the positions of these words as headers for two columns of graphs in Figure 5.2. The graphs also show 'error bars' indicating the reliability or warrantability, and so probability of error, in the data: a visual presentation of a mathematical formulation of an orientational meaning.

The peatland sites, their botanical and nutritional characteristics, pH and annual N_2O emissions

Site number and type*	Dominating plant species in surface vegetation and changes in vegetation after drainage	Tree stand	Total N in peat (%)	pH†	N_2O emission‡ (g N M^{-2} yr^{-}) 1991	1992
1 Mesotrophic sedge pine mire	Drained: *Pleurozium schreberi, Polytrichum commune, Sphagnum angustifolium, Vaccinium myrtillus, Vaccinium vitis-idaea.*	160 m³ per hectare 93% pine§ 7% birch‖	1.8	4.3	0.143	0.125
	Virgin: *Sphagnum papillosum, S. angustifolium, S. magellanicum* (hummocks), *Trichophorum caespitosum, Betula nana* (hummocks).	< 5 m³ per hectare	n.d.	5.0	< 0.004	< 0.004
	Drained: vegetation scarce because of abundant birch leaf litter. Much less sphagnum species than in virgin area. Typical new species: *Polytrichum commune* and *P. strictum.*	50 m³ per hectare 95% birch 5% pine and spruce¶	n.d.	4.6	n.d.	0.065
2 Mesotrophic flark fen						
3 Tall sedge fen	Virgin: *Carex rostrata, Sphagnum fallax, S. papillosum.*	< 1 m³ per hectare 100% pine	1.9	5.0	< 0.004	< 0.004
	Drained#: *Polytrichum commune, P. strictum.* Much less sphagnum species than in virgin area.	90 m³ per hectare 99% pine 1% birch	2.1	4.6	0.135	0.051

Site	Vegetation		pH		
4 Cottongrass pine bog with *Sphagnum fuscum* hummocks	Virgin: *Sphagnum angustifolum, S. fuscum, Eriophorum vaginatum, Empetrum nigrum.*	5 m³ per hectare 100% pine	0.5	4.3	< 0.004 < 0.004
	Drained: less sphagnum species than in virgin area. The proportion of forest mosses has increased (*Pleurozium schreberi, Polytrichum strictum.* The proportion of *Eriophorum vaginatum* and *Empetrum nigrum* slightly decreased.	20 m³ per hectare 100% pine	0.5	4.1	< 0.004 < 0.004
5 Low-sedge bog	Virgin: *Sphagnum angustifolium, S. fuscum, Empetrum nigrum Eriophorum vaginatum.*	1 m³ per hectare 100% pine	0.4	4.2	< 0.004 < 0.004
	Drained: clearly less shagnum species. The proportion of hummock species has increased (*Pleurozium schreberi, Betula nana*)	15 m³ per hectare 100% pine	0.4	4.0	< 0.004 < 0.004

Notes: n.d., Not determined.
* Sites 1, 2 and 3 are minerotrophic, 4 and 5 are ombrotrophonic. Site type names according to Finnish peatland classification[24].
† Soil pH, measured in soil–water suspension.
‡ Annual emissions are calculated from average monthly fluxes, winter emissions are estimated from winter measurements (see measuring frequency in Fig. 1).
§ *Pinus sylvestris.*
‖ *Betula pendula* and *B. pubescens.*
¶ *Picea abies.*
# Fertilized in 1966 with 10 kg N per hectare 6 kg P per hectare, and 6 kg K per hectare. The site received 53 kg P per hectare and 63 kg per hectare in 1984.

Figure 5.2 Table 1 from Martikainen *et al.* (1993: 52). Reproduced from *Nature*, by permission

Abstract graphs and diagrams

It is not very far historically from a table with numerical, or repeated symbol, entries, to a primitive bar graph, and from there to a line graph. Even Cartesian line graphs and their corresponding mathematical functions can to a certain extent be 'read' as text insofar as the axes have numerical scales, allowing the graph to be read as a geometrical condensation of a table like that in Bernoulli, 'when x has the value . . ., y will have the value . . . .' This is certainly true for data-graphs, but even here, visual semiotics begin to allow us to see 'trends' and 'functional dependencies' in the data, which no textualisation of it as information would lend itself to so directly. We apprehend the 'patterns' in the data when displayed as a graph differently than we do when it is displayed as text, or even as a table.

Such patterns are important in the value-scheme of natural science. Mathematical functions abstract these patterns from the data and even the variables, the thematic items, the measured phenomena among which they are the patterns. In scientific theory, patterns are generated from assumptions. Initially these are verbal–semantic statements, then they are mathematical expressions and/or graphical images or imagined or displayed dynamical simulations, but always primarily of quantitative patterns and covariations, the very things language has not evolved to present very well. So, in addition to mathematical expressions, scientific practice makes use of *abstract graphs* which only show conceptual relations, and not actual data. Here we leave behind any possibility of textualisation in the manner for tables, but now there is a new sort of textualisation possible, by way of mathematics. The abstract graph has a mathematical formulation, and that in turn is rooted in an extension of the semantics of natural language and its grammar.

Abstract graphs are more nearly pictures than text. Or they sit about mid-way. If we begin from the other end of the typology (text and verbal semantics) to topology (continuous variation and interaction) spectrum, we must start from our visual perception of real objects, and then their holographic or photographic representation. A photograph can be abstracted into a drawing (with third-dimensional perspective or without), and from the drawing it is only a few more steps to the abstract diagram, which is still interpreted as if it were a drawing or a photograph or a visual percept. For each step we foreground some features as more important, as more significantly in contrast with potential alternatives and so more in need of specification, or else by mere convention we let the part stand for the whole, we suggest a whole, which the reader must supply, fitting intertextual (interpictorial?) information to the presumptive pattern. This is not at all unlike the corresponding process with thematic formations for verbal meaning.

Abstract diagrams and abstract graphs are sufficiently close in their visual semiotics that they can be directly combined visually and read as two parts of the same visual presentation. As an example, consider Figure 5.3 (from Berge *et al.* 1984: 84). The fine horizontal dotted lines visually integrate (organisational function) the abstract graph at right with the abstract diagram at left. This is possible here because one of the variables, 'z', in the graph is a measure of spatial position, and the scale of the graph has been set to correspond exactly to the visual representation of the same spatial distance in the diagram. But otherwise we are still in two visual worlds on the two sides of this figure. At the left, the bold arrow of 'g' points down to indicate the pull of gravity and the horizontal dimension is still spatial. At the right, 'z' on its vertical axis is only an arbitrary, scaleable measure of spatial position, oriented to 'real space' only by the visual connection here (and by the conventional use of the co-ordinate name 'z' for vertical positioning); the horizontal direction now represents the value of the temperature of places with vertical position 'z', it is not spatial at all, except metaphorically.

On the same page of this text appears footnote 58 (see Figure 5.4), which is both textually linked to, and visually echoes, the diagram portion of Figure 5.3. The diagram is rotated by 90 degrees, exchanging vertical for horizontal and vice versa. This change would not matter at all to the meaning of an abstract graph, but in this case the diagram is once again oriented on the page to 'real space' with the force of gravity still acting down, even though the meaning of the downwards arrow is now ambivalent (the footnote text refers both to the fall of the liquid and to the force, gravity, which produces that fall). The full meaning of footnote 58 requires an integration of presentational, orientational, and organisational contributions from its diagram, the footnote text, the main text, *and* its relation to the diagram portion of Figure 5.3.

The abstract graph portion of Figure 5.3 is itself a visual metaphor, showing a relation between position and temperature *as if* it were a shape in space, something that might be gestured and understood as a

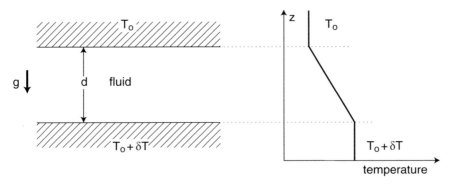

Figure 5.3 Figure V.3 from Berge *et al.* (1984: 84). Reproduced by permission

104   *Jay Lemke*

This is not so if the temperature gradient is horizontal rather than vertical. In this case, the liquid tends to rise along the warmer boundary and fall near the colder boundary. The forces are no longer opposed, but instead create a nonzero torque. No matter how small the temperature difference, δT, *even infinitesimal,* this torque induces motion in the fluid. Hence we see the necessity of avoiding horizontal temperature gradients in a R.B. experiment if we wish to have a well-marked convective threshold.

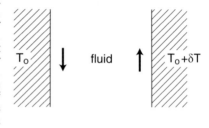

Figure 5.4 Footnote 58 from Berge *et al.* (1984: 84). Reproduced by permission

relationship among possible positions or motions. It brings to problems of continuous co-variation in all sorts of phenomena our intuitions and perceptual pattern-recognition capacities for spatial–motor phenomena. Those intuitions are supplemented by the mathematisation of the abstract graph, itself an extension of an original, textualisable description of numerical data to a pure mathematical abstraction of pattern. Mathematics is more powerful than visualisation, even though it is less intuitive, because it can represent patterns that cannot be visualised, and allow them to be compared, manipulated, combined, etc.

The abstract graph in this figure is not mathematised in the text because it is much too simple. Any competent reader could do the mathematisation immediately, but does not need to because this pattern is so familiar that it also has a verbal textualisation, e.g. 'The temperature rises linearly with depth in the fluid from T_o to T_o + dT.' Or any one of many thematically equivalent textualisations, such as: 'The temperature is directly proportional to depth in the fluid', or 'The temperature decreases linearly with height in the fluid', or 'There is a linear vertical temperature gradient in the fluid, with the bottom at higher temperature'. Any specialist reader could *draw* a substantially identical graph, or write the equivalent equation, from any of these verbal statements. The abstract thematic formation which unites all these representations is semiotically multimodal, as it is in principle for all scientific concepts and their relationships.

Figure, caption, and text

Consider, as a final example, Figure 5.5, which reproduces Figure 1 of an article from *Nature* on the spontaneous movement of a biological molecule, kinesin (Svoboda *et al.* 1993). Careful inspection will show a subdivision, visually and by labels, into Figures 1a, 1b and 1c (as they are labelled in the original), of which the latter two are of the data graph genre, and Figure 1a is an extraordinarily complex visual integration of abstract diagrams and relatively abstract drawings of several sorts, as well as one semi-abstract graph. Important as visual codes, especially presentational and organisational ones (orientational ones, too) are to the interpretation of Figure 1a, it could not be readily interpreted without substantial reliance on thematic formations formulated in the semantics of natural language and indexed by the verbal labels in the figure. For many of these, recourse to at least the caption text, and perhaps to the main text, is necessary, as well as prodigious intertextual connections to complete the formations and unpack their *thematic condensations* (Lemke 1988a): all that is left unsaid for the expert reader.

Quite apart from the complexities of the implicit mathematisations here, there are some very simple questions about how scientific texts are to be read so as to combine canonically figures with captions with main text. When we read the main text, there are references outward to the figures, such as '(see Figure V.3)'. We need to use verbal thematic formations at that point to construct meaning connections between the main text from which we have come and what we find in the figure. Those connections are most readily made either through the labels in the figure or through the intermediary of the caption text. Captions as extensive as this one (equivalent to almost a full page of main text) are somewhat unusual; it contains a great deal of very important information necessary for the interpretation of the main text, which certainly has major thematic gaps without it. In fact the visual figure itself is probably necessary for an interpretation of the main text adequate to the purposes of professional readers, and this is not at all unusual. Visual figures in scientific text, and mathematical expressions also, are generally *not* redundant with verbal main text information. They do not simply 'illustrate' the verbal text, they add important or necessary information; they complement the main text, and in many cases they complete it.

I want to consider here only a few points concerning the ways in which visual semiotics contribute to and interact with verbal semiotics in constructing presentational, orientational, and organisational aspects of the meaning of this multi-semiotic text. Accordingly, I will begin from the figure rather than from the main text, and refer first to text from its caption and only then to main text. My comments are based on a very thorough analysis of the visual–verbal relations among these elements.

Since we have concentrated so far more on presentational and organisational aspects of meaning in these scientific texts, let me here begin with orientational aspects. Orientational meaning includes (1) the stance or attitude a text seems to take to its own presentational content (e.g. warrantability, importance, desirability, usuality); (2) the stance it takes to prospective readers/viewers (*users*; e.g. solidary or antagonistic, deferential or condescending), including their anticipated attitude to the presentational content; and (3) the orientation of the text to other possible attitudes and viewpoints in the intertextual community (e.g.

opposed, allied, complementary). Orientations to users can be analysed by considering what the text seems to construct as its ideal prospective user, e.g. what the user is expected to know or be able to construe, what the user's expectations and attitudes are likely to be. Scientific research articles generally construct users as highly knowledgeable in relevant technical matters, and mildly critical or sceptical, especially of warrant-ability claims, but also of importance claims. It is generally assumed that text voice and user stance share the same values as to what is desirable in scientific research.

The orientational attitudes to presentational content which are most salient in this genre are evaluations of warrantability, usuality or surpris-

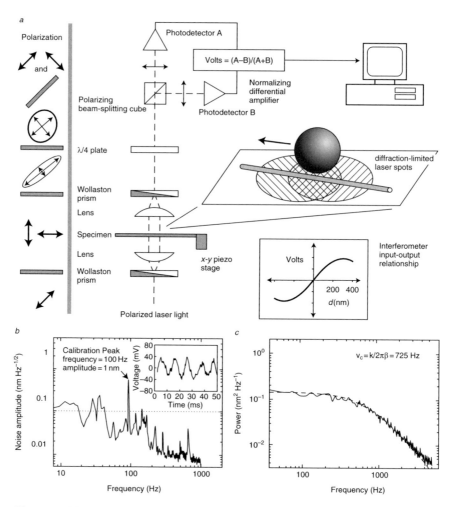

Figure 5.5 Figure 1 from Svoboda *et al.* (1993: 723). Reproduced from *Nature*, by permission

ingness, and importance. Desirability is generally backgrounded since it is assumed not to be in contention between text voice and user stance. It does however appear to mark this presumptive solidarity (see also Lemke 1988a). Consider some of the ways in which *importance* is constructed visually in Svoboda *et al.*'s Figure 1.

Importance is generally signalled by various conventions of visual prominence (see analyses by Kress and van Leeuwen 1990, O'Toole 1994, Arnheim 1956, Tufte 1983), one of which is *relative* size. Thus among the graphs in Figure 1, the *inset* graph in 1b is much smaller in scale than the other graphs and is thus marked as of less importance, particularly relative to the larger graph in 1b. In the caption text for 1b there is a title, followed by two sentences (twenty-seven words) on the larger graph, and then one (ten words) on the inset graph. In the main text, a paragraph begins with reference to the larger graph (one sentence), and then a sentence on the inset graph follows. To understand *why* text and users would evaluate the inset graph as of lesser importance requires intertextual reference to the canons of experimental science regarding the best measures of instrument sensitivity *and* the most honest and revealing ways to display data on this important issue (important for the warrant of experimental claims made by using the instrument).

In fact, rhetorically, a major claim of this article is not just for its factual findings, but for the 'advantages' (p. 722, a rare explicit claim of desirability) of its instrumental design over those in use by other researchers. This in turn accounts in part for the visual prominence of the whole of Figure 1, which is quite visually striking as a composition compared to typical diagrams of experimental apparatus, as well as for the prominence of 2b, which has a high visual density (compare 2c) and such additional highlights as the arrow pointing to the peak of the graph. When reading 2b, the two most important visual features, relative to the claim for sensitivity of the instrument, are the downward trend of the graph and the fact that it lies mostly beneath a dotted line (visually foregrounding a fact that would be evident without this feature) representing a 10:1 signal to noise ratio. The inset graph not only provides subsidiary information, it also presents it in a way that makes a strong visually intuitive case for the irrelevance of noise in the signal, even though canonically the main graph is considered the more reliable measure of this effect. The inset is 'icing on the cake', a sort of intuitive backup to the more technical evidence of the main graph it accompanies.

It is interesting that while the expert reader can get far more from the main graph, its implications for the issue of sensitivity are more indirect and must be mediated by considerable verbal discourse and reference to mathematical operations and relationships (which are provided in the caption text, in its subsidiary 'methods' section). On the other hand, the inset graph can be read topologically and intuitively as *showing* the relative size of signal and noise (the large wave of ups and downs is the signal, the lesser wiggles are minor distortions of it, the noise). The one shows what the other proves. A scientific understanding integrates both these modes of warrant.

The most visually prominent feature of the entire figure is surely the abstract drawing I will call the *sphere and rod* element (in 1a), including the shaded circles and their plane just below. We need in fact some reference to organisational visual semiotics here just to determine what constitutes a likely thematic unit in this part of the page. Proximity of elements, the enclosure effect of the parallelogram, and the specifically organisational visual device of the 'enlargement' or 'detail' lines diverging at an angle from the *specimen stage* (to the left and below) contribute. The diverging lines subtend in their angle the visual unit we are describing. They also call for us to perform a very complex visual–motor operation, in imagination, to co-orient the two different visual spaces (that of the microscope *stage* and that of the *sphere and rod*) in a single coherent space of representation. This is a practised operation for expert users.

The *sphere and rod* region is visually prominent on the page in part because it contains the only three-dimensional representation, as well as the largest areal concentration of ink (especially the large dark sphere), and the boldest surface and contrast (black–white) effects. The prominent visual *vectors* (cf. Arnheim 1956) of the arrow, the parallel line of the rod's axis, and the near-parallel sides of the parallelogram all contribute to the effect. Why is this visual complex so important? Presentationally, we are seeing here the heart of the clever design of this experiment: a silica bead (the sphere) reflects laser light (cf. the highlight on the sphere, the 'shadows' in the plane) as it is pulled (the arrow) along a microtubule (the rod) by a kinesin molecule (the small black blob connecting rod and sphere). The experiment is about the properties of the kinesin molecule, and the main claim is about how this molecule moves along a microtubule, but it is not the biological molecule that is visually prominent here (you might mistake it for a slip of the draughtsman's pen), it is the 'optical trapping interferometer', the clever experimental design to study the molecule indirectly by observing the bead.

As in all semiotic constructions, the visual qualities of an element mean in relation to those of other elements, especially those in the same presentation. All visual presentational forms in Figure 1 are highly abstract. The most recognisable is the schematic drawing of a computer, which is reduced in relative importance despite (or because of) its likely visual interest, by being small in scale compared to the sphere and rod drawing, and rendered only two-dimensionally. Abstract as these drawings are, they still show what counts in our culture as pictorial representation. By contrast, the 'optical bench' representation (elements such as lenses, stacked vertically and connected by dashed line, to the right of the long gray vertical dividing bar at left) and its continuation at the top into an electronic circuit schematic ('photodetector', 'amplifier') are purely abstract diagrams. They too could have been presented in more realistic renderings, or even in a photograph.

At the far left, we find an echo of the optical bench elements marking off the stages of transformation of the polarisation of the laser light as it passes through the various lenses and prisms. The arrows and arrows with ellipses are conventional symbolic representations of polarisation, descended from actual graphs. The lens or photodetector symbols follow arbitrary conventions, one residually iconic. The algebraic symbols of the *Volts formula* (boxed, top centre) descend from words and sentences of natural language, represented here by the orthography of the nearby word labels. We have here a large swath of the spectrum from visual–pictorial representations to verbal–semantic ones. They have been visually integrated (organisationally) and modulated for relative importance (orientationally).

Note that the organisational aspects of this figure, what we need to know in order to construe its wholes and parts, its sequences and internal relationships, depend not just on visual information and conventions. Much of the interpretation depends on thematic (presentational) information from the verbal text, or verbal intertexts, in some cases mediated by mathematical operations. This is also true in reverse. Figure 1c provides a view of data on the basis of which the weak forces with which the beads were 'trapped' by the beams of laser light could be calculated. The relevant caption text reads, '[the bead's] brownian motion [was] recorded, from which a power spectrum was computed. The corner frequency provides the ratio . . . [needed for the calculation].' The corresponding main text has: '[bead] dynamics corresponds to brownian motion . . ., which has a lorentzian power spectrum. Experimental spectra are well fitted by lorentzians, and the corner frequency provides the ratio . . . [needed].'

Inspection of Figure 1c, even without a knowledge of the mathematics of the lorentzian function or its canonical graphical forms, indicates visually what must be meant by the 'corner frequency' and lets us interpret the legend on the graph as telling us that 725 Hz is the exact frequency at which we can see the graph of the power spectrum suddenly bending, as if around a corner. On the one hand we could interpret 'corner frequency' merely as a quirky name for an algebraic parameter in an equation (for the lorentzian function), but the expert user here is expected *also* to interpret it visually, and perhaps physically, in terms of the shape of the graph, and in terms of the randomised motion to which it corresponds. Some users will rely more on one realisation of the underlying multimodal thematics (verbal, mathematical, visual, physical), others on another, and the same user may shift and combine these as the particular situation requires.

MAKING MEANING WITH MULTIPLE SEMIOTICS

I will not provide the details here for lack of space, but it is quite possible, working from the caption text and the main text, to establish item by item correspondences between verbal elements and structures in the text and visual ones in the figure, particularly for the description of the passage of light (and so of information about the bead and kinesin molecule) in its various states of polarisation along the optical bench to the electronic analyser. This shows particularly well how the user must integrate visual and verbal realisations of objects, concepts, relations and processes in the joint interpretation of text and figure. On the basis of this and similar analyses, it seems most reasonable to assume a joint visual–verbal thematic formation as the basis for interpretation, integration and intertextual (and interpictorial) contextualisation in making sense with multimedia texts. Thus, the 'concept' of polarisation, for example, must have not only a verbal semantic component, based in its canonical semantic relations to its usual collocates and contrast items (cf. Lemke 1983, 1990), but it must also have a visual–presentational component with similar relational meaning, as well as a mathematical component, and a technical–operational (sensorimotor) one, in order to be canonically useful in making meaning with a multimedia scientific article such as this.

It is sometimes argued that the various representations of a 'concept' are entirely 'redundant' with one another, that they can be placed in one-to-one correspondence, so that meanings which can be made in one semiotic modality can be equally well made in the others. This is not the way scientific communication appears to work: meanings are made by the *joint co-deployment* of two or more semiotic modalities, and such co-deployment of resources is likewise needed for canonical interpretation. In my opinion, semiotic modalities (e.g. language, depiction) are essentially *incommensurable*: no verbal text can construct the same meaning as a picture, no mathematical graph carries the same meaning as an equation, no verbal description makes the same sense as an action performed. As with all abstractions, we learn how to construct relations and connections among these different semiotic acts and their traces; we learn how to count them as the same for some restricted purposes. But insofar as their meanings are not determined entirely by these correspondences with one another, but also by their relations to other forms within their own semiotic (picture to picture, and word to word; cf. Saussure's *valeur* principle), even what they mean *within* these correspondences adds specificity of meaning in each semiotic modality beyond the common meaning shared across modalities.

'Concepts' as they are used in scientific communication, and in scientific work generally, are not defined by the common denominator of their representations, but by the sum, the union of meanings implied by all these representations. Nothing is really being 're-presented' here; there is no separate entity, no pure mental idea, apart from the meanings made with the specific material systems of semiotic resources our culture provides us with. What we call the abstract concept is only a shorthand for a multimodal semiotic construction, a simultaneous and multiply-articulated cluster of interdependent practices. At the level of specificity that matters here, the different semiotic constructions that together and in relation to one another constitute 'the concept' have *nothing* in common; there is no common denominator, and certainly no higher Platonic idea of which they are each pale shadows. It is in the nature of scientific concepts that they are semiotically multimodal in this sense, and this may well be true in other systems of semiotic practices as well.

When we investigate how meaning is made, we can no longer assume that actual social meanings, materially made, consist only in the verbal–semantic relations (paradigmatic, syntagmatic, intertextual) by which we have previously defined them. We must now consider that meaning-in-use normally organises, orients and presents, directly or implicitly, through the resources of multiple semiotic systems. What the logocentrism of a few prominent genres of purely verbal text (e.g. unillustrated novels, academic articles in philosophy and the humanities) has distracted us from, perhaps the pervasively multimodal disposition of scientific and technical text can remind us of. As computer technologies make multimedia genres more convenient and accessible for all purposes, it will become increasingly important to understand how the resources of different semiotic systems have been and can be combined.

Language, for all its power, has had relatively little to tell us about topological, as opposed to typological, modes of meaning-making. We understand far too little about quantitative and mathematical meaning, about affective and bodily meaning, about dynamic and emergent meaning, about all the dimensions of material interaction and social being that are not well represented in categorial terms.

Language, and typological modes of semiosis generally, have evolved to work in partnership with other, often more topologically grounded, semiotic systems. It is my hope that by studying scientific and computer hypermedia genres, we can explore the powerful mysteries of that partnership in order to understand better just how we make sense of our world and ourselves.

REFERENCES

Arnheim, R. 1956. *Art and Visual Perception*. London: Faber.
Bakhtin, Mikhail Mikhailovich. 1935. Discourse in the novel. In M. Holquist (ed.) *The Dialogic Imagination* (1981). Austin, TX: University of Texas Press pp. 259–422.
Bazerman, C. 1988. *Shaping Written Knowledge*. Madison, WI: University of Wisconsin Press.

112 *Jay Lemke*

Berge, P., Pomeau, Y. and Vidal, C. 1984. *Order Within Chaos: Towards a Deterministic Approach to Turbulence*. New York: Wiley.

Bernoulli, Johan. 1734. *De motu musculorum*. Bound in Giovanni Alfonso Borelli, *De motu animalium*. Napoli [Naples]: Felix Mosca. [Item 105 in the Cole Collection of the New York Academy of Medicine Library].

Gregory, M. 1967. Aspects of varieties differentiation. *Journal of Linguistics 3*: 177–198.

Halliday, M.A.K. 1978. *Language As Social Semiotic*. London: Edward Arnold.

—— 1982. The de-automatization of grammar. In J. Anderson (ed.) *Language Form and Linguistic Variation*. Amsterdam: John Benjamins pp. 129–159.

—— 1985. *An Introduction to Functional Grammar*. London: Edward Arnold.

—— 1991. Towards probabilistic interpretations. In E. Ventola (ed.) *Recent Systemic and Other Functional Views on Language*. Berlin and New York: Mouton/de Gruyter pp. 39–62.

Halliday, M.A.K. and Hasan, R. 1976. *Cohesion in English*. London: Longman.

—— 1989. *Language, Context, and Text*. London: Oxford University Press.

Hasan, R. 1984. Coherence and cohesive harmony. In J. Flood (ed.) *Understanding Reading Comprehension*. Newark, DE: International Reading Association pp. 181–219.

—— 1995. The conception of context in text. In M. Gregory and P. Fries, (eds) *Discourse in Society: Functional Perspectives*. Norwood, NJ: Ablex Publishing pp. 183–283.

Kress, G. and van Leeuwen, T. 1990. *Reading Images*. Geelong: Deakin University Press.

Kress, G. and Threadgold, T. 1988. Towards a social theory of genre. *Southern Review 21*: 215–243.

Latour, B. 1987. *Science in Action*. Cambridge, MA: Harvard University Press.

Lemke, J.L. 1983. Thematic analysis: Systems, structures, and strategies. *Semiotic Inquiry 3*(2): 159–187.

—— 1985. Ideology, intertextuality, and the notion of register. In J.D. Benson and W.S. Greaves (eds) *Systemic Perspectives on Discourse*. Norwood, NJ: Ablex pp. 275–294.

—— 1987. Strategic deployment of speech and action: A sociosemiotic analysis In J. Evans and J. Deely (eds) *Semiotics (1983) Proceedings of the Semiotic Society of America 'Snowbird' Conference*. University Press of America pp 67–79.

—— 1988a. Discourses in conflict: Heteroglossia and text semantics. In J.D. Benson and W.S. Greaves (eds) *Systemic Functional Approaches to Discourse*. Norwood, NJ: Ablex Publishing pp. 29–50.

—— 1988b. Text structure and text semantics. In R. Veltman and E. Steiner (eds) *Pragmatics, Discourse, and Text*. London: Pinter pp. 158–170.

—— 1989a. Social semiotics: A new model for literacy education. In D. Bloome (ed.) *Classrooms and Literacy*. Norwood, NJ: Ablex Publishing pp. 289–309.

—— 1989b. Semantics and social values. *WORD 40*(1–2): 37–50.

—— 1990. *Talking Science: Language, Learning, and Values*. Norwood, NJ: Ablex Publishing.

—— 1991. Text production and dynamic text semantics. In E. Ventola (ed.) *Functional and Systemic Linguistics: Approaches and Uses*. Berlin: Mouton/de Gruyter (*Trends in Linguistics*: Studies and Monographs 55) pp. 23–38.

—— 1992. Interpersonal meaning in discourse: Value orientations. In M. Davies and L. Ravelli (eds) *Advances in Systemic Linguistics: Recent Theory and Practice*. London: Pinter pp. 82–104.

—— 1993a. Making meaning with language and other semiotic systems. Paper presented at International Congress of Systemic and Functional Lingusitics, Victoria BC, Canada.

Lemke, J.L. 1993c. Intertextuality and educational research. *Linguistics and Education* 4(3–4): 257–268.

—— 1993d. Hypermedia and higher education. In T.M. Harrison and T.D. Stephen, (eds) *Computer Networking and Scholarship in the 21st Century University.* Albany, NY: SUNY Press pp. 215–232.

—— 1994. Multiplying meaning: Literacy in a multimedia world. Paper presented at the National Reading Conference, Charleston, SC (December 1993). Arlington, VA: ERIC Documents Service (ED 365 940).

—— 1995a. *Textual Politics: Discourse and Social Theory.* London: Taylor & Francis.

—— 1995b. Intertextuality and text semantics. In M. Gregory and P. Fries (eds) *Discourse in Society: Functional Perspectives.* Norwood, NJ: Ablex Publishing pp. 85–114.

—— 1996. Self-organization and psychological theory. Review of L.B. Smith and E. Thelen (eds) *A Dynamic Systems Approach to Development. Theory and Psychology* 6(2): 352–356.

—— in press, a. Metamedia literacy: Transforming meanings and media. In D. Reinking, L. Labbo, M. McKenna and R. Kiefer (eds) *Literacy for the 21st Century: Technological Transformation in a Post-Typographic World.* Hillsdale, NJ: Erlbaum.

—— in press, b. Semantic topography and textual meaning. In R. Stainton and J. DeVilliers (eds) *Communication and Linguistics.*

Lynch, M. and Woolgar, S. 1990. *Representation in Scientific Practice.* Cambridge, MA: MIT Press.

Mann, W. and Thompson, S. 1986. Relational propositions in discourse. *Discourse Processes* 9(1): 57–90.

Martikainen, P.J., Nykanen, H., Crill, P. and Silvola, J. 1993. Effects of a lowered water table on nitrous oxide fluxes from northern peatlands. *Nature* 366: 51–53.

Martin, J.R. 1991. Intrinsic functionality: Implications for contextual theory. *Social Semiotics* 1(1): 99–162.

—— 1992. *English Text.* Philadelphia, PA: John Benjamins.

Matthiessen, C.M.I.M. 1992. Interpreting the textual metafunction. In M. Davies and L. Ravelli (eds) *Advances in Systemic Linguistics: Recent Theory and Practice.* London: Pinter pp. 37–81.

Ochs, E., Gonzales, P. and Jacoby, S. 1996. When I come down I'm in the domain state: Grammar and graphic representation in the interpretive activity of physicists. In E. Ochs., E. Schegloff and S. Thompson (eds) *Interaction and Grammar.* Cambridge University Press pp. 328–369.

Ochs, E. Jacoby, S., and Gonzales, P. 1994. Interpretive journeys: How physicists talk and travel through graphic space. *Configurations* 2(1): 151–172.

O'Toole, M. 1994. *The Language of Displayed Art.* London: Leicester University Press.

Percival, I.C. 1987. Chaos in Hamiltonian systems. In M.V. Berry, I.C. Percival and N.O. Weiss (eds) *Dynamical Chaos.* Princeton, NJ: Princeton University Press pp. 131–143.

Scheflen, A.E. 1975. Models and epistemologies in the study of interaction. In A. Kendon, R. Harris and M. Key (eds) *Organization of Behavior in Face-to-Face Interaction.* The Hague: Mouton.

Svoboda, K., Schmidt, C.F., Schnapp, B.J. and Block, S.M. 1993. Direct observation of kinesin stepping by optical trapping interferometry. *Nature* 365(6448), 721–727.

Tufte, E. 1983. *The Visual Display of Quantitative Information.* Cheshire, CT: Graphics Press.

6 The greening of school science
Ecogenesis in secondary classrooms

Robert Veel

One of the most significant changes in scientific philosophy, research and education this century has been in the way we view and construe the relationship between humans and their physical environment. The term 'environmentalism' has been coined to distinguish these ostensibly new ways of thinking from 'conventional' or 'traditional' thinking about humans and the environment. Although comprising a wide range of philosophical, ideological and political positions, and far from unified, environmentalism is a phenomenon which is widely recognised by both academics and the wider community (Pepper 1994, 1996, O'Riordan 1981, Schumaker 1973). The increased prominence of environmentalist perspectives in the community is now reflected in school education. In most industrialised countries, disciplines which deal with human/physical environment relations, such as geography, science, economics and history, have all been reformulated in recent years so as to include content which deals directly with human impact on the environment or to take an 'environmentalist perspective' on traditional content.

This chapter examines how and to what extent the language of environmentalism is different from the language of traditional science. As for Halliday (this volume) the question of 'how' entails a consideration of 'in what respects' and 'by what means' the language is different. In order to make meaningful comparisons I have selected 'apprenticing' texts from primary and secondary schooling which are representative of both 'traditional' school science and environmentalism.

In order to understand how the language of environmentalism in schooling is different, it is necessary first to consider how traditional science construes relationships between humans and the environment. We will then examine how environmentalist texts construe this relationship, using a range of texts published for school students. The third section of the chapter deals with the use of visual images in environmentalist publications. As we will see, the dominant role of visual images is one of the main features of environmentalist texts and is a powerful resource for construing particular kinds of relationships between humans and the environment. The analysis and discussion of texts is based on the model of text/context relations and functional grammar provided by Systemic Functional Linguistic (SFL) theory (Halliday and Hasan 1985, Halliday 1994, Matthiessen 1996) as well as on closely related register genre theory (Martin 1992, 1997). The analysis of visual images is based on the work of Kress and Van Leeuwen (1990, 1996).

TRADITIONAL SCHOOL SCIENCE AND REPRESENTATIONS OF THE ENVIRONMENT

The ways of theorising, investigating and explaining events which most of us recognise as 'traditional' science remain pervasive in schooling. This tradition derives from what has been called the 'Cartesian–Newtonian Paradigm' of scientific knowledge (Capra 1982). Its principles include those of 'natural' observation and collection of raw data from the physical environment as well as those of rational hypothesis-making and induction. As the tradition has evolved, strict definitions of what constitutes valid scientific knowledge have developed. Legitimate observations, for example, must derive from quantifiable base attributes (length, mass, time, temperature, etc.), and scientists from Galileo onwards stressed the importance of measurability and mathematics in explaining the physical environment. At the same time, through the work of Newton and others, the 'naturalness' of scientific observations was being claimed. Quantitative observations of the physical environment were not only true, they were also objective and universal. Through a process of observation and induction traditional science uncovers the 'laws' by which the natural world operates.

As Pepper (1984) argues, the very clearly circumscribed way of investigating the physical world in traditional science predisposes us to construe human relations with the environment in very particular ways; ways that may not always be either complete, accurate or conducive to our long-term survival. Clearly written scientific language, as it has evolved over the centuries as a means of organising and producing scientific knowledge (see Halliday 1993, this volume), is one of the chief meaning-making resources for construing human–environment relationships.

If we consider Halliday's research in terms of how it construes relations between humans and the environment, we see that the language of science plays an active role in embodying, or realising, the 'external' or 'object-oriented' ways of viewing nature inherent in the traditional Cartesian–Newtonian paradigm. The cumulative effect of scientific writing is to make the logical links we draw between physical phenomena appear as 'natural', and therefore immutable, as possible. It is possible to identify several grammatical features of scientific texts which play a role in this process. These features include:

- the use of grammatical metaphor to create natural-like cause-and-effect links between events

- the use of middle and passive voice clauses to create texts where events are carried forward by a simple Process + Medium structure
- 'taxonomy-construing' texts such as reports, which use Theme, nominal group and Relational Processes to organise knowledge into natural-like taxonomies.

GRAMMATICAL METAPHOR

Consider the following text.

Text 1

Ice movement
As much as 10 per cent of the Earth's present day land area is covered by ice. We have evidence that, in the past, the area covered by ice was much greater.

  In high mountain areas, large thicknesses of snow can collect. This is compressed by its own weight and hardened. The compression of the snow can cause it to form into large bodies of ice. The weight of the snow and ice causes the ice to move slowly down the valley. This moving body of ice is called a glacier. The slow but powerful movement of this ice erodes sediments from the mountains and eventually carves out a large U-shaped valley, which is quite different from a river valley. The movement of the ice as it goes downhill also results in cracks, called crevasses, forming in the glacier.

(Heffernan and Learmonth 1988: 129)

At first glance the events described in this text seem connected to one another in an entirely 'natural' manner; the text seems at one with the physical world (or 'iconic' as Martin [1992: 516–523] describes it). Yet the language of the text, particularly the use of *grammatical metaphor* (see Halliday, this volume), construes events which are actually dispersed in time and place (e.g. 'large thicknesses of snow can collect' and 'carves out a large U-shaped valley') as a compact cause-and-effect chain located within a single semiotic space, the text itself. In this way a particular kind of *non-relationship* between humans and the environment is construed. In Text 1, like so many other scientific texts, the role of human observation and reasoning in construing 'natural' relations is completely effaced.

  Looking at the text as a whole, we see that a cause-and-effect chain, or 'implication sequence' is created (cf. Wignell, Martin and Eggins 1993, Veel 1997). Physical phenomena are linked together as if 'natural' and the human semiotic processes which establish these links are backgrounded. Ice movement, like so many other physical phenomena, appears to simply be following the 'laws of nature'. Table 6.1 sets out the metaphorical cause-and-effect links in Text 1.

Table 6.1 Metaphorical cause-and-effect links in Text 1

Cause	Effect
by its own weight	This is compressed . . .
The compression of the snow	can cause it to form into large bodies of ice.
The weight of the snow and ice	causes the ice to move slowly down the valley. This moving body of ice is called a glacier.
The slow but powerful movement of this ice	erodes sediments from the mountains and eventually carves out a large U-shaped valley, which is quite different from a river valley.
The movement of the ice as it goes downhill	also results in cracks, called crevasses, forming in the glacier.

MIDDLE AND PASSIVE VOICE CLAUSES

An analysis of patterns of *ergativity* in texts reveals the key participants around which a text unfolds. Such an analysis is useful for demonstrating to what degree scientific texts construe a world in which things simply happen and to what degree agency, particularly human agency, is involved. In an ergative analysis the core of a clause is the Process and the key participant (the 'Medium') associated with the process. Other participants, such as the Agent, are viewed as more peripheral to the process. In discussing ergativity Halliday states,

> Every process has associated with it one participant that is the key Figure in that process; this is the one trough in which the process is actualised, and without which there would be no process at all. Let us call this process the MEDIUM, since it is the entity through the medium of which the process comes into existence . . .. The Process and Medium together form the nucleus of an English clause; and the nucleus determines the range of options that are available to the rest of the clause.
>
> (Halliday 1994: 163–164)

The use of active, middle and passive voice clauses is a vital grammatical resource for construing different kinds of ergative patterns across texts. The preference for middle and passive voice clauses in scientific writing, noted by Halliday (1993), constructs particular kinds of relationships between humans and the environment. Middle and passive (non-agentive) clauses present events as simply *occurring*, rather than being *made* to happen, as the following example shows.

Thus the air in contact with the ground	is heated,	and	tends to rise
	Passive		**Middle**
	Voice		**Voice**

These clause types are well suited to presenting the physical environment as if it were external to human existence and independent of it, and our representations of the phenomena in language as if they were iconic with the physical environment and not mediated through semiotic processes. The use of middle and passive voice clauses in scientific texts thus complements the use of grammatical metaphor, where non-human agency can be generated. Through grammatical metaphor events are construed as causing other events. In the middle and passive voice clauses events *just happen*. In both cases human agency is absent and the human process of construing logical links between events is kept outside the text.

The following text, written for secondary school students and discussed by Martin (1993a), follows a typical ergativity pattern. An analysis of these patterns is displayed on p. 119.

Text 2

Sea Breezes
Sea breezes begin during the afternoons of hot days when the air over the ground becomes heated. Radiant energy from the sun is absorbed by the ground and this energy is converted into heat energy which raises the temperature of the rocks and soil. Thus the air in contact with the ground is heated, and tends to rise. Because water requires more heat than other substances to produce the same rise in temperature, the temperature of the sea surface does not rise as much as that on the land. Thus the air above the sea is cooler than the air over the land. The result is that the heated air above the land rises, causing the cooler air from the sea to flow in to take its place.

The analysis (Table 6.2) reveals the very great extent to which this text revolves around a chain of Process + Medium clauses. The effect is to present an explanation which seems at once both logical and natural: event A leads to event B, event B leads to event C, etc. The two agents that are present in the text are non-human. Note, however, that the very linearity of this text is itself an artefact. In the physical environment all the events described in the text would be happening simultaneously, not in sequence. Because language must proceed word-by-word and clause-by-clause, a written explanation, simply because it is written, must be to some extent linear (cf. diagrams and flow charts which may be cyclical). Moreover the text is forced to evoke abstract categories such as 'radiant energy from the sun' and 'temperature' in order to create a logical sequence.

Table 6.2 Ergativity in 'Sea Breezes' text

Process	Medium	Agent	Circumstance, beneficiary, range
begin	sea breezes		during the afternoons of hot days
becomes heated	the air over the ground		
is absorbed	Radiant energy from the sun	by the ground	
is converted	this energy		into heat energy
raises	the temperature of the rocks and soil.	which [i.e., conversion into heat energy]	
is heated	the air in contact with the ground		
tends to rise	(the air in contact with the ground)		
requires	more heat than other substances		water
to produce	the same rise in temperature		
does not rise	the temperature of the sea surface		as much as that on the land
the air above the sea	is		cooler than the air over the land
rises	the heated air above the land,		
causing . . . to flow in	the cooler air from the sea		
to take	its place		

TECHNICAL TAXONOMIES

Technical taxonomies are another feature of scientific texts, and they too work to construe particular relations between humans and the environment. A distinctive kind of text, the *taxonomic report*, is the usual textual vehicle for presenting taxonomic knowledge (Martin 1993a). The chapters by Wignell and White in this volume discuss some of the grammatical resources used to construe taxonomic knowledge (typically Theme, nominal group and Relational Processes). In taxonomising texts it is the observation of base attributes (length, mass, etc.) which renders the knowledge natural. The taxonomies are 'true' because their basis lies in 'objective' measurement of observable key attributes.

The taxonomic organisation of knowledge through language, so prominent in school science, also predisposes us to view the physical environment in particular ways. First, by viewing the environment as a set of objects, it reinforces the subject–object distinction of Cartesian philosophy, in which unknowable human subjects examine naturally occurring and knowable physical objects. In this way the role of human social subjectivity in constructing and organising knowledge is divorced from the knowledge itself. Second, the division of the physical world into discrete objects and classes of objects promotes the 'nature as a machine' view of the environment, encouraging us to view physical systems as discrete and mechanical, and discouraging us from thinking of them as interactive and complex. Such a view, critics have argued, often prevents us from understanding the full effects of human activity on the environment.

In this section I have attempted to illustrate how the language of 'traditional science' cultivates particular ways of viewing the physical environment: ways which tend to render invisible the link between human thought, language and activity from the ways we think about the physical environment.

ENVIRONMENTALISM AND ECOLOGY

In modern environmentalism and ecology we can recognise fairly well-defined ways of conceptualising the environment and human relations with the environment. Like traditional science these ways of looking at the environment have developed over many centuries. Both environmentalism and ecology share the view that humans and human activity need to be seen as *part* of the physical environment, and that any account of this environment must allow for the impact of human activity. This is not to say that humans interact with the environment in the same way as other entities, but simply that they should not be ignored or actively excluded from our accounts. In particular, many environmentalists and ecologists stress the need to scrutinise closely the role played by humans themselves in creating the dominant models of human–environment interaction.

Environmentalism can best be described as an ideology, an '-ism'. It is not comprised of any specific body of knowledge, but is rather a particular way of relating information and accounting for phenomena. Through the lens of environmentalism it is possible to reorganise and reinterpret information developed through traditional disciplinary knowledge. As well as attempting to model the human relationship with the environment in distinctive ways, environmentalism is often described as being about reform. O'Riordan, an influential researcher and writer in environmentalism, states, for example, that environmentalism is 'about conviction – conviction that a better mode of existence is possible . . . opening up our minds and our organisation to new ideas about fairness, sharing, permanence and humility' (O'Riordan 1981: vi).

As we shall see this orientation to reform has profound effects on the language of environmentalism.

Ecology, on the other hand, presents itself much more as a 'hard science', an '-ology'. The term was coined in 1866 by Ernst Haeckel, a trained biologist and evolutionist to refer to the study of the interaction of organisms (not just humans) with the physical world. Ecology uses the epistemological resources of science: hypothesis testing; the collection, sorting and analysis of empirical data; written genres of report, explanation, etc. to construct a model of the world based on a kind of dialectical interaction between humans and the environment, rather than on seperation and isolation. Like other sciences, ecology claims to be objective in the way it gathers and presents data.

Despite these different histories and different orientations, environmentalism and ecology are frequently linked in practice. In educational settings the study of ecosystems (ecology) is almost invariably accompanied by some moral or ethical discussion of the impact of human activity (environmentalism). In Australia, for example, the National Science Profiles include the following linked outcomes. (Significantly the more reformist outcomes are also the higher level ones.)

- identify events that affect balance in an ecosystem (level 4)
- analyse the effects of environmental change on living things in an ecosystem (level 6)
- evaluate scientific evidence about the long-term impact on ecosystems of human intervention (level 7)
- identify the role of scientific disciplines in an interdisciplinary approach to understanding and managing ecosystems (level 8)

(Curriculum Corporation 1993: 51)

In research and publishing contexts, the collection of 'objective evidence' in ecology is inexorably linked to the desire to reform society. Prominent, established ecologists such as David Suzuki also act as spirited advocates of environmentalism.

According to Pepper (1984) there are two distinct schools of thought running through environmentalism. The first derives from an aesthetic and moral rejection of industrialisation, and has its roots in nineteenth-century romanticism. The second takes a more scientific and rationalist approach to the accumulation and organisation of information and reflects the scientific and rationalist heritage of Malthus and Darwin. Although there is no one-to-one correlation between these two strands and the distinction between environmentalism and ecology, it is clear that ecology relies more solely on the rationalist tradition whereas environmentalism tends to blend the two approaches.

Both of these schools of thought can be identified in environmentalist texts written for and by school students, as the following examples show.

The first extract, written by a seventeen-year-old student, illustrates the more romantic kind of environmentalism:

> Environmental imperialism represents another area where the manifestations of an unsustainable growth-and-green society are further broadening the chasm between North and South . . . The consequences of this failure to address the problem of greed are displayed in the growing ecological crisis gripping the planet in the form of acid rain, deforestation, ozone depletion, desertification and the pollution of the world's hydrological resources. The manifestation of greed is posing fatal consequences on the global community.
>
> (Board of Studies 1993b: 29)

The second extract, from a book written for junior secondary students, illustrates the more scientific/rationalist tradition:

> *The limiting factor*
> In 1944 a small group of 27 reindeer was introduced on to St Matthew Island, off the north west coast of Alaska. In less than 20 years the population had grown to 6,000. Following a hard winter at the end of 1963, the population then crashed to just 42 individuals. The lichen on the island, the deer's usual food, had almost disappeared and an examination of the dead deer revealed that they had starved to death. In the absence of any predators, the density dependent factor that had so dramatically reduced the number of reindeer was clearly the food supply.
>
> (Pollock 1993: 31)

It is evident then that environmentalism is a very broad concept, encompassing both humanities-based ideas about the social and economic organisation of society as well as a scientifically based body of knowledge. It is this combination of disparate discourses which makes environmentalism and environmentalist language distinct. The remainder of this chapter will investigate in more detail how language works to realise environmentalist discourse in schools.

THE LANGUAGE OF ENVIRONMENTALISM IN SCHOOLS

This section draws upon texts from a range of sources. These include texts from a book for upper primary aged children, *Man-made Disasters: Atmosphere in danger* (Walker 1993), a book on *Ecology* for junior secondary students (Pollock 1993), a text from a traditional science text book (Heffernan and Learmonth 1988) and an essay written by an eighteen-year-old student for her final year school exams in General Studies in New South Wales, Australia (Board of Studies 1993b). Although this sample of texts is small compared to the volume of published materials for school students, it does give an idea of the range of language used in environmentalism.

Turning first to the book for upper primary children, *Man-made Disasters: Atmosphere in danger*, we find that most of it combines a romantic, humanities-like approach to the environment with a scientific one. This is not surprising given the integrative approach to knowledge in primary school education. As the educational sociologist Basil Bernstein notes, it is not until secondary school that most disciplines declare themselves and become strongly classified as humanities or sciences (Bernstein 1977: 85–116). Here is a text from *Man-made Disasters: Atmosphere in danger*.

Text 3

Polluting the air
Human beings are making the air dirtier and dirtier. As the demand for energy has increased, more and more harmful gases have been produced as a result of burning fossil fuels, such as coal, oil and gas. Two of the principal air pollutants are sulphur dioxide (SO_2) and nitrogen oxides (NO_2), which are the main causes of acid rain.

We are also increasing the quantity of gases which trap heat in the atmosphere. These include carbon dioxide (CO_2), which is caused by the burning of fossil fuels and rainforest destruction, and methane, which is released from rice fields, swamps, and animal waste.

Another type of pollution comes from man-made chemicals such as chlorofluorocarbons (CFCs). These rise into the atmosphere and damage the ozone layer.

(Walker 1993: 8)

The generic structure of this text is typical of discursively mixed writing, and allows the text to combine emotive meanings with scientific ones. The opening sentence is very much like the *thesis* stage in an exposition, as described by Martin (Martin 1985, Martin and Peters 1985). At this point the intent of the text seems to be to show that 'Human beings are making the air dirtier and dirtier'. The arguments which support this thesis are minimal, and consist of a listing of human-made contributions to air pollution. The generic structure of the text is shown in Figure 6.1.

Simultaneously, however, the text construes knowledge in the manner of an taxonomy-construing report. A taxonomy of different kinds of air pollutants is established in this text, and is represented in Figure 6.2.

The result of this mixture is to create a text which is not uncommon in environmentalism, where a genre concerned with interpersonal mean-

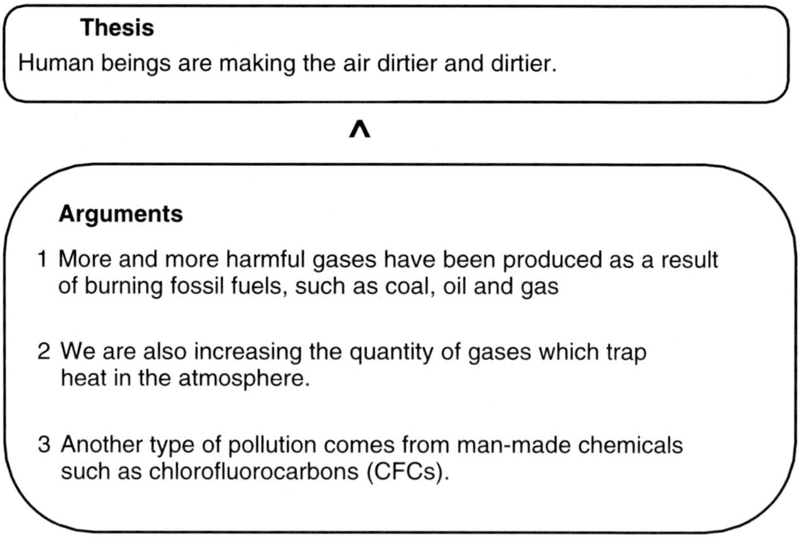

Thesis
Human beings are making the air dirtier and dirtier.
^
Arguments
1 More and more harmful gases have been produced as a result of burning fossil fuels, such as coal, oil and gas
2 We are also increasing the quantity of gases which trap heat in the atmosphere.
3 Another type of pollution comes from man-made chemicals such as chlorofluorocarbons (CFCs).

Figure 6.1 Generic structure of Text 3, viewed as exposition

Air pollutants
from increased burning of fossil fuels
sulphur dioxides
nitrogen oxides
[...]
from increased production of heat-trapping gases
carbon dioxide
[...]
from man-made chemicals
chlorofluorocarbons
[...]

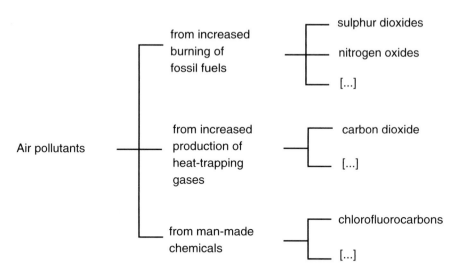

Figure 6.2 Field taxonomy of Text 3, viewed as report

ing, here an analytical exposition, also works to construe knowledge which is traditionally presented in a more information-oriented genre, such as a report. This kind of dual-purpose text, where one genre 'stands for' another genre, and simultaneously construes forms of knowledge typically found in both genres, has been described by Martin as *register metaphor* (Martin 1997), akin to Halliday's notion of grammatical metaphor. Text 3 is able to be read in two ways: as analytical exposition which persuades the reader that 'Human beings are making the air dirtier and dirtier', *and* as a report which construes a taxonomy of different types of pollutants. In this way more scientifically driven information about the environment is presented within a text which is primarily about confronting the reader with an issue. It is important to note that the taxonomic knowledge is projected *through the exposition*, and not the other way around. The effect of this is to construe the humanities-like rhetoric as motivating the scientific knowledge; scientific knowledge is presented as a means to a (social) end and not an end in itself. Figure 6.3 displays the dual purpose of this text.

The grammatical patterns in this text reflect the dual expository/information-giving function of this text. The text is 'personalised' in a way which is typical of exposition. This is achieved in a number of ways, including the representation of humans as grammatical agents, acting upon their physical environment:

Human beings   are making the air dirtier and dirtier.
Agent

We   are also increasing the quantity of gases
Agent   which trap heat in the atmosphere.

and the use of amplification to inflate the value of epithets in the opening stage of the text:

Human beings are making the air **dirtier and dirtier.**

more and more harmful gases have been produced . . .

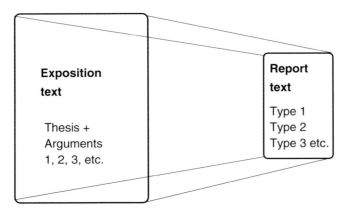

Figure 6.3 Register metaphor in Text 3: exposition projecting report

At the same time the text exploits some of the same linguistic resources as traditional science. These include the use of Classifier + Thing structures in nominal groups to imply taxonomic relationships:

sulphur	dioxide
Classifier	**Thing**

nitrogen	oxides
Classifier	**Thing**

carbon	dioxide
Classifier	**Thing**

and the use of grammatical metaphor to construe cause-and-effect relationships between events:

> As the <u>demand</u> for energy has increased, more and more harmful gases have been produced as <u>a result of burning</u> fossil fuels, such as coal, oil and gas.

> These include carbon dioxide (CO_2), which <u>is caused by</u> the <u>burning</u> of fossil fuels and rainforest <u>destruction</u>.

We will now examine the language of *Ecology*, a book written for junior secondary students. In this book we find that the scientific information is mixed far less freely with persuasive or emotive language than is the case in *Man-made Disasters: Atmosphere in danger*. Most of the book is dedicated to systematically building up students' field knowledge in ecology. The organisation and sequence of 'two-page spreads' in the book, given in the page titles listed in Figure 6.4, demonstrate this clearly. Notice in particular the shift from information about more *abstract* patterns in the environment in the first half of the book (food webs, energy transfer, water cycle, etc.) to information about *actual* ecosystems in the second half (ocean, arid lands, grasslands, etc.).

When dealing with fairly simple levels in an ecosystem, many of the texts in *Ecology* closely resemble those of traditional science. The following text, for example, explains an environmental phenomenon at the level of 'population'.

Text 4

Feeding the young
When the adults of some species of salmon have migrated upriver and spawned, they are so exhausted that they die. Their bodies lie in great numbers in the shallows of the river's headwaters, where they rot down, providing a readily available supply of nutrients for the growth of the eggs and for the young salmon when they hatch. The young are effectively made up of carbon from their parents.

(Pollock 1993: 19)

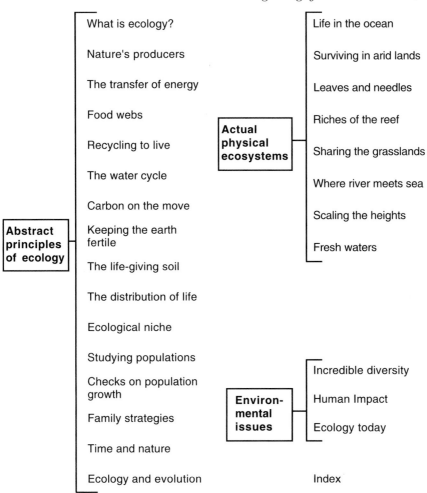

Figure 6.4 Titles of page spreads in *Ecology*: organisation of knowledge from abstract to actual

   In structure and grammatical features this text is very similar to that of an explanation in traditional science (cf. Text 2). The world is construed as a place where things just happen, rather than being caused to happen. This is achieved largely through the use of middle voice clauses in the text. Rather than being a text about 'who does what to salmon', this is a text about 'what happens to salmon'. Like Text 2, it has the effect of objectifying nature, representing it as something 'out there' which we unobtrusively observe and document. Table 6.3 shows an ergative analysis of this text.

   Not all of the texts in *Ecology*, however, resemble those of traditional science so closely. Differences begin to appear in those texts which deal with higher levels of ecological abstraction, such as 'community' or

Table 6.3 Ergativity in Text 4

Medium	Process	Agent
the adults of some species of salmon	have migrated	–
( )	spawned	–
they	are	–
they	die	–
their bodies	lie	–
they	rot down	–
( )	providing	–
they	hatch	–
carbon from their parents	are . . . made up of	the young

'ecosystem'. Most of these differences arise from a tension between the desire for universality and generalisability in traditional science on the one hand, and the need to recognise the context-specific nature of an ecosystemic world view on the other. Roughly stated this tension is, 'How can one derive abstract and universal laws of nature from a meaning system whose very basis lies in the connectedness of things within actual physical contexts?' This kind of tension is not unique to ecology. It is a feature of any theory which tries to talk about context and still be recognisable as a theory, as anyone who has worked in the fields of functional linguistics, sociology or cultural studies will know.[1]

One text in *Ecology* demonstrates this tension well. In 'Carbon on the move' (Text 5) we see an attempt to combine theoretical ideas about energy transfer in the biosphere with the actual physical locations in which the energy transfer occurs. The negotiation between theoretical laws and the actual physical contexts occurs at all levels in the text: generic structure, discourse semantics and grammar.

Text 5

Carbon on the move
All life on earth is based on the element carbon. It is constantly being passed between different parts of the biosphere in various chemical forms. It is found in the bodies of all living things, in the oceans, in the air, and in the Earth itself. In the atmosphere, when combined with oxygen, it forms carbon dioxide (CO_2). In plants, it becomes carbohydrate, the source of energy for plants and eventually for the animals that eat them. In the ground, and in the bones and shells of animals, carbon is found in the form of chalky calcium carbonate. Plants are the main point of exchange, converting atmospheric carbon dioxide into carbohydrate through photosynthesis (p. 8). Decomposition (p. 14) eventually returns all the carbon to the atmosphere.

(Pollock 1993: 20)

The overt generic structure of the text is that of a report (Martin 1993a). The general statement, which opens the text, clearly locates the knowledge in the realm of abstract models of the environment. This is construed through the use of generic Participants ('the element carbon', 'various chemical forms', 'the bodies', etc.) in 'timeless' present tense processes ('is based', 'is . . . being passed', 'is found') and is emphasised through choices of Deixis in the Nominal Group ('*All* life on earth', *all* living things') and through a Modal Adjunct ('constantly'):

> All life on earth is based on the element carbon. It is constantly being passed between different parts of the biosphere in various chemical forms. It is found in the bodies of all living things, in the oceans, in the air, and in the Earth itself.

The Description stage of the text, however, moves away from the abstract model and instead organises information around the actual physical parts of ecosystems. This is clearly signalled through the use of Marked Themes, locating the information in observable physical spaces.

In the atmosphere,	when combined with oxygen, it forms carbon dioxide (CO_2).
<u>Marked Theme</u>	
In plants,	it becomes carbohydrate, the source of energy for plants
<u>Marked Theme</u>	
In the ground, and in the bones and shells of animals	carbon is found in the form of chalky calcium carbonate.
<u>Marked Theme</u>	

The taxonomic organisation of knowledge in this text is unambiguous. Figure 6.5 shows this.

The ordering of information in the Description stage of 'Carbon on the move' is not random. Within the non-temporal taxonomic arrangement of information there is also a sequence, which allows the text to explain the *cycle* through which carbon moves; from the atmosphere, to plants, to animals, to the ground and back into the atmosphere. This

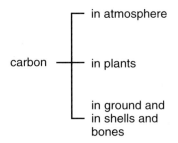

Figure 6.5 Field taxonomy in Text 5

sequence transcends the context-specific nature of each part of the Description stage of the texts and thus contributes to the abstract propositions about carbon being made in the text. Thus the text simultaneously fulfils the purpose of a report and an explanation, and is another example of register metaphor, in this case a report 'standing for' an explanation. Figure 6.6 models the co-existence of a context-specific taxonomy and a universal sequence in the text.

At the level of discourse semantics, the resource of *identification* works to hold disparate elements of the text together (Martin 1992: 93–157). This is most clearly shown by the lexical string and reference chain for 'carbon', shown in Figure 6.7. The role of identification in unifying the text is highlighted by the fact that there is little consistency in the use of the item 'carbon' in other lexico-grammatical systems. In terms of information structure, 'carbon' appears both as 'given' and 'new' information, as well as in intermediate positions. In the transitivity system, it appears as Circumstance, Carrier, Actor, Goal and as a Classifier in a Nominal Group ('Carbon Dioxide'). The reference chain therefore plays a vital role in holding the text together.

The tension between the abstract and the actual is also manifested through the clause grammar of 'Carbons on the move'. Looking once again at ergativity, one sees that the Process + Medium 'nub' of the text is concerned with construing the *abstract* sequence relating to the carbon cycle. Those elements concerned with locating events within *actual ecosystems* are assigned a more peripheral role, usually as Circumstances. As Martin notes (1992: 316), the meaning of the Process/Circumstance relationship is analogous with that of a main clause/enhancing clause relationship, with the Circumstance qualifying the meaning of the Process + Medium nub. Following Matthiessen (1992), Martin notes the 'peripherality' of this kind of relationship; it is one of the least strong bonds between constituents in a clause. Table 6.4 shows an analysis of ergativity for 'Carbon on the move'.

Although the effect of ergative relations in this text is to keep separate the abstract and the actual elements in each clause of the text, it should also be noticed that the very consistency of this pattern across the whole text gives it a kind of unity or harmony. Elements of the text referring to specific places consistently appear as Circumstance, and elements relating to the universal carbon cycle consistently appear in the Process + Medium nub. The effect is to build up two distinct strands through the text, each of which has an internal consistency. In this way patterns in the clause grammar 'redound' with the register metaphor in the text (report 'standing for' explanation), with the peripheral Circumstances realising the overt report function of the text, and the references to carbon, occupying a central role in the clause grammar, realising the explanation function. Perhaps the best description of the pattern is one of *parallel worlds*, where the specific information about different ecosystems is built up through the text parallel with abstract information about the carbon cycle.

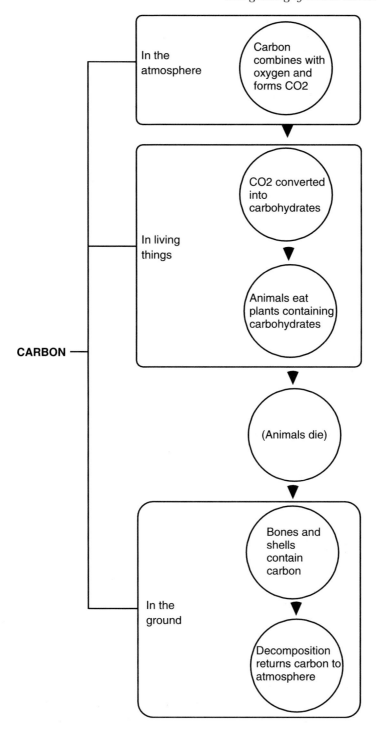

Figure 6.6 Register metaphor in Text 5: report construing explanation

Carbon on the move

1   All life on earth is based on the element carbon.

2   It is constantly being passed between different parts of the biosphere in various chemical forms.

3   It is found in the bodies of all living things, in the oceans, in the air, and in the Earth itself.

4a   In the atmosphere, when combined with oxygen,

4b   it forms carbon dioxide (CO_2).

5   In plants, it becomes carbohydrate, the source of energy for plants and eventually for the animals [that eat them].

6   In the ground, and in the bones and shells of animals, carbon is found in the form of chalky calcium carbonate.

7a   Plants are the main point of exchange,

7b   converting atmospheric carbon dioxide into carbohydrate through photosynthesis (p. 8).

8   Decomposition (p. 14) eventually returns all the carbon to the atmosphere.

Key: ——————— Reference chain
          - - - - - - · lexical string

Figure 6.7 Identification in 'Carbon on the move': reference chain and lexical string for the item 'carbon'

To summarise this analysis of 'Carbon on the move', we can say that patterns in the generic structure, discourse semantics, clause grammar and nominal group structure which are patterned in a way to allow the text to move back and forth between a world of abstract, theoretical knowledge, concerned with the carbon cycle, and a world in which knowledge is localised and contingent upon the particular physical features of ecosystems. These patterns are summarised below.

Stratum	'Theorising' features	'Physicalising' features
Genre	Explanation-like sequence of process + medium relating to carbon cycle	Report-like taxonomy of different locations in which carbon cycle occurs (atmosphere, plants, animals, ground)
Discourse semantics	Lengthy reference chain associated with carbon extending throughout text	Consistency of physical-location-as-Circumstance gives overall coherence to diverse locations

Table 6.4 Ergativity in 'Carbon on the move'

Medium	Process	Agent	Range	Circumstance (Enhancement)
the element carbon	is based on		All life on earth	
It	is being passed			constantly; between different parts of the biosphere in various chemical forms.
It	is found			in the bodies of all living things, in the oceans, in the air, and in the Earth itself.
it	forms	carbon dioxide (CO_2)		In the atmosphere
( )	combined			with oxygen
it	becomes		carbohydrate, the source of energy for plants and eventually for the animals that eat them	In plants
carbon	is found			In the ground, and in the bones and shells of animals; in the form of chalky calcium carbonate
the main point of exchange	are	plants		
atmospheric carbon dioxide	converting	( )		into carbohydrate; through photosynthesis
all the carbon	returns	decomposition		to the atmosphere

| **Lexico-grammar** | Processes associated with carbon cycle consistently in process + medium nub of clause, references to physical world appear peripherally as circumstances | Marked themes of location making places 'point of departure' for clauses |

INTERPERSONAL MEANING IN ENVIRONMENTALIST TEXTS

So far I have been concerned to show how, and to what extent, environmentalist texts differ from traditional scientific texts in the way that they construe a *field* of knowledge; how they represent things, events, places, times and what kind of relation these elements have to one another. Some of the greatest differences between traditional science texts and environmentalist texts lie, however, not in the way they construe field, but in the types of reader/writer relationship realised through language. Within SFL this aspect of context is referred to as *tenor*. The chief grammatical structures which realise different tenor relationships are grouped together as *interpersonal meaning*. The question of tenor often receives scant attention in school science. It is often simply assumed that scientific texts are 'impersonal', even though this term has little meaning in relation to language which is essentially a shared communicative act. The tenor of many environmentalist texts is so obviously different from traditional science, however, that we cannot possibly ignore this dimension here.

It is perhaps significant that one must go outside of the discipline area of science and beyond published textbooks to find the most striking examples of different tenor roles in environmentalist texts. The text we shall examine here, for example, is an exam script written by a seventeen-year-old student, not by a teacher or a textbook writer, and comes from the subject area of general studies, not science. The text was deemed excellent by the examination committee.

Text 6

Question

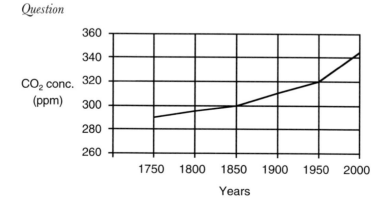

By analysing gas trapped in glacial ice, scientists have found CO_2 levels have risen steadily since the Industrial Revolution. CO_2 concentrations are presently rising by 3–4% a decade and have increased by 25% over the last 200 years. Adapted from *New Internationalist.*

Explain the trend indicated in this graph.
If this trend continues, how might it affect the environment?

Student's response
Carbon dioxide levels have increased dramatically over the past two hundred years. Increased burning of fossil fuels and deforestation are the main contributors to this increase. If such trends continue the climatic changes due to the 'Greenhouse Effect' may have disastrous consequences.

The opinion held before the 1960's was generally that resources were there to be exploited; they would not run out. Since that time it has become increasingly obvious that resources will run out and attempts are being made to decrease our resource usage and hence cut down our pollution. However the damage has been done and people and companies, are set up in their ways and to change their methods is a hard task. This is evidenced in the graph by the continuing rise in the carbon dioxide levels in the glacial ice.

Fossil fuels such as coal and oil, are our major providers of energy. Hence, we tend to overuse them. The problem is, upon combustion these fuels release carbon dioxide, a 'Greenhouse gas'. Most resources show that we are consuming too much energy or wasting energy billions of tonnes of carbon dioxide are being released into the atmosphere. Even though there are alternative energy sources such as wind, water, nuclear power, industry tends to be centred around the fossil fuels for provision of energy.

Our forests are a great resource; they offer a diverse 'gene pool' for providing medicines, cotton, timber for industry etc. Yet through exploitation the forests are disappearing at a rate of two football fields per second – an alarming rate. These forest actually 'breathe in' carbon dioxide from the atmosphere. Carbon dioxide is needed in the chemical process of photosynthesis which provides food for the plants. In theory, these plants and trees should be able to keep a biological balance. However this is not true. The level of carbon dioxide in the atmosphere is simply too high and the forest are disappearing at an alarming rate. This balance can never be achieved if the industries are going to continue logging our forests.

Carbon dioxide is often described as a 'greenhouse gas'. This means that it contributes to what we call the 'Greenhouse Effect'. The sun beams down onto the earth and heat passes through the atmosphere and warms our planet. However, due to the large concentrations of carbon dioxide in the atmosphere, the heat cannot radiate back out into space from earth. This means the earth's atmosphere slowly warms up. A common term for this process is 'global warming'.

'Global warming' can have devastating effects on the environment. Scientists have suggested that the average temperature of the earth may rise 3–4% would mean the floating ice caps would melt meaning an overall rise in the level of the ocean. Snowfall patterns would change dramatically. Organisms would have to adapt to a hotter environment. For many organisms, quite sensitive to changes in temperature, this could mean relocating to a cooler climate or facing extinction. The effects on the environment due to the greenhouse effect could be quite severe and it is mainly due to the ever increasing amounts of carbon dioxide being released into the atmosphere each year.

It can be seen that the increasing levels of carbon dioxide found in the glacial ice is due to over use of fossils fuels and deforestation. If man does not put a stop to this exploitation of resources, the 'Greenhouse Effect' may have devastating consequences for the environment and humanity in general.

(Board of Studies 1993b: 40–41)

Like 'Polluting the atmosphere', Text 6 is structured as an exposition, with a Thesis and a number of supporting Arguments. Into this structure it interpolates other genres, especially explanation, in order to form recognisably scientific arguments.[2] Structurally the text is a synthesis of scientific and humanities discourses. The writer must adopt the tenor role of an 'informed advocate' in order to achieve this synthesis. This kind of role is markedly different from those of 'information giver' or 'information consumer' typically found in school science. Figure 6.8 models the generic structure of the text. The interpolated genres are shown in parentheses on the right of the figure.

An important distinguishing feature of interpersonal meaning is that it is realised prosodically across texts (Martin 1992:11). Rather than appearing at particular points in a text or as a particular pattern of constituents in a clause, interpersonal meaning is spread across a text, combined with ideational and textual elements. As well interpersonal meaning is usually gradable from 'low' to 'high' realisations (e.g. 'rather hot' vs 'really hot') and are used to intensify ideational meanings. This is a feature which the writer controls well in the 'Carbon dioxide' text. In the paragraph below the items which most clearly can be interpreted interpersonally are shown in italics.[3]

Our forests are a *great* resource; they offer a diverse 'gene pool' for providing medicines, cotton, timber for industry etc. Yet through *exploitation* the forests are disappearing at a rate of two football fields per second – an *alarming* rate. These forests *actually* 'breathe in' carbon

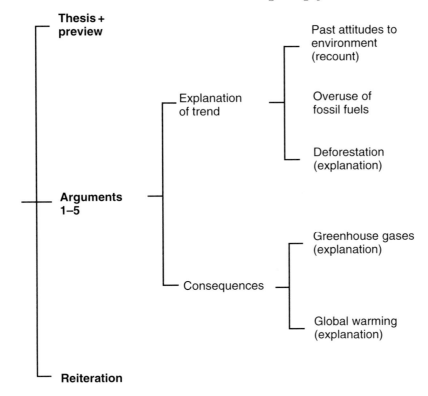

Figure 6.8 Generic structure of 'carbon dioxide' essay (Text 6)

dioxide from the atmosphere. Carbon dioxide is needed in the chemical process of photosynthesis which provides food for the plants. In
theory, these plants and trees should be able to keep a biological
balance. However this is *not true*. The level of carbon dioxide in the
atmosphere is *simply too high* and the forest are disappearing at an
alarming rate. This balance can never be achieved if the industries are
going to continue logging our forests.

At the level of clause, a range of grammatical resources is deployed to
combine humanities and scientific discourse and realise an environmentalist text. Like 'Polluting the atmosphere', *human agency* appears in the
text, explicitly linking humans to events occurring in the physical environment:

people and companies, are set up in their ways and to change their
methods is a hard task.

Hence, *we* tend to overuse them

we are consuming too much energy

industry tends to be centred around the fossil fuels for provision of energy.

Scientists have suggested that the average temperature of the earth may rise 3–4%.

If *man* does not put a stop to this exploitation of resources, the 'Greenhouse Effect' may have devastating consequences for the environment and *humanity* in general.

Possessive deixis also helps to link humans to the physical environment, this time in the role of custodians of nature:

Our forests are a great resource; they offer a diverse 'gene pool' for providing medicines, cotton, timber for industry etc.

The sun beams down onto the earth and heat passes through the atmosphere and warms *our planet*.

The writer also uses *modalisation* to create a 'contingent field' in the text. This contingency reflects a trade-off between disparate local contexts and the desire to make generalisable statements. The paragraph on global warming illustrates this well.

'Global warming' *can have* devastating effects on the environment. Scientists have suggested that the average temperature of the earth *may rise* 3–4% *would mean* the floating ice caps *would melt* meaning an overall rise in the level of the ocean. Snowfall patterns *would change* dramatically. Organisms *would have to adapt* to a hotter environment. For many organisms, quite sensitive to changes in temperature, this *could mean* relocating to a cooler climate or facing extinction. The effects on the environment due to the greenhouse effect *could be* quite severe and it is *mainly due* to the ever increasing amounts of carbon dioxide being released into the atmosphere each year.

In addition to this field-oriented contingency, the use of *if/then clause complexes* construes a kind of 'moralistic contingency', in which the fate of the world depends upon human decisions about the environment.[4] Significantly the two examples below occur in the Thesis and Reiteration stages of the text, the two stages in an exposition most oriented to *persuading* the reader.

If such trends continue the climatic changes due to the 'Greenhouse Effect' may have disastrous consequences.

If man does not put a stop to this exploitation of resources, the 'Greenhouse Effect' may have devastating consequences for the environment and humanity in general.

Even through the examination of a single text it is possible to see the important role played by tenor and interpersonal meaning in creating environmentalist discourse. Like the construal of field, the construal of tenor is realised through a range of levels in the language system, from the selection of particular genres such as exposition, the prominence of prosodic systems of appraisal and grammatical features such as agency, possessive deixis and modalisation. A different orientation to tenor is perhaps the key feature which distinguishes environmentalism from ecology.

MERGING IDEATIONAL AND INTERPERSONAL GRAMMAR – CONTROL OF THE WRITTEN MODE

The 'carbon dioxide' essay does not consist solely of interpersonal meanings. A sophisticated control over the resources for construing scientific fields, such as *grammatical metaphor* and the *nominal group*, is necessary for the writer to merge scientific information with humanities rhetoric. The thesis stage demonstrates the writer's control over these resources.

> Carbon dioxide levels have increased dramatically over the past two hundred years. *Increased burning of fossil fuels* and *deforestation* are the main contributors to this *increase*. If such trends continue the climatic *changes* due to the 'Greenhouse Effect' may have disastrous consequences.

Through grammatical metaphor the writer is here able to construe cause-and-effect links between events (e.g. *burning + deforestation →* increase) as well as abstract categories with which to talk about human activity (*exploitation, contributors, humanity,* etc.). Because grammatical metaphor allows these categories to be represented as nouns in the text, they can be combined with other clause constituents to realise a persuasive discourse. Once the noun group 'carbon dioxide levels' is created, for example, the writer is able to pass interpersonal comment on it:

> Carbon dioxide levels have increased *dramatically.*

Nominalisation of the verb 'increases' then allows this environmental phenomenon to be linked to human activity:

> *Increased burning of fossil fuels and deforestation* are *the main contributors* to *this increase.*

Through one abstraction (*trends*) this link between human activity and the environment is judged sternly via another rhetorical abstraction (*consequences*):

> If such *trends* continue *the climatic changes due to the 'Greenhouse Effect'* may have *disastrous consequences.*

The point here is that without control of grammatical resources which characterise the *written mode* of language, it would be difficult for the writer to take up the role of 'informed advocate'. The text would risk becoming either a 'human-free' piece of scientific information (i.e., informed but not advocating), or an emotive tirade, full of opinion but with little 'scientific' evidence to support it (i.e., advocating but not informed).

Environmentalism, being an ideology, mobilises both the resources of humanities rhetoric and scientific knowledge. It is this merging of the scientific and the rhetorical in the written mode which characterises the language of environmentalism. It allows writers both to mobilise the kinds of technical meanings made possible by scientific discourse and simultaneously to explore the issue of the relationship between humans and the environment, presenting the reader with propositions about humans and the environment and making proposals for action. Unfortunately for the emergent writer, it also requires a sophisticated control over a large number of linguistic resources in the written mode.

VISUAL IMAGES

To conclude our discussion of language of environmentalism it is worth expanding our definition of 'language' briefly to consider the role of images in producing meanings. As the technology of graphic design and printing has developed, the use of visual images in teaching materials, particularly diagrams, tables and charts, has increased both in quantity and prominence. Kress and van Leeuwen (1990, 1996) argue that it is important to see visual images as independent vehicles for meaning in their own right. They suggest that visual images do not simply accompany text in teaching materials: they actively organise and construe meaning and often play a more dominant role than written text itself.

What is the potential for visual images to construe particular kinds of relationship between humans and their environment, and how much do recently published materials rely on visual images to construe them? Visual images and the visual organisation of written text appear to play a significant role in environmentalist texts for students. This is particularly so in the book *Ecology*, whose written language we have examined closely. It is impossible to say if the comparatively prominent role accorded to visual images in books like *Ecology* is inevitable — visual images being necessary to create the kinds of meanings the book does, or whether it is simply due to the simultaneous development of technological resources in graphic design and the rise of environmentalism. In either case the role of visual images in constructing meaning in a book like *Ecology* cannot really be ignored.

Figure 6.9 shows a two-page spread from *Ecology*, which includes a text whose language we have examined, 'Carbon on the move' (Text 5). The design of textbooks according to graphic principles such as a two-page spread is now commonplace in textbook materials. Using the analysis techniques developed by Kress and Van Leeuwen a number of points can be made regarding the relationship between images and text on the page, the relative size of print amongst the texts, the composition and the contrasting use of photographic images and diagrams in these pages.

The most striking feature of these pages is the interspersed use of text, diagrams and images. Not only is the arrangement of these features aesthetically pleasing, it also works to address the viewer in a range of ways. Kress and Van Leeuwen call this area of visual semiosis 'interactive meaning' (cf. interpersonal meaning in SFL) and argue that in scientific texts, full-saturated colour photographs, such as those of the burning trees, squirrel, salmon and carbon molecules in Figure 6.9, are the most 'local' resource available, providing an empirical picture of 'what we see' and relating to the viewer's everyday experience of the world. The diagrams and text, on the other hand, are related to scientific renderings of 'what we know' and present knowledge which is at a greater 'semiotic distance' from the viewer's first-hand experience of the world. The effect is to take the reader from what they have experienced and can relate to personally towards the world of shared, abstract scientific knowledge. This kind of movement is very similar to the negotiation between the 'abstract' and the 'actual' which occurs in the written language of the most prominent text on this page ('Carbon on the move'). The effect of these images is to make links between what may be part of the reader's first-hand experience and abstract knowledge about ecosystems. Thus a relationship is created between the abstract knowledge and the most important human agent in the context, the reader. It is important to note, however, that the reader–text relationship in Figure 6.9 is quite different to other, more obvious, ways of construing reader–image relationships. Like most other scientific texts, no image on these pages addresses the viewer directly. Even the animals are shown in profile! This contrasts sharply with the use of images in advertising, for example, where the reader is frequently addressed directly.

The organisation of these two pages conveys 'representational meaning' as well (cf. ideational meaning in SFL). The use of contrasting larger and smaller fonts, for example, suggests that the information in the text 'Carbon on the move' is more important than the other texts. Examining the language we find, not surprisingly, that 'Carbon on the move' *is* at a higher level of abstraction, dealing with phenomena at the level of biosphere. The other texts deal with phenomena at lower levels of ecological abstraction (population and species) or provide background information to the 'Carbon on the move' text. Thus the visual organisation of the page is in sympathy with the linguistic organisation. The photographic images each complement one of the texts in the smaller font, further reinforcing their place in the environmentalist hierarchy as empirical, localised knowledge. The diagram, on the other hand, a more abstract kind of image, supports a more abstract text. The arrangement

142   *Robert Veel*

Figure 6.9 A two-page spread from *Ecology* (Pollock 1993: 18–19)

CARBON CYCLE

Of all the carbon on Earth, less than 1 per cent is in active circulation in the biosphere. The remainder is locked up as inorganic carbon in rocks and as organic carbon in fossil fuels (coal and oil). Growing plants take in carbon from the atmosphere (in the form of CO_2) and incorporate this in solid compounds in their structure. In this form, carbon passes into the food chains. Different ecosystems take up carbon at different rates. In a tropical rainforest, where plants grow quickly, carbon is incorporated at a rate that is 100 times greater than in a desert.

Marine algae absorb CO_2 for photosynthesis

CO_2 taken in by plants for photosynthesis

CO_2 released into atmosphere

Respiration

Bacteria release CO_2 from dead material

Plants

Marine algae

Shells deposited as chalk

Dead material

Animals

Humans

Human energy use

Fossil fuels

RISING LEVELS OF CO_2

This graph shows a rapid increase in the concentration of carbon dioxide in the atmosphere between 1958 and 1985. This was due mainly to the burning of fossil fuels. Evidence from ice cores shows that atmospheric carbon dioxide has increased by at least 25 per cent since the industrial revolution in the 18th century. Carbon dioxide prevents heat radiating from the Earth into space (the "greenhouse effect"), so this increase may cause the planet's overall temperature to rise – the phenomenon known as global warming.

Rise in atmospheric carbon dioxide since 1958, measured in Hawaii

SECOND-HAND ENERGY

Animals depend on plants to obtain their carbon, whether they feed on plants directly or eat animals that feed on plants. This chipmunk is eating a nut produced by a tree that has converted atmospheric carbon into carbohydrates through photosynthesis. All animals are living stores of carbon, but all release some carbon (as carbon dioxide) in the breath that they exhale. When animals die, the carbon in their bodies is released as the complex chemicals decompose.

FEEDING THE YOUNG

When the adults of some salmon species have migrated upriver and spawned, they are so exhausted that they die. Their bodies lie in great numbers in the shallows of the river's headwaters, where they rot down, providing a readily available supply of nutrients for the growth of the eggs and for the young salmon when they hatch. The young are effectively made up of carbon from their parents.

CARBON STORES

Carbon becomes locked up in the remains of animals and plants that fail to decompose completely – for example, in conditions of insufficient oxygen. In the shallow swamps of the Carboniferous period, which ended some 280 million years ago, trees and other plants died in just such conditions, forming thick layers. Over millions of years, the heat of the Earth and the pressure of material building up above them turned the carbon in these plants into coal. In a similar way, heat and pressure turned vast deposits of minute dead sea creatures, like these seen under a microscope, into a liquid store of carbon – oil. When these "fossil fuels" are burned, this carbon is released into the atmosphere. It has been estimated that there may be 50 times as much carbon locked up in the Earth's coal and oil as there is in all the living organisms in the world.

19

of the two pages into recognisable sub-units also indicates that the representational meaning is oriented to structured, analytical, 'conceptual' knowledge rather than 'presentational' meaning (Kress and van Leeuwen 1990: 86). Figure 6.10 gives a schematic rendering of the elements on these pages.

The composition of these pages also conveys meanings which compliment the linguistic texts. Kress and van Leeuwen argue that the arrangement of images along top-to-bottom and left-to-right axes creates 'waves' of textual prominence, rather like that of Theme and Rheme in verbal texts. The top of an image tends to be the space of 'ideal' images and/or text. In scientific texts this is where generalised, abstract knowledge will appear. The bottom of the image will be more 'real', oriented to the here-and-now. The left hand-side of an image tends to represent 'given' information (that which is assumed to be known to the reader) of 'medium salience'. The right-hand side of an image is for new information of high salience. Kress and van Leeuwen use the following diagram shown in Figure 6.11 to summarise this.

Using Kress and van Leeuwen's analysis we can see how the compositional meaning of the two pages helps the text to negotiate both 'abstract' and 'actual physical' meanings. The more abstract elements, the text on 'Carbon on the move' and the diagram of the carbon cycle, are both at the top of the page suggesting they are more idealised kinds of knowledge and that they are highly valued, which they certainly are in traditional science. The left-to-right axis of the page, on the other hand, takes the reader from 'given' information about the carbon cycle to a new representation of this knowledge in a diagram or to specific pieces of information about aspects of the carbon cycle in specific contexts. The

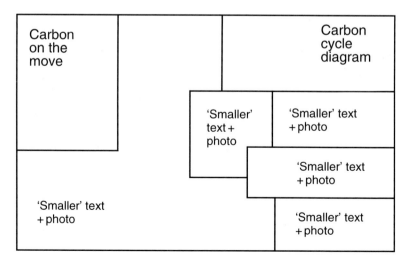

Figure 6.10 'Conceptually' arranged constituents of pp. 18–19 of *Ecology*

The ideal/most highly valued;	The ideal/most highly valued;
the given	the new
medium salience	high salience
The real, less highly valued;	The real, less highly valued;
the given	the new
low salience	medium salience

Figure 6.11 Compositional meaning in visual images, adapted from Kress and van Leeuwen 1990: 108

least prominent position on the page, the bottom left-hand corner, is nearly empty! Figure 6.12 schematises the compositional structure of these pages.

As well as the overall arrangement of images and text on the page, the construction of individual diagrams in *Ecology* plays an important role in the meaning making process. The large food web diagram on pages 12–13 of the book, reproduced here as Figure 6.13, is an interesting example. In this image we see a combination of the photographic and the diagrammatic, where the photographs clearly represent 'what we see' in our environment whereas the network of arrows connecting various images represents 'what we know', what ecologists have contributed to our understanding of the physical world.

Another important aspect of this image, common to many diagrams in environmentalist texts, is the representation of humans as participants in

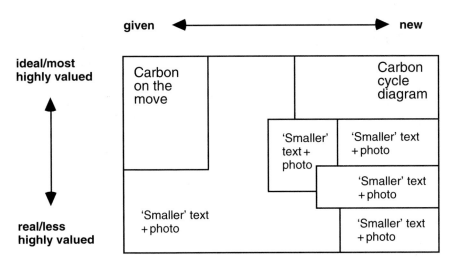

Figure 6.12 Compositional structure of pp. 18–19 of *Ecology*

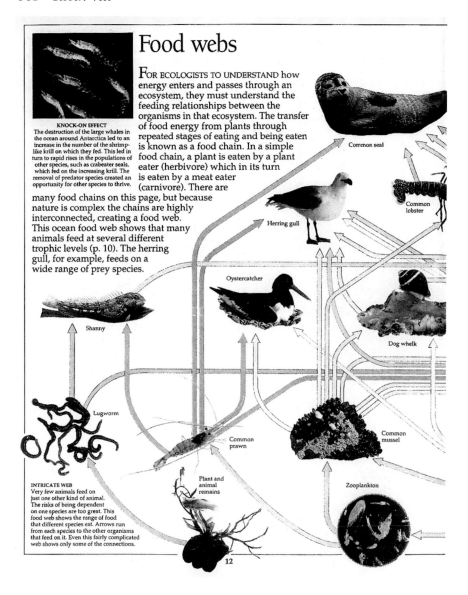

Food webs

KNOCK-ON EFFECT
The destruction of the large whales in the ocean around Antarctica led to an increase in the number of the shrimp-like krill on which they fed. This led in turn to rapid rises in the populations of other species, such as crabeater seals, which fed on the increasing krill. The removal of predator species created an opportunity for other species to thrive.

FOR ECOLOGISTS TO UNDERSTAND how energy enters and passes through an ecosystem, they must understand the feeding relationships between the organisms in that ecosystem. The transfer of food energy from plants through repeated stages of eating and being eaten is known as a food chain. In a simple food chain, a plant is eaten by a plant eater (herbivore) which in its turn is eaten by a meat eater (carnivore). There are many food chains on this page, but because nature is complex the chains are highly interconnected, creating a food web. This ocean food web shows that many animals feed at several different trophic levels (p. 10). The herring gull, for example, feeds on a wide range of prey species.

Common seal

Common lobster

Herring gull

Oystercatcher

Shanny

Dog whelk

Lugworm

Common prawn

Common mussel

INTRICATE WEB
Very few animals feed on just one other kind of animal. The risks of being dependent on one species are too great. This food web shows the range of food that different species eat. Arrows run from each species to the other organisms that feed on it. Even this fairly complicated web shows only some of the connections.

Plant and animal remains

Zooplankton

12

Figure 6.13 A two-page spread from *Ecology* (Pollock 1993: 12–13)

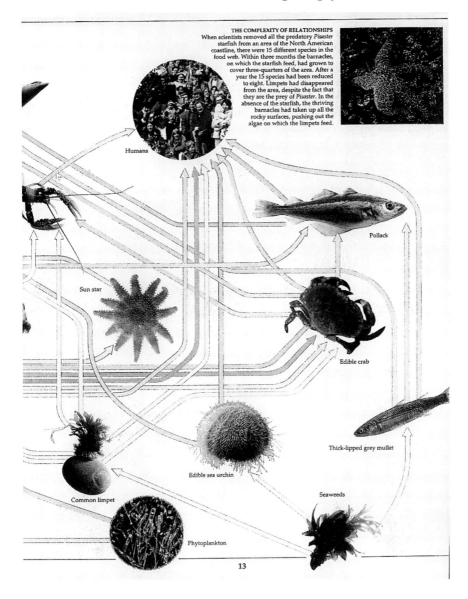

THE COMPLEXITY OF RELATIONSHIPS
When scientists removed all the predatory *Pisaster* starfish from an area of the North American coastline, there were 15 different species in the food web. Within three months the barnacles, on which the starfish feed, had grown to cover three-quarters of the area. After a year the 15 species had been reduced to eight. Limpets had disappeared from the area, despite the fact that they are the prey of *Pisaster*. In the absence of the starfish, the thriving barnacles had taken up all the rocky surfaces, pushing out the algae on which the limpets feed.

Humans

Pollack

Sun star

Edible crab

Thick-lipped grey mullet

Edible sea urchin

Common limpet

Seaweeds

Phytoplankton

13

a food web. The meanings given here are contradictory. On the one hand the many people shown in the photograph are much smaller than the single plants and animals shown in other photographs, suggesting that single human beings are less significant than plants and animals. On the other hand, the humans are placed in the top right-hand corner of the image, a position of high value and high salience.

This very brief examination of visual images has been far from complete. However it does show that visual images are an important semiotic resource in environmentalist texts, perhaps more so than traditional scientific texts. In particular visual images seem to play an important role in negotiating between abstract forms of knowledge and context-specific facts, a difficult and unstable facet of the environmentalist view of the physical world.

THE LANGUAGE OF ENVIRONMENTALISM: REVOLUTIONARY OR EVOLUTIONARY?

Academic and educational debate places much emphasis on the new. Every decade or so we are told of a new approach which will 'completely revolutionise the way we look at' the world. The ascendancy of environmentalist perspectives in the sciences has produced perhaps the greatest change to scientific thinking this century. In many ways the discourse of environmentalism *is* revolutionary. It challenges and attempts to combine some very fundamental philosophical divisions in Western society, such as those between 'scientific' and 'non-scientific' ways of thinking about the world, and attempts to negotiate one of the most difficult disjunctions in scientific thought, that between the local and contextually dependent and the abstract and generalisable. In language this has resulted in distinctive textual and grammatical configurations and patterns which make it possible to talk of a 'language of environmentalism'. As well, environmentalist discourse appears to make original use of other semiotic systems, especially visual images, to construe new meanings (see Lemke, this volume).

While the *discourse* of environmentalism might be new, how new is the *language*? Within language we have a large, but limited, set of resources for realising meanings. As with other innovative discourses, environmentalism takes resources which already exist within 'natural language' (i.e., language used by humans) and re-configures them in original ways. Thus the linguistic building blocks of environmentalism are *the same as those of other academic disciplines*: genres of report, explanation and exposition, sequential, cause-and-effect and taxonomically organised fields, prosodic realisation of appraisal, grammatical metaphor, lengthy nominal groups, etc. *What is new is the way these elements are put together.* The language of environmentalism is revolutionary not because it rejects the linguistic resources used to construe meanings in traditional science (and other disciplines) but because it takes up these resources, combines them with other resources – in particular humanities-style rhetoric and visual images – and construes new meanings. The purpose in doing this, if we are to accept the assertions of environmentalists, is to enable us to construct an epistemological relationship between humans and the environment that values scientific knowledge in a different way, as a tool that will permit the survival of the human race and promote responsible use of finite physical resources.

This notion of re-configuration and re-construal of existing linguistic resources, common to many studies of functional varieties of English within SFL, has important implications for language education. It suggests that the basis for change, be it in the way knowledge is discursively construed or in who has access to that knowledge and who does not, lies within the language system as it is currently used and not outside of it. If we are interested in developing school students' abilities to understand and accept an environmentalist world view, it would seem both possible and indeed desirable to build on the meaning potential of existing disciplines, including traditional science, with all its faults and limitations, rather than rejecting them in favour of an unspecified alternative.

NOTES

1 Within SFL this tension is represented in the notions of 'system' and 'instance', where it is the accumulation of many instances which construes the language 'system' and yet no single instance typifies the system in general.
2 Note that this is not an example of register metaphor, discussed earlier, but a 'macro-genre' in which a large-scale generic structure (here exposition) incorporates other genres within stages of the text. The incorporated texts serve an auxiliary function to the macro genre.
3 This is a grossly simplified account of ongoing work on interpersonal discourse semantics, which has identified networks of judgement, appreciation and amplification in the general network of appraisal. See Martin (in press), Iedema, Feez and White (1994) and Veel (1994) for more detailed analysis.
4 Martin (1992) actually describes if/then clause complexes as a modalised causal relationship.

REFERENCES

Bacon, F. 1976. *De sapientia veterum London, 1609 and The Wisedome of the Ancients* (trans. Arthur Gorges) New York: Garland Publishing.
Bernstein, B. 1977. *Class, Codes and Control* (Volume 3) London: Routledge and Keegan Paul.
Board of Studies, New South Wales 1993a. *Science and Technology K-6 Syllabus and Support Document* Sydney: Board of Studies, New South Wales.
Board of Studies, New South Wales 1993b. *Sample HSC Answers, General Studies 1993* Sydney: Board of Studies, New South Wales.

Capra, F. 1982. *The Turning Point* London: Wildwood House.

Coghill, G. and P. Wood 1989. *Spectrum Science 3* Melbourne: Heinemann.

Curriculum Corporation 1994. *Science: A curriculum profile for Australian schools* Melbourne: Curriculum Corporation.

Goudie, A. 1989. *The Human Impact on the Natural Environment* Oxford: Blackwell.

Halliday, M.A.K. 1993. 'On the language of physical science' in M.A.K. Halliday and J. Martin 1993 *Writing Science* London: Falmer Press.

Halliday, M.A.K. 1994. *An Introduction to Functional Grammar* 2nd Edition. London: Edward Arnold.

Halliday, M.A.K. 1993. 'The act of meaning' Paper presented to the Georgetown Round Table of linguistics, Georgetown, DC.

Halliday, M.A.K. and R. Hasan 1985. *Language, Context and Text: Aspects of language in a social-semiotic perspective* Geelong: Deakin University Press.

Halliday, M.A.K. and J. Martin 1993. *Writing Science* London: Falmer Press.

Heffernan, D.A. and M.S. Learmonth 1988. *The World of Science: Book One*, Melbourne: Longman Cheshire.

Iedema, R., S. Feez and P. White 1994. *Media Literacy* (Write It Right Literacy in Industry research project, Stage Two) Sydney: Disadvantaged Schools Program, New South Wales Department of School Education, Metropolitan East Region.

Kress, G. and T. Van Leeuwen 1990. *Reading Images* Geelong Victoria: Deakin University Press.

Kress, G. and T. Van Leeuwen 1996. *Reading Images: The grammar of visual design* London: Routledge.

Martin J. 1985. *Factual Writing: Exploring and challenging the experiential world* Geelong: Deakin University Press.

Martin, J. 1992. *English Text: System and structure* Amsterdam: Benjamins.

Martin, J. 1993a. 'Literacy in Science: learning to handle the text as technology' in M.A.K. Halliday and J. Martin 1993 *Writing Science* London: Falmer Press.

Martin, J. 1993b. 'Life as a noun: Arresting the universe in science and humanities' in M.A.K. Halliday and J. Martin 1993 *Writing Science* London: Falmer Press.

Martin, J. 1997. 'Analysing genre: functional principles and parameters' in F. Christie and J. Martin (eds) *Genres and Institutions: Social processes in the workplace and school* London: Cassell.

Martin, J. and P. Peters 1985. 'On the analysis of exposition' in R. Hasan (ed.) *Discourse on Discourse: Workshop reports from the Macquarie workshop on Discourse Analysis*, Applied Linguistics Association of Australia (Occasional Papers 7), pp. 61–92.

Mattheissen, C. 1996. *Lexicogrammatical Cartography: English systems* Tokyo: International Language Science Publishers.

O'Riordan, T. 1981. *Environmentalism* London: Pion.

Pepper, D. 1984. *The Roots of Modern Environmentalism* Beckenham, Kent: Croom Helm.

Pollock, S. 1993. *Ecology* (Collins Eyewitness Science) Sydney: Collins Angus and Robertson.

Sauer, C. 1938. 'Destructive exploitation in modern colonial expansion' *Proceedings of the International Geographical Congress, Amsterdam*, vol. III, sect. IIIC: 494–9.

Schumacher, F. 1973. *Small Is beautiful: Economics as if people really mattered* London: Abacus.

Veel, R. 1992. 'Engaging with scientific language: A functional approach to the language of school science' *Australian Science Teachers Journal* 38 (4).

Veel, R. 1993. *Exploring Literacy in School Science* MS Sydney: Disadvantaged Schools Component, New South Wales Department of School Education.

Veel, R. 1997. 'Learning how to mean – scientifically speaking' in F. Christie and J. Martin (eds) *Genres and Institutions: Social processes in the workplace and school* London: Cassell.

Walker, J. 1993. *Man-made Disasters: Atmosphere in danger* London: Gloucester Press.

Wignell, P., J. Martin and S. Eggins 1993. 'The discourse of geography: Ordering and explaining the experiential world' in M.A.K. Halliday and J. Martin *Writing Science* London: Falmer Press.

7 Science and apprenticeship

The pedagogic discourse[1]

Frances Christie

INTRODUCTION

The pedagogic device, so Bernstein (1994, 1996) has suggested, is a device for shaping consciousness. It gives rise to the operation of a pedagogic discourse, the nature of which is such that it inducts subjects into various institutionally sanctioned values and practices. The operation of a pedagogic discourse involves the building of subjectivity: the building of aspects of identity, as well as the structuring and ordering of experience in some way. In Bernstein's terms, a pedagogic discourse will be found in many relationships apart from those that are purely educational. They include, for example, not only the relationships of teacher and taught, but of social worker and client, or of doctor and patient, among others.

This chapter discusses the pedagogic discourse of schooling – in particular the discourse of upper primary school science. At issue in the operation of an instance of pedagogic discourse in science teaching is much more than the learning of a scientific 'content', however we may conceive that. At issue too, is the learning of a range of values, attitudes and ways of working, all critical to the development of social beings, able to operate within a set of socially approved practices, and to interpret and employ scientific knowledge of a kind recognised and used in many contexts outside those of school.[2]

Scientific knowledge, like much other school knowledge, is uncommonsense.[3] Commonsense knowledge is habitual and constructed in familar language: that which is uncommonsense is esoteric and its expression requires some new uses of language. Uncommonsense knowledge is not immediately available to the uninitiated, and its mastery usually requires some effort over time. Any attempt to understand the manner in which the uncommonsense knowledge of schooling is learned makes it necessary to explore teaching and learning over time, tracing those shifts and changes that occur, both in the relationship of teacher and taught and in the emergent control by the learners of the knowledge and skills involved. The attempt to trace such matters of itself necessitates a departure from much conventional classroom discourse analysis, and the articulation of new models of classroom discourse analysis.

Various traditions of classroom language-related research have developed over the last twenty to thirty years. Early work, such as that by Bellack *et al.* (1966) or Flanders (1970), sought to identify, albeit rather informally, different categories of classroom talk, and to develop methods for documenting the frequency of these. Other researchers still such as Barnes (Barnes, Britton and Rosen 1971) offered commentary (rather than detailed analysis) upon the talk that students engage in when learning together. Sinclair and Coulthard (1975), Stubbs and Delamont (1976) and Stubbs (1983) developed more linguistically motivated models for analysing classroom talk, where the focus was generally on the moves in the discourse construction in which students and teachers engaged. Such research pointed, for example, to the asymmetrical nature of classroom talk, especially as characterised by the so-called IRF (Initiation, Response, Followup) or IRE (Initiation, Response, Evaluation) pattern found in many classrooms, and subsequently often criticised for the constraints it has been said to impose on students (e.g. Lindfors 1981, Perrott 1988). Other work still has drawn upon ethnographic and/ or sociolinguistic traditions. The latter, represented for example by Mehan (1979), Cazden (1988) Cicourel *et al.* (1974), Green (cited by Cazden, 1986), Green and Kantor-Smith (1988), Green and Harker (1988), Shuy (1988), Kantor *et al.* (1992), Baker and Freebody (1989), Green and Dixon (1993), Wells (1993) has variously explored ways classroom talk functions in structuring classroom behaviour generally. Sometimes, such research has focused on the ways the talk appears to be constituted of different segments or phases, some of them to do with management, some with more or less explicit teaching and learning of content.

While these bodies of research have added to the general understandings about classroom talk and processes, there have been limitations. First, with some exceptions (e.g. Lemke 1990) the research has not generally addressed the manner in which the contents of different school subjects are constructed in talk. Where content has been considered, it has been in rather general terms: a very delicate means of language analysis is actually needed to bring out the differences between school subjects. (See Hasan, in press, for a discussion of impoverished models of language and their failure to address issues of meaning in language education theory.) Second, again with notable exceptions (e.g. Wells 1993; Green and Dixon 1993) the research has tended to focus on particular teaching episodes, rather than upon the overall sequences in which such episodes occur. However, the most effective way to demonstrate what constitutes successful teaching–learning activity must focus upon sustained sets of lessons in which teaching and learning activities pass through different phases to achieve specific goals. Third, the research has not generally addressed the relationship of talk to the literacy students must learn to use in the different subjects. Both literacy and oral language remain important to the teaching of all school subjects, and for that reason both merit serious attention. Yet most models of classroom discourse analysis have tended to focus upon speech, while the study of writing, or of literacy more generally, has normally engaged other researchers. In the development of a model of pedagogic discourse as outlined here, an attempt is made to address these limitations.

Thus, it will be argued, the effort to trace the changes that are effected in a pedagogic discourse takes us into tracing the growth in the overall organisation of the classroom text, building, expanding and sustaining its meanings, so that a momentum develops as the text unfolds and draws to a close. Such growth has been characterised by Halliday in Halliday and Martin (1993) as growth in logogenesis. In the logogenetic sense, any text unfolds, building its meanings as it develops from its beginning, to its middle, to its end. When it does so, the text builds cumulatively, constructing meanings later in the text made possible by the operation of its meanings earlier in the text. Where an instance of pedagogic discourse works well, it functions successfully in a logogenetic sense. Much of the success depends upon the skill with which the teacher and students establish a logos for working together, generating and sustaining its growth in an ever-cumulative way.

THE NOTION OF A CURRICULUM MACROGENRE

One way to address the issue of the unfolding of a pedagogic text logogenetically will be to interpret it as an instance of a curriculum macrogenre (see Martin 1994, 1995 for discussion of the notion of a macrogenre). A curriculum macrogenre is a cycle of teaching–learning activity in which a teacher and students engage with some 'content area', progressing from some introductory stage through a series of stages until a conclusion is reached. The term 'curriculum macrogenre' is used to capture the point that the total unity or sequence involved has an overall structure, which in turn may be shown to consist of a series of individual curriculum genres (Christie 1989, 1995a, 1995b, 1996), each of them having particular phases within them. Just as any instance of a curriculum genre may be said to be staged, purposeful and goal-directed, so too is the macrogenre of which each forms a part held to be staged and purposeful, working towards the achievement of particular curriculum goals.

Functioning within the curriculum macrogenre will be two registers or sets of language choices: a first order or regulative register, and a second order or instructional register. The first order register is to do with the teacher's goals for the curriculum activity. The second order register is to do with the actual 'content' or field of knowledge taught. The regulative register is said to 'project' the instructional register, in that it fundamentally determines the introduction, ordering and pacing of the latter register. The discourses, say, of physics, or of mathematics or of history, are taken from contexts outside schools and in Bernstein's terms (1990) 'relocated' within pedagogic discourses for the purposes of school learning. Bernstein, whose terms 'regulative and instructional discourse' have been adapted here, writes thus:

> We shall define pedagogic discourse as the rule which embeds a discourse of competence (skills of various kinds) into a discourse of social order in such a way that the latter always dominates the former. We shall call the discourse transmitting specialised competences and their relation to each other *instructional* discourse, and the discourse creating specialised order, relation and identity *regulative* discourse.
>
> (Bernstein 1990: 183)

Later, making clearer the significance of a pedagogic discourse Bernstein states: '*Pedagogic discourse is a principle for appropriating other discourses and bringing them into a special relation with each other for the purposes of their selective transmission and acquisition.*' (Bernstein 1990, 183–4, original italics). The school is *par excellence* an institution in which discourses are taken and relocated for their 'selective transmission (to) and acquisition' (by) students.[4]

Use of a functional grammar (Halliday 1994), with its model of grammar in metafunctional terms, helps us explain how the school appropriates the discourses of fields of knowledge outside and relocates these for the purposes of students' learning. We will begin to demonstrate how a functional grammar can be used to demonstrate this. First, we will give an overview of the particular science curriculum macrogenre to be examined.

A SCIENCE CURRICULUM MACROGENRE

The instance of a curriculum macrogenre to be discussed comes from an Australian upper primary classroom, in which a composite Year 6–7 class of twenty-seven students was studying science. The students were aged eleven to twelve years, and while all were proficient users of English, about one-third of them were from non-English-speaking backgrounds. The topic concerned the notion of the 'mechanical advantage' conferred by the invention of machines. The primary school science curriculum from which the teacher drew his topic stated that students should develop scientific understandings through 'investigations'. In these investigations they should develop 'seven core skills': observing, classifying, measuring, using space–time relationships, communicating, inferring and predicting (Northern Territory [NT] Education Department 1986:

8). Under the topic 'Forces and Motions', students were to cover 'ways of moving objects – pushing, pulling, lifting, sliding and rolling' (NT Education Department 1986: 25). In transposing this entry to his class program, the teacher had added that the students should develop 'attitudes' of being able 'to co-operate in a group'. The unit of work on machines was planned for a fortnight, with nine substantial teaching periods devoted to it.

As the analysis will seek to demonstrate, the macrogenre showed a movement from explicit teacher direction in the introductory genre through a middle stage, in which the students assumed a great deal of the control of their learning, to a final stage, represented in the final curriculum genre, where the students produced texts – oral and written – largely independently of their teacher. The nature of the pedagogic discourse had changed fundamentally over the fortnight's work.

The structure of the science curriculum macrogenre concerned is represented initially in Figure 7.1, and then expanded upon in Figure 7.2, where a more delicate level of description is attempted.

Figure 7.1 indicates there are three genres involved: the Curriculum Initiation, the Curriculum Collaboration and the Curriculum Closure. The symbol ^ indicates sequence. A curriculum macrogenre will typically have an opening initiating genre, whose function is to point goals and define directions for the teaching–learning activity that is to come. No less typically, a curriculum macrogenre will have a closing genre, whose function is to bring the macrogenre to a conclusion, normally marked by the completion of some task(s). The 'middle' genre or genres, where students undertake tasks necessary to the achievement of goals, will show the greatest variation, depending on the age of the students, the subject taught and the teacher's purposes. Though the pattern normally involves the three types of genres identified, in practice curriculum macrogenres differ quite markedly. Figure 7.2 attempts to capture something of the complexities involved in the science curriculum macrogenre considered. It is not suggested, however, that this macrogenre is definitive of science teaching generally.

Figure 7.2 reveals the layered pattern by which the curriculum macro-

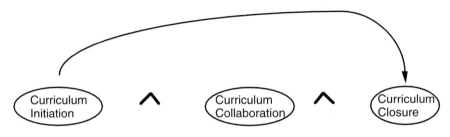

Figure 7.1 Upper primary science curriculum macrogenre: initial view

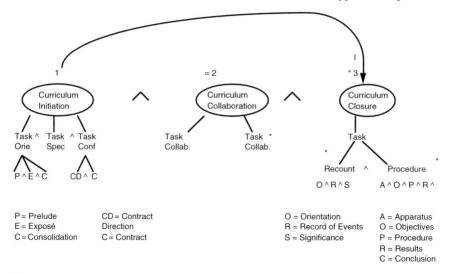

Figure 7.2 Upper primary science curriculum macrogenre: expanded
Note: * = recursive

genre is built up through its genres and their elements of structure. Sometimes these elements of structure have other phases within them, so the total picture is multi-layered.

The functional labels capture something of the experiential significance of the various genres, their schematic structures, and the phases within these. The Curriculum Initiation, consisting of one genre, has three elements of schematic structure. The first of these is a Task Orientation, where the teacher points directions and sets purposes for the whole macrogenre. This element has within it three phases referred to as the 'Prelude' (the opening, intended to indicate themes and directions), the 'Exposé' (intended to explore and identify aspects of machines) and the 'Consolidation' (where some essential information regarding machines is established in order to proceed further). The second element of schematic structure is the Task Specification, where the students' tasks are established. This element has only one phase. The third element of structure is the Task Conference, in which the students and teacher confer over the distribution of the tasks to different working groups. This element has two phases, a 'Contract Direction' where the teacher indicates a range of possible tasks, and the 'Contract', where students negotiate those tasks they will undertake. The Curriculum Collaboration involves several recursive genres within it, referred to as Task Collaborations, in which the students work together on their scientific tasks. Finally, in the Curriculum Closure the students both reconstruct what they have done and direct others about how to do what they have done, as well as comment on its significance. Two genres – one oral, the other written – operate recursively here. The oral genres are procedural recounts of what was done (consisting of three elements: an 'Orientation', a 'Record of Events' and a statement of 'Significance'). The written genres are scientific procedures, written to direct others about how to build machines, and to identify the significance of building such machines. The latter have five elements of structure: 'Apparatus', 'Objectives', 'Procedure', 'Results' and 'Conclusion'.

The genres are logically linked, and the logical relationships are suggested, metaphorically at least, in Figure 7.2, through a series of symbols taken from Halliday's (1994: 215–273) description of the relationships of clauses to each other. (See Martin 1995 for some discussion of the logical relations among genres.) Thus, the Curriculum Collaboration stands in a relation of elaboration (=) to the Curriculum Initiation, where, as the word suggests, the second genre expands upon the former, primarily by exemplifying what has been opened up in the Curriculum Initiation. The Curriculum Closure is said to stand in a relation of projection (") upon the Curriculum Initiation, in that the oral recounts and written scientific procedures produced here represent completed tasks projected by the teacher in the very early stages of the Curriculum Initiation. The notion of projection is also intended to be captured by the use of the arrow →, showing the direction the projection takes.

Textually, the genres are related in the manner of their ordering. That is, there is a particular sequential movement established through the overall text of the macrogenre, as the genres and their elements of structure and phases build, unfold and come to a conclusion.

Interpersonally, there is an unfolding and shifting character to the relationship of teacher and students, captured across the bottom of Figure 7.2. In the Task Orientation and Task Specification there is a great deal of teacher authority and direction, even, as we shall see later, in that phase labelled 'Exposé', where the teacher engages the students in working with him in joint construction of some relevant field knowledge. The nature of the relationship changes as the students move into some negotiation with the teacher of their group tasks in the Task Conference. Their relationship changes again as the students move into direction of their own group work in the Task Collaboration. Finally, in the Curriculum Closure, the students operate independently of their teacher, assuming the authoritative role as they explain what they have learned.

The curriculum initiation

In the Curriculum Initiation, the first order register is marked, because the teacher is defining goals and establishing with the students commonly understood purposes. The sense of purpose depends upon understanding both the principles for working that apply, and upon developing a shared language for dealing with the second order field or 'content' to be taught and learned. In practice – and this is one significant measure of the success with which a pedagogic discourse operates – the first order or instructional register becomes less marked as the total macrogenre proceeds, so that by the Curriculum Closure, it has effectively disappeared. However, it continues to operate invisibly. Its presence is critical to the successful learning that takes place.

It is in the Prelude, the first phase in the Task Orientation that the teacher introduces the nature of the tasks to be undertaken, both in terms of the 'hands on' scientific activities to be developed, and in terms of the projected writing tasks that will arise from doing these. While the first order or regulative register is foregrounded, the second order or instructional register has some expression. One would expect this, since the goal of a lesson is always to teach about *something*. On occasion (though not often here) the regulative register will operate in such a way that the instructional register has no expression. Where this occurs, it means the teacher devotes attention to establishing principles for working, before engaging with the second order or instructional field.

The prelude

In a manner characteristic of those elements where the regulative register is foregrounded, the teacher talk in the Prelude is monologic, and there is a strong expectation that the students listen attentively. The teacher's authority is thus marked:

Teacher: Right, OK now we are going to start our theme next week, but we are actually starting a bit earlier because of it. The main requirement is for various things to be done. The main one is on science day . . . (*inaudible*). So we've got to do a lot of concentrating. There will be two pieces of writing, one is a procedural text . . . (*inaudible*). The other one is to write an explanation as to why parts of a machine work. So a bit of concentration. Um, you can start by looking up the basis of how the machines work in a series of science books. . . . (*inaudible*) For instance a catapult. You'll be making an exact replica of a catapult, not the full size of course. Think about it. This is your problem for the the next couple of weeks. The other thing you might do is making a lift or wishing well or even a spanish windlass, it's basically a barrel. What's a barrel?

Textually, the discourse reveals a cluster of textual themes, some of them continuatives (indicated with italics):

right, OK now we are going to start our theme next week,

while others are structural:

> *but* we are actually starting a bit earlier because of it
> *so* we've got to do a lot of concentrating
> *so* a bit of concentration.

Their effect is to signal to the students that directions are being pointed for the activity. As a general principle, such linguistic features are less characteristically a feature of students' talk than of teachers' talk. However, as we shall see below in the Curriculum Collaboration, the students' talk makes frequent use of such textual themes. This is evidence of the actual independence the students enjoy in their learning at this point. As we shall see, it is also part of the linguistic evidence for the claim that the discourse changes as the students grow in understanding throughout the total macrogenre. Still focusing on the the textual, it is noticeable that the teacher frequently thematises the students, using *we* and sometimes *you*, indicating that it is they who are being directed in their behaviour. Sometimes too, the task itself is thematised, as in:

> *the main requirement* is for various things to be done, or
> *the main one* is on science day . . .

This is in contrast, as we shall see later, with those elements where it is the second order field which is foregrounded, for on these occasions, it is the latter field that is thematised.

Experientially, the transitivity choices in the text reveal a great deal of the manner in which both fields are realised. In general, material, behavioural or mental processes realise the children's behaviour, while relational or existential processes realise the nature of the tasks to be done.

Examples of processes realising aspects of the children's behaviour include (italicised):

> we *are going to start* our theme next week
> but we *are* actually *starting* a bit earlier because of it

Here, while class members are identified in the participant role of actor (*we*), it is the educational activity itself which is identified in the other participant role of goal, *our theme*. It is noticeable, too, that the nominal group used to realise the latter participant role is of a general kind; this is consistent with the teacher's taking the first step in building the logos of the regulative field. Later, the choices will become more specific.

Other processes realising aspects of the students' behaviour include:

> so we*'ve got to do a lot of concentrating*, or
> you*'ll be making* an exact replica of a catapult.

In the latter case again, the second order or instructional field is realised in the participant role of goal (*an exact replica of a catapult*). This is part of a consistent pattern found across many classroom texts.

It provides evidence that the second order field is realised in transitivity at points where the first order register is foregrounded, but in a manner which gives the former a secondary, if nonetheless essential, significance.

Relational and existential processes establishing the nature of the tasks include (italicised):

the main requirement *is* for various things to be done,
there *will be* two pieces of writing.

Here the nominal group realising the existent role *two pieces of writing* is still reasonably general. The subsequent choices become more specific:

one is *a procedural text*
the other one is *to write an explanation as to why parts of a machine work.*

(In practice, by the time the Curriculum Closure is reached, this requirement has changed, so that there are one oral and one written text required.)

Interpersonally, the Prelude establishes the teacher at his most authoritative. He addresses the students using the first-person plural (*we*), building solidarity with them in the common enterprise of working together; elsewhere he addresses them with the second person (*you*), signalling that the students' behaviour is being directed. At points such as this, the teacher rarely uses the vocative, and this is an observation borne out by study of other classroom texts (Christie 1989, 1995a, 1995b, 1996). There is an important functional explanation for the uses of the first-person plural and the second person in the regulative register. It is here that the children *generally and collectively* are being urged towards appropriate learning goals: it would be inappropriate and a distraction to use vocatives, serving as they do to single out individuals.

The mood choice is declarative, and information is being given out. But a strong sense of obligation is suggested, as for example in the nominal groups in 'the main requirement', or 'the main one'. Elsewhere, high modality builds the obligation: 'we've got to do a lot of concentrating'. A strong attitudinal significance attaches to the word 'problem' in 'this is your problem'. Notable too is the consistent use of positive polarity. This builds a strong sense of an overall positive commitment to a set of tasks worth doing.

The effect of all the above interpersonal choices is to build a strong sense of a series of commands to activity. The teacher's authority in giving such commands is never in doubt, and it says much for the relationship enjoyed by him with his students that they listened with attention and interest.

The Prelude is considerably longer than the extract dealt with, though to save space no more will be discussed. Suffice it to note that, after some short discussion, the teacher shows the students a short film which

demonstrates the principles by which machines work and hence introduces the notion of a mechanical advantage.

The Exposé

In the Exposé the teacher constructs a simple taxonomy of machines
on the board, involving the children in its joint construction, drawing
upon what they have seen in the film. This is a long and important
phase, because it is here that significant language is established specific
to the second order field of machines. We can do no more here than
capture some of the major linguistic features in which the activity is
developed.

Figure 7.3 represents the taxonomy constructed on the board. It
depends upon a basic distinction, suggested by the film, drawn between
levers and inclined planes. Within the group of levers a further distinction was made between machines without a wheel, such as a rake, and
those with a wheel, such as a wheel and axle.[5]

It has already been noted that this phase is marked by *joint construction*
of the instructional field. Wherein is this realised linguistically?

Organisationally, the text is highly dialogic, as students and teacher
together construct the instructional field. The teacher's textual themes
help marshall the children towards the joint activity:

Teacher: *Right* let's have a summary of what was the film basically about.
            They seem to mention two basic machines. Um, Andrew?
Andrew: Levers.
                                                                          6
. . . .
Teacher: Lever (*writes 'lever' on the board*) and (*said on a high rising tone, intended
            to invite a response*)
Brad: An inclined plane.
Teacher: An (*pause*) inclined plane (*he writes 'inclined plane' on the board*).

The pattern here is pursued throughout most of this phase. It is a
pattern by which the teacher sets up a transitivity structure, and the
students help complete it. It is this which accounts for the claim that
what is involved is joint construction, and it is in marked contrast to the
language of the Prelude, examined in part above. The implicit transitivity pattern may be shown thus:

Teacher: They seem to mention two basic machines. Um, [What are the
            two basic machines] Andrew?
Andrew: [The two basic machines are] levers.
Teacher: [They are] lever[s] and
Brad: An inclined plane.
. . . .

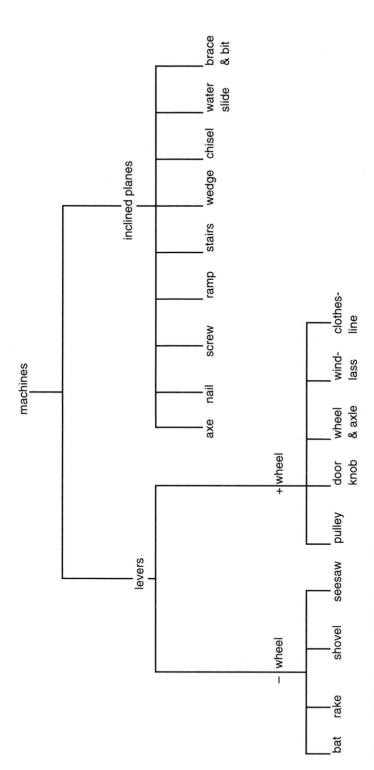

Figure 7.3 Taxonomy of simple machines constructed in the Exposé

Teacher:	They extended out some of the machines. They used the lever. Hold on. Hold on (*children are calling out*).
. . . .	
Naomi:	[They used] a seesaw.
. . . .	
Brad:	[They used a] baseball bat.
. . . .	
Joanne:	[They used a] flying fox.
. . . .	
Several children:	[They used a] pulley.

Here the technical language of the second order field is jointly constructed, and the students' participation is essential. It is worth noting at this point that the pattern at work where the teacher involves the students in joint construction of a transitivity structure in this manner, referred to as the IRE (Mehan 1979) or IRF (Sinclair and Coulthard 1975) pattern has been often criticised, on the grounds that it is held to 'constrain' the students' capacity to contribute to the discourse and hence to the development of a lesson. The evidence here is to the contrary. The pattern has an essential role in such a teaching–learning phase. (Wells 1993 has made a similar observation.) It is the only sustained phase in the whole fortnight's work devoted to machines where this pattern occurs. If it could be shown to be a constant feature of the talk, there would be grounds for concern. As it is, in a complex and linguistically varied pattern of discourse across the fortnight, this is a functionally useful and relevant feature of the talk. It is critical to the logogenetic unfolding of the total macrogenre.

Interpersonally, the stretch of text is of interest in at least two senses. First, it is marked by frequent teacher use of the interrogative mood, in contrast to the largely declarative mood choice of the Prelude. Second, it is interesting in that here the teacher makes frequent use of vocatives, as he attempts to draw as many students as possible into helping him build the taxonomy on the board:

Um, Andrew?
Joanne?
All right, all right, come on, come on Naomi.
Isabel?
Um, Aranthi?
Um, Anna, you got anything for us?
Um, Yvonne?
Daniel, nothing? Raymond?
Martin?
Nicole Smith?

This is in contrast with the linguistic pattern observed in the opening of the Prelude, where, as was noted, vocatives had no functional relevance at all. Here, their presence is an important measure of the fact that the teacher works hard to involve students in the joint construction. Elsewhere, and towards the end of this phase, the teacher offers praise for the contributions of the students:

> All right, that is the finish, pretty good, people. Don't you think so, Ms E? (*addressed to the person recording the activity*)

Consolidation

In the Consolidation the teacher moves the students forward to a new understanding, with a generalisation about the instructional field: namely, the abstract principle of the mechanical advantage exploited in using machines. Linguistically, there is a further shift. Textually, the teacher returns to monologue, while once again he takes up the declarative mood to inform:

> Now (*pause*) tomorrow (*pause*) tomorrow[7] all those machines are going to make work easier, you find that if you do something you trade, make a trade off, um (*writes 'trade force for distance or distance for force'*) either force for distance, or perhaps distance for force. The whole lot, whatever it does, it does work. . . . And each machine is used to give you a mechanical advantage (*writes 'work – mechanical advantage' on the board*).

The new nominal group 'mechanical advantage' introduces an important piece of technical language, an understanding of which is crucial to the students' developing control of the instructional field. The viewing of the film and the subsequent building of the many specific instances of machines in the Exposé have led to this new stage, and it is noticeable that an example of grammatical metaphor (See Halliday elsewhere in this volume) is involved in the new technical term. Note the way the meaning involved is constructed first by the teacher:

machines are going to make work easier.

A more congruent way to make the point might have been to say:

machines work for you.

In both cases, the piece of experiential information is constructed in a transitivity process, in which the process itself is material while 'machines' operates in the participant role of actor.

The same point is made, but metaphorically, when the activity is turned into a thing, through the resource of a nominal group: 'mechanical advantage'. With the entry to some awareness of the latter, the students have reached a new, more abstract stage of understanding.

They now have a phenomenon they can discuss: the principle of the mechanical advantage. They are ready to move to a new practical activity demonstrating the phenomenon.

The task specification and the task conference

Space will not permit a lengthy discussion of either the Task Specification or the Task Conference. A very brief account will be given of the Task Specification, while a little more will be said of the Task Conference. The Task Conference is an important element both of the Curriculum Initiation and of the macrogenre overall, because here the students begin to assert themselves in pursuing their own learning.

In the Task Specification the teacher outlines the 'variety of problems' the students can take up in building machines. He distributes sheets of paper with directions for making such things as a catapult, a lift using a windlass, a pulley or a robot. The text is largely monologic. Earlier in this chapter it was noted that what was at issue in the building of a macrogenre of the kind under discussion was not only the learning of a 'content', but also the learning of ways of working. Development of 'attitudes' of being able 'to co-operate in a group' were specified as of concern in the teacher's class program. Development of satisfactory patterns of behaviour thus far has been of concern, not often overtly referred to, but implicit in much that the teacher has done and expected. It was for instance an aspect of his expectations in the Exposé where he got the students to join him in construction of the instructional field, and subsequently praised them.

It is of interest that within the Task Specification element, it is not only the matter of selection of machines for building that concerns the teacher. He is also concerned that the students recognise the desired manner of working. He says at one point:

> Now on your piece of paper, I want, Brad, Shane (*addressed to gain attention*), once you've selected your group I want, one of the things for you to do, is stick by that group right until the end of the project and the machine is set up to show the kids and adults of the school, there might be a few parents.

Here the first order or regulative register is prominent. Interestingly, the teacher begins to invoke his own authority twice – 'I want'. But then he changes to a more abstract expression of authority, in the marked nominal group, and in the strong attitudinal force carried in the process 'stick':

> one of the things for you [to do], is stick by that group right until the end of the project and the machine is set up to show the kids and adults of the school.

In discussing the language of authority in administrative texts, Iedema (1994, 1997) has argued that authority is at its most powerful in the relatively abstract form made possible in such a nominal group, where the source of the authority is hidden. In this case, it is the authority of the teacher that is hidden. A very strong expectation about acceptable student behaviour is at work. Thus does the pedagogic discourse do its work, building the kinds of knowledge the students are to learn and the kinds of subjects they are required to be.

In the Task Conference there are two phases: the Contract Direction, where the details of the tasks for working together are pursued, and the Contract, where the students settle their working groups. In the Contract Direction, the text is again largely teacher monologue. But it is in the Contract that the teacher's and students' roles in the discourse construction begin to shift interpersonally. The students use the interrogative mood frequently in order to negotiate with the teacher what they are to do:

> how big do they (*i.e., the working groups*) have to be?
> can we change the size of the groups?
> Patricia wants to know if you can chuck money in it (*i.e., a wishing well with a windlass*)
> do you want that (*i.e., a particular task*)?
> Mr K what do we do?
> Mr K what are they doing, the wishing well or the spanish windlass?

Most of the students' questions relate to the terms and conditions by which they are to work. Their role is very important in marking the point in the macrogenre where the students begin to assume responsibility for their activities.

The Curriulum Collaboration

This genre falls in the 'middle' of the overall macrogenre, and it was itself made up of several recursive genres, as the students worked in groups to build their machines and draft the procedural genres they also wrote. Two instances of Task Collaborations were recorded, small extracts from one of which will be reproduced here, focusing on some girls making a lift to demonstrate the principle of a windlass. The most decisive shift linguistically at this point in the macrogenre is a shift with respect to mode and the textual metafunction. The students are directing their own behaviour, demonstrating co-operative activity, much as the teacher intended when he wrote that the students should develop habits of working together.

The language – in which the teacher is not much involved – shows extensive use of exophoric reference as the girls refer to their implements:

Chanoa: OK we are doing this one (*points to illustration*).
Aranthi: So we need that.
Chanoa: OK.
Katrina: Hey I got it (*refers to implement needed*).
Chanoa: Oh, excellent!
Yvonne: Looks good.
Chanoa: We need a heavy nut.

. . . .
Naomi: Go ask Bill.
Aranthi: We need a thin saw blade.
Chanoa: Use this (*gives her a stanley knife*).

. . . .
Aranthi: Do you have a matchbox anywhere?

. . . .
Katrina: We need to tie some string.

One notes here, but elsewhere in the Task Collaboration, extensive use of textual themes ('oh', 'OK', 'so'). Earlier it was observed that such themes were very much a feature of the teacher monologues, as in the Prelude, where the teacher was pointing directions. Their marked presence here in the children's talk is a measure of the independence the students enjoy in directing their own learning activity.

Interpersonally, the text shows frequent use of the interrogative mood as the students direct and ask each other things:

> OK, do we have that wire?
> How we going to cut it?
> This the string?
> How much string do you people have?

while elsewhere the imperative mood is also involved:

> Careful please. Please be careful! (*said to a child using a sharp knife*).
> Give us the wire.
> Make it a bit deeper.

Experientially, it is the second order field which is foregrounded here, as the students use the various implements necessary to building their machine, often, as already noted, referring to them exophorically:

> At least it turned.
> Maybe this end can be bent more.
> You've got to hold it this way.

Overall, the Task Collaboration is remarkable for its linguistic differences from the earlier genres. Logogenetically, the text has developed, and the students have progressed to a new understanding of some uncommonsense knowledge, to do with the principle of the mechanical

advantage. They have in fact been pursuing some fundamental principles in Newtonian science, and the fruits of their pursuit will become
clearer in the Curriculum Closure.

The Curriculum Closure

The Curriculum Closure consists of two genres, both operating recursively. The former is an oral one, in which the groups of students give
oral recounts and demonstrations of how their machines work. In the
latter, they display the written procedural genres they have constructed.
Both genres accord closely with those described by Veel (1992, 1997) in
junior secondary school science.

The oral procedural recount

The complete procedural recount provided by the girls working on a lift
is reproduced here, setting out its elements of structure:

ORIENTATION
Naomi: Hi my name is Naomi. (*points to the others in the group*) Aranthi,
Yvonne, Katrina and Chanoa. Our project was to make, um, a
lift using a windlass. We needed a cork, bendable wire and about
thirty-five centimetres of string, a cork, a match box, a heavy
nut, and eight pins and a coil (*indicates for the next person to continue*).

RECORD OF EVENTS
Aranthi: Um, we cut the coil and stuck the bendable wire in and we bent
it like that (*demonstrates*) and we put a cork in the wire and
wrapped the string around a couple of times and attached the
string to a match box and a heavy nut and, um, and then turn
the handle and (*demonstrates*) it should go up and down.

SIGNIFICANCE
The mechanical advantage of this is, um, when you wrap it
around, um, it's easier to, um . . .
Yvonne: Turn the cork.
Aranthi: Yeah.
Yvonne: And the windlass is the wire and the cork and it helps it lift
(*demonstrates*).

The text is monologic, though collectively produced, and the girls probably rehearsed it. The monologic character is in marked contrast with
the highly dialogic character of the Curriculum Collaboration, looked at
above, and evidence that a new stage has been reached logogenetically.
In the Orientation, the first order or regulative register is foregrounded, partly through the theme choices (italicised):

> *our project* was to make um, a life using a windlass
> *we* needed a cork

Unlike the language of the Task Collaboration, the language here is 'context independent', as the girls are aware of the particular needs to be met in offering an oral reconstruction of what they have done. Hence, they even identify themselves, and by use of indefinite referential items, they go on to introduce the various items needed to undertake 'our project': 'a lift', 'a cork', 'bendable wire', 'a match box', 'a heavy nut', 'eight pins', 'a coil'.

The Record of Events unfolds the steps taken to build the machines. A series of textual themes links and carries forward the steps involved:

> *and* stuck the bendable wire in
> *and* we bent it like that
> *and* we put a cork in the wire
> *and* wrapped the string around a couple of times
> *and* attached the string to a match box and a heavy nut and, um
> *and* then turn the handle
> *and* it should go up and down

Interpersonally, the Record of Events, like the Orientation, uses the declarative mood, signalling that information is being given. By the end of the Record, an element of modality creeps in:

> and then turn the handle
> and it *should* go up and down.

Experientially, the processes involved are material, reconstructing the actions undertaken:

> we *cut* the wire
> and *stuck* the bendable wire in

With the entry to the element called 'Significance', it is noticeable that the previous tendency to identify group members in topical theme position is now abandoned. Gone is the personal, and the sense of reconstructing what 'we' did. Instead, two essentially non-personal items appear in topical theme, indicating that a further shift in the unfolding of the genre and of the second order register has occurred:

> *the mechanical advantage of this* is, um . . .
> and *the windlass* is . . .

Experientially, the students use a relational process to unpack the grammatical metaphor involved in the principle of the mechanical advantage:

> the mechanical advantage of this is, um, when you wrap it around, um, it's easier to, um, turn the cork

A new level of understanding is achieved here as the students abstract away from the details of the steps reconstructed in the Record of Events, and as they offer the generalisation about the mechanical advantage.

The process which the students have followed in order to complete their procedural recount accords very closely with the process as described by Halliday (in Halliday and Martin 1993: 57–62) in Newton's language. Paralleling much that Bazerman (1988) has also argued about the emergence of Newtonian language, Halliday sees Newton's language as 'registering the birth of scientific English' (Halliday and Martin 1993: 57) because it 'creates a discourse of experimentation'. Halliday identifies two types of processes as centrally involved, although only one such type is found in the children's oral procedural recount. The two are material processes, involved in recreating what Newton did, and mental processes, involved in recreating what he observed or what he reasoned.

By the same token, we can argue that the young learners who produced their oral procedural recount had recreated what they did and then, through a use of grammatical metaphor, reflected upon the principle that emerged. In that they did not use mental processes to record their observations or thoughts, this is perhaps a feature of the fact that they were young learners, or it may have been influenced by the fact that they were using the oral rather than the written mode used by Newton. In either case, the procedural recount is testimony that the students had gone a long way towards learning the scientific behaviours characteristic of modern scientific inquiry.

The written procedure

The students' written procedure follows what is fairly orthodox scientific practice, of the kind alluded to by Halliday in discussing Newton's scientific English. Thus, they begin by identifying materials needed to undertake their study, then proceed to set out their objective, after which they detail the steps to be taken to achieve that objective. They subsequently outline the results of the study, indicate their conclusions, and refer briefly to applications of the windlass. To do these things, the students foreground the second order register throughout. The first order or regulative register has disappeared in the text, though its operation must be held to remain at a tacit level nonetheless. The text is set out, with elements of schematic structure shown as labelled by the students themselves.

THE LIFT

Apparatus: a cork, bendable wire, about 35 cm of strong string, a matchbox, a heavy bolt, 8 pins, a plastic drink container [Coke bottle].

Objective: to find the mechanical advantages [of] using the windlass.

Procedure:

- Get a medium-sized bottle (approx. 30 cm in height).
- Cut the bottle about 6 cm down from the top.
- Cut a doorway about 6 cm.
- Make two holes opposite each other around 5 cm from the base of the bottle.
- Get the piece of wire, e.g. a coat hanger.
- Thread wire a quarter way through one of the holes in the bottle.
- Make a hole [going through the centre of the cork].
- Holding the cork inside the bottle, push the wire through the other hole in the cork. Put the remaining wire through the other hole in the bottle.
- On one end of the wire leave 3–4 cm protruding from the bottle and on the other end leave around 11 cm.
- Bend 3–4 cm wire at a right-angle turn. Then get the other end of the wire, leave 3 cm, then bend down at a right angle. Then leave 4 cm of wire and bend at a right angle sideways. Refer to diagram.
- Get the matchbox, take the inner part of the box out, put a hole in the side of it and thread the string 35 cm in. Tie a knot so the string does not slip out. Reassemble matchbox.
- Take the heavy bolt and tie it on the other end of the string. Wind one end of the string around the cork a couple of times so both the matchbox and bolt are dangling downwards.
- Rotate the handle and the matchbox should go up and down.

Result: Problems were encountered because the string had unstable balance, therefore it was consistently sliding off when the handle was turned. To fix this problem pins were pushed in the cork to make a pathway for the string [to follow].

Conclusions: This concludes the experiment of the lift. The model [that has been made] shows one of the uses of mechanical advantages – the windlass. It changes the direction of force to help lift things.

Applications: The lift may be used in tall or large buildings, in the office, home or school. Variations of the lift can be used almost everywhere.

The opening element 'Apparatus' lists items needed, while the 'Objective' asserts what is sought. The Procedure is built round a series of topical themes realised in the process choices (italicised):

> *get* the medium-sized bottle . . .
> *cut* the bottle . . .

The Procedure also makes use of an occasional marked topical theme (in italics):

holding the cork inside the bottle push the wire through . . .
on one end of the wire leave . . .

Experientially, the processes are all material, indicating that a series of actions is under construction:

thread the wire a quarter way . . .
tie it on the other end of the string
bend at a right angle sideways

Interpersonally, the procedure uses the imperative mood to direct the reader's behaviour.

The move to the element 'The Results' marks a decisive shift. The object is no longer to direct behaviour, but to reflect upon what was learned. The opening theme choice is significant:

problems were encountered.

Interpersonally, the element is authoritative, as the students inform their readers of the results.

In the Conclusion, the students signal closure:

This concludes the experiment of the lift

where this introduces a series of clauses having no textual themes, only topical ones.

There is one verbal processes in the conclusion, the only one of its kind in this genre:

that model that has been made *shows* one of the uses of mechanical advantages.

This adds to the sense that reflection upon events and results is now of concern.

In the Applications, the reflection is removed a little more, into considering ways the lift that made the windlass can be used. Here a sense of the technological consequences of inventions like the lift is involved. It will be sufficient to comment on the introduction of modality, not a feature of the earlier elements, but a part of an element in which some judgement is offered:

the lift *may* be used in tall buildings . . .
variations in the lift *can* be used almost everywhere . . .

Thus is the written scientific procedure constructed, and thus too, is the science curriculum macrogenre concluded.

THE PEDAGOGIC SUBJECT IN SCIENCE

Above it was suggested, following Bernstein, that a pedagogic discourse is designed to induct subjects into various institutionally sanctioned values and practices. A pedagogic discourse is a consequence of the operation of a pedagogic device, whose purpose is to shape particular forms of consciousness. The school is an important institution in which pedagogic discourses operate, taking forms of knowledge and their discourses from other institutional sites, and relocating these for the purposes of their selective transmission to learners. Teachers are the agents of the processes of relocation, and these processes bring about transformations in the nature of the discourses because of the recontextualisation involved. Where the discourse of physics, for example, may be found in the institutional site of a university, it will be recontextualised and hence changed for the purposes of its transmission to school students. It is not the logic of the original physics discourse that determines its transmission, but rather the logic of the pedagogic activity, as this is realised in what Bernstein calls the regulative discourse, and we have called the regulative register. It is the operation of the regulative register then, that controls the operation of the instructional register; where the pedagogic discourse is successful the instructional register is ultimately foregrounded, though the regulative register continues to operate tacitly. A successful operation of the pedagogic discourse in school will produce particular pedagogic subject positions, such that persons are apprenticed into ways of reasoning and valuing deemed of importance in a culture.

This chapter has sought to demonstrate how a pedagogic discourse works by reference to an instance of upper primary school science teaching. We have sought to examine some of the complex linguistic changes that take place in a curriculum macrogenre, effecting the building of a pedagogic discourse. The learning of science in the manner outlined is a matter of developing both an understanding of particular scientific fields of knowledge, and an understanding of how those fields of knowledge may be applied. In the case examined, it was the Newtonian principle of mechanical advantage which the students were to learn. In a series of steps across the curriculum macrogenre, the students moved from an opening genre in which goals and directions were explicitly identified by the teacher, to subsequent steps in which they jointly constructed some sense of the scientific field, before they moved on to relatively independent activity as they made their own machines. Subsequently, they reconstructed orally what they had done, and displayed written procedures.

As we demonstrated, the two registers functioned in particular ways as the curriculum macrogenre unfolded. In the opening stages the first order or regulative register was foregrounded, but there were subsequent later stages in which the second order or instructional register was foregrounded and the students increasingly assumed responsibility for their own learning. They became authoritative about the scientific topic in question, and as they did so, the teacher's authority dropped away, its operation still tacit, but no longer marked in the text.

A logogenetic growth in the organisation and development of the curriculum text had occurred, such that a cumulative series of changes had taken place, indicating the students' progress to new understandings with which to learn in further new ways. In this sense, then, the students' subjectivity had been shaped, preparing them for the many learning tasks that lay ahead.

NOTES

1 The research reported in this paper was funded by the Australian Research Council.
2 To put the matter in these terms is not to argue a determinist position. Bernstein (e.g. 1996: 52) suggests that for both intrinsic and extrinsic reasons, the pedagogic device always admits of instability, and hence of challenge to the knowledge that is taught. Elsewhere (Christie 1997) I have argued that it is never the case that all students equally acquire the discourses of schooling, and hence adopt the same desired pedagogic subject positions: on the contrary, these are a matter of the different meaning orientations with which students function.
3 The distinction between 'commonsense' and 'uncommonsense' knowledge is one used by Bernstein e.g. 1971: 214–15. Hasan (1986) attributes the distinction as originally used to Whorf (1956).
4 Bernstein does not use the metaphor of projection to characterise the relationship of a regulative and an instructional discourse, but rather one of 'embedding' (e.g. Bernstein 1990). The notions of the two registers and the metaphor of projection are taken from systemic functional linguistic theory, and used to try to find linguistic evidence for the pedagogic discourse.
5 Authorities differ about the principles by which machines are grouped. While all authorities consulted would recognise the machines identified, they would not necessarily group them this way. The teacher apparently chose this grouping because it was in the film, and because it was appropriate for the age group of the children.
6 A row of dots indicates that some of the discourse has been left out.
7 The reference to 'tomorrow' indicates it is then that the students will commence building their machines.

REFERENCES

Baker, C.D. and P. Freebody 1989. *Children's First School Books: Introductions to the Culture of Literacy.* Oxford: Blackwell.
Barnes, D. Language in the secondary classroom, in Barnes, D., Britton, J. and Rosen, H. (eds) *Language the Learner and the School.* Middlesex: Penguin (revised edition 1971), 11–77.
Bazerman, C. 1988. *Shaping Written Knowledge. The genre and activity of the experimental article in science.* Madison, WI: University of Wisconsin Press.
Bellack, A., H. Kliebard, R. Hyman and F. Smith 1966. *The Language of the Classroom.* Columbia, NY: Teachers College Press.
Bernstein, B. 1971. *Class, Codes and Control vol. I Theoretical studies towards a sociology of language.* London: Routledge and Kegan Paul.
Bernstein, B. 1990. *The Structuring of Pedagogic Discourse. Class, codes and control vol. IV.* London: Routledge.

Bernstein, B. 1994. The pedagogic device. A plenary paper at the 21st International Systemic Functional Congress, held University of Ghent, 1–5 August 1994.

Bernstein, B. 1996. *Pedagogy, Symbolic Control and Identity. Theory, research, critique.* (Critical perspectives on literacy and education, Series Editor, Allan Luke). London: Taylor & Francis.

Cazden, C.B. 1986. Classroom discourse in M.C. Wittrock (ed.) *Handbook of Research on Teaching* (third edition). New York: Macmillan, 433–63.

Cazden, C.B. 1988. *Classroom Discourse. The language of teaching and learning.* Portsmouth: Heinemann.

Christie, F. 1989. Curriculum genres in early childhood education: a case study in writing development. Unpublished PhD thesis, University of Sydney.

Christie, F. 1995a. The teaching of literature in the secondary English class. *Report 1 of a Research Study into the Pedagogic Discourse of Secondary School English.* A study funded by the Australian Research Council. University of Melbourne.

Christie, F. 1995b. The teaching of story writing in the junior secondary school. *Report 2 of a Research Study into the Pedagogic Discourse of Secondary School English.* A study funded by the Australian Research Council. University of Melbourne.

Christie, F. 1996. Geography. *Report of a Research Study into the Pedagogic Discourse of Secondary School Social Sciences.* A study funded by the Australian Research Council. University of Melbourne.

Christie, F. 1997. Curriculum genres as forms of initiation into a culture in Christie, F. and Martin, J.R. (eds) *Genres and Institutions: Social processes in the workplace and school.* London: Cassell Academic, 134–160.

Cicourel A. *et al.* 1974. *Language Use and School Performance.* New York: Academic Press.

Flanders, N. 1970. *Analysing Teacher Behaviour.* Reading, MA: Addison Wesley.

Green, J. 1986 cited in Cazden, C.B. 1986 Classroom discourse in M.C. Wittrock (ed.) *Handbook of Research on Teaching* (third edition). New York: Macmillan, 433–63.

Green, J. and R. Kantor-Smith 1988. Exploring the complexity of language and learning in the life of the classroom. A paper given at the Post World Reading Congress Symposium on Language and Learning, University of Queensland, Brisbane, 10–15 July 1988.

Green, J. and C. Dixon (eds) 1993. Special Issue: Santa Barbara Classroom Discourse Group. *Linguistics and Education,* 5, 3 and 4.

Green, J. and J.O. Harker (eds) 1988. *Multiple Perspective Analysis of Classroom Discourse.* Norwood, NJ: Ablex.

Halliday, M.A.K. 1994. *Introduction to Functional Grammar* (revised edition). London: Edward Arnold.

Halliday, M.A.K. and J.R. Martin 1993. *Writing Science. Literacy and discursive power.* (Critical perspectives on literacy and education, Series Editor, Allan Luke). London: Falmer.

Hasan, R. 1986. The ontogenesis of ideology: An interpretation of mother–child talk in T. Threadgold, E.A. Grosz, G. Kress and M.A.K. Halliday (eds) *Semiotics, Ideology, Language.* Sydney: Sydney Studies in Society and Culture, 3. Association for Studies in Society and Culture, 125–146.

Hasan, R. in press. The disempowerment game: Language in literacy in C.D. Baker, J. Cook-Gumperz and A. Luke (eds) *Literacy and Power.* London: Blackwell.

Iedema, R. 1994. *The Language of Administration.* Disadvantaged Schools Program, East Sydney.

Iedema, R. 1997. The language of administration: Organising human activity in formal institutions in F. Christie and J.R. Martin (eds) *Genres and Institutions: Social processes in the workplace and school.* London: Cassell Academic, 73–100.

Kantor, R. *et al.* 1992. The construction of schooled discourse repertoires: An interactional sociolinguistic perspective on learning to talk in preschool. *Linguistics and Education,* 4, 2, 131–172.

Lemke, J.L. 1990. *Talking Science. Language, learning and values.* Norwood, NJ: Ablex.

Lindfors, J.W. 1981. *Children's Language and Learning.* New York: Prentice-Hall.

Martin, J.R. 1994. Macro-genres: the ecology of the page. *Network* 21, 29–52.

Martin, J.R. 1995. Text and clause: fractal resonance. *Text* 15, 1, 5–42.

Mehan, H. 1979. *Learning Lessons: Social organisation in the classroom.* Cambridge, MA: Harvard University Press.

Northern Territory Education Department 1986 *1–7 Primary Science Core Curriculum.* Darwin: NT Education Department, Darwin.

Perrott, C. 1988. *Classroom Talk and Pupil Learning.* Sydney: Harcourt Brace Jovanovich.

Shuy, R. 1988. Identifying dimensions of classroom behaviour in J.L. Green and J.O. Harker (eds) *Multiple Perspective Analysis of Classroom Discourse.* Norwood, NJ: Ablex, 113–134.

Sinclair, J. McH. and Coulthard, R.M. 1975. *Towards an Analysis of Discourse. The English used by teachers and pupils.* Oxford: Oxford University Press.

Stubbs, M. and Delamont, S. (eds) 1976. *Explorations in Classroom Observation.* Chichester: Wiley.

Stubbs, M. 1983. *Language, Schools and Classrooms.* London: Methuen.

Veel, R. 1992. Engaging with scientific language: A functional approach to the language of school science. *The Australian Science Teachers Journal.* 38, 4, 31–5.

Veel, R. 1997. Learning how to mean – scientifically speaking: Apprenticeship into scientific discourse in the secondary school in F. Christie and J.R. Martin (eds) *Genres and Institutions: Social processes in the workplace and school.* London: Cassell Academic, 161–195.

Wells, G. 1993. Reevaluating the IRF sequence: A proposal for the articulation of theories of activity and discourse for the analysis of teaching and learning in the classroom. *Linguistics and Education,* 5, 1, 1–38.

Whorf, B.L. 1956. *Language, Thought and Reality. Selected writings of Benjamin Lee Whorf.* (J.B. Carroll, ed.) Cambridge, MA: Massachusetts Institute of Technology.

Part IV
Discourses of science

Introduction to part IV

Like most schools of functional linguistics, Systemic Functional Linguistics (SFL) has long been interested in the language of science. Scientific language appeals to linguists for a number of reasons. It is one of the most instantly recognisable and widely recognised varieties of English. It performs distinct functions in society, has a distinct set of users and has distinct grammatical and textual structures.

Because SFL is particularly concerned with describing the relationship between language and social context, the kinds of questions it asks about scientific language tend to focus on the relationship between the language system and broader questions of human semiosis. Of special interest is the relationship between the *forms of language* used in science and the *forms of knowledge* construed/construable by that language. In other words, SFL has attempted to map out the *meaning potential* of scientific discourse, and how it varies from other specialist forms of language as well as from everyday, non-specialist language. Such explorations allow us to understand the functionality of scientific language: how it allows us to know things that were previously unknowable, and to do things (through technology) that were previously undoable. It gives us a better understanding of what is required in order to learn and control scientific knowledge. A clear understanding of the functionality of scientific language also allows us to question what scientific discourse does *not do* – the kinds of meanings it leaves out, or deals with inefficiently, and the kind of language users it excludes.

We begin this section with a chapter by Michael Halliday. The analyses of scientific language by Halliday have played a central role in understandings of scientific language within SFL. The chapter in this volume brings together in a definitive form Halliday's work on how the grammar of the clause works in scientific English to reconstrue human experience as technical knowledge. Central to Halliday's discussion is the resource of *grammatical metaphor* in linguistically reorganising our experience into new categories and placing these new categories into new semantic and textual relations with one another. Of particular interest in this chapter is Halliday's systematic categorisation of *different types of grammatical metaphor* and the 'general drift' of grammatical metaphor towards construing a world of 'virtual entities' – fundamental to the construal of technical taxonomies and causal relations in science.

Among the many pieces he has written in this area, his 'On the language of physical science' (Halliday and Martin 1993: Chapter 3), an exploration of the evolution of scientific language from Chaucer to the present day, has been especially influential. All the other chapters in this section are heavily influenced by Halliday's study. Halliday's influence comes not only through the use of a historical perspective (this is present in Wignell and Mattheissen's papers) but in taking up the idea that scientific and technical language involves a *systematic reconstrual of meanings* to create new kinds of meaning and new relationships between objects and events.

Rose's chapter applies the Hallidayan idea of reconstrual-through-grammar to the field of science-based industries, examining how everyday activity – here the industrial production of goods – is systematically reconstrued in increasing levels of technicality and abstraction according to the hierarchical structure of the workplace. The potential of the language system is activated in different ways at different levels in the industrial production hierarchy, with a general drift towards more metaphorical modes of expression at more senior levels of the hierarchy. These senior levels are also the point, Rose argues, where the worlds, and the language, of research science and industrial science meet.

The chapter by White extends Halliday's studies of the language of science with a linguistically delicate examination of the differences between technological and scientific discourse. White shows that, although technology is usually considered a sub-field within scientific discourse, there are substantial differences between science and technology, particularly in the relationship between lexical items and the taxonomic organisation of knowledge, and proposes the recognition of a process of 'techno-cality' in language, to complement Martin's (Halliday and Martin 1993: Chapter 10) notion of technicality. White's contribution is typical of the evolving nature of understandings about scientific language within SFL. Just as it has become necessary to distinguish between 'technical' and 'abstract' lexis as our understandings of the function of grammatical metaphor develop (Martin 1997), so too further and more delicate investigation reveals the need to distinguish different tendencies within the grammar of different kinds of scientific language.

In considering the language of social science, Wignell uses Halliday and Martin's descriptions of the language of science to investigate the ways in which social science is both similar to and from different to science. Like Halliday for science, Wignell traces the development of the language of social science over several centuries, and notes the diverse linguistic and political influences which have resulted in a modern discourse that appropriates meanings both from the humanities and the sciences, creating a new meaning potential by setting them in a new relationship with one another, albeit a relationship of considerable semantic tension. Wignell's conclusions about the language of social science resonates with Veel's remarks (Chapter 10) about the language of environmentalism, even though these two discourses have very different origins.

Wignell's study also shows a very important by-product of the research into the language of science. By establishing the characteristic linguistic and semantic tendencies in one discourse, one is able then to proceed to a comparative study of another similar, but different, discourse. Over time we are able to build up an overall topology of the relationship between discourses and the resources of the language system. Such understandings develop not only our understanding of the discourses themselves, they also enhance our understanding of the language system itself, and point to areas where our understanding of the language system needs to be developed. Research into the language of school disciplines conducted in the early 1990s (see Hasan and Williams 1996 and Christie and Martin 1997), for example, resulted not only in new understandings about school disciplines, but in the development of a whole new set of techniques for analysing the discourse semantics of appraisal (see Martin 1996, Iedema, Feez and White 1994 for examples of this).

Mattheissen also uses Halliday's insights about scientific language to investigate another discursive realm: in this case cognitive science. Like the term 'social science', 'cognitive science' identifies itself as a subbranch of scientific discourse. Like social science, cognitive science activates many of the grammatical structures used by research science in order to reconstrue meanings, creating new orders of meaning, new categories of meaning within these orders and new relationships between the categories. In examining one area of the lexico-grammar, the representation of mental activity, Mattheissen shows that although cognitive science uses sophisticated techniques for generating abstract and technical categories, its view of the mind is still very much a 'folk' one – a minimal reconstrual of the way we talk about the mind in everyday language. He argues that cognitive science and artificial intelligence have much to gain by taking a more social–semiotic approach to the representation of mind.

REFERENCES

Christie, F. and J. Martin (eds) 1997. *Genre and Institutions: Social processes in the workplace and school* London: Cassell.

Halliday, M. and J. Martin 1993. *Writing Science: Literacy and discursive power* London: Falmer Press.

Hasan, R. and G. Williams 1996. *Literacy in Society* London: Longman.

Iedema, R., S. Feez and P. White 1994. *Media Literacy* (Write It Right Literacy in Industry research project, Stage Two) Sydney: Disadvantaged Schools Program, New South Wales Department of School Education, Metropolitan East Region.

Martin, J. 1996. Evaluating disruption: Symbolising theme in junior secondary narrative in R. Hasan and G. Williams (eds) *Literacy in Society* London: Longman. pp. 124–171.

Martin, J. 1997. Analysing genre: Functional principles and parameters in F. Christie and J. Martin (eds) *Genre and Institutions: Social processes in the workplace and school* London: Cassell. pp. 3–39.

8 Things and relations

Regrammaticising experience as
technical knowledge

M.A.K. Halliday

QUESTIONS AND ASSUMPTIONS

The question I am asking in this chapter is: how does the language of
science reconstrue human experience? By *how* I mean both 'in what
respects' and 'by what means'. By *the language of science* I mean the various
forms of discourse in which the activities of 'doing science' are carried
out – but seen as a systemic resource for creating meaning, not as a
collection of instances of text. By *reconstrue* I mean 'reconstruct semiotically': that is, replace one semiotic construction by another. I leave open
the possibility that, in the end, the question might be dismissed – we
might conclude that no such reconstrual takes place; although I have
expressly formulated the question so as to suggest that I think it does.

I am concerned specifically with the scientific discourses of English,
although it seems that the critical features are present in other languages
as well. (I myself have examined scientific writings in Chinese [Halliday
and Martin 1993: Chapter 7]; Biagi [1995] discusses their history in
Italian.) My approach is through the grammar, and specifically through
systemic functional 'grammatics', theorising the grammar in such a way
that it is possible to interpret texts as instantiations of a meaning-creating
system and its sub-systems. The most general sources for the grammatics
are Halliday (1985/1994), Martin (1992), Eggins (1995), Matthiessen
(1995) and Davidse (1991). The discussion as a whole takes off from the
issues raised in Halliday and Martin (1993); in particular, I hope it will
help to clarify the relationship between what appears there as two rather
distinct motifs: one, that of technicality and categorising (foregrounded
in Martin's chapters), the other that of logicality and reasoning (foregrounded in my own).

I shall make two assumptions about grammar at the start. One is that
the grammar of every (natural) language is a theory of human experience. The other is that this is not all that it is. The grammar of a natural
language is also an enactment of interpersonal relationships. These two
functions, the reflective and the active, are each dependent on the other;
and they, in turn, are actualised by a third function, that of creating

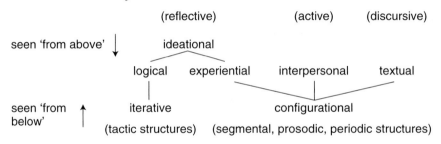

Figure 8.1 The metafunctional framing of the grammar

discourse. Thus grammar brings into being a semiotic mode of activity that models the material mode while being itself a component of what it is modelling (cf. Lemke 1993). This functional framing of the grammar can be summarised as in Figure 8.1. These assumptions constitute the core of the 'metafunctional' hypothesis that has evolved over three decades of systemic functional grammatics and will not be elaborated further here.

GRAMMAR AS THEORY OF EXPERIENCE

When one talks about the grammar as a theory of human experience one is, obviously, focusing on the ideational metafunction; and since this is the aspect of grammar that is almost always given greatest prominence I want to reject, explicitly, the suggestion that it has some kind of priority. Neither historically nor functionally is ideational meaning more basic or more potent than the other components of human semiosis. To say this is not simply to give value to the interpersonal and textual domains. Grammar evolved in the human species, and develops in the human brain, as a form of consciousness in which each instance – each act of meaning – simultaneously both construes (some portion of) experience and enacts (some portion of) the social process. Typically these take place below the level of our (adult) awareness and attention; but when we focus our attention we become aware first of all of the grammar's representational power – its potential for referring to perceptual phenomena; and theories of meaning have usually fixated on that. This potential is critical to the present argument; for that reason, especially, it is important to put it in perspective. In our construction of meaning, the representational has no priority over the other, conative and expressive (to use terms derived from Bühler [1934]), semantic domains. The most abstruse scientific theory becomes actualised only in taking at the same time the form of a social act (Lemke 1990, 1995).

What the grammar does, in its ideational guise, is to transform human experience into meaning. The grammar construes a universe of things and relations, imposing categories on our perceptions of phenomena; in other words, it sets up a *theory* of experience, modelling the immensely complex interaction between the human organism and its environment. In mainstream twentieth-century philosophy of language this has been interpreted as a largely passive process of correspondence, whereby the grammar fulfils its experiential role by recognising patterns – forms of likeness among different phenomena – that are 'given' in the material world, so that a lexicogrammatical category (a lexical item, or a term in a grammatical system) simply reflects, or codifies, something that is already there. But, as Ellis (1994) points out, this notion is mistaken. In fact there are no such natural classes; or (what amounts to the same thing) there are indefinitely many of them: that is, indefinitely many ways in which the phenomena of our experience can be seen to be related to one another. What the grammar does is to impose a categorisation: it treats a certain cluster of phenomena as alike in certain respects, and hence sets this cluster apart from others which it treats as being different.

It is easy to demonstrate this principle with meanings that are construed lexically: it comes down to the question of what phenomena we call by the same name. Of the various objects sticking out of the ground that I can see outside my window, some are *trees*, some are *bushes* and some are *shrubs*; and of the humans that are passing by some are *walking* and some are *running* (and some are *driving* in cars). We can observe small children working hard to construct the category meanings of words in their mother tongue, and we become aware of the problem for ourselves when we learn a language that is culturally distant from our own. But the more pervasive categories of our experience are those that are construed grammatically, since they provide us with a general foundation for understanding our environment and ourselves.

In the most general terms, the grammar construes experience as *process*, in the form of a grammatical *unit*, a *clause*. Each process, in turn, is construed as *configuration*, in the form of a grammatical *structure*; the components of this configuration are (1) the process itself, (2) certain entities that participate in the process and (3) various circumstantial elements that are associated with it; these are construed in the form of grammatical *classes*, the verbal, the nominal, and some more or less distinct third type. Then, one process may be construed as being related to another, by some form of grammatical *conjunction*.

The way things are is the way our grammar tells us that they are. In the normal course of events we do not problematise this construal; it is our 'taken for granted reality', and we do not reflect on why the grammar theorises experience the way it does or whether it could have been done in some other way. If we do reflect, we are likely still to appeal to a sense of what is natural. We might reason that, as long as to our perceptions things stay just as they are, we do not 'experience' them; experience begins when the organism becomes aware of some change taking place in its environment (or in itself). Hence the grammar construes experience around the category of 'process': a process typically represents some sort of change, of which staying the same – not changing – becomes just the limiting case.

But sorting out a *process* of change from the *entities* that remain in existence throughout and despite the change (let alone from other phenomena that are seen as circumstantial to it) is already a major enterprise of semiotic construction. If we consider a simple clause such as *the sun was shining on the sea* (immortalised as the first line of *The Walrus and the Carpenter*), a considerable amount of semiotic energy has gone into the grammar's construal of this as a configuration of process 'shine', participating entity 'sun' and circumstance 'on the sea'. Taken purely in its own terms, as perceptual phenomenon, it would have been simpler to construe it as a single unanalysed whole. It is only when the whole of experience is being construed as an ideational *system* that the analytical model – breaking down a complex perception to recognise likenesses of many different kinds – shows up as infinitely more resourceful and more powerful. (To pursue the same text further, the sun's shining may be attended by other circumstances, *with all his might*; and the sun may participate in other processes than shining, trying *to make the billows smooth and bright*.)

What is significant for the present discussion, however, is not so much the particulars of the experiential model, as it evolved in human grammars; rather, it is the fact that the same evolutionary processes which make it possible to construe experience, by transforming it into meaning in this way, also provide the means with which to challenge the form of the construal. When experience has once been construed, it can be reconstrued in a different light.

STRATIFICATION AND METAPHOR

It is, I think, acknowledged that human consciousness is the product of natural selection (Edelman 1990) – that there is no need to postulate some mysterious entity called 'mind' (itself, as Matthiessen [1993] has shown, the rather one-sided product of the grammar's construing of inner experience) that lies outside the processes of biological history. Neuroscientists have shown that the brain (including the human brain) evolved in the context of the increasingly complex relationship between the organism and its environment; I would just want to add here, since this formulation overprivileges the ideational (see p. 186): and in the context of the increasingly complex social interactions among the organisms forming a group. These evolutionary processes have engendered what Edelman calls 'higher order consciousness', something that appears to be unique to *Homo sapiens*.

Higher order consciousness is semiotic consciousness; it is this which transforms experience into meaning. From my point of view in this chapter, with its focus on language, higher order consciousness depends on two critical steps by which language evolved. One I have already introduced: that of functional diversity, or *metafunction* – the principle that 'meaning' is a parallel mode of activity (the semiotic, alongside and in dialectic relation with the material) which simultaneously both construes experience and enacts the social process. The other critical step is stratal organisation, or *stratification*.

Primary semiotic systems – those of other species, and the 'protolanguage' of human infants before they embark on the mother tongue – are not stratified; they are inventories of signs, without a grammar. Such systems cannot create meaning; their contexts are 'given' constructs like 'here I am', 'let's be together', 'I want that' (which we distort, of course, by glossing them in adult language wordings). Language, the semiotic of higher order consciousness, is *stratified*: it has a stratum of lexicogrammar 'in between' the meaning and the expression (Halliday and Martin 1993: Chapter 2). The 'signified' part of the original sign has now evolved into a meaning space, within which the meaning potential can be indefinitely expanded (Figure 8.2). Such a system can *create* meaning; its text-forming resources engender a discursive flow which is then modified (rather like the airstream is modified, on the expression plane, by articulation and intonation) so that it becomes at the same time both interactive (dialogic) and representational.

In the primary semiotic, 'content' is formed directly at the interface with the experiential world – hence it is 'given', as described above. In the higher order stratified semiotic, meaning is created across a semiotic space which is defined by the *semantic* stratum (itself interfacing, as before, with the world of experiential phenomena) and the *lexicogrammatical* stratum, a new, purely abstract level of semiotic organisation which interfaces only with the two material interfaces. The semiotic energy of the system comes from the lexicogrammar.

This 'thick', dimensional semiotic thus creates meaning on two strata, with a relation of *realisation* between them: the semantic, and the lexicogrammatical – analogous to Hjelmslev's 'content substance' and 'content form' within his 'content plane'. If we focus now on the ideational

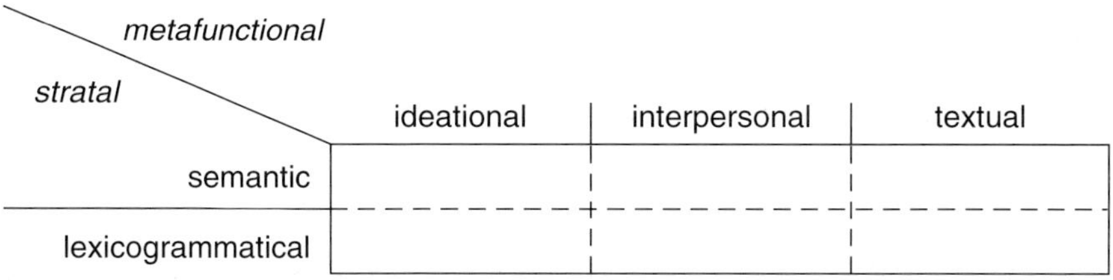

metafunctional / stratal	ideational	interpersonal	textual
semantic			
lexicogrammatical			

Figure 8.2 The 'meaning space' defined by stratification and metafunction

function, we can represent the outline of the way experience is construed into meaning in the grammar of English along the following lines:

	semantic		*lexicogrammatical*
ranks	sequence (of figures)	realised by	clause complex
	figure	"	clause
	element (of figure)	"	group/phrase
types of	process	realised by	verbal group
element	participating entity	"	nominal group
	circumstance	"	adverbial group or prepositional phrase
	relator	"	conjunction

For example: *the driver drove the bus too rapidly down the hill, so the brakes failed* (Figure 8.3).

Thus the grammar, in a stratified system, sets up categories and relationships which have the effect of transforming experience into meaning. In creating a formal distinction such as that between verb and noun, the grammar is theorising about processes: that a distinction can be made, of a very general kind, between two facets: the process itself, and entities that are involved in it.

But, as remarked above, since the grammar has the power of construing, by the same token (that is, by virtue of being stratified) it can also deconstrue, and reconstrue along different lines. Since stratification involves mapping meanings into forms, 'process' into verbal and 'participant' into nominal, it also allows remapping – say, of 'process' into a nominal form: the previous clause could be reworded as a nominal group *the driver's overrapid downhill driving of the bus*. The experience has now been retransformed – in other words, it has undergone a process of metaphor. A stratified system has inherent metaphoric power.

Of course, the initial categorising of experience is already a kind of metaphorical process, since it involves transforming the material into the semiotic. But, having said that, I will go on to use the term 'metaphor'

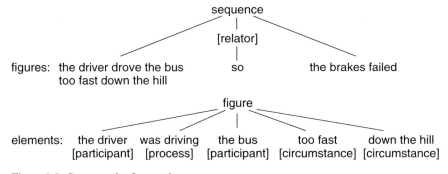

Figure 8.3 Construal of experience

just in its canonical sense, that of transformation *within* the semiotic mode. Traditionally the term is applied only to *lexical* transformations, and it is theorised as 'same signifier, different signified' (e.g. *spoonfeed*: 'literal meaning', 'feed baby or invalid with small quantities of easily digested food on a spoon'; 'metaphorical meaning', 'provide learner with small quantities of carefully chosen instructional materials'). But here I shall be talking about *grammatical* transformations, and I shall theorise these as 'same signified, different signifier', for example 'brake + fail': 'congruent construal' *the brakes failed*, 'metaphorical construal' *brake failure*. Notice however that what varies is not the lexical items, which are the same in both cases; it is the grammatical categories, so that the metaphor actually proceeds as follows: 'process + participant', 'congruently' clause; nominal group + verbal group, 'metaphorically' nominal group – noun + noun. This same grammatical metaphor is then present in numerous other such exemplars: not only with 'fail', such as *engine failure, crop failure, heart failure, power failure*, but with many thousands of other processes besides, as in *cloud formation, bowel movement, tooth decay, tissue growth, particle spin, rainfall* and the like.

If we consider a pair of expressions such as those above:

the driver drove the bus too rapidly down the hill, so the brakes failed

the driver's overrapid downhill driving of the bus resulted in brake failure,

it is clear that there is a highly complex relation of grammatical metaphor between the two; a number of transformations are taking place simultaneously: *the driver / the driver's*; *drove / driving*; *the bus / of the bus*; *too rapidly / overrapid*; *down the hill / downhill*; *fail / failure*; *the brakes / brake*; *so / resulted in*. These may be represented diagrammatically as in Figure 8.4.

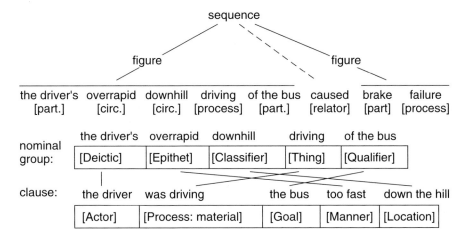

Figure 8.4 Metaphoric reconstrual

It will be seen that the metaphorical shift involves two kinds of grammatical movement: one in rank, the other in structural configuration (the latter will be more effectively modelled in terms of grammatical functions, rather than simply in terms of classes). On the one hand, there has been a movement *down in rank*: (1) a (semantic) sequence, congruently construed as a (grammatical) clause complex, is reconstrued as a (grammatical) clause, which congruently construes a (semantic) figure; (2) a figure, congruently construed as a clause, is reconstrued as a group, which congruently construes an element in a figure. On the other hand, there has been a movement *across in function / class*; this is very much more complex, since it involves (1) reconstruing each configuration of elements as a whole:

i 'driver + drive + bus + too fast + down hill'
   from clause functioning as primary clause in paratactic clause nexus to nominal group functioning as Token in clause

ii 'brake + fail'
   from clause functioning as secondary clause in paratactic clause nexus to nominal group functioning as Value in clause

and in addition (2) reconstruing each individual element, from a function in the clause to a function in the nominal group:

i 'driver'   from Actor   (in clause) to Deictic   (in nominal group)
   'drive'   Process   Thing
   'bus'   Goal   Qualifier
   'too fast'   Manner   Epithet
   'down hill'   Location   Classifier

ii 'brake'   Actor   Classifier
   'fail'   Process   Thing

as well as (3) reconstruing the relator 'therefore' from Conjunctive in the configuration of one of the two clauses (in this case, the secondary one) to Process in the single remaining clause.

Thus grammatical metaphor, like metaphor in its traditional, lexical sense, is a realignment between a pair of strata: a remapping of the semantics on to the lexicogrammar; hence the term 'reconstrual' being used here to refer to it. It depends entirely on the stratal organisation of language; there could be no metaphor without stratification – and once the content plane has become stratified, such transformation automatically becomes possible. (Note that this transformation is distinct from 'transformation' in the early Chomskyan grammar, which was a purely formal, syntactic operation. Here we are talking rather of 'cross-coupling' between the grammar and the semantics.) If this takes place in isolated instances, scattered more or less randomly throughout the discourse, it probably has only local significance in the text. But if it becomes a regular, sustained feature of discourses of a particular kind, then certain questions about it seem to arise:

1 What is the payoff? What effect has such reconstrual on the construction of the discourse?
2 What different kinds of metaphorical shift take place, and is there any general principle lying behind them?
3 What are the systemic consequences? To put this in other terms, in what way is 'regrammaticising' experience also 'resemanticising' it?

I shall try to take each of these questions up in turn.

GRAMMATICAL METAPHOR IN SCIENTIFIC ENGLISH

The example discussed in the last section was of course contrived. But it was contrived on the model of what is in many ways the favourite grammatical pattern ('syndrome' of grammatical features) in modern scientific English. In this pattern, (1) a sequence of two figures is construed as a single clause, typically a relational clause of the intensive or circumstantial type (cf. Halliday 1985/1994, Chapter 5); (2) each figure is construed as a nominal group, and (3) the logical–semantic (conjunctive) relation between them is construed as a verbal group. Here are some text examples:

rapid changes in the rate of evolution   are caused by   external events

the thermal losses typical of an insulating system   are measured in terms of   a quantity called the thermal loss coefficient

the absolute indistinguishability of the electrons in the two atoms gives rise to   an 'extra' attractive force between them

this breeding effort   was anchored in   the American species' resistance to phylloxera

the theoretical programme of devising models of atomic nuclei   has been complemented by   experimental investigations

the growth of attachment between infant and mother   signals   the first step in the child's capacity to discriminate among people

many failures   are preceded by   the slow extension of pre existing cracks

fire intensity   has a profound effect on   smoke injection

Griffith's energy balance approach to strength and fracture   also suggested   the importance of surface chemistry in the mechanical behaviour of brittle materials

the model   rests on   the localised gravitational attraction exerted by rapidly oscillating and extremely massive cloud loops of cosmic string

increased responsiveness   may be reflected in   feeding behaviour

this acidification   was caused mainly by   the burning of coal containing high levels of sulphur

Let me put this into the context of the present discussion. I began by observing that a natural language embodies, in its grammar, a theory of human experience. This is a commonsense theory evolving in daily life, and usually remains below the level of attention. A scientific theory differs from this in that it is a dedicated and partially designed semiotic subsystem which reconstrues certain aspects or components of human experience in a different way, in the course of opening them up to be observed, investigated and explained. The problems addressed by modern theories in the physical and biological sciences often involve phenomena that are far removed from the experiences of every day, like human genomes or gravitational waves; but they are still such as to permit an ultimate renewal of connection, and – what is significant here – they derive steadily and unbrokenly from the origins of modern science in the theories of Newton, Galileo and beyond. And when we examine the discourse in which these earlier theories are propounded, the grammatical continuity is very clear. When I first looked into the history of this pattern of reconstrual, I took as two of my principal sources Newton's *Opticks*, published in English in 1704, and Priestley's *History and Present State of Electricity* from the middle of the same century (published in 1767). In these texts the features that characterise the grammar of modern scientific writing in English, while they have since become much more highly elaborated, are already beginning to emerge. Here are two brief examples:

> Now those Colours argue a diverging and separation of the heterogeneous Rays from one another by means of their unequal Refractions, as in what follows will more fully appear. And, on the contrary, the permanent whiteness argues, that in like Incidences of the Rays there is no such separation of the emerging Rays, and by consequence no inequality of their whole Refractions.
>
> (Isaac Newton, *Opticks*)

> [Some authors] say that, as the dense electric fluid, surrounding two bodies negatively electrified, acts equally on all sides of those bodies, it cannot occasion their repulsion. Is not the repulsion, say they, owing rather to an accumulation of the electric fluid on the surfaces of the two bodies; which accumulation is produced by the attraction of the bodies, and the difficulty the fluid finds in entering them?
>
> (Joseph Priestley, *The History and Present State of Electricity*)

These passages already display, in an evolved form, what we have recognised above as grammatical metaphor. This looks at first sight like a loose and rather random assembly of unrelated grammatical effects. Can we make any observations that might suggest whether these writers are exploiting the metaphorical resources of the grammar in such a way as to extend the overall meaning potential – and to extend it in a way which is systematically related to the context in which this is happening, that of the development of forms of discourse for pursuing experimental science?

There seem to be two most general motifs; and they relate to the two features referred to above (p. 189) as properties specific to a semiotic that is stratified: namely, its potential for referring and its potential for expanding. In these discourses, the semiotic power of *referring* is being further exploited so as to create *technical taxonomies*: constructs of virtual objects that represent the distillation of experience (typically experience that has itself been enriched by design, in the form of experiment). The semiotic power of *expanding* – relating one process to another by a logical–semantic relation such as time – is being further exploited so as to create *chains of reasoning*: drawing conclusions from observation (often observation of experimental data) and construing a line of argument leading on from one step to the next.

Grammatically, these two discursive processes, which lead out of the daily language into an elaborated language of systematic, theory-modulated knowledge, both depend first and foremost on the same basic resource: the metaphoric transformation of a clausal into a nominal mode of construal. Put like that, this sounds a simple enough operation; but, as we have seen, it actually involves a highly complex series of cross-couplings, culminating in a kind of knight's move within the grammar: down in rank, and sideways in class and function. The two motifs we have identified – technicalising, and rationalising – exploit this grammatical potential in rather different ways; although it should be possible to show that, at a more abstract level, they are complementary aspects of an integrated semiotic process.

Appendix Text 1 taken from a modern scientific text shows both these motifs at work. The technical terms are generally obvious: there are some that have already been established, like *transport mechanisms* and *catabolic and biosynthetic pathways*; and others that are being introduced here for the first time. Since the book from which the passage is taken is a textbook, new terms are flagged: highlighted in italic type, and sometimes explicitly defined. The use of grammatical metaphor in carrying forward the argument can be seen in sequences such as . . . *until one essential nutrient in the medium falls to a very low value, approaching exhaustion. At this limiting nutrient concentration,* . . . , where the second sentence recapitulates the preceding point but in a grammatical form such that it can serve as the departure point for the next step in the reasoning. I shall draw further illustrations from this text in the later sections of this chapter.

GRAMMATICAL ENERGY: THE SEMOGENIC POWER OF NOMINALISATION

The nominal group is a powerful resource for making meaning – in English, and in many other languages besides. The main reason for its semogenic power is that it can be expanded to a more or less indefinite extent. In a historical perspective, a 'group' is an expanded word; both verbs and nouns get expanded into groups, but while the verbal group expands grammatically, with complex tenses, modalities, phases and the like (processes get elaborated on the temporal dimension), the nominal group expands lexically, by the device known as modification: one noun functions as a kind of keyword, and other words are organised around it, having different functions with respect to this head noun. For example,

one of the	last few	viable	subtropical	rainforests	in Australia
Deictic	Numerative	Epithet	Classifier	Thing	Qualifier

The semantic principle of this expansion, and its significance for discourse, is that it locates the participating entity along certain parameters ranging from the most instantial to the most systemic; in English, this appears as a movement in the pre-modifying segment of the group 'from left to right', beginning with the Deictic and ending up with the Classifier. The Deictic element is the one which locates the entity instantially, with respect to the speech situation; the Classifier locates it systemically, by subclassifying; other elements lie on the continuum in between.

The nominal group also accommodates expansion by down-ranked figures (congruently, clauses and phrases). These may be grammaticised as words and fitted in to the pre-modifying schema, as in *a four-legged animal*, where *four-legged* is Classifier; but in their (more) congruent form, as clauses or phrases, they occupy a special place in the group, as the Qualifier: *an animal with four legs* (phrase) / *having four legs* (non-finite clause) / *which has four legs* (finite clause). Such figures are often ambiguous when they occur in a pre-modifying function; contrast the following pair:

| four-legged animal | where four-legged is Classifier | [lɛgɪd] |
| long-legged animal | where long-legged is Epithet | [lɛgd] |

(Here the two are usually pronounced differently, although that is not a typical feature.) If such modifying elements are grammaticised as finite clauses, the difference between these two functions is realised as a difference in tense, provided that the process is of a certain type (material, including behavioural, rather than mental/verbal or relational); thus contrast:

our forces need low-flying aircraft: Classifier . . . which fly low
hit by a low-flying aircraft: Epithet . . . which was/is flying low

Thus the nominal group has, in its grammar, the potential for organising a large quantity of lexical material into functional configurations, in which lexical items operate either directly (as words) or indirectly (through rankshifted phrases or clauses). This potential that nominal groups have for structural expansion is clearly related to their role in the construal of experience. Congruently, nominal groups construe participants – entities that participate in processes; these are the more stable elements on the experiential scene which tend to persist through time, whereas the processes themselves are evanescent. When leaves have fallen, the leaves are still around; but the falling is no longer in sight. Two things follow. One is that participants are more likely than processes to be subcategorised – to be assigned to classes, and to carry attributes (there are more classes of leaves than classes of falling). The second is that participants are more likely than processes to function as anchorpoint for the figure in which they occur. Given a figure 'fall + leaves', we are more likely to construe it message-wise as 'as for the leaves, (they) were falling' than as 'as for the falling, it was (being done by) leaves'.

When a figure (congruently construed as a clause) is reworded, by grammatical metaphor, in a nominalised form, a considerable amount of energy is released, in terms of the two semantic potentials mentioned above: the potential for referring, and the potential for expanding – that is, for transforming the flux of experience into configurations of semiotic categories, and for building up such configurations into sequences of reasoned argument. These are spelt out more fully in the course of the next two sections.

THE PAY-OFF: (1) CATEGORISING, TAXONOMIC ORGANISATION

We have noted that the grammar, in its guise as a theory of experience, construes phenomena into classes. The primary resource for doing this is the vocabulary: a lexical item, like *bird*, constitutes an experiential category, more or less indeterminate at the edges but in explicit paradigmatic contrast with others, e.g. *reptile, fish*. The lexis also allows for taxonomising (constructing classes of classes): *swift, magpie, owl, toucan* are all classes of *bird*. The taxonomic relationship may or may not be made explicit in the word structure: in *swift, toucan* it is not, whereas in *blackbird, lyrebird* it is.

It is in the nominal group structure that this taxonomising potential is fully opened up, through the iterative character of modification. Thus, one kind of *toucan* is a *mountain toucan*; one kind of *mountain toucan* is a *greybreasted mountain toucan*; and so on. Such taxonomies are already a feature of everyday language; the semi-designed registers of technology and science simply take over the same potential and systematise its application (see Wignell, Martin and Eggins 1993, for a discussion of folk, expert and scientific taxonomies of living creatures). The prototypical form is of course the categorising of concrete objects in the perceptual world; and the organising concept is that of hyponymy, '*a* is a kind of *x*'. The grammar also allows for classes to be intersected; thus an *immature grey-breasted mountain toucan* shares the feature *immature* with a subclass of birds as a whole.

In a taxonomy of this kind, the relationship is one of generality; the superordinate category is more general than its hyponyms. It is not any more abstract: a *bird* is not more abstract than a *grey-breasted mountain toucan*. It is simply a more inclusive set. But at the same time assigning a class to a larger, more general class is a theoretical operation. If it is a feature of the everyday grammar of English that *toucan* is a hyponym of *bird*, along with other lexical items as co-hyponyms, then *bird* is a theoretical construct, in the grammar's overall theorising of experience. It has a value in people's theory of the living environment. Suppose now that this 'folk' taxonomy is reconstrued as an expert or a scientific taxonomy, the category of *bird* is likely to get more explicitly defined, in an attempt to show what is 'in' the category and what is outside it. This is a way of recognising both its *place* in the taxonomy, and its *value* as a theoretical construct. It has now become what is called a 'technical term'.

In the course of this process, the meaning may get a new name: so a *bird* becomes an *avis*. *Avis* is, of course, merely the Latin word for 'bird'. But a subtle change has taken place: it has now become a more abstract bird, a link in a chain of explanations of how species evolved. The metaphoric shift into another tongue, one which is both exotic and highly valued, symbolises the move to a higher, technical status; it is not a necessary feature of technicalisation – just relocating the term in a designed theoretical schema would suffice; but it is typical of the technicalising process in many languages, and very markedly so in scientific English.

To that extent, therefore, this new 'bird' – the *avis* – does function at a somewhat more abstract level. In becoming technicalised, it has also become condensed: it is no longer just the name of a list of members but embodies certain other semantic features besides. Hence its relationship to one particular specimen no longer appears as one of simple instantiation; when we are woken by the dawn chorus we don't say, 'Listen to those noisy aves' – or if we did, it would be as a rather self-conscious joke. The noun *avis* still retains the category meaning of a noun; but it has something else besides – some meaning that we might gloss as 'theoretical abstraction'.

But this opens up the possibility of extending the theoretical power of the grammar still further, by technicalising elements which construe phenomena of other kinds: not only things, but qualities of things, and even processes themselves. Nouns like *length* and *motion* construe 'be(ing) long' and 'mov-e/-ing' as theoretical entities. In doing so, they are exploiting a further resource which has always been part of the grammar of everyday language: that of (not merely categorising but) *trans*categorising – deriving one grammatical category from another. Specifically, they are exploiting the grammar's potential for *nominalising*: turning verbs and adjectives into nouns, as in these prototypical examples from ancient Greek:*

(1) verb: active (actor) noun
'one who/that which . . . -s'

ποιέω make: ποιητής maker
πράσσω do: πράκτωρ doer

(2) verb: passive (goal) noun
'that which is . . . -n'

be made: ποίημα thing made
be done: πρᾶγμα thing done, deed

(3) verb: middle (medium) noun
'. . . -ing' (abstract)

make: ποίησις making

do: πρᾶξις doing, action

(4) adjective: noun of quality/degree
'being . . . ; how . . . ?'

μέγας big: μέγεθος size; greatness, magnitude

βαθύς deep: βάθος depth; deepness, altitude

*The Greek forms provided the model for scientific terminology in Europe; they were translated into Latin (which was fairly close to Greek both in its grammatical structure and in its semantic organisation), and the Latin terms were subsequently borrowed into the modern European languages. In Greek and Latin transcategorisation always involved some morphological alternation; the morphology was also borrowed, so that from the late middle ages new terms were typically coined from Latin and Greek resources. (Transcategorising does not necessarily entail morphological change; in Chinese and Vietnamese, for example, words do not usually change in form when they shift from one class to another – as also in much of the Anglo-Saxon component of English.)

The nouns in 1 and 2 originate as concrete, or at least perceivable, 'things'. Type 1 is an entity, typically a person, identified as actor in, or causer of, a process; type 2 is an object coming into being as product or as outcome of a process (it may then develop a more abstract sense; e.g. πρᾶγμα coming to mean something like 'affair'). The nouns in 3 and 4, on the other hand, do not represent entities. Here some process itself 3, or else some quality 4, is being construed *as if it was* a 'thing': that is, as an ongoing, stable – and hence, in 4 measurable – phenomenon. It is these latter types, 3 and 4, that are particularly potent, because they are reconstruing the process or quality *as a kind of entity* – and hence as something *which can itself participate in other processes*.

In other words, there is no metaphor involved in 1 and 2; these are entities *defined by* processes, but they do not themselves contain any semantic feature of 'process'. However, 3 and 4 embody a semantic *junction*: 3 contains *both* the feature 'entity', which is the congruent meaning of the grammatical category 'noun', and the feature 'process', which is carried over from their original status as verbs. Likewise, 4 combine 'entity' with the feature 'quality' that is present in their adjectival form. Types 3 and 4 provided the semiotic foundation for ancient Greek science and mathematics: qualities transcategorised into vectors and units of measurement like *length, distance, straight line*; processes transcategorised into abstract, theoretical 'things' like *motion, change, growth*.

It is type 3, above all, that opens up the full semogenic potential of metaphoric nominalisation in the grammar. A process, such as 'move', is observed, generalised, and then theorised about, so that it becomes a virtual entity 'motion'; as a noun, it now has its own potential (a) for participating in other processes, as in:

> The Rays of Light, whether they be very small Bodies projected, or only Motion or Force propagated, are moved in right Lines . . .
>
> (*Opticks*, p. 268)

and (b) for being expanded into a taxonomy, such as *linear motion, orbital motion, parabolic motion, periodic motion* . . . . Semantically, *motion* realises the junction of two features, (i) that of 'process', the category meaning of the congruent form *move*, and (ii) that of 'entity' or 'thing', which is the category meaning of the class 'noun' of *motion*. This kind of semantic junction is what is meant by saying that the meaning of the term is 'condensed'. But, as Martin has shown, technicality involves more than the condensation of ideational semantic features. The term *motion* is now functioning as a theoretical abstraction, part of a metataxonomy – a theory which has its own taxonomic structure as a (semi-)designed semiotic system (see Lemke 1990, for scientific theories as semiotic systems). Martin (Halliday and Martin 1993: Chapter 9) refers to this semantic process as *distillation*. We can get a slight sense of the gradual 'distilling' effect of progressive nominalisation from a simple morphosyntactic sequence in English such as

> moves – is moving – a moving – movement – motion
> planets move – the planet is moving – a moving planet – the planet's moving – the movement of planets – planetary motion

culminating perhaps in the Greek *kinesis* (the most distilled terms in English tend to be those from Greek; cf. *ornitho-* for 'bird' at its most theoretical level).

The gradual distillation of terms such as these, in ancient Greek science (κίνησις in the original Greek will serve as example), so that they became technical abstractions, was the beginning of the evolution of scientific theory in the west. This nominalising metaphor is the principle on which all technical terminology is ultimately based. (The difference between technological and scientific discourse, in this respect [cf. discussions elsewhere in the present volume], is that, of the overall nominalising potential, technological nomenclatures depend relatively more heavily on the taxonomising and less heavily on the metaphorical; and they also develop taxonomies based on meronymy [*b* is a part of *y*] – the semantic analogy between meronymy and hyponymy, and the fact that both use the structural resources of the nominal group, explains the familiar impression we have that the smaller an object is, the longer its name is likely to be.)

The potential for creating technical language, therefore, is one aspect of the pay-off derived from metaphoric nominalisation. As Martin expresses it,

> Technical language both *compacts* and *changes the nature of* everyday words . . . For the biologist [marsupials] are warm-blooded mammals that give birth to live young with no placental attachment and carry the young in a pouch until they are weaned; and they contrast with the two other groups of mammals, monotremes (egg-laying) and placentals.
>
> (Martin 1992: 172)

This kind of distillation is a necessary resource for theory building. At the same time, there is another aspect of the pay-off which we become aware of in the unfolding of the discourse itself; this is now taken up in the following section.

THE PAY-OFF: (2) REASONING, LOGICAL PROGRESSION

The features discussed in the last section (creating technical language by categorising, taxonomising and distilling) depend on the *ideational* resources of the nominal group – its potential for expanding through an iterative pattern of modification. They also depend on the *systemic* effect of these resources – the terms created are not transient constructs that serve for one moment of discourse and then disappear. They become part of a sub-system within the overall semantic space that constitutes the experiential domain of the grammar.

But technicality by itself would be of little value unless accompanied by a discourse of reasoning: constructing a flow of argument based, in its prototypical form in experimental science, on observation and logical progression. Here is another example from Newton's *Opticks*:

> If the Humours of the Eye by old Age decay, so as by shrinking to make the Cornea and Coat of the Cystalline Humour grow flatter than before, the Light will not be refracted enough, and for want of a sufficient Refraction will not converge to the bottom of the Eye but to

some place beyond it, and by consequence paint in the bottom of the Eye a confused Picture, and according to the Indistinctness of this Picture the Object will appear confused. This is the reason of the decay of sight in old Men, and shews why their Sight is mended by Spectacles. For those Convex glasses supply the defect of plumpness in the Eye, and by increasing the Refraction make the Rays converge sooner, so as to convene directly at the bottom of the Eye if the Glass have a due degree of convexity. And the contrary happens in short-sighted Men whose Eyes are too plump.

(pp. 15–16)

This passage contains numerous instances of reasoning from one process to another; largely in congruent form, with the processes construed clausally and the logical–semantic relations realised by conjunctions functioning as relator: *if, so as to, for, why, by*. But some of the reasoning depends on a different grammatical resource, illustrated in the following pairs of wordings:

make . . . grow flatter than before	: supply the defect of Plumpness
will not be refracted enough	: for want of a sufficient Refraction
paint . . . a confused picture	: according to the Indistinctness of this Picture

In each case, we are first told something in a clausal form; then, when it is brought in again to further the argument, it becomes nominalised, with the process or quality construed metaphorically by a noun functioning as thing: *defect (of Plumpness), (sufficient) Refraction, Indistinctness (of this Picture)* – other elements being accommodated in the nominal group as its modifiers. Compare this with a modern example:

> If electrons weren't absolutely indistinguishable, two hydrogen atoms would form a much more weakly bound molecule than they actually do. The absolute indistinguishability of the electrons in the two atoms gives rise to an 'extra' attractive force between them.
>
> (David Layzer, *Cosmogenesis*, 1990: 61)

Here the grammatical metaphor has a discursive function: it carries forward the momentum of the argument.

At the same time as construing instances of human experience the grammar also has to construe itself, by creating a flow of discourse. This is often referred to as 'information flow'; but this term – as always! – privileges the ideational meaning, whereas the discursive flow is interpersonal as well as ideational. It is as if the grammar was creating a parallel current of semiosis that interpenetrates with and provides a channel for the mapping of ideational and interpersonal meanings. The metafunctional component of the grammar that engenders this flow of discourse is the 'textual' (cf. Martin 1992, especially Chapter 6; Matthiessen 1992, 1995).

Many features contribute to the discursive flow; those that primarily concern us here are those that form part of, or are systemically associated with, the grammar of the clause – because it is there that the explicit mapping of textual and ideational meanings takes place. The two systems involved, in English, are those of theme and information. The 'theme' system is a system of the clause, where it sets up a structural pattern that we can interpret as a configuration of the functions Theme and Rheme. The 'information' system has its own distinct structural domain, the 'information unit', where it sets up a configuration of the functions Given and New. The management of these two systems is one of the factors that contributes most to the overall effectiveness of a text (Martin 1992: Chapter 6; Hasan and Fries 1995).

(1) The theme system maps the elements of the clause into a pattern of movement from a point of departure, the Theme, to a message, the Rheme. The point of departure may be a consolidation of various elements; the part that is relevant here is its experiential module, defined grammatically as that part which has some function in the transitivity of the clause (semantically, some participant, circumstance or process). This thematic structure, in English, is realised lineally – the Theme comes first; furthermore there is a stong bond between the (textual) system of theme and the (interpersonal) system of mood, such that, if the clause is declarative, then other things being equal the same element will function both as Subject and as Theme – which means that it will be a nominal of some kind, since only a nominal element can function as Subject. So *those Convex glasses*, in the clause *for those Convex glasses supply the defect of Plumpness in the Eye*, is a typical 'unmarked' Theme of this kind.

(2) The information system maps the discourse into a pattern of movement between what is already around, the Given, and what is news, the New. The 'Given' is what is being presented in the discourse as recoverable, to be taken as read; while the 'New' is what is being foregrounded for attention. This system is not directly represented in written English because it is realised by patterns of intonation and rhythm, especially the pitch contour of speech; it constructs its own domain, in the form of a 'tone group', and hence is independent of the grammatical clause – which means that the movement of 'information' (in this technical sense) can vary freely with the thematic movement. However, the two systems are associated: other things being equal, one information unit will be mapped on to one clause – and, within the information unit, the Given will precede the New, so that, in the 'unmarked' case, the Theme of a clause is located within the Given portion, and the New, that which is under focus of attention, within the Rheme. What this means is that, typically, a speaker takes as point of departure something that is (or can be presented as being) already familiar to the listener, and puts under

focus of attention something that forms part of (and is typically at the culmination of) the message.

It is this pattern of association between the information system and the thematic system which guides the readers – and the writers – of written text. Unless there is some clear indication to the contrary, the default condition will be assumed. (Such counterindication might be lexical – repetition, or synonymic echo, marking a later portion as Given; or grammatical – the predication of the Theme, as in *it was the drummer who stole the show,* marking *the drummer* as New.) The two systems together give a rhythm to the discourse, at this micro level, creating a regular pattern whereby in the unmarked case each clause moves from one peak of prominence to another – but the two prominences are of different kinds. The initial prominence, that of Theme, is the speaker/writer's angle on the message: this is the point from which I am taking off. The culminative prominence, that of New, is still of course assigned by the speaker/writer; but it carries a signal to the listener/reader: this is what you are to attend to. Of course, this underlying discursive rhythm gets modulated all the time by the other meaning-making currents that are flowing along in the grammar, as well as being perturbed by the larger-scale fluctuations – moves in dialogue, shifts of register and the like. But it provides the basic semiotic pulse, not unlike the chest pulse that gets modulated by the sound-making antics of the organs of articulation.

The discourse of experimental science depended on an ordered progression in which not just this or that single element but *any chunk of the argument* could be given prominence in the unfolding of a clause. Let us look again at the example from David Layzer (for the complete paragraph see Appendix Text 8.2). The first part of the paragraph builds up the story that in the quantum world all electrons are alike; and this motif is stated, in a congruent form, as the first step in an illustration of the principle: *if electrons weren't absolutely indistinguishable, two hydrogen atoms . . . .* The next clause is going to give the reason; so the writer recapitulates – but this time the whole figure 'electrons + indistinguishable' becomes part of a larger motif in which it is functioning simply as point of departure. Previously, this figure occupied a clause on its own; but now it becomes the Theme of another clause, which (like most clauses of written science) is declarative – hence it gets conflated, in typical fashion, with the Subject. Subjects are nominal groups, so the writer uses a nominalising metaphor: *the absolute indistinguishability of the electrons in the two atoms.* The quality 'indistinguishable' is now construed as a 'thing', *indistinguishability*; and the electrons, previously functioning as Carrier in a Carrier + Attribute clause structure, now appear inside this nominal group, as a postmodifying element *of the electrons.*

Most noticeably it is the Theme that is metaphorised in this way: the writer carries the argument forward by 'packaging' some semantic construct from the discourse to serve as point of departure for a further step. As already noted, there is a strong association between Theme and Given; so such packages are typically condensations of material that has gone before. This may be material that has extended over a long and complex sequence of preceding argument (it is of course impossible to illustrate this without citing large passages of text). It is important to reiterate, however, that the Theme may not be informationally Given; and in discourse such as that of written science, where the Given/Theme conflation is powerful and highly favoured, considerable effect may be achieved by departing from it. And conversely, considerable confusion may be brought about when such departure is unmotivated and unannounced (cf. Halliday and Martin 1993: Chapter 4).

But there is also a tendency – a kind of secondary discursive motif – whereby such nominalised packages occur in culminative position in the clause, where they are Rheme not Theme and hence in strong association with the New. Fries (1992, 1995) refers to this conflation as the 'N-Rheme'; this is an important concept for written text because it embodies the culminative principle – that the way the writer ensures that something is read as New is by making it (a part of) the Rheme of a ranking clause. If we look again at the Layzer text: the N-Rheme [*gives rise to*] *an 'extra' attractive force between them* is also a metaphoric nominalization, in this case one based on an established technical term, *force.* This is locally New – it is what is called to the reader's attention *in this particular clause;* but it also picks up on what the reader has just been told (it does not add any new content; but it moves up to a higher level of abstraction, expressing 'would otherwise be more weakly bound' in more theoretical terms – compare in this connection, from another source, the clause *solid particles are held together by the strong attraction between them,* where by simply rewording the congruent form of the process as a metaphoric variant in the N-Rheme the writer establishes 'are held together' as a construct within the theory). The first passage cited from Newton (p. 194) also contains a metaphoric nominalisation as N-Rheme: [*those colours argue*] *a diverging and separation of the heterogeneous Rays from one another by means of their unequal Refractions,* where 'diverge' and 'separate' are nominalised for the occasion and contrast with *there is no such separation . . . and by consequence no inequality of their . . . Refractions* in the succeeding sentence.

The complex interplay of Theme + Rheme in the clause with Given + New in the information unit constitutes an immensely powerful discursive resource; it is the primary source of energy for the dynamic of scientific and technical argument. The reason it works so powerfully is that it is a structure of the clause: a configuration embodying the system of transitivity, which is the grammar's theory of *process.* But because it is a clause, the parts which are configured in it are bound to be elements of clause structure; and the defining elements of clause structure are groups and phrases. It is possible to incorporate unreconstructed clauses by means of rank shift. But, as we saw, the nominal group has the potential for expanding to include all the elements of the (congruent) clause (and the noun, likewise, has the potential for transcategorising processes and qualities); moreover, unlike a rankshifted clause, a nominal group moves freely within the textual systems of theme and information. This is the pay-off of these nominalising metaphors in the instantial context of the discourse.

UNPACKING THE METAPHORS: THE 'FAVOURITE CLAUSE TYPE'

Let me stay with the Layzer example for one further step. (We should however be aware of the problem of exemplification in a discussion of grammar: in a semiotic system, every instance is unique, with its own particularities, so that any one instance is an example only in respect of certain specific features.) We can 'unpack' the metaphors in the clause in question and produce a more congruent rewording such as the following:

> Because the electrons in the two atoms are absolutely indistinguish-able, they attract each other 'extra' strongly.

We now have a clause nexus consisting of two clauses in a hypotactic interdependency. The relationship to the semantics is congruent both in rank and in status; compare Figure 8.3 above. (The grammar puts the relator inside one of the figures, as a conjunction at the beginning of the clause.)

In the metaphoric version, that in the original text, each figure has been nominalised – reworded in the form of wording that congruently construes 'things', with nouns for the quality (*indistinguishability*) and the process (*attraction*). But things do not stand up in the grammar by themselves; they gain entry only as participants, by virtue of being configured with some process. The 'process' here is *gives rise to*. This, however, is the outcome of another metaphoric transformation, whereby the relator (the logical–semantic relationship *between* the two processes, congruently construed as a conjunction [or cohesive conjunctive; cf. Halliday and Hasan 1976: Chapter 5]) is metaphorised as a verbal group, the form of wording that congruently construes a process. The effect is the same as in the contrived example of the bus driver: *the driver's overrapid downhill driving of the bus resulted in brake failure.*

This combination of metaphoric features is what we can regard as the 'favourite clause type' of English scientific writing. It is a fuzzy type; but we could perhaps characterise it as follows:

semantic:	sequence of two figures, linked by a logical–semantic relation

grammatical

[congruent]: nexus of two clauses, with Relator/conjunction in secondary clause (optionally also in primary clause)

[metaphoric]: one clause, 'relational: identifying/intensive, circum-stantial or possessive', of three elements:

Identified   + Process   + Identifier
nominal group   verbal group   nominal group

There are variant forms (1) with 'relational: attribu-tive' process, where the second nominal group may have adjective as Head; (2) with 'relational: existen-tial' process, with one nominal group only. These have slightly different semantic profiles. The second nominal group (if present) may be inside a preposi-tional phrase.

All examples given above on pp. 193–4 are of the canonical type. Examples of the variant types are: (1) *the indistinguishability of electrons is also responsible for the structure of the periodic table*; *a total head range of less than 10 m was inadequate to account for this variation*; (2) *the phylloxera resistance collapsed*; *rapid bonding occurs*; *viability exists*.

In saying that these are the 'favourite clause type', I am not asserting that they are the most frequent (there would be no sensible way of estimating this; at the least, they are certainly very common). But they are the most critical in the semantic load that they carry in developing scientific argument. What is interesting about them is that their clause structure is extremely simple: typically one nominal group plus one verbal group plus a second nominal group or else a prepositional phrase. But packed into this structure there may be a very high density of lexical matter; again, compare the examples cited in the earlier section (pp. 193–4), which have up to thirteen lexical words within this single clause. (The average lexical density for spontaneous spoken English barely exceeds two lexical words per clause.) If the agnate, more congruent variant is always just one nexus of two clauses, then the lexical density will be simply halved. Often, however, the 'favourite' has gone through more than one cycle of metaphoric transformation, and the most plausible 'congruent' rewording will have three, four or even more clauses in it.

It is clear from all the examples that a great deal more is happening at the rank of the word than simply construing processes and qualities as nouns. We need to look more systematically at grammatical metaphor considered as a stratal phenomenon – that is, as the exploiting of the 'play' that arises at the interfacing of the grammar and the semantics;

and to ask what metaphoric processes actually take place there. We noted above (p. 192) that grammatical metaphor involves a complex move, both 'down' in rank and 'across' in status (function/class). We have not yet examined the possible range of metaphoric cross-couplings in status. The question that arises is: do all the logically possible shifts take place? Or are only certain of those that are possible in principle actually taken up?

TYPES OF GRAMMATICAL METAPHORS

Let me first return to the congruent pattern – noting that 'congruent' means that pattern of relationships between the semantics and the grammar in which the two strata initially co-evolved (I come to the evidence for this in the next section). I shall arrange the entries in a different order from that in which they were given previously; and – since we are now looking at processes taking place at word rank – I will express the grammatical realisation as a class of word. The categories, as always, are those of English.

Congruence of status (semantic functions with word classes):

semantic function	[construed by]	*grammatical class*
relator (in sequence)		conjunction
minor process (in circumstance)		preposition
process		verb
quality		adjectkve
entity ('thing')		noun

Table 8.1 shows the types of grammatical metaphor that I have found in investigating scientific discourse. I am sure that the list is not exhaustive; but it includes those that I have identified in the course of analysing instances that seemed to me significant in the unfolding of the text. The entries are classified according to the following design:

shift in semantic type	shift in grammatical class
shift in grammatical function	example(s)

(not shown in Table 8.1)

For example, the metaphoric transformation of *unstable* to *instability* would represent a shift from 'construed as quality' to 'construed as entity', from 'adjective' to 'noun' and from the typical function (here, in the nominal group) of Epithet to that of Thing. A text example illustrating this pattern was: *diamond is kinetically unstable . . . the kinetic instability of diamond leads to . . . .*

It seems that not all possible metaphoric moves actually occur; the

Table 8.1 Types of grammatical metaphor

#	semantic type congruent	metaphorical	class shift	example
1	quality	entity	adjective – noun	unstable – instability
2i	process	entity	verb – noun	transform – transformation
2ii	aspect of phase of process		tense/phase verb (adverb) – noun	going to/try – prospect/attempt
2iii	modality of process		modality verb (adverb) – noun	can, could – possibility; potential
3	circumstance	[minor process] entity	preposition – noun	with – accompaniment
4	relator	entity	conjunction – noun	so – cause, proof; if – conditions
5i	process	quality	verb – adjective	[poverty] is increasing – increasing [poverty]
5ii	aspect or phase of process		tense/phase verb (adverb) – adjective	begin – initial
5iii	modality of process		modality of verb (adverb) – adjective	[always] will – constant
6i	circumstance	manner quality	adverb – adjective	[acted] brilliantly – brilliant [acting]

Table 8.1 (continued)

#	congruent semantic type	metaphorical	class shift	example
6ii	time, place etc.	quality	prepositional phrase – adjective	[argued] for a long time – lengthy [argument]
6iii	"	(class)	prep. phase – noun premodifier	[cracks] on the surface – surface [cracks]
7	relator	quality	conjunction – adjective	before – previous
8	circumstance	process	be/go + preposition – verb	be about – concern; be instead of – replace
9	relator	process	conjunction – verb	and – complement; then – follow; so – lead to
10	relator	circumstance	conjunction – prepositional (phrase)	when – in times of; so – as a result
11	0	entity	0 – noun	[x] – the fact of [x]
12	0	process	0 – verb	[x] – [x] occurs
13	entity	modifier (of entity)	noun – [various]	engine [fails] – engine [failure]; glass [fractures] – [the fracture] of glass; cabinet [decided] – government's [decision]

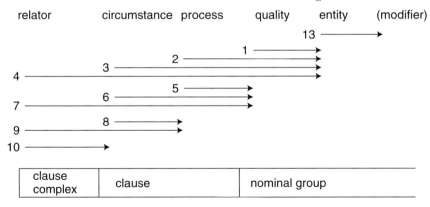

Figure 8.5 The 'general drift' of grammatical metaphor

ones that do occur can be summarised as in Figure 8.5, where they are set out in terms of semantic function. Figure 8.5 shows that it is possible to order the semantic functions from left to right in such a way that (i) all possible moves to the right can occur, but (ii) no move can take place to the left. The ordering is:

relator → circumstance → process → quality → entity

What this means is that (1) any semantic element can be construed as if it was an entity (i.e., grammaticised as a noun); (2) a relator, a circumstance or a process can be construed as if it was a quality (i.e., grammaticised as an adjective); (3) a relator or a circumstance can be construed as if it was a process (i.e., grammaticised as a verb); (4) a relator can be construed as if it was a (minor process within a) circumstance (i.e., grammaticised as a preposition, in a prepositional phrase). But not the other way round: entities cannot be construed as if they were processes; and so on.[1]

Here, therefore, we can recognise what we might call a general drift: this is the drift towards 'thinginess'. The direction of metaphor is a move towards the concrete – with nouns, typically the names of *participants* (concrete objects, animals and persons) as the terminal point. The noun is the most metaphorically attractive category: everything else can end up as a noun. This drift towards the concrete is, of course, exactly what one finds to be a feature of metaphor in its traditional, lexicalised sense.

We can now see the close relationship between the two aspects of the metaphorical process: the shift in rank, and the shift in status. Let us try to show these two things happening together; in order to do this, however, we shall have to focus on one single semantic element at a time – otherwise there will be too much happening at once. The figures in the left hand column refer to the numbering in Figure 8.5. I will present two examples: one of the relator 'therefore', the other of the process 'grow, become greater', each of them shifting step by step towards the metaphoric status of a noun.

Example 1: relator 'therefore'. Congruent rank: clause complex; congruent status: conjunction

move in status	move in rank	example
– relator: conjunction	clause nexus	(*a* happened) so (*x* happened)
10 (minor process in) circumstance: preposition	clause	(*x* happened) as a result of (happening *a*)
9 process: verb	clause	(happening *x*) resulted from (happening *a*)
7 quality: adjective	nominal group	the resultant (happening of *x*) . . .
4 entity: noun	nominal group	the result (of happening *a*) . . .

Example 2: process 'grow'. Congruent rank: clause; congruent status: verb

move in status	move in rank	example
– process: verb	clause	(poverty) is increasing
5 quality: adjective	nominal group	increasing (poverty)
2 entity: noun	nominal group	the increase (in poverty)

There is one apparent exception to the drift towards the concrete: this is what I have recognised as type 13, where participants are metaphorised from being nominal groups to being modifiers inside other nominal groups: for example *the driver's driving of the bus*, where the driver has become a possessive Deictic and the bus is inside a prepositional phrase functioning as Qualifier. Two things may be noticed about these. One is that they do not occur alone; they occur only in combination with other metaphorical shifts – whereas others can occur by themselves; e.g. 5(ii) *possible* in *possible enemies* '(creatures) that may be enemies', or perhaps 'enemies that may be around'. The other is that the Thing (the main noun) of the nominal group in which they occur is always itself a metaphoric entity – a transformed quality or process. When the process has been nominalised, the grammar still has to incorporate somehow the displaced participants and circumstances from the congruent figure. If 'failed' in 'brakes + failed' becomes *failure*, what happens to the 'brakes'? The controlling metaphor is that of process to entity; the others are carried along with it, so that the 'brakes' take over some modifying function in the nominal group: Range (in Qualifier), *failure of the brakes*; possessive Deictic, *the brakes' failure*; or, as in the original example, Classifier: *brake failure*. In other words, these 'entities' become expansions of the new nominalised entity. The grammar is exploiting the potential of the nominal group to give functional status to the participating entities (as they would be) in the congruent clause. Thus:

[congruent]				
the cat's	old	wicker	basket	for sleeping in in winter
Deictic	*Epithet*	*Classifier*	*Thing*	*Qualifier*
the driver's	overrapid	downhill	driving	of the bus
the	natural	buffering	capacity	of the agricultural soils
Griffith's		energy balance	approach	to strength and fracture
[metaphoric]				

One question that arises with these secondary metaphors, if they do occur as the structural consequence of the controlling metaphor of nominalisation (rather than as metaphors in their own right), is whether they also entail semantic junction: do they also acquire the congruent semantic features of the categories into which they have shifted? Are *engine failure, heart failure, crop failure, power failure, brake failure* classes of a 'thing' called *failure?* We may note that (since a stratified system has so much play in it) the grammar tends to become playful at this point; given the metaphoric progression

the president decreed → the president's decree → the presidential decree

we construct, by analogy,

the president's pyjamas → the presidential pyjamas

– where the humorous effect of *the presidential pyjamas* shows that there is an anomaly between the function Classifier and the lexical collocation of *president* with *pyjamas*. If *presidential* is not a class of *pyjamas*, this suggests that *engine, heart, crop, power, brake* are not classes of *failure*; an *energy balance approach* is not a class of *approaches*, and so on. It seems that these should be explained as secondary effects, consequential on another metaphoric movement, and that for this reason they do not undergo semantic junction.

SYNDROMES OF GRAMMATICAL METAPHOR

Lexical metaphor usually presents itself as a simple opposition between two terms; for example, *fruit/result*, where a more concrete, metaphorical expression, *the fruit(s) of their efforts*, contrasts with a more abstract, 'literal' expression, *the result(s) of their efforts*. If, as sometimes happens, we are able to set up longer chains this is because they embody a piece of semiotic history in which a metaphor has 'died' and a new one has taken over.

In grammatical metaphor, where the shift is not from one lexical item to another but from one grammatical category to another, the situation becomes more complex. As Figure 8.5 brings out, there may be more than one degree of metaphoric displacement; so if, to take the most extreme case (namely type 4), a relator is construed grammatically as a noun, there may well be a number of intermediate steps, as suggested by the example of 'therefore' in the previous section (p. 212). In any given instance not all of the intermediate manifestations may be plausible; but typically at least some of them are, so that in 'unpacking' a highly complex metaphor we have to choose how far to go. To follow up one of the earlier examples,

fire intensity has a profound effect on smoke injection,

we might unpack the metaphor in the word *effect* in any of the following ways (proceeding step by step towards the congruent):

the intensity of a fire profoundly affects (2) the injection of smoke according to (3) the intensity of a fire more or less smoke is injected as (4) a fire grows more intense, so (4) more smoke is injected

Again, figures in parentheses refer to the types of metaphoric shift set out in Figure 8.5: thus, if the verb *affects* was to be taken as the congruent form (that is, if the semantic element was being interpreted as 'process') the metaphoric shift whereby it appears as a noun *effect* would be one of type 2. If on the other hand we interpret it semantically as a relation between processes, congruently construed as a conjunction *as* (. . . *so*), then the metaphoric shift to the noun *effect* is of type 4.

But since the metaphoric process is taking place in the grammar, any transformation is likely to reverberate throughout the clause, and may affect an entire clause nexus. Almost inevitably one displacement in rank and status will involve a number of others. So grammatical metaphors tend to occur in *syndromes*: clusters of interrelated transformations that reconfigure the grammatical structure as a whole. The limiting case of such a syndrome is that which was discussed in the previous section in explaining the maverick type 13, whereby a noun is driven out of its functional role as a participant (congruently, as Thing in a nominal group) by a controlling metaphor of type 1 or 2; for example (from sentences cited on pp. 193–4):

the child's capacity . . .   (the child is able to . . .)
    13   2(ii)
the burning of coal   (coal was burnt)
    2(i)   13
the indistinguishability of the electrons   (the electrons are
        1   13   indistinguishable)
the American species' resistance to phylloxera (the American species
        13   2(i)   13   resisted phylloxera)

In other syndromes, however, while a cluster of metaphors is clearly functioning in association, there is no single controlling type and each one could in principle occur alone.

Below is a paragraph of text with the instances of grammatical metaphor marked according to the same notation.

Even though the fracture of glass can be a dramatic event, many
             2.i   13   11
failures are preceded by the slow extension of preexisting cracks. A
   2.i   9   6.i   2.i   13   7 or 5.i
good example of a slowly spreading crack is often found in the wind-
                              5.i   12
shield of an automobile. The extension of a small crack, which may
                              2.i
have started from the impact of a stone, can be followed day by day as
             2.i   13
the crack gradually propagates across the entire windshield. In other

cases small, unnoticed surface cracks can grow during an incubation
             5.i   6.iii   2.i   13
period and cause a catastrophic failure when they reach a critical size.
             9   6.ii   2.i   8   1
Cracks in glass can grow at speeds of less than one trillionth of an inch
                                              1
per hour, and under these conditions the incubation period can span
                              4   2.i   13
several years before the catastrophic failure is observed. On an atomic
   8   6.ii   2.i   12
scale the slow growth of cracks corresponds to the sequential rupturing
       6.i   2.i   13   9   6.ii   2.i
of interatomic bonds at rates as low as one bond rupture per hour. The
13   6.iii   1   13   2.i
wide range of rates over which glass can fracture – varying by 12
       3   1
orders of magnitude (factors of 10) from the fastest shatter to the
       1   6.i   2.i
slowest creep – makes the investigation of crack growth a particularly
   6.i   2.i   9   2.i   13   2.i
engaging enterprise.
   5.i   11

(from Terry A. Michalske and Bruce C. Bunker, 'The
fracturing of glass', *Scientific American*, December 1987)

In analysing this passage I have interpreted the elements 'crack' and
'bond' as theoretical entities, and hence considered their wording as
nouns to be congruent. If we treat 'crack' and 'bond' as processes, this
will necessitate further unpacking; the difference between these two
interpretations may be illustrated by reference to one sentence which
happens to contain both these terms. The analysis given above corresponds to a congruent version as follows:

The slow growth of cracks corresponds to the sequential rupturing of
[6.i   2.i   13]   9   [6.ii   2.i   13
interatomic bonds at rates as low as one bond rupture per hour.
      6.iii]   1   [13   2.i]
Cracks grow slowly – as slowly as when the bonds between the atoms
rupture one after another only once an hour.

If 'bond' and 'crack' are treated as metaphoric, the analysis, together
with the corresponding congruent rewording, will be as the following:

The slow growth of cracks corresponds to the sequential rupturing of
[6.i   2.i   13   2.i]   9   [6.ii   2.i   13
interatomic bonds at rates as low as one bond rupture per hour.
      6.iii   2.i]   1   [2.i   13   2.i]
Glass cracks slowly – as slowly as when one atom stops being bonded
to another atom only once every hour.

As is to be expected, given that grammatical metaphor involves two
distinct moves in rank (clause nexus to clause; clause to group), the 'syndromes' of metaphoric features fall into two groups along these same lines:

(a) Lower rank syndromes: figures reconstrued as if elements
    [A figure, congruently construed as a clause, is instead reworded as a
    nominal group, which congruently construes an element]
(b) Higher rank syndromes: sequences reconstrued as if figures
    [A sequence, congruently construed as a clause nexus, is instead
    reworded as a clause, which congruently construes a figure]

I will look briefly at each of these in turn.

(a) Lower rank syndromes: figures reconstrued as if elements. These
are the clusters of features that co-occur in metaphoric nominal groups
(the 'limiting case' of type 13, discussed earlier (p. 212), fall within this
group). Here the key metaphors are the nominalisations of qualities (type
1) and processes (type 2); these are then accompanied by transformations
of other elements of the figure, either participants (which are already
realised as nouns, but change their *function* from Thing to Deictic,
Epithet, Classifier or [part of] Qualifier; hence type 13) or circumstances
(type 6). Examples:

indistinguishability of electrons   (electrons are indistinguishable)
          1   13
fire intensity   (how intense fire is)
13   1
the fracture of glass   (glass fractures)
        2.i   13
Griffith's approach to . . .   (Griffith approached . . .)
      13   2.i

slow extension   (extend slowly)
  6.i   2.i

Any given nominal group may of course contain a number of these together:

the sequential rupturing of interatomic bonds
      6.ii   2.i   13 6.iii
              (the bonds between atoms rupture one after another)

the importance of surface chemistry in the mechanical behaviour of
      1   13 6.iii   6.iii   2.1   13
brittle materials
                (that the chemistry of the surface is important in
           relation to how brittle materials behave mechanically)

And metaphors of other types may also be involved in these lower rank syndromes:

increased responsiveness (. . . becomes more responsive)
    5.i   1
feeding behaviour[2]   (how . . . feed)
    5.i   11
the slow extension of preexisting cracks
    6.i   2.i   13   5.i
             (cracks which existed before slowly extend)

a consequence of the differing contributions of . . .
    7   6.i   2.i
          (because . . . contribute different[ial]ly)

(b) Higher rank syndromes: sequences reconstrued as if figures. These were referred to earlier, with illustration from the intemperate bus driver: where a semantic *figure* (congruently construed as a grammatical *clause*) is reconstrued in the grammar as a *group* (which congruently construes a semantic *element*), the *clause* now comes to construe a *sequence*. See Figure 8.6.

In characterising type b in these terms, I am not suggesting that either

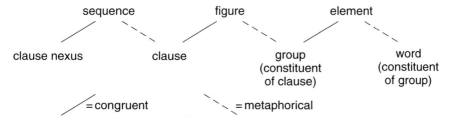

Figure 8.6   Reconstrual of semantic units by grammatical metaphor

metaphoric movement *causes* the other. In terms of the discussion on pp. 197–206, the lower rank movement (figure as group, and element as constituent of group: type a syndromes) is more directly associated with taxonomic categorising, while the higher rank movement (sequence as clause, and figure as constituent of clause: type b syndromes) is more directly associated with logical reasoning. But the metaphoric grammar hangs together as a whole, and there is no reason, either logical or historical, for supposing that any one component is driven by any other.

The grammatical manifestation of this unity of the metaphoric process is what I referred to earlier as the 'favourite clause type' of scientific English, which consists of two nominalised processes or qualities (each one a nominal group) joined by a verbalised relator (a verbal group), illustrated in all the examples set out in the earlier discussion (pp. 193–4). The higher rank syndrome in question can be generalised as [1/2] + 9 + [1/2], where [1], [2] stand for any possible syndrome of type a; for example,

increased responsiveness may be reflected in feeding behaviour
          [1]   9   [2]
this breeding effort was anchored in the American species' resistance . . .
          [2]   9   [2]
the rate of glass crack growth depends on the magnitude of the applied
          [1]   9   [1]
stress

There is then a secondary type b syndrome in which there is only one process, likewise nominalised, and the verbal group simply indicates that it happens, or does not happen; for example,

rapid bonding occurs   (. . . bond rapidly)
     [2]   12
a difference in osmotic pressure exists (osmotic pressure differs)
          [1]   12
the phylloxera resistance collapsed   (. . . ceased to resist
          [2]   12   phylloxera)

I shall not attempt to enumerate further specific types of metaphoric syndrome here. The text included as Appendix Text 2 offers an excellent example of scientific writing, containing instances of all the categories given in Table 8.1. Two points remain to be noted. One is that the grammar, in its metaphoric potential, typically accommodates a series of steps intermediate between the most congruent and the most metaphorical. I can perhaps best illustrate this by constructing a paradigm of agnate forms on the basis of a text example:

increases of osmolarity cause rapid excretion of putrescine

1 Osmoslarity increases, so putrescine is rapidly excreted.
(clause nexus: paratactic)

2 Because osmolarity increases, putrescine is rapidly excreted.
(clause nexus: hypotactic)

3 That osmolarity increases has the effect that putrescine is rapidly excreted.
(clause: two rankshifted clauses, finite)

4 Osmolarity increasing leads to putrescine being rapidly excreted.
(clause: two rankshifted clauses, non-finite)

5 Increasing of osmolarity causes rapid excreting of putrescine.
(clause: two nominal groups, verb as Head)

6 Increase of osmolarity causes rapid excretion of putrescine.
(clause: two nominal groups, mass noun as Head)

7 Increases of osmolarity cause rapid excretions of putrescine.
(clause: two nominal groups, count noun as Head)

Starting from a rather congruent form of wording I have kept the two processes at more or less the same degree of metaphoricity; in real texts, of course, they will often diverge – compare the clause that concludes the immediately following sentence:

> ionic strength is maintained approximately constant as a result of the excretion of putrescine.

The other point to bring out is that, while I have illustrated this 'favourite' syndrome with the generalised category of cause, there are other categories of conjunctive relationship that appear as the verbal element in clauses of this type. Perhaps the most widely encountered are:

complex causal (e.g. *prevent, increase*)
temporal (e.g. *follow*)
identifying (e.g. *be, constitute*)
symbolising (e.g. *signal, mark*)
projecting, 'cause to know/think' (e.g. *prove, suggest*)
additive (e.g. *complement, accompany*)

I will give a very brief sketch of these, together with examples.
    In the 'complex causal', the relator 'cause' is fused with some other semantic feature, typically 'negative' ('cause not to') or some quantity or quality ('cause to become more, stronger', etc.):

> the presence in the medium of the amino acid proline dramatically increases a bacterium's ability to grow in a medium of high osmotic strength

> movement of the solute across the membrane can be prevented by applying a certain hydrostatic pressure to the solution

osmotic tolerance . . . is accomplished in bacteria by an adjustment of the internal osmolarity

The 'temporal' relationship construes the two processes as being related in time:

many failures are preceded by the slow extension of existing cracks

In the 'identifying' and 'symbolising' types, some Token + Value relationship is set up between the two parts; for example:

the most efficient energy-producing mechanism is respiration

the growth of attachment between infant and mother signals the first step in the child's capacity to discriminate amongst people

the ionic strength of a solution is defined by the equation . . .

the slow growth of cracks corresponds to the sequential rupturing of interatomic bonds at rates as low as one bond rupture per hour

In some instances, taken by themselves, there can be ambiguity between the senses of 'symbolising' and 'causing':

increased responsiveness may be reflected in feeding behaviour

– where it is left open whether the feeding behaviour is sign or effect. The 'projecting' relationship is exemplified by:

Griffith's energy balance approach to strength and fracture also suggested the importance of surface chemistry in the mechanical behaviour of brittle materials

relative osmotic tolerance can be deduced from their relative K^+ contents

Here the prototypical sense is not cause but proof: not 'because *a* happens, *x* happens', but 'because *b* happens, I know that *y* happens' – the intersection of causing and symbolising. Finally, the 'additive' are those which simply conjoin two figures in a relationship of 'and', or sometimes 'but'; e.g.

the theoretical program of devising models of atomic nuclei has been complemented by experimental investigations

the induction of mutations by causing base-pair transitions is to be contrasted with the mechanism of induction of mutations by certain acridine dyes

the inheritance of specific genes is correlated with the inheritance of a specific chromosome

These syndromes of higher and lower rank constitute the syntagmatic dimension of grammatical metaphor. They are of course represented in the description of the grammar as structural configurations in their own right; in presenting them as 'syndromes' I am emphasising their metaphoric status – the fact that they arise from a cross-coupling between the semantics and the grammar, and are significant because, taken as a whole, they manifest a reconstrual of the experiential world.

THE DISTILLATION OF TECHNICAL MEANING

In trying to understand how, and why, this reconstrual has taken place, I have postulated two distinct metafunctional environments for grammatical metaphor: one textual – creating reasoned argument through managing the information flow of the discourse; the other ideational – creating ordered taxonomies of abstract technical constructs. I used different, though overlapping, (lexical) metaphors for the two: packaging and compacting for the former, and (following Martin) condensing and distilling for the latter. It is helpful, I think, to recognise these as two distinct contexts for grammatical metaphor, if only because in any given text instance either factor may be present without the other. Thus, many of the wordings that are textually motivated, like *the indistinguishability of the electrons* (following *all electrons . . . are indistinguishable*), *movement of the solvent across the membrane* (following *the solvent tends to be drawn through the membrane into the solution*) (and compare Newton's *the permanent whiteness*, which follows *continues ever after to be white*), are not, and do not become, technical terms. They are and remain *instantial* constructs, created for the immediate requirements of the discourse (typically, functioning as Theme, or else as focus of New information). Thus they can always be 'unpacked' – reworded in a more congruent form. Likewise, many occurrences of the terms with a technical status have no motivation in the particular discursive environment; they may be occurring in titles, headings, abstracts, definitions and so on. These are *systemic* constructs, created for the long-term requirements of the theory; and they *cannot be unpacked* – there is no agnate rewording in a more congruent form. So there seem to be two independent factors at work leading to grammatical metaphor: one textual and instantial, the other ideational and systemic.

But they are not, in fact, as separate as they seem. If we view the discourse of science in the longer term, we can observe the instantial *becoming* the systemic. Technical terms are not, as a rule, created outright, in isolation from the discourse; they emerge discursively, as the 'macrotext' of the discipline unfolds. In this respect they are just one manifestation of the general phenomenon whereby instantial effects flow through into the system – because there is no disjunction between system and instance: what we call the 'system' of language is simply the potential that evolves over time. Thus any wording that is introduced discursively as a resource for reasoning *may* gradually become *distilled*; and in the course of this distillation out of successive instances of its occurrence, it becomes a new 'thing', a virtual entity that exists as part of a theory. It now 'stands to reason' as a part of our reconstrued experience; it can enter into figures, as a participant; and, as already remarked, it can no longer be unpacked. As a metaphor, it is 'dead' – because it has taken on a new, non-metaphoric life of its own.

Since this process – the instantial becoming systemic, compacting turning into distilling, the semantic junction of the two grammatical categories – typically takes place over a long period of text time, it is impossible to illustrate it adequately in a short chapter. But writers of scientific textbooks often recapitulate the process as a way of introducing technical terms to the learners; so it is possible to gain some impression of it from an extract such as that in Appendix Text 1: for example, the build-up of the term *osmotic tolerance*:

> some halophiles . . . can tolerate high concentrations of salt

> the tolerance of high osmolarity

> Osmotic Tolerance. Osmotic tolerance – the ability of an organism to grow in media with widely varying osmolarities – is accomplished in bacteria by an adjustment of the internal osmolarity

Compare the lead-up to *'redox' potential* (which is likewise first introduced as the heading) in the *New Scientist* text reproduced as Appendix Text 3. Compare also Appendix Text 2, where we might speculate whether (*electron*) *indistinguishability* could be taking the first steps towards becoming a technical term.

All these processes take place in real time – but in different dimensions of time. I shall distinguish logogenetic, phylogenetic and ontogenetic time. Logogenetic time is the time of unfolding of the text: the history of the *instance*. I have cited elsewhere the gradual building up of the technical concept of *glass fracture growth rate* in the text on 'The Fracture of Glass' (Halliday 1995). Martin and his colleagues have documented the construal of technicality in the context of science textbooks (see e.g. Halliday and Martin 1993: Part 2).

Phylogenetic time is the time of evolution of the language, in the particular registers in question (e.g. 'scientific English'): the history of the *system*. In the metaphoric processes taking place in the grammar, these two histories intersect; and it is this that enables us to speak about the ordered relationship between the metaphorical and the congruent. Taken out of time, each of a pair of expressions such as

> the solvent tends to be drawn through the membrane

> movement of the solvent across the membrane

is metaphoric with respect to the other; there is no way of identifying one or other as 'congruent' (cf. the bus driver example on pp. 190–1). As soon as we view them historically, however, the picture changes: both instantially and systemically the clausal mode precedes the nominal one. It is this that explains our 'intuitive' sense of congruence. Experience is first construed clausally, and only later is it reconstrued in nominalised form. (Once again there is a parallel with metaphor in its traditional, lexical guise.)

What of the third dimension of history – ontogenetic time? Ontogenetic time is the time of growth and maturation of the user of the language: the history of every human child. And here again the picture is the same: children first construe experience in the clausal form, in the grammar of daily life. For them the nominalising grammar of scientific discourse demands a massive act of reconstruction, one of the major barriers to the technical, discipline-based knowledge of secondary education.

ONTOGENETIC NOTES

Clare Painter says of young children's speech that 'meaning and lexical class are congruent with one another' [Painter 1993: 112]. What this means is that, when children first move from their infant protolanguage into the mother tongue, they build up their picture of the world according to the same principles on which the grammar itself evolved. Painter adds that 'control of experiential grammatical metaphor is a late development' (1993: 111).

The protolanguage has no grammar: there is no stratification of the content plane into a lexicogrammar and a semantics (Halliday 1975, Painter 1984). Hence it has no possibility of metaphor, which depends on cross-coupling between the two strata – decoupling, and then recoupling in a different fashion. What distinguishes *language*, in its prototypical sense (that is, post-infancy human language), from infant protolanguage is precisely that it is stratified in this way. We can observe the effect of this early in life when children start constructing discourse; here are two clear examples:

Hal [age 1;8, watching seagulls eating]: breàd; eàt; birdies.

Nigel [age 1;7, seeing a cat run into a house]: blā' miào; rān doòr.

In each case the child in question is able to form a semantic figure but is not yet able to construe it as a grammatical clause. The semantics runs ahead of the grammar – and it stays ahead throughout our lives. Semantically, we can construe a whole book as a single text, whereas grammatically we can create structure only up to the rank of the clause complex, or at most perhaps to something like a paragraph.

But for those units which do fall within the compass of the grammar, as long as the coupling of semantics to grammar remained congruent it would not matter whether we labelled the categories in grammatical or in semantic terms: either (1) semantic or (2) grammatical representations would suffice (see Figure 8.7). It is only when cross-coupling begins that we cannot avoid theorising both semantic and lexicogrammatical patterns and keeping them terminologically apart. Painter describes a child's early attempts to come to terms with this cross-coupling, with examples such as:

Stephen [4;8, whose father has said that the hired car can't go as fast as the usual one]: I thought – I thought all cars could – all cars could go the same – all cars could go the same . . . fast.
Mother: The same speed.
Stephen: Yes, same speed.

(1993: 136)

Beverly Derewianka (1995) provides a detailed and insightful account of one child's language development from childhood to adolescence (ages 4–14), with the development of grammatical metaphor as the central theme. Here is one of her examples of a child (her main subject's younger brother, at age 12) consciously construing metaphoric modes of expression:

Stefan: Mum, is 'preservation' a word?
Mother: Why?
Stefan: Because I need it for my project. I've written 'Mummification was necessary . . . ' – you know, to keep the body intact and keep the corpse from decaying. Can I say 'Mummification was necessary for the preservation of the corpse'?

(1995: 128)

In the way that educational knowledge is organised, at the present

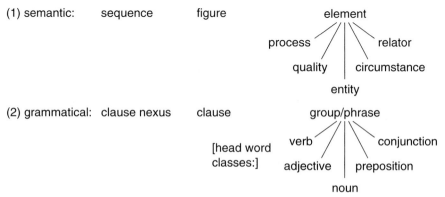

Figure 8.7 Congruence of semantic and grammatical categories

stage of our history, children have to undertake this secondary reconstrual of experience before they can succeed in secondary edcuation. They are initiated into grammatical metaphor in the upper years of primary school; note how *animal protection* and *capacity* are brought in in these examples:

> Put a label on each [container] to show two things:
> (a) The quantity it holds.
> (b) What fraction of a litre in it. [sic]
> Put all that measure one litre together. Some will be tall, some short, some rectangular, some cylindrical for milk or drinks, some wine bottles or carafes. But they all contain 1 LITRE. A litre is a litre, whether long, round or square. . . . So all kinds of shapes can be made to have the same capacity.[3]
>
> (K. Perret and G. Fiddes, *New Primary Maths 5*,
> Sydney: School Projects, 1968/1977, p. 71)

> ANIMAL PROTECTION. Most animals have natural enemies that prey upon them. To survive, these animals need some protection from their enemies.
> Animals protect themselves in many ways.
> Some animals rely on their great speed to escape from danger. . . .
> Animals like snakes and spiders protect themselves with bites and stings, some of which are poisonous. These bites and stings can also help the animals capture food.[4]
>
> (R.L. Vickery *et al.*, *The Process Way to Science*,
> Book C, Sydney: Jacaranda, 1978, p. 85)

Soon after reaching secondary school, they may have to cope with:

> Braking distance increases more rapidly at high speeds.

(This is not easy to unpack: one would have to say something like *the faster you're going, the more quickly the time it takes you to stop gets longer.* It recalls the well-known footnote on 'acceleration' in Whorf [1941/1956: 151].)

Derewianka sums up by saying 'grammatical metaphor is intimately involved in the development of experiential meanings and is particularly implicated in the shift from commonsense to uncommonsense' (1995: 198). This is in no way to imply, of course, that young children do not engage in logical reasoning – of course they do, from the time they are able to talk at all. Commonsense knowledge is no less dependent on rationality (see especially Hasan 1992). But (whether or not it could have evolved in other grammatical formations) scientific knowledge in fact evolved as a metaphoric reconstrual of experience; and it is this that has determined how it is pursued by those who are 'doing science' and how it is transmitted to those who are learning.

REWORDING; REMEANING?

Young children's world of meaning is organised congruently; this is how they are able to move into it, at one and the same time both construing the grammar and using the grammar to construe their own experience (cf. Wells 1986). The world is, in Edelman's words, an 'unlabelled place'; grammar is our way of categorising it, enabling us to analyse out the elements that are commutable – that you can vary while leaving the remainder constant. This is the significance of the clause (or rather, of the category that is congruently both clause and figure): it is an organic configuration of elements having different, complementary functions with respect to the whole.

Then, as children are approaching adolescence, and as a condition of entry into the world of adult knowledge, children have to reconstrue their clausal grammar in a different, nominalised form. It is this reconstrual that I have been exploring in the present chapter.

Using the concept of 'grammatical metaphor' I have tried to set up a taxonomy of types of rewording which would make it possible to examine both the inherent directionality of the reconstrual and the patterns of co-occurrence or 'syndromes'. This has meant 'unpacking' the metaphors and plotting the types of cross-coupling that occur between the semantic and the lexicogrammatical stratum. Such unpacking is not a unique operation; as in other metatextual activities, such as translation, or error analysis, there will usually be more than one possible route to travel. I have suggested a classification of grammatical metaphor based on the terminal point – the category into which the metaphoric shift takes place; this makes it possible to vary the degree of congruence in the analysis: that is, to decide how far any instance is to be unpacked.

So is the grammatical metaphor simply a rewording, saying the same things in different ways? Or is it also a 're-meaning' – saying something different from the congruent form?

It is noticeable how ambiguous the metaphoric variants are. When a figure, which is congruently a clause, is reworded as a nominal group, much of the semantic information becomes hidden. Thus *animal protection* might be the realisation of 'how animals are (or should be) protected (by humans)', 'how animals protect themselves', or 'how we protect (or should protect) ourselves from animals'; or even of 'how animals protect other things (such as humans, or the environment in general)'. The slightly less metaphorical wording *the protection of animals* rules out one or two of these; and if we then replace *of* by a true preposition such as *by* or *from* we recover some more semantic information – but only when we reach the congruent, clausal form can we be sure what function animals have in the protecting process. This suggests that the nominal grammar would not have served very well in the primary construal of experience: you have to know the answers before you start.

From this point of view it seems as if there is a loss of meaning potential in the nominal, metaphoric mode of discourse. But this is a misleading impression. There is, certainly, a great deal of neutralisation taking place when a figure is reworded as a nominal group; but the result (in almost all cases; there are some exceptions)[5] is not loss of semantic distinction but ambiguity: the different possible meanings are still discrete. This may – indeed it often does – create problems for the learner, who has to guess right, often without realising there is more than one possible interpretation. (The textbook writer may provide the answer, using the text as a key to metaphorical modes of expression: for example, the heading *Animal Protection* is followed in the first paragraph by the clause *animals protect themselves in many ways*.) But the total semantic range is not reduced. On the contrary: in shifting into the metaphoric mode the grammar actually creates new meanings, by the semantic junction across ranks and across categories.

Let me briefly summarise this part of the argument. Language – every human language – is a stratified system in which the content plane is split into a semantics, interfacing with the world of human experience (and of human social relationships), and a grammar, which is a purely abstract level of organisation; the two are coupled through a relation of congruence, but they can be decoupled and recoupled in other ways (which I am calling 'grammatical metaphor'). This gives the system indefinitely large semogenic power, because new meaning is created at the intersection of the congruent and the metaphoric categories ('semantic junction').

This potential seems to be exploited particularly at moments of major change in the human condition. We find one such reconstrual of experience in the languages of the iron age cultures of the Eurasian continent (of which classical Greek was one), which evolved discourses of measurement and calculation, and ordered sets of abstract, technical terms – the registers of mathematics and science (cf. Dijksterhuis 1950/1986: Part III). This grammar was carried over through classical and medieval Latin, and also with a significant detour via Syriac and Arabic, into the national languages of modern Europe.

A further reconstrual then took place in the 'modern' period, with the evolution of the discourses of experimental science from Galileo and Newton onwards; and it is this secondary reconstrual that I have been describing in the present chapter. This new semiotic potential provided the foundation for our discipline-based organisation of technical knowledge. It could perhaps be summed up under five headings:

1 **expanding** the noun as a taxonomic resource (this was the goal of language planning in the 1600s, especially in England and France [cf. Salmon 1979]);
2 **transcategorising** processes and qualities into nouns, relators into verbs, etc., with resulting semantic junction (pp. 197–201);
3 **compacting** pieces of the argument to function (e.g. as Theme of the clause) in an 'information flow' of logical reasoning (pp. 201–6);
4 **distilling** the outcomes of (2) and (3) to create technical taxonomies of abstract, virtual entities (pp. 221–3);
5 **theorising:** constructing a scientific theory through the reconstruing of experience as in (1)–(4), with a 'favourite clause type' in which virtual entities (instantial and/or systemic) participate in virtual processes based on logical–semantic relations ('relational processes' [cf. Halliday 1985/1994: Chapter 5]).

A scientific theory is a specialised, semi-designed sub-system of a natural language; constructing such a theory is an exercise in lexico-grammar. Science and technology are (like other human endeavours) at one and the same time both *material* and *semiotic practices*; knowledge advances through the combination of new techniques with new meanings. Thus 'reconstruing experience' is not merely rewording (regrammaticising); it is also resemanticising. The languages of science are not saying the same things in different ways – although they may be appropriated for this purpose by others wishing to exploit their prestige and power.

On the contrary; what is brought into being in this reconstrual is a new construction of knowledge; and hence, a new ideology. The connection between metaphor and ideology – metaphor in its traditional sense – is well enough documented (cf. Lakoff 1992); we shall not be surprised that grammatical metaphor has ideological import. There are two aspects to this: in metafunctional terms, the ideational and the interpersonal. Ideationally, the nominalising grammar creates a universe of things, bounded, stable and determinate; and (in place of processes) of relations between the things. Interpersonally, it sets itself apart as a discourse of the expert, readily becoming a language of power and technocratic control. In both aspects, it creates maximum distance between technical scientific knowledge and the experience of daily life. These are familiar enough motifs (cf. Lemke 1995, Thibault 1991, Fairclough 1992, Halliday and Martin 1993, especially Chapters 2, 6, 9–11); my concern here is to emphasise how the ideology is constructed in the grammar, by the same reconstrual of experience that was central to the development of modern science in the first place. With this in mind we can hope to exploit 'grammatics' to keep track of what is happening today, and perhaps predict what may happen in the next phase of semiotic reconstruction (cf. Martin's comment [1992: 409–10] on the verbs in current use in computer discourse).

Every human language is stratified in the same way, and the grammar of every language has the same potential for reconstruing experience. It happened that, in the case of the particular reconstrual that accompanied the development of modern science, this potential was taken up, in the first instance, by a few languages that became the standard or literary languages of the European nation states; and many more languages around the world have taken it up in the present century. It is worth remarking, perhaps, that it was not taken up in the non-standard varieties of these languages: the rural dialects of Italy, England or Germany did not evolve these elaborated grammatical metaphors – they were not, after all, expected to serve in the contexts of advanced education and science. To ask whether modern science could have developed without such semiotic reconstrual is of course one of the unanswerable questions of history. Any major restructuring of knowledge is likely to demand some remodelling of grammar. But the particular form this took was the product of specific historical (including semohistorical) circumstances: and if these had been different – for example, if modern science had developed first in China or India – the grammar of scientific discourse might have taken a rather different route. But then again, it might not.

APPENDIX: TEXT 1

(from Roger Y. Stanier, John L. Ingraham, Mark L. Wheelis and Page R. Painter, *General Microbiology*, fifth edition, Basingstoke and London: Macmillan Education, 1987, pp. 204–5. First published Englewood Cliffs, NJ: Prentice-Hall, 1957)

Effects of solutes on growth and metabolism

Transport mechanisms play two essential roles in cellular function. First, they maintain the intracellular concentrations of all metabolites at levels sufficiently high to ensure operation of both catabolic and biosynthetic pathways at near-maximal rates, even when nutrient concentrations in the external medium are low. This is evidenced by the fact that the exponential growth rates of microbial populations remain constant until one essential nutrient in the medium falls to a very low value, approaching exhaustion. At this limiting nutrient concentration, the growth rate of the population rapidly falls to zero (Chapter 7). Second, transport mechanisms function in *osmoregulation*, maintaining the solutes (principally small molecules and ions) at levels optimal for metabolic activity, even when the osmolarity of the environment varies over a relatively wide range.*

Most bacteria do not need to regulate their internal osmolarity with precision because they are enclosed by a cell wall capable of withstanding a considerable internal osmotic pressure. Bacteria always maintain their osmolarity well above that of the medium. If the internal osmotic pressure of the cell falls below the external osmotic pressure, water leaves the cell and the volume of the cytoplasm decreases with accompanying damage to the membrane. In Gram-positive bacteria, this causes the cell membrane to pull away from the wall; the cell is said to be *plasmolysed*. In Gram-negative bacteria the wall retracts with the membrane; this also damages the membrane.

Bacteria vary widely in their osmotic requirements. Some are able to grow in very dilute solutions, and some in solutions saturated with sodium chloride. Microorganisms that can grow in solutions of high osmolarity are called *osmophiles*. Most natural environments of high osmolarity contain high concentrations of salts, particularly sodium chloride. Microorganisms that grow in this type of environment are called *halophiles*. Bacteria can be divided into four broad categories in terms of their salt tolerance: *nonhalophiles*, *marine organisms*, *moderate halophiles*, and *extreme halophiles* (Table 8.3). Some halophiles, for example *Pediococcus halophilus*, can tolerate high concentrations of salt in the growth medium, but they can also grow in media without added NaCl. Other bacteria, including marine bacteria and certain moderate halophiles, as well as all extreme halophiles, require NaCl for growth.

---

* When a *solution* of any substance (*solute*) is separated from a *solute-free solvent* by a membrane that is freely permeable to solvent molecules, but not to molecules of the solute, the solvent tends to be drawn through the membrane into the solution, thus diluting it. Movement of the solvent across the membrane can be prevented by applying a certain hydrostatic pressure to the solution. This pressure is defined as *osmotic pressure*. A difference in osmotic pressure also exists between two solutions containing different concentrations of any solute.

The osmotic pressure exerted by any solution can be defined in terms of *osmolarity*. An osmolar solution is one that contains one *osmole* per liter of solutes, i.e., a 1.0 molal solution of an ideal nonelectrolyte. An osmolar solution exerts an osmotic pressure of 22.4 atmospheres at 0°C, and depresses the freezing point of the solvent (water) by 1.86°C. If the solute is an electrolyte, its osmolarity is dependent on the degree of its dissociation, since both ions and undissociated molecules contribute to osmolarity. Consequently, the osmolarity and the molarity of a solution of an electrolyte may be grossly different. If both the molarity and the dissociation constant of a solution of an electrolyte are known, its osmolarity can be calculated with some degree of approximation, as the sum of the moles of undissociated solute and the mole equivalents of ions. Such a calculation is accurate only if the solution is an ideal one, and if it is extremely dilute. Therefore, it is preferable to determine the osmolarity of a solution experimentally, e.g., by freezing-point depression.

The tolerance of high osmolarity and the specific requirement for NaCl are distinct phenomena, each of which has a specific biochemical basis.

Osmotic tolerance

Osmotic tolerance – the ability of an organism to grow in media with widely varying osmolarities – is accomplished in bacteria by an adjustment of the internal osmolarity so that it always exceeds that of the medium. Intracellular accumulation of potassium ions (K^+) seems to play a major role in this adjustment. Many bacteria have been shown to concentrate K^+ to a much greater extent than Na^+ (Table 8.4). Moreover, there is an excellent correlation between the osmotic tolerance of bacteria and their K^+ content. For bacteria as metabolically diverse as Gram-positive cocci, bacilli, and Gram-negative rods, relative osmotic tolerance can be deduced from their relative K^+ contents after growth in a medium of fixed ionic strength and composition. Studies on *E. coli* have shown that the intracellular K^+ concentration increases progressively with increasing osmolarity of the growth medium. Consequently, both the osmolarity and the internal ionic strength of the cell increase.**

The maintenance of a relatively constant ionic strength within the cell is of critical physiological importance, because the stability and behavior of enzymes and other biological macromolecules are strongly dependent on this factor. In bacteria, the diamine putrescine (Chapter 5) probably always plays an important role in assuring the approximate constancy of internal ionic strength. This has been shown through studies on *E. coli*. The concentration of intracellular putrescine varies inversely with the osmolarity of the medium; increases of osmolarity cause rapid excretion of putrescine. An increase in the osmolarity of the medium causes an increase in the internal osmolarity of the cell as a result of uptake of K^+, ionic strength is maintained approximately constant as a result of the excretion of putrescine. This is a consequence of the differing contributions that a multiply charged ion makes to ionic strength and osmotic strength of a solution; a change of putrescine^{2+} concentration that alters ionic strength by 58 percent alters osmotic strength by only 14 percent.

Changes in osmotic strength or ionic strength of the growth medium also trigger a cellular response that changes the proportions in the outer membrane of *E. coli* of the two major protein constituents, OmpC and OmpF. These changes are thought to be adaptive, but the mechanism by which they alter the cell's ionic or osmotic tolerance remains unclear.

** The ionic strength of a solution is defined by the equation $1 - \frac{1}{2}\Sigma M_j Z^2$, where M_j is the molarity of a given ion and Z is the charge, regardless of sign. Since the Z term is squared, the ionic strength of an ion increases exponentially with the magnitude of its charge either positive or negative. The magnitude of ionic charge, however, does not affect osmolarity.

APPENDIX: TEXT 2

(from David Layzer, *Cosmogenesis: The growth of order in the universe*, New York and Oxford: Oxford University Press, 1990, pp. 61–62)

The classical world is populated by individuals; the quantum world is populated by clones. Two classical objects – a pair of ball bearings, for example – can't be precisely alike in every respect. But according to quantum physics, all electrons are exact replicas of one another. They are indistinguishable not only in practice but also in principle, as are all hydrogen atoms, all water molecules, and all salt crystals (apart from size). This is not simply a dogma, but a testable and strongly corroborated hypothesis. For example, if electrons weren't absolutely indistinguishable, two hydrogen atoms would form a much more weakly bound molecule than they actually do. The absolute indistinguishability of the electrons in the two atoms gives rise to an 'extra' attractive force between them. The indistinguishability of electrons is also responsible for the structure of the periodic table – that is, for the fact that elements in the same column of the table (inert gases, halogens, alkali metals, alkali earths, and so on) have similar chemical properties.

APPENDIX: TEXT 3

(from William Stigliani and Wim Salomons, 'Our fathers' toxic sins', *New Scientist* 1903, 11 December 1993)

Redox potential: the chemical switch

One of the fundamental requirements of life is the need to generate biochemical energy by the oxidation of organic carbon to carbon dioxide. The most efficient energy-producing mechanism is respiration, in which molecular oxygen (O_2) is the oxidising agent. In soils, waters and sediments, however, the supply of O_2 is often limited. Nonetheless, the Earth's aquatic and terrestrial ecosystems contain microorganisms which can extract oxygen from other oxygen-containing compounds. These include nitrate, manganese and iron oxides, sulphate and organic carbon.

The type of molecule used first depends on how good an oxidising agent it is in relation to others – in chemical terms, its 'redox' potential. Oxidation by molecular oxygen has the highest redox potential, so molecular oxygen is the first compound to be consumed. Nitrate has the next highest redox potential, so it is consumed next. The sequence continues with manganese oxide, ferric hydroxide, sulphate, and finally to organic carbon. The redox potential is a kind of 'chemical switch' which determines the order in which oxygen-containing chemicals are used by microorganisms to extract oxygen.

NOTES

1 Note the important difference here between transcategorisation and metaphor [cf. pp. 199–200]. There is nothing metaphorical about *poiētēs* 'maker'; it is simply an actor noun derived from a verb 'make' ['one who makes']. In the same way one can derive an adjective from a noun; e.g. in English, *venom*: *venomous*. In such cases there is no semantic junction: *venomous* is not the name of an entity, just as *poiētēs* is not the name of a process. In metaphor, on the other hand, there is semantic junction between the 'vehicle' and the 'tenor': thus *venomousness* contains not only the feature 'entity' but that of 'quality' as well.

2 Note the difference between *behaviour* as metaphorised process 'behave' (which is accented; cf. *mechanical behaviour* = how (they) behave in terms of mechanics) and *behaviour* as dummy noun introduced in the nominalising of another process (unaccented; cf. *feeding behaviour* = how (they) feed).

3 It is interesting to compare this with children's own theories of conservation, illustrated in these two examples:

Nigel [4;11]:   Why does as plasticine gets longer it gets thinner?
Father: That's a very good question. Why does it?
Nigel: Because more of it is getting used up.
Father: Well . . . (looking doubtful)
Nigel: (patiently) Because more of it is getting used up to make it longer, that's why; and so it goes thinner.

(M.A.K. Halliday)

Nick [8;0]:   (in car, explaining *high beam* to his brother) On low beam the light is all spread out but on high beam it is thick, it has texture. It's like plasticine – on low beam it's like plasticine all spread out but on high beam it's like when you roll out the plasticine into a long shape like a snake so it all goes forwards instead of to the sides.

(Beverly Derewianka 1995: 108)

4 Compare Nigel's observation on the same topic at age 3:

Nigel [3; 5]: Cats have no else to stop you from trossing them . . . cats have no other way to stop children from hitting them; so they bite.
(M.A.K. Halliday, 'Towards a language-based theory of learning'. *Linguistics and Eduation* 5.2, p. 110)

5 Perhaps the most striking example is the class of verbs such as *correlate with*, *be associated with*, *mean*, *reflect* which neutralise the decoding/encoding distinction in intensive relational processes (i.e., the opposition of Token identified as Value vs. Value identified as Token [cf. Halliday 1965/1966, 1985/94; Davidse 1992]); for example:

the inheritance of specific genes is correlated with the inheritance of a specific chromosome

But this could also be interpreted positively: neutralising a semantic distinction is, from another point of view, creating a new semantic category (a 'new meaning').

REFERENCES

Biagi, M.L.A. 1997. 'Diacronia dei linguaggi scientifici', in R. Rossini, G. Sandri and R. Scazzeri (eds) *Incommensurability and Translation*. Cheltenham: Elgar.

Bühler, K. 1934. *Sprachtheorie: die Darstellungsfunktion der Sprache.* Jena: Fischer.

Davidse, K. 1991. *Categories of Experiential Grammar.* PhD thesis, University of Leuven.

Davidse, K. 1992. 'Transitivity / ergativity: The Janus-headed grammar of actions and events', in M. Davies & L. Ravelli (eds) *Advances in Systemic Linguistics: recent theory and practice.* London and New York: Pinter. 105–135.

Derewianka, B. 1995. *Language Development in the Transition from Childhood to Adolescence: The role of grammatical metaphor.* PhD thesis, Macquarie University.

Dijksterhuis, E.J. 1950/1986. *The Mechanization of the World Picture: Pythagoras to Newton.* Princeton, NJ: Princeton University Press.

Edelman, G.M. 1992. *Bright Air, Brilliant Fire: On the matter of the mind.* New York: Basic Books.

Eggins, S. 1994. *An Introduction to Systemic Functional Linguistics.* London: Pinter.

Ellis, J.M. 1993. *Language, Thought, and Logic.* Evanston, IL: Northwestern University Press.

Fairclough, N. 1992. *Discourse and Social Change.* Cambridge: Polity Press.

Fries, P.H. 1992. 'The structuring of written English text' *Language Sciences.* 14.4. 461–488.

Fries, P.H. 1995. 'Themes, methods of development, and texts', in R. Hasan & P.H. Fries (eds), *On Subject and Theme: A discourse functional perspective.* Amsterdam and Philadelphia: Benjamins. 317–359.

Halliday, M.A.K. 1965–1966. 'Notes on transitivity and theme in English', Parts 1–3 *Journal of Linguistics* 3.1, 3.2, 4.1. 37–81, 199–244, 175–215.

Halliday, M.A.K. 1975. *Learning How to Mean: Explorations in the development of language.* London: Edward Arnold.

Halliday, M.A.K. 1985/1994. *An Introduction to Functional Grammar.* London: Edward Arnold (second edition).

Halliday, M.A.K. 1997. 'The grammatical construction of scientific knowledge: The framing of the English clause', in R. Rossini, G. Sandri and R. Scazzeri (eds) *Incommensurability and Translation.* Cheltenham: Elgar..

Halliday, M.A.K. and Hasan, R. 1976. *Cohesion in English.* London: Longman.

Halliday, M.A.K. and Martin, J.R. 1993. *Writing Science: Literacy and discursive power.* London & Washington, DC: Falmer.

Hasan, R. 1992. 'Rationality in everyday talk: From process to system' in Jan Svartvik (ed.), *Directions in Corpus Linguistics: Proceedings of Nobel Symposium 82.* Berlin and New York: Mouton de Gruyter. 257–307.

Hasan, R. and Fries, P.H. (eds) 1995. *On Subject and Theme: A discourse functional perspective.* Amsterdam and Philadelphia: Benjamins.

Lakoff, G. 1992. 'Metaphor and war: The metaphor system used to justify war in the Gulf', in M. Pütz (ed) *Thirty Years of Linguistic Evolution.* Amsterdam: Benjamins. 463–481.

Lemke, J.L. 1990. *Talking Science: Language, learning, and values.* Norwood, NJ: Ablex.

Lemke, J.L. 1993. 'Discourse, dynamics, and social change' *Cultural Dynamics,* 6.1–2. 243–275.

Lemke, J.L. 1995. *Textual Politics: Discourse and social dynamics.* London and Bristol, PA: Taylor & Francis.

Martin, J.R. 1992. *English Text: System and structure.* Philadelphia and Amsterdam: Benjamins.

Matthiessen, C. 1992. 'Interpreting the textual metafunction' in M. Davies & L. Ravelli (eds) *Advances in Systemic Linguistics: Recent theory and practice.* London and New York: Pinter. 37–81.

Matthiessen, C. 1993. 'The object of study in cognitive science in relation to its construal and enactment in language' *Cultural Dynamics.* 6.1–2. 187–242.

Matthiessen, C. 1995. *Lexicogrammatical Cartography: English systems.* Tokyo: International Language Sciences Publishers.

Painter, C. 1984. *Into the Mother Tongue: A case study in early language development.* London and Dover, NH: Frances Pinter.

Painter, C. 1993. *Learning Through Language: A case study in the development of language as a resource for learning from 2½ to 5 years.* PhD thesis, University of Sydney.

Salmon, V. 1979. *The Study of Language in Seventeenth Century England.* Amsterdam: Benjamins.

Thibault, P. 1991. 'Grammar, technocracy and the noun: Technocratic values and cognitive linguistics', in E. Ventola (ed.) *Functional and Systemic Linguistics: Approaches and uses.* Berlin and New York: Mouton de Gruyter. 281–306.

Wells, C.G. 1986. *The Meaning Makers: Children learning language and using language to learn.* Cambridge: Cambridge University Press.

Whorf, B.L. 1941/1956. 'The relation of habitual thought and behaviour to language' in J.B. Carroll (ed.) *Language, Thought and Reality: Selected papers of Benjamin Lee Whorf.* Cambridge, MA: MIT Press. 134–159.

9 Science discourse and industrial hierarchy

David Rose

INTRODUCTION

In an inspiring paper, On the Language of Physical Science, Halliday (1993) charts the history of scientific English from the late fourteenth to the late twentieth centuries. He exemplifies the evolution of its grammar with texts from the physical sciences by Chaucer 1391, Newton 1675–1687, Priestley 1760s, Dalton 1827, Maxwell 1881 and a contemporary research report. To begin with, he summarises the 'diatypic variation' of this register 'in field, extending, transmitting or exploring knowledge . . .; in tenor, addressed to specialists, to learners or to laymen . . .; in mode, phonic or graphic channel'.

These variables of field and tenor apply to two general domains of scientific practice – research and training, as well as to its reporting in public discourse. The semiotic features of both these domains have been explored extensively in a systemic functional framework (e.g. Lemke 1990, Halliday and Martin 1993), and more generally in discourse studies (e.g. Hunston 1993). However there is a third domain of science which is only partially covered in the definition above, and in the literature. That is the application of science in industrial production. In fact the scientific domains of research, training and industrial application constitute a common enterprise of modern culture, in which universities, research institutions and industry laboratories co-operate to extend our ability to control the physical, biological and social world, and schools are co-opted to train potential researchers, teachers and appliers.

Representations of the scientific enterprise in public discourse do tend to foreground the growth and teaching of scientific knowledge, and the industrial basis for its development is often backgrounded. But of course modern science would not have happened without the evolution of industrial capitalism. From Chaucer's Treatise on the Astrolabe, to the astronomy, mathematics and physics of Galileo, Descartes and Newton, the impetus and application of scientific discovery was in the maritime expansion of European trading and colonisation, and warfare between imperial powers. From Priestley to the present day, physical, chemical and geological sciences have developed in tandem with the beginnings, expansion and technologisation of mass industrial production, for which mercantile and imperial expansion provide the capital. Darwin made his biological discoveries in the context of expanding global agriculture, across Europe's nineteenth-century empires. Developments in social sciences, from Adam Smith, through Marx to Weber and Taylor, were made in the context of rapidly changing social structures, and the need to design new management systems brought on by imperial expansion and the industrial revolution.

So the growth of scientific knowledge has been implicated from the beginning in the evolution of modern economic systems and the global power structures they support. But the transmission of scientific knowledge is also implicated in the maintenance of power structures within industry. At the top of scientific industrial hierarchies are postgraduate trained researchers and managers and at the bottom are the 'de-skilled' operators of Fordist production lines. Between these two poles, access to income, control and life opportunities depend on the level of technical literacy people are able to acquire through school education and vocational training.

In Australia these educational differences have been intersected by ethnic ones as its economic base has shifted from agriculture to the manufacturing industry since World War II. While the dominant Anglo-Celtic population has tended to move up the industrial ladder, with the acquisition of higher levels of training, successive Australian governments have encouraged mass immigration from non-industrialised regions of the world. Few immigrants had English literacy skills on arrival, so most tended to fill the lowest de-skilled positions in expanding manufacturing industries. While children of non-English speaking immigrants may acquire technical literacy and move up the ladder to trades or higher positions, new waves of immigrants arrive to take up the lower positions. Gender is also an issue at skilled and higher levels, since historically men have tended to acquire technical literacy and associated positions more readily than women, and have tended to be paid more. At the bottom rungs however, there are as many immigrant women as men on the factory floor, with both partners having to work on the low incomes these positions award.

Changes in the world economy over the past twenty-five years have caught up with this rigidly stratified production system. Western Fordist economies are giving way to 'flattened' production hierarchies, in which each member of a production unit must be 'multiskilled' rather than de-skilled (Harvey 1989). Whole sectors of the Fordist manufacturing base of Australia's economy are collapsing in the face of cheaper or more efficient production in newly industrialised regions. In order to survive Australian government and industry have decided that its workers must become more skilled, and this means becoming literate enough to enable formal training and participation in the management of production.

This is the context in which Australian government, capital and labour began to collaborate from the late 1980s, to define a course for the restructuring of its industries on the principles of quality cell production, multiskilling, and retraining. This has led to promotion of education and training pathways for all workers, in schools, training institutions and workplaces. To help inform the literacy dimension of this training program, the *Write It Right* project was commissioned by the Australian National Training Board (NTB) to research literacy demands at all levels in industry. This chapter summarises some of the findings of this research project in manufacturing industries, in which technical literacies are a major feature (Rose, McInnes and Korner 1992).

The NTB (1991) provided a framework for interpreting the three-way relationship between science, education and industry, in the form of a hierarchical 'competency scale' of occupations from the least skilled or qualified production worker to the most highly trained researchers and managers. This hierarchy of educational qualifications is explicitly correlated with a hierarchy of authority and control in the workplace. It is an open statement of the class structure of Fordist industrial organisation, and the relationship of that class structure to the education system. These correlations are brought out in Table 9.1 of extracts from the NTB competency scales.

From this perspective, scientific research and training appears integral

Table 9.1 NTB competency scales

	Training level	Workplace authority level
1	job specific training, mainly in the workplace	routine, predicatable, repetitive and proceduralised tasks . . . under close supervision
2	job specific or generalised training	proceduralised tasks under general supervision
3	trade certificate or equivalent	self-directed application
4	post-trade or equivalent certificate	highly developed . . . capacity for self-directed application
5	advanced certificate to diplomas	limited supervisory functions
6	associate diploma to degree	significant supervisory functions
7	degree or higher degree	accountability and responsibility for the output of others
8	appropriate degree or higher degree . . . post-doctoral research	managerial functions with full accountability and responsibility for the output of others

to the industrial base of modern society, and the hierarchical relations between its participants, rather than an independent enterprise for 'extending, transmitting or exploring knowledge'. Education emerges as the device for reproducing this stratification, with levels of technical/ science education as integral to the hierarchy of Fordist manufacturing.

The *Write It Right* researchers collected a variety of text types, in a hierarchy of worksites that corresponded closely with the NTB's eight competency levels. The varieties of language features displayed by text types at each level of industry were then compared with analyses of secondary school science texts. The hierarchy of industrial scientific text types were found to share grammar and discourse features with text types at each stage of science education. For example, while no science education is required for manual production work, some junior secondary science is essential for trades courses that involve formal science and technology course work, and senior secondary science is an essential prerequisite for tertiary science and engineering training. At each of these educational stages, the language of science texts, read and written, becomes more specialised, technical and abstract, leading eventually to the extremely dense written texts exchanged by research scientists.

In the written texts found in both industrial workplaces and science education, three complementary semantic developments take place as we move up the industrial ladder and the educational sequence. One axis of change is in the ways that reality is represented as sequences of activities. The second is in the ways that social relations are enacted by degrees of obligation and probability. The third is in the ways that these meanings are presented as written text, moving further from the patterns of speech as the hierarchy is ascended.

The changes in representations of activity sequences can be exemplified by developments in the grammar of causal relations between events. In procedural texts found at the manual end of the industrial hierarchy, cause tends to be represented congruently as a conjunctive relation between material processes, for example:

1 The gas must pass through the brassert at a reasonably slow velocity.
2 *Thus* the semi-clean gas enters the bottom section of the brassert . . .

In research reports found at the other end of the hierarchy, cause is represented metaphorically, for example as a process relating nominalised events (3), or as a preposition (4).

3 Defects have been shown to *be related to* surface and sub-surface cracks.
4 Plate surface defects were probably *due to* brittle failure.

Changes in the grammar of cause, as we move up the hierarchy, are comparable with Halliday's (1993) 'highly schematic interpretation' of the evolution causal grammar in scientific English since the fourteenth century, reproduced in Figure 9.1.

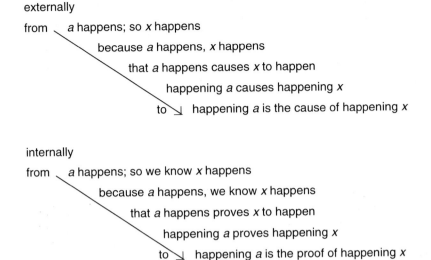

externally

from   *a* happens; so *x* happens

         because *a* happens, *x* happens

            that *a* happens causes *x* to happen

               happening *a* causes happening *x*

            to   happening *a* is the cause of happening *x*

internally

from   *a* happens; so we know *x* happens

         because *a* happens, we know *x* happens

            that *a* happens proves *x* to happen

               happening *a* proves happening *x*

            to   happening *a* is the proof of happening *x*

Figure 9.1 Evolution of causal grammar in scientific English (after Halliday 1993)

The general direction of change in this schema is from more fluid structures of spoken language, to the more crystalline structures of writing. In the first step, one event follows another as in our subjective experience, as external effect follows cause, or internal knowing follows observation. In the second step the causal event is thematised, enabling a choice in textual organisation of the clause complex, and disconnecting the sequence from subjective experience. In the third step, the sequence is realised by a single clause: the cause and effect are embedded clauses, and the conjunctive relation between them is realised metaphorically as a process: externally 'causes', and internally 'proves'. The latter effaces the subjectivity of the observer, ascribing modal reponsibility instead to the observed effect. In the fourth step the cause and effect are fully nominalised, i.e., more 'thing-like' than embedded clauses. In the fifth, the causal relation is itself nominalised, so that events, observations and logical relations between them all become abstract entities.

This sequence of steps in the evolution of scientific English closely reflects the pattern of increasing abstraction, of both events and subjectivity, as we move up the scientific industrial hierarchy. Scientific English is apparent from NTB levels 5 to 8, in which university science training is a prerequisite for employment, and is reflected in the texts written by and for workers at these levels, including technical notes, reports and research articles. However there is no sharp division between these and the vocationally oriented texts found at lower levels. Rather there is a cline of scientific/technological English across all levels, from language most closely resembling the fluid iconic patterns of everyday speech, to the most dense, crystalline forms of research reporting.

In the realm of social relations, we have already noted that subjective interpersonal intrusions recede in Halliday's schema for internal cause, from 'so we know' to '*a* proves *x*'. However causal relations in general in English incorporate interpersonal meanings as gradations of obligation, inclination and probability. Martin (1992) interprets causal/conditional relations in English along interpersonal lines, as *modulating* and *modalising* relations of temporal succession between events; that is, they incorporate the interpersonal resources of modality into the logical system of interdependency. These metafunctional relationships are outlined in Table 9.2.

In the semantic domain of causality, the two functions of language as representation and exchange are realised in the same causal motif: whereas degrees of obligation, inclination and probability typically grade a speaker's intention that s/he or the listener will perform an action, they may also be applied to grade causal relations between events that involve neither speaker nor listener. The lexis of cause in scientific English includes a large, delicate range of possible expressions of these meanings. Halliday (1993) exemplifies these from Maxwell writing in 1881, externally with 'cause, lead to, accompany, follow, produce, dictate, stimulate, demand, require, correspond to, apply to, arise from, flow from, cover, result from, be associated with, be measured by', and internally with 'prove, show, predict, illustrate, suggest, attest, be explained by, indicate, confirm'.

By means of this range of finely graded judgements, science writers negotiate their relationships with their peers, masters and apprentices (see also Hunston 1993, 1994). At the bottom of the science industrial hierarchy, interpersonal meanings tend to be direct and subjective, e.g. imperative commands to perform actions. As we move up the ladder, such direct expressions of status and control recede, resurfacing in the lexicogrammar of causes and effects, observations and conclusions.

Table 9.2 Consequential logic and modality (from Martin 1992: 194)

Logical relation	Modulation	Modalisation
time (when, while)	–	–
manner (thus, by)	ability	–
reason (so, because)	obligation	–
condition (then, if)	obligation	probability
purpose (so that)	obligation and inclination	probability

ANALYSIS

These parallel semantic movements, in the representation of reality, in the negotiation of social relations, and in their presentation as written text, are exemplified here with text extracts and analyses at each NTB competency level. To facilitate comparison, the field is restricted to metals manufacturing, from the factory floor to the research laboratory. Up to NTB level 4 the most common types of texts are procedures, designed to direct and enable more or less trained operators or technicians to control the technology they are working with. Procedures are not simply concerned to command the reader to action, they also need to give information about the production process and the technology involved. As we move up the industrial hierarchy, more information is given to the worker, and the commanding function of the procedures recedes.

At levels 1–2 the commanding function is foregrounded, it is realised directly and less negotiably as a series of imperatives – a *simple procedure*. At Level 3 workers need to make choices about what actions to take. These decision-making functions are realised in *conditional procedures*. At this level workers also need to know how the technology operates in order to 'select and use appropriate techniques and equipment required to perform tasks of some complexity' (NTB ibid.). These descriptions of the workings of the technology are realised as *technological explanations*. Many tasks involve multiple participants, including operators and technicians so the procedure must foreground the identity of the worker to carry out each step in the task. We have called this type a *co-operative procedure*.

Each of these procedures is concerned with operating technology – the field is technological and more or less specialised. They may also involve some knowledge of scientific measurement, but generally limited knowledge of scientific theory. At level 4 procedures involve scientific laboratory work – testing products and materials. While this work also involves operating technology, it is generally highly technical and demands significant knowledge of scientific theory. We called this genre *technical procedures*.

From level 5 up, texts are not written directly for the operators of technology, but for their managers. At Levels 5–7, *technical notes* are written by technicians and applied scientists, analysing features of production processes and making recommendations for technological changes. Technical notes resemble scientific *research articles*, written by research scientists at level 8, whose role is to research more general production issues, rather than specific processes. Their findings inform the applied scientists who design production processes.

The relations of these text types to their industrial contexts and their degrees of specialised or technical English are illustrated in Figure 9.2.

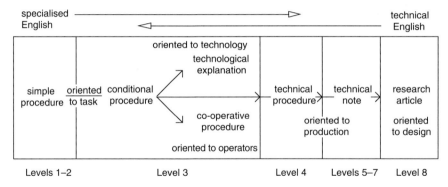

Figure 9.2 Relations between text types in manufacturing industries

These text types are exemplified as follows, up to level 7. Level 8 is excluded for the sake of brevity. The language features of research articles are adequately exemplified in technical notes at level 7.

Levels 1–2: job specific or generalised training

At its simplest, a workplace procedure consists of a sequence of commands. Minimal information is given about the technology being operated. Either the reader does not need to know this information, or it is assumed that the reader already knows the necessary information. These types of procedures are very common at the basic operator level of manufacturing, in the 'Standard Operating Procedures' (SOPs) written for process workers.

In common with more complex procedures, simple procedures typically begin with a statement of purpose. This may be simply a title for the activity sequence, which embodies the purpose of the procedure as in the following title:

Text 1: simple workplace procedure (from BHP Steel, Slab and Plate Products Division 1990–1991)

TO ISOLATE PRECIPITATOR ELECTRICALLY

1 Move the main isolator switch (CFS) in the precipitator switch room to the OFF position
+ and tag, 'OUT OF SERVICE'.
2 Lock the main isolator switch switching arm using 'Castell Key 2'
3 Remove the 'Castell Key 2'
+ and attach an 'OUT OF SERVICE' tag to the key identifying No. 12 Tar Precipitator.
4 Place the 'Castell Key 2' in the shift supervisor's office.

The representation of experience here differs little from that found in everyday spoken English, except in the specialised terms used to refer to the technology to be operated. Such specialised terms are often constructed as complex nominal groups, subclassifying to the left and subcomposing to the right, illustrated in Figure 9.3.

Despite their potential complexity these technological entities are still realised congruently as nominal groups, acted on by the operator: e.g. *Move the main isolator switch,* or the location or means of actions: *in the precipitator switch room, using 'Castell Key 2'.* Processes are represented congruently as the verbs, *move, tag, lock, remove, attach and place,* and the text unfolds iconically with the action sequence proposed in the text. Likewise the enactment of workplace social relations is congruently realised as imperative mood in each clause, commanding the operator to action, without explanation, argument, or choice.

Another site where written procedures are very common is in the secondary science classroom. Here their function of enabling a specialised task is secondary to learning something more general about the world; the specialised task is not an end in itself, but rather a learning experience leading to some scientific knowledge (see Veel 1992). However the secondary function of classroom procedures is to learn tasks associated with scientific research, such as the use of measuring equipment. In this way school science procedures train students to follow workplace procedures, a skill that is assumed in trades and technical training, and an example of the largely implicit functional relation between school science and workplace technology. If students learn to read and act on classroom science procedures, they will be well equipped to do the same with workplace procedures up to the NTB level corresponding to the stage of their secondary science education.

Text 2: simple classroom procedure (from a Year 8 science class)
    Aim: To see if plants need soil to germinate
    [. . .]
    Firstly, get 2 Petri dishes
    Put a thin layer of soil in one dish and some cotton wool in the other dish
    Next spread 20 seeds in each dish
    Then pour 50ml of water into each dish
    Finally, place both dishes in a warm sunny spot

At this school level the grammar is entirely congruent, both ideationally

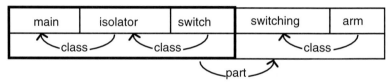

Figure 9.3 Specialised terms: subclassifying to the left and subcomposing to the right

and interpersonally, as in simple workplace procedures. But as well as specialised terms such as 'Petri dish', we find technical terms from biology such as 'germinate'. Specialised terms enter into technological taxonomies of machinery and its parts, technical terms into scientific taxonomies of the natural world.

Level 3: trade certificate or equivalent

At NTB level 3, the grammar of technological texts starts to move away from the patterns of everyday spoken discourse, in both interpersonal and ideational dimensions. Ideationally it becomes a resource for explanation of complex technological processes. The operator requires schematised knowledge of these processes to make independent decisions for controlling them. At this level the operator is construed as a relatively free agent, so that interpersonally the grammar enables choices, giving reasons and purposes as bases for potential actions.

The general grammatical shift is from congruent representation and enactments to metaphorical variants. For example, obligation is infrequently expressed as imperative mood, but rather as modulated declaratives, and is often objectified. Text structure is no longer simple succession. Temporal relations between processes may be simultaneous, and are frequently modulated by cause or condition, operators are given reasons and choices for their actions, including the sequence in which they carry them out. At this level causal relations are usually expressed congruently as conjunctions or prepositions, but may also be expressed metaphorically as verbal or nominal groups. Grammatical metaphor is associated with technical written discourses, which members of industrialised cultures generally begin to learn in junior secondary school. The functions and grammar of texts at this level are comparable to the stage of technological English Halliday identifies in Chaucer's Treatise on the Astrolabe, with some later grammatical developments less frequently employed.

We will exemplify these grammatical developments first with technological explanations. Technological explanations track the manufacturing sequence through the 'topography' of the manufacturing machinery. They typically occur as part of manuals which describe the composition and operation of plant and equipment. The primary function of this genre is to enable an operator to perform a technological procedure requiring knowledge about the process. To do so it must give information to the operator about the manufacturing technology.

The text we will examine here is from one such manual describing the gas cleaning system in a BHP blast furnace. Similar manuals are found in all plants at BHP (a major Australian steel manufacturer), and generally in manufacturing enterprises where award restructuring is underway. Scientific/technological literacy is indispensable for this level of operator.

Text 3.1: technological explanation (from Abeysingha 1991).

Brassert

1   The main function of the brassert is [to **cool down** the blast furnace gas **discharged** *from the furnace*] and [to also partially **remove** dust and grit *from the gas*].

2β To **achieve** this increased gas cleanliness,

α the gas must **pass** *through the brassert* at a reasonably slow velocity.

3   Thus, the semi-clean gas **enters** *the bottom section of the brassert via a main from the dustcatcher*.
    [. . .]

4   *Inside the brassert* two ring mains (top and bottom sprays) **supply** salt water *to the brassert sprays*.

5α There are 24 sprays [*on each ring main*],

β each spray projecting *into the brassert*.
    [. . .]

6   The primary salt water **is supplied** *to the top ring main* by one of two (2) pumps, [*located in the recirculating fresh water (RFW) pumphouse*, [*located under the emergency head tank*].

7   Secondary salt water **is supplied** *to the lower ring main from the power house*.

8.1 The water spray *in the brassert* **cools** the gas stream

8.2 and also **combines** with the gas, dust, etc.,

8.3 and **precipitates** (by gravity) *at the base of the brassert*.

9   The mud precipitated is periodically **removed** by the brassert dump valves [*located at the base of the brassert*]

The technological explanation is mostly realised as a sequence of 'doing' processes (**bold type**) – an activity sequence. Like the simple procedure, these clauses follow one after the other in succession as the manufacturing process unfolds. As in the simple procedure these material processes typically unfold in concrete spatial locations (*italic type*). Each of these locations realises a new part of the manufacturing technology. The function of the technological explanation is simultaneously to explain the manufacturing process as an activity sequence, and to build up the composition taxonomy of the manufacturing technology. The activity sequence is realised as a succession of material processes; and the composition taxonomy is realised as a sequence of circumstances of location in which these processes occur. The composition taxonomy of the blast furnace gas cleaning system, realised in this technological explanation, is illustrated in Figure 9.4.

The activity sequences in this text are similar to those of secondary science explanations described by Wignell *et al.* (1992/1993). These authors describe the sequence of temporal and causal relations between events in an explanation as an *implication sequence*. This means that each

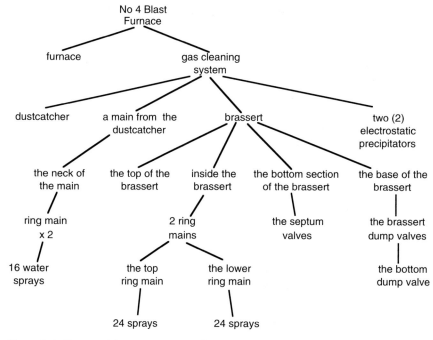

Figure 9.4 Composition taxonomy of the blast furnace gas cleaning system

step in the sequence is logically implied by the preceding step as a chain of cause and effect. An example of such an implication sequence is the introductory section of the technological explanation:

1   The main function of the brassert is . . . [to also partially remove dust and grit from the gas].
2β To achieve this increased gas cleanliness,
α   the gas must pass through the brassert at a reasonably slow velocity.
3   Thus, the semi-clean gas enters the bottom section of the brassert via a main from the dustcatcher.

Here we find some of the grammatical features Halliday identifies as coming to the fore in the scientific English of Newton's time. Clause 1 is an identifying relation, with a nominalised *process* function as the Theme of the message. This is identified by an embedded clause *to also partially remove dust and grit from the gas* as New information.

1 The main function of the brassert	is	[to also partially remove dust and grit from the gas]
Value/Theme	Process	Token/New

This embedded clause is picked up in the Theme of the following step, and itself nominalised *this increased gas cleanliness*. Figure 9.5 illustrates how the congruent wording of the material clause is 'translated' into the metaphorical wording of the nominal group.

There are three movements in nominalisation from clause 1 to 2. (1) the Quality *partially* becomes an Epithet *increased*, (2) the Process plus Goal *remove dust and grit* becomes a Thing *cleanliness* and (3) the Location *from the gas* becomes the Classifier *gas*. These steps in nominalisation exemplify the options for ideational metaphor in English described by Halliday (Chapter 8, this volume).

The logical relation between clauses 1 and 2 is causal: the reason for following activity sequence is *to partially remove dust and grit from the gas*, although this relation is left implicit – there is no conjunction to mark it. Nevertheless this implicit causal relation signals to the reader that what is to follow is an explanation, of how the dust and gas is removed. The remainder of text is devoted to explaining this process, as an implication sequence. Its goal is to explain the technological sequence to the operator responsible for removing *the mud precipitated* at the end, and is followed in the operating manual by a procedure for doing so.

Technological explanations are closely related to similar sequences in scientific explanations of the kind that junior secondary students meet. The following is an example from Wignell *et al.* (1992):

Text 3.2: scientific explanation (from Sale *et al.* 1980)

1   After flash floods, desert streams **flowing** *from upland areas* **carry** heavy loads of silt, sand and rock fragments.
2β   As they **reach** *the flatter area of desert basins,*
  α   they **lose** speed and their waters may also **soak** quickly *into the basin floor.*
3   The streams then **drop** their loads, the heaviest materials first – the stones – then the sand and finally the silt.

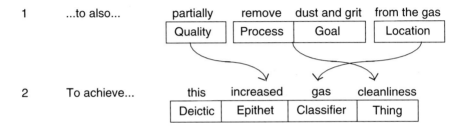

Figure 9.5 Congruent wording 'translated' into the metaphorical wording

4β **Choked** by their own deposits,
  α these short lived streams frequently **divide** *into a maze of channels* **spreading** their load *in all directions.*
5   In time fan or cone shaped deposits of gravel, sand, silt and clay **are formed** *around each valley or canyon outlet.*
6   These are called alluvial fans.

This text exhibits similar resources to the technological explanation for tracking something through time and space – in this case *desert streams*. (1) There is a sequence of 'doing' processes. (2) These take place *from, in, into and around* circumstances of location in space. (3) The participant being tracked: *desert streams* is in Theme position in most clauses. (4) Stages of the sequence are announced by marked Themes: enhancing clauses or prepositional phrases.

The difference is that this is an explanation of a natural, rather than technological, feature. The function of the science explanation genre is not to teach us about parts of technology; the circumstances are simply spatial locations, and not as significant as in the technological explanation. The function is to explain the sequence of the formation of *alluvial fans*, and finally to give them a name – a technical term that fits into the classification system of the scientific field. This is done by the means of an identifying clause (6).

These (fan or cone shaped deposits of gravel, sand, silt and clay)	are called	alluvial fans
Value	Process	Token

The function of the technological explanation on the other hand is to enable the reader to operate a section of technology. To this end, the final clause gives us the part of technology that we will use to perform the operation *the brassert dump valves*. This is a specialised rather than a technical term; its significance lies not in its place in a classification system, but in its function in the manufacturing process.

Written procedures in the workplace can become very complex when the operator needs to make choices about a course of action. These decisions depend on what is happening in the manufacturing process, so at each point there are a number of possible decisions to take. We call this type of procedure a *conditional procedure*. An operator at this level has to understand the effect of his actions on the technology, and is given reasons for each step in the procedure, as set out following step 1 in the following example, Text 3.3.

Text 3.3: conditional procedure (from BHP Coke Ovens By Products Dept 1991)

STOP GAS FLOW THROUGH PRECIPITATOR

1 Check the number of the tar precipitators on line to assure an uninterrupted gas flow.

Currently four (4) tar precipitators are the minimum number that have to be on line to maintain an acceptable back pressure range of 8–14 kPa.

If after this precipitator is isolated:

    i There will be fewer than four (4) tar precipitators in operation, go to step 2.

    ii There are four (4) or more tar precipitators in operation, go to step 3.

2 Open tar precipitators by pass gas valve (5 or 6 turns).
3 Close the inlet gas valve slowly,
  and tag, 'OUT OF SERVICE' in two positions:
  • Rotork isolator with the lugs tied together,
  • Manual valve handle.
4 Exhauster driver to monitor back pressure
  which must be in the acceptable range
  if enough precipitators are on line (Range 8–14 kPa).

The complex conditional relations in a conditional procedure are already remote from everyday spoken English, and may be difficult to follow. However similar complexity of conditions is a common feature of secondary school science texts, at junior and senior levels. The genre where these types of conditions are found are explanations of abstract physical phenomena, such as pressure, upthrust in a fluid, flotation, etc.

Text 3.4: conditional explanation (from Heading 1967)

Buoyancy and Density

1β If the object is completely submerged
 α it displaces its own volume of fluid.
2 The weight of displaced fluid, and therefore the upthrust, will depend on the density of the fluid.

3β If the density of the fluid is less than the average density of the object,
α1 the weight of the displaced fluid will be less than the weight of the object
 2 and the object will sink.

4β If, on the other hand, the density of the fluid is greater than the average density of the object, α the weight of the displaced fluid will therefore exceed the weight of the object.

5α The net upward force will then cause the object to rise to the surface
β where it will float.

In this case, clauses 1–2 set up the overall conditions in which the following two choices, 3 and 4, unfold. But in general the grammatical complexity of this text is very similar to that of the conditional procedure. In both cases the reader is asked to *imagine alternative possible eventualities.* In the science explanation, these imagined events are intended to lead to the students' understanding of an abstract physical relationship – that 'buoyancy' is dependent on 'density'. And the way this understanding is achieved is through the grammatical resource of conditional relations between clauses. In the conditional procedure, the imagined events are possible outcomes of actions the operator might take, and the same grammatical resource is used.

Both texts display features of the written mode of English. In these written texts, the grammar is constructing possible worlds that are independent of the immediate context in which they are being read. This kind of grammar has evolved in written English to be able to do this, to construct texts that are independent of any particular context. It enables scientifically literate readers and writers to generalise across different possible contexts, and to construct abstract models of reality. These abstractions can then be translated back into concrete situations, whether it is to make operating decisions, or to design industrial technology. On the other hand, the everyday spoken English that most students begin secondary school with does not enable them to generalise and abstract along scientific lines. To be able to do so, they need to be taught how to read scientific writing.

Level 4: post-trade or equivalent certificate

NTB level 4 is at a junction between trades and professional levels of industry and education. Texts at this level show features of lower rank procedures, e.g. sequences of commands, expressed not in imperative mood, but as declaratives and objectified. But they also show features of higher rank texts, e.g. the apparent effacement of interpersonal intrusion except as causal relations. And these relations are expressed by relational verbs, e.g. . . . is taken to be . . ., realising internal result.

Text 4: technical procedure (from BHP Metallurgical Technology 1991)

[. . .]

Sample preparation (Sequence of technological activities)

1.1 The test section **shall be** sectioned transverse to the weld joint,

1.2 ground to a 1200 grit
1.3 and etched with 2% nital.
2β To assist metallographic examination,
  α the test piece **should be** cut down to the approximate dimension
  shown in Fig. 2.

Here the sequence of commands is iconic with the activity sequence to
be carried out. However the commands are realised by modulated
declaratives, simultaneously grading obligation as high *shall be* or median
should be, and enabling the technology to be thematised *The test section, the
test piece*. In addition we find experiential metaphors such as the verbalised *sectioned* 'cut into sections', and the nominalised *metallographic examination* 'examine with metallography', which function in a marked
thematic purpose for the activity.

[. . .]

Results (Sequence of scientific activities)

3 The vertical crack length **is expressed** as a percentage of the vertical
  leg length (I/L) x 100
4 The four results obtained **are averaged to give** a result to the
  nearest 10%.
5 This number **is** then **taken to be** the amount of cracking in the weld.

Each identifying relational process in the Results stage of the technical
procedure is made up of technical verbs from the field of mathematics *is
expressed, obtained, are averaged to give, is taken to be* . . . Participants are
nominalised processes or mathematical abstractions. By means of passive
voice, each step is organised as a sequence of Theme/Value and New/
Token, with the next step picking up the New of the preceding step, and
redeploying it as Theme, illustrated in Figure 9.6.
   This kind of textual pattern, with nominalisations and mathematical
abstractions built up as Themes and News, Halliday (1993) sees beginning in Newton's writing, evolving to this level in Maxwell's writing

The vertical crack length is expressed **as a percentage of the vertical leg length**

The four results obtained are averaged to give **a result to the nearest 10%**

This number is then taken to be **the amount of cracking in the weld**

Figure 9.6 Picking up the News of the preceding step, and redeploying it as
Theme

| The amount of heat which enters or leaves the body | is measured | **by the product of the increase or diminution of entropy...** |

| The consequences which flow from this conjecture | may be conveniently described | **by an extension of the term 'entropy' to electric phenomena** |

Figure 9.7 Nominalisations and mathematical abstractions built up as Themes and News

by the late nineteenth century. For example, from Maxwell (1881) illustrated in Figure 9.7.

These are the kinds of textual/ideational patterns that students are learning to read by late junior or senior secondary school, in the science and maths classrooms.

From an interpersonal perspective, this stage of the procedure is still functioning as a sequence of commands, but the obligation inherent in each step is objectified and implicit to the point of invisibility. The operator's obligation to perform these mathematical tasks is implicit in her role in the organisation and in the overall function of the text as a procedure for this role. The information giving function of the procedure at this stage has overtaken its commanding function, as the status inherent in a technical qualification replaces the explicit control to which less qualified workers are subject.

Level 5: advanced certificate to diplomas

In materials and product testing areas of manufacturing enterprises it is necessary to produce written reports on testing to customers. These extended texts are typically known as technical notes. Technical notes are written by technicians and applied scientists, often with data recorded on pro formas as the Results of technical procedures by technical assistants. They follow similar overall stages as scientific research articles, but their goal is to solve a specific production problem, whereas research articles are typically concerned with more general scientific problems.

At tertiary trained levels, obligation is almost completely depersonalised, realised only as degrees of causation. Written texts are no longer procedures for action, but reports on actions and observations performed. In the ideational grammar of these texts we find a lot of information packed tightly into series of post-modifiers in nominal groups. This includes classification of things, as well as sequences of nominalised activities. This nominal density increases as we move up the ladder, beginning with **technical notes** on technological investigations carried out by diploma level engineers.

Text 5: technical note (specialised) (from Drmota *et al.* 1991)

GTA Welds on hi-silicon coil plates without filler rod addition

1α Consistency of weld shape and form was difficult to achieve
  β with burn through occurring both in welds showing good penetra-
    tion as well as welds made at lower current levels which showed lack
    of penetration.
2α We found
  β that only a slight increase in amperage of say 5 amps, after a
    previous weld giving a good clean weld without full fusion, would
    cause the next weld to burn through with good weld penetration
    observed on intermittent sections.

(1) Classifying by means of post-modifiers

A common pattern in both specialised and technical/scientific discourse
is for things or processes to be classified within nominal groups. The
entity being classified is typically the Head of the nominal group, and the
criteria by which they are classified occur as post-modifiers. We saw in
Text 1 how classification occurs in pre-modifiers, and composition in
post-modifiers in specialised terms. In scientific writing strings of post-
modifiers can get very dense, and we find the beginning of this density in
the technical note.

  In clause 1β, there is a long nominal group complex with the structure
'x as well as y'.

  welds showing good penetration *as well as* welds made at lower current
  levels which showed lack of penetration.

Here there are two nominal groups linked by the conjunction 'as well as',
illustrated in Figure 9.8:

  This nominal group complex classifies two types of welds for which
there are no existing specialised terms.

welds	showing good penetration
Thing	Qualifier

'as well as'	welds	made at lower current levels	which showed lack of penetration
	Thing	Qualifier	Qualifier

  These two classes of weld can be re-expressed as a taxonomic diagram,
in Figure 9.9:

  In both nominal groups the characteristics of the weld are the *criteria*
for their classification and occur as post-modifiers to 'welds' as Head.

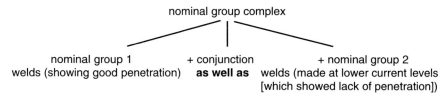

nominal group 1   + conjunction   + nominal group 2
welds (showing good penetration)   **as well as**   welds (made at lower current levels
                                              [which showed lack of penetration])

Figure 9.8 Two nominal groups linked by the conjunction 'as well as'

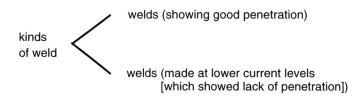

Figure 9.9 Two classes of weld re-expressed as a taxonomic diagram

There are two criteria here: (1) quality/quantity of penetration (good vs lack), and (2) current level (higher vs lower). These criterial *characteristics* are construed in the same way as *parts* in a specialised term, i.e., as post-modifiers in the nominal group which represents a technological entity. This pattern redounds with that in scientific taxonomies, in which the compositional parts/characteristics of an entity determine its place in a classification taxonomy.

(2) *Compressing activity sequences as clause elements*

Another common pattern in technological/scientific discourse is for activity sequences to be compressed into a single clause, with most of the information packed into sequences of post-modifiers in nominal groups. Clause 2β shows the beginning of this pattern.

Actor	Location:time	Pro-	Goal	-cess	Accompaniment
only a slight increase in amperage of say 5 amps,	after a previous weld giving a good clean weld without full fusion,	would cause	the next weld	to burn through	with good weld penetration observed on intermittent sections.

As in clause 1, clause 2β also classifies two kinds of welds, *a previous weld* and *the next weld*, with their characteristics expressed as circumstances or embedded clauses.

> a previous weld [giving a good clean weld (without full fusion)]
> the next weld . . . with good weld penetration [observed on inter-
> mittent sections]

But there is also a temporal relation between these two nominalised processes of 'welding'. The sequence is expressed both circumstantially and as nominal Classifiers **after** a **previous** weld. There is also a causal relation between two processes, 'burning through' and 'increasing the amperage', the latter nominalised to become Theme of the clause. A congruent representation of the activity sequence might read:

> we first welded (the metal) ^ then we increased the amperage ^ so it got burnt through

The whole clause might be unpacked as a dependency sequence:

1α   we first welded (the metal)
=β1   which made a good clean weld
 +2   but did not fully fuse (the metal)

x2β   then the next weld would burn through (the metal)
xα1   because we increased the amperage by 5 amps
+2α   and we observed
 'β   that the weld penetrated well on intermittent sections (of the metal)

At this level we find a mixture of congruent and metaphorical resources used to represent the unfolding of time, and classification of entities. These two semantic domains are starting to coalesce into the same grammatical pattern of nominalisation and post-modification. In Text 5, temporal relations are construed circumstantially between nominalised or embedded events. Interpersonally, writers at this level are still subjectively taking responsibility for their investigation, explicitly as personal pronouns in 'like-type' mental processes, *We found that* . . ., and implicitly in passives *good weld penetration [that we] observed*, and 'please-type' mentals *welds showing [us] good penetration*. They also express their feelings in attitudinal lexis such as *difficult to achieve, a good clean weld*, etc. Above this level such explicit personal intrusions become rare.

The interpersonal goal of the text is to make a recommendation for change in a particular production process. The interpersonal features we have noted above are evident in the Conclusions and recommendation stage, in which the writers subjectively make (1) a claim of proof, flowing indisputably from their experiments, (2) a tentative 'suggested' command to their managers/clients.

> Conclusion and recommendation
>   From our weld trials we have proven
>   that these steel grades are capable of being welded by the GTA process.
>   However all process variables have to be 'spot on'
>   to achieve consistent full penetration.
>   [. . .]
>   We suggest further trial welding

using an automatic filler wire feeder
to produce more consistent welds.
Unfortunately we do not have this equipment at present.

The recommendations leave the reader's response relatively open to spend money on further trialling and on new equipment. The latter is subtly recommended by a subjective invitation to solidarity, *Unfortunately we do not have . . . at present*, a discursive strategy familiar more in oral and non-technical contexts than in technical writing.

Level 6: associate diploma to degree

The following excerpt is from a technical note written by a senior chemist in a testing laboratory. This position would typically require a university degree in chemistry, engineering or metallurgy, as well as considerable experience. However the text itself was relatively brief and accessible to maintenance or production supervisors who may not be professional scientists. It reports the results of chemical testing of a maintenance problem, the chemical testing for which would probably have been done by technical assistants or technicians who record their results as figures in printed pro formas. The tertiary trained supervisor then writes these up as a technical note with a Discussion and Recommendations for the client.

Text 6: technical note: technical (extract from BHP Steel, Slab and Plate Products Division 1991)

SUBJECT: OPTIMUL BM460 OIL EX BOS No 1 CHARGER
          CRANE MAIN HOIST WORM DRIVE GEARBOXES.

1 Infrared examination of the oil suggested contamination with per-chloroethylene (tetrachloroethylene).
2 Confirmation of this finding was the fact that the gearbox had been flushed out with perchloroethylene.

First we can note the complexity of the specialised term in the title. As we found in the simpler specialised terms, while pre-modification classifies, specifying more general classes, post-modification de-composes, specifying smaller parts of wholes, illustrated in Figure 9.10.

At this level, activity sequences tend to be compressed into identifying relational clauses. Participants in these clauses are most frequently full nominalisations, embedded clauses less so, whereas in the previous text at level 5, embedded clauses or prepositional phrases are more frequent. This is comparable to the third stage in Halliday's historical schema, from embedding to full nominalisation. Once again, the textual function of this is to organise sequences of messages as Themes and News, as in Figure 9.11.

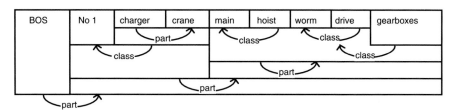

Figure 9.10 Pre-modification classifies, post-modification de-composes

Infrared examination of the oil suggested **contamination with perchloroethylene**

Confirmation of this finding was **the fact that the gearbox had been flushed ...**

Figure 9.11 Nominalisation-organised sequences of messages as Themes and News

In this example we also see the final step in the historical development of nominalisation. In clause 1 internal cause is realised verbally *suggested*, expressing low obligation and probability. This meaning is picked up and realised nominally as the Theme in clause 2 *Confirmation . . .*, in which the obligation/probability is graded as high.

As with Text 5, these two clauses can be unpacked as an implication sequence of observation and reasoning, illustrated in Figure 9.12.

However the implication sequence in Text 6 is more implicit than in Text 5, in which temporal sequence is explicitly signalled by conjunctions *after* and temporal Classifiers *previous* and *next*, and the verbs *caused to* and *observed* congruently realise external and internal causes. Interpersonally, the original metaphorical realisation in Text 6 also effaces the person-alities engaged in the investigation, shifting responsibility for judgements

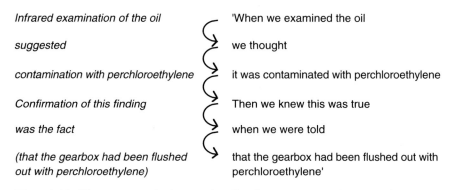

Figure 9.12 Clauses unpacked as an implication sequence of observation and reasoning

of cause and proof, from people to the observed phenomena. As at level 5, implication sequences are nominalised and conflated with composition and classification taxonomies, but at this level interpersonal judgements also become part of the edifice of abstract entities, grading relations between them as more or less necessary and evident. The world of people and power has been reconstrued as a structure of things and truths. These truths are accumulated in the Theme/New text development, as evidence supporting the final Recommendations stage, in which authority is more congruently expressed as a set of commands:

Recommendations
Due to the critical nature of these gearboxes it is recommended that:

(1) A regular checking programme be instituted to monitor the oil quality for physical properties and wear metals.
(2) Whenever flushing and oil changes are carried out, viscosity checks should be carried out to determine the possible presence of residual flushing fluid.

The same recommendation should be applied to other similar critical units.

These recommendations are more highly obligated than those of Text 5, (a) because the technology affected is 'critical' to the production process, and (b) because the writers have greater institutional authority. This authority is rendered non-negotiable by objectifying it. Modal responsibility for the obligation is shifted away from the writer to the technology, by a Thematic nominalised reason *Due to the critical nature of these gearboxes it is recommended . . .*, in which high obligation is expressed objectively as classifying an abstraction *the critical nature*. A subjective conguent reading might be 'we very strongly recommend', which is the pattern in Text 5, except that those writers' lower authority is also evident in the low obligation modulating their recommendations.

Level 7: degree or higher degree

The following excerpt is from a text written by a post-graduate level applied scientist to other applied scientists in the client organisation. It addresses a particular problem in the production process in the enterprise, so it is still a technical note rather than a research article (which typically addresses more general scientific problems). The detail of the field and the scientific grammar approaches that of post-graduate research articles, but is still accessible to applied scientists and engineers in industrial production. Nevertheless, the text assumes maximum field knowledge on the part of the reader.

Text 7: scientific technical note

SUBJECT: METALLOGRAPHIC EXAMINATION OF BIS 40 SLAB SAMPLES FOR CRACKING AND PRECIPITATION AT COLUMNAR GRAIN BOUNDARIES

1   Defects have been shown in the past to be related to surface and sub-surface cracks associated with columnar grain boundary precipitation of aluminium nitride films which in the case of BIS 40 had grown upon boron nitride precipitates.

2α Results of this investigation suggest

β that plate surface defects were probably due to brittle failure along subsurface films at columnar grain boundaries during initial stages of rolling or during early stages of slab casting.

Partly for reasons of space, the scientific field must be summed up very briefly and the result is very dense writing. The structure of each clause or clause complex is simple relation, but the information is packaged as nominalisations with long strings of post-modifiers.

Defects   have been shown in the past to be related   to surface and sub-surface cracks . . .

Token	Process/internal cause	Value

As we have seen in similar clauses types in Texts 4 and 6, internal cause is realised verbally *have been shown . . . to be related to*. But here the direction of cause is left implicit; do *defects* cause *surface and sub-surface cracks*, or vice versa? The direction of causality is also effaced in the post-modifiers which realise an implication sequence.

surface and sub-surface cracks	associated with columnar grain boundary precipitation of aluminium nitride films	which in the case of BIS 40 had grown upon boron nitride precipitates.
Thing	Qualifier	Qualifier

Do *surface and sub-surface cracks* cause *columnar grain boundary precipitation* or vice versa? The whole of clause 1 can be unpacked in steps, to reveal the causal sequence lurking in these strings of bi-directional relations, as in Figure 9.13.

Figure 9.13 Causal sequence lurking in strings of bi-directional relations

The bi-directional relations *shown to be related to* and *associated with*, can be re-expressed as explicit causal relations modalised by degrees of evidentiality and probability, as in Figure 9.14.

Third, the entire metaphorically realised implication sequence can be unpacked in a more spoken form, illustrated in Figure 9.15.

The same procedure of unpacking can also be applied to the projected clause 2β, as in Figure 9.16. First the nominalised causal relation *due to* is verbalised as *caused by*.

Second, the long nominal group functioning as Token/New is analysed as a string of Qualifiers.

brittle failure	along subsurface films	at columnar grain boundaries	during initial stages of rolling	or during early stages of slab casting
Thing	Qualifier	Qualifier	Qualifier	Qualifier

Third, the nominalisations are unpacked as steps in the implication sequence, as in Figure 9.17.

These unpacked sequences of cause give us a *scientific explanation*, an implication sequence where one event is made to imply the next event as a sequence of cause and effect. It is a feature of science beyond the basic

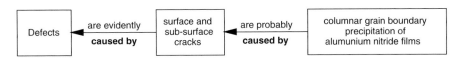

Figure 9.14 Causal relations modalised by degrees of evidentiality and probability

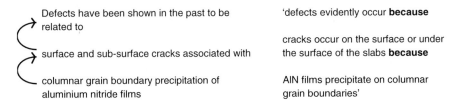

Figure 9.15 Metaphorically realised implication sequence unpacked in a more spoken form

Figure 9.16 Nominalised causal relation *due to* verbalised as *caused by*

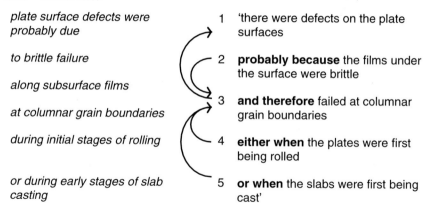

plate surface defects were probably due	1	'there were defects on the plate surfaces
to brittle failure	2	**probably because** the films under the surface were brittle
along subsurface films		
at columnar grain boundaries	3	**and therefore** failed at columnar grain boundaries
during initial stages of rolling	4	**either when** the plates were first being rolled
or during early stages of slab casting	5	**or when** the slabs were first being cast'

Figure 9.17 Nominalisations unpacked as steps in the implication sequence

junior secondary level that such extended explanations can be packed into a few clauses, by means of nominalisation and layers of post-modifiers in relational clauses. The junior secondary explanations (such as we saw in Text 3.3) are the starting point for understanding how science constructs causal relations between processes. But to get beyond this point, students must learn how to read the highly metaphorical realisations we are seeing here.

As we have seen in both Text 6 and Text 7, the writers are cautious about stating causal relations between events. They use a wide range of causal verbs to temper their claims of obligation and direction, probability and evidentiality, and refer often to previous research in the field 'it has been shown', 'it was reported' etc. The interpersonal function of this tendency is to negotiate the accumulation of evidence. Each cause or proof is modulated and modalised with degrees of truth, allowing more or less potential for counter-claims. An unmodalised statement may be scientifically unacceptable, since one example of counter-evidence negates it. The truth value of the text lies in its accumulation of probabilistic statements of evidence, leading to a conclusion that is acceptable to the writer's professional community (Hunston 1993, 1994). Following the Conclusion stage in the chain of reasoning of Text 7 (not shown in the excerpt here), the writers consider that enough evidence has been accumulated to justify the principle recommendation:

Recommendations

To minimise the likelihood of grain boundary precipitate film formation and resultant plate surface defects, it is recommended that

(1) Harder mould cooling and faster casting speeds be employed.

Whereas Texts 5 and 6 were concerned with local production processes, in Text 7 a phase of the general steel production process, worth hundreds of millions of dollars, rides on this recommendation. It is not therefore surprising that the writers are tentative about determining causative factors for the problem. But this pattern of probabilistic statements and accumulation of evidence is characteristic of scientific discourse in general. Furthermore, all of the grammatical resources for constructing an explanation, employed at this industrial level, can be found in educational science texts at senior secondary and undergraduate level. The specialisation in field and professional role identification evident in this text are products of further tertiary science training, built on the discursive resources and behaviours acquired in late adolescence.

CONCLUSION

The drift towards grammatical metaphor that Halliday has documented over the modern history of science discourse, and that we have documented here through the industrial hierarchy, also corresponds to the stages of a science apprenticeship, from junior secondary to postgraduate levels, illustrated in Figure 9.18.

Halliday focuses on textual pressures as a source of these grammatical developments in the written mode, and these are amply illustrated in our analyses of industry texts. From level 3 up, the grammar that workers read and write is increasingly remote from everyday spoken English. The pressure to organise more and more information that is more and more technical, into coherent written text, has produced highly metaphorical forms of grammar. This information includes (1) taxonomies of specialised and technical terms, and (2) causal explanations of technological and scientific processes. Because the English clause packages information as nominal groups in Theme and News, both taxonomic relations and causal relations come to be expressed within nominal groups.

However, while its primary pressure may be textual, the semiotic drift in science's evolution, its educational sequence and the industrial hierarchy is also ideational and interpersonal. Processes become things that act on other processes as things, then this relation of 'acting upon' itself becomes a thing. The unfolding of activity sequences are finally

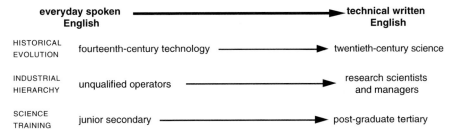

Figure 9.18 Correlated tendencies in historical evolution, industrial hierarchy and science training

re-expressed as parts of composition taxonomies, as criteria for classifying the abstract entities they modify. Instead of a sensually experienced world of unfolding processes involving actual people, things, places and qualities, reality comes to be experienced virtually as a generalised structure of abstractions. Instead of a subjectively negotiated social order, in which status and solidarity are enacted in personal exchanges, interpersonal meanings are subsumed in the relations between abstract things, graded as more or less necessary or evident.

Of course the scientists, engineers, educators and managers that live this abstract reality in their working roles, also know the older spoken construal. They learn it first as children and continue to deploy it in personal relationships. This is an aspect of what Bernstein refers to as an 'elaborated' coding orientation, simply put: to have access to more than one set of options for making meaning (Bernstein 1971–1990). However the scientific construal is dominant in modern industrial society, and is integral to the maintenance and development of its stratified social structure; the theories of natural reality it realises have evolved in tandem with the relations of production in industrial capitalism. It is the property of the class which benefits most from this system, and reflects the structures of institutional roles which its members occupy in the course of making their living and sharing control.

A secondary science education is probably essential for participating powerfully in modern economic and political processes. But this entails more than just learning new ways of construing the natural world; it also involves learning new ways of being in the world, remote from kin and local community relations, a world of impersonal, objectified roles whose occupants must continually negotiate their status and solidarity. The language barriers erected by these forms of discourse currently exclude the majority of the world's peoples from participating in its control. As we learn how to teach effectively more than the few students who currently acquire technical literacies, the rigid scientific industrial hierarchies I have outlined in this chapter may metamorphose into more efficient production systems, exploiting the intellectual potential of all workers.

REFERENCES

Abeysingha, K. 1991. *No. 4 Blast Furnace Gas Cleaning Manual.* BHP Steel, Slab and Plate Products Division, Port Kembla.

Bernstein, B. 1971–1990. *Class, Codes and Control: The structuring of pedagogic discourse.* London: Routledge.

BHP Coke Ovens By Products Dept 1991. *Isolate No. 12 Tar Precipitator.* BHP Steel, Slab and Plate Products Division, Port Kembla.

BHP Metallurgical Technology 1991. *CTS Testing Procedure.* BHP Steel, Slab and Plate Products Division, Port Kembla.

Byron, J. and P. Renwick 1991. *Metallographic Examination of BIS Slab Samples for*

Cracking and Precipitation at Columnar Grain Boundaries. BHP Steel, Slab and Plate Products Division, Port Kembla.

Drmota, R. and P. Draper, Welding Development 1991. *GTA welding on high silicon coil plates without filler rod addition.* BHP Steel, Slab and Plate Products Division, Port Kembla.

Finn, B. *et al.* 1991. *Young People's Participation in Post Compulsory Education and Training: Report of the Australian Education Council Review Committee.* Canberra: DEET.

Halliday, M.A.K. 1990. New ways of meaning: A challenge to applied linguistics. *Journal of Applied Linguistics* 6.

Halliday, M.A.K. 1993. *On the language of physical science.* In Halliday and Martin 1993.

Halliday, M.A.K. and J.R. Martin 1993. *Writing Science: Literacy and discursive power.* Pittsburgh: University of Pittsburgh Press.

Harvey, D. 1989. *The Condition of Post-Modernity.* London: Basil Blackwell.

Heading, K.E.G., D.F. Provis, T.D. Scott, J.E. Smith and R.T. Smith 1967. *Science for Secondary Schools*, 2. Adelaide: Rigby.

Hunston, S. 1993. Evaluation and ideology in scientific English. In M. Ghadessy (ed.) *Register Analysis: Theory and practice.* London: Pinter (Open Linguistics Series). 57–73.

Hunston, S. 1994. Evaluation and organisation in a sample of written academic discourse. In M. Coulthard (ed.) *Advances in Written Text Analysis.* London: Routledge. 191–218.

Lemke, J. 1990. *Talking Science: Language, learning and values.* Norwood, NJ: Ablex.

Martin, J.R. 1992. *English Text.* Amsterdam: Benjamins.

Maxwell, J.C. 1881. *An Elementary Treatise on Electricity.* Oxford: Clarendon.

National Training Board 1991. *National Competency Standards: Policy and guidelines.* Canberra: NTB.

Rose, D., D. McInnes and D. Korner 1992. *Write It Right: Scientific literacy in industry.* Sydney: Disadvantaged Schools Program.

Sale, C., B. Friedman and G. Wilson 1980. *Our Changing World. Book 1: The vanishing natural ecosystem.* Melbourne: Longman Cheshire.

Veel, R. 1992. Engaging with scientific language: a functional approach to the language of school science. *The Australian Science Teachers Journal* 38.4. 31–35.

Wignell, P., J.R. Martin and S. Eggins 1993. *The discourse of geography: Ordering and explaining the natural world.* In Halliday and Martin 1993.

10 Extended reality, proto-nouns and the vernacular

Distinguishing the technological from the scientific

P.R.R. White

INTRODUCTION

It is a commonplace within the academic literature and more generally in the wider community for the discourses of western experimental science and modern industrial technology to be represented as occupying the same socio-semiotic space, as constituting the same functional variety of language. The linkage of the two is such that they frequently share the same nominal group, being referenced together as 'the language of science and technology'. Thus we find that a recent study of the literacy needs of science-based industries in Australia makes no distinction between the scientific and the technological and refers simply to 'the language features of scientific/technological writing' (Rose *et al.* 1992) Similarly, the general-ist science magazine, *Australasian Science*, carries the subtitle 'Exploring Science and Technology in Everyday Life'.

From a commonsense perspective, there are, of course, differences in the social context in which the two discourses operate. Science is typi-cally understood to constitute the practices by which systematic theories are formulated about the constitution of the natural world, by means of repeatable observation and experiment. Technology, in contrast, is con-stituted of the practices by which tools are developed with which humans interact with each other and with their physical environment. This contrast is reflected in the distinction made, by way of example, between the 'technologists' and the 'scientists' within the research laboratories of Australia's primary telecommunications provider, Telstra. Research by the author in 1994 revealed that staff at the laboratories operated with this broad conceptual division, designating as 'scientists' those workers involved with 'pure', 'theoretical' research and as 'technologists' those involved with developing new devices or new modes of operation for telecommunications equipment.

The two domains are, nevertheless, intimately interconnected as social institutions. Science relies on technology to provide the devices by which it conducts its experimentation just as technology relies upon science to provide the theoretical basis for its development of new or more efficient devices. The two enterprises are therefore mutually implicated, the one serving both as the other's servant and as the other's beneficiary.

Should we assume, however, that the texts which enact these two domains necessarily share the same key linguistic features? Should we assume that the semantic, lexico-grammatical and text-organisational features which distinguish scientific texts also characterise technological discourse?

This chapter will argue that it is possible to identify systematic patterns of difference in the lexico-grammatical preferences of the two discourses and that these can be explained by reference to a fundamental difference in the communicative purposes of their respective specialist lexis. (In this, I am picking up on the distinction made by Halliday between 'concrete technological' terms and 'abstract scientific' terms in his discussion of Chaucer's *Treatise on the Astrolabe*, a text which is both technological and proto-scientific, Halliday and Martin 1993.) While the two discourses rely on the same range of lexical resources when developing new specialist terminology, they differ, however, in their preferences for particular resources, in the degree that they mobilise particular resources when construing the phenomenon of their respective 'non-commonsensical' ideational domains. English-language science, for example, favours morphologically non-native forms derived from Greek and Latin, while modern technology favours elaborately premodified nominal groups built from items drawn from the vernacular lexicon and the acronyms derived from these complex groupings. They differ also with respect to certain grammatical phenomena, the most significant of which are the structures associated with specialist category definition. Science favours modes of definition which clearly articulate a taxonomic space, foregrounding and systematising both cohyponym-to-cohyponym and hyponym-to-superordinate relationships. The definitional structures of technology, in contrast, are much less directly focused on such a mapping of taxonomic spaces. They typically act to identify the functionality of items rather than to locate them in a systematised set of taxonomic relationships.

The chapter will argue that these differences can be explained by reference to the semantics of what I will term 'lexicon revaleurisation' and 'lexicon extension'. Martin (Halliday and Martin 1993) has demonstrated how much of the specialist lexico-grammar of scientific texts acts to establish experiential categories which reconstrue and hence revaleurise commonsense experiences of reality, a syndrome which he has termed 'technicality'. The chapter will argue that there is a second communicative purpose operational in the specialist lexis of scientific and technological texts by which the lexico-grammar acts not to challenge or displace the vernacular system of valeur but to extend it. I will term this 'lexicon extension', a process by which the language develops new categories and new names for these categories as the potential range of vernacular experience is expanded over time. It will be shown that while at least a key sub-component of scientific discourse is characterised by its strong association with lexicon revaleurisation, the specialist lexis characteristic of technological discourse is that of lexicon extension.

The chapter will give special attention to the technological acronym since it is such a salient feature of technological discourse. It will be shown that many technological acronyms are no longer simply abbreviations of longer forms but have taken on at least some of the qualities of established lexical items. They have become what I will term 'proto nouns' and have features which specifically equip them for lexicon extension in the domain of modern technology where the new, extended reality to be mapped is one of constant innovation, instability and provisionality.

THE SPECIALIST LEXICONS OF SCIENCE AND TECHNOLOGY

Terminology – modes of naming

Science and technology draw on the following resources for naming their specialist, non-vernacular categories (although both vocabularies are non-vernacular, they are non-vernacular for different reasons, a point which will be demonstrated below):

- the reuse of established, vernacular lexical items: (science) *desert, fruit;* (technology) *memory, scanner, Web, bug, mouse, to mirror, firewall, to flame, Trojan Horse, worm;*
- the use of established, vernacular lexical items in nominal groups where specific reference is established through premodification: (science) *saturated fat, dark matter;* (technology) *floppy disk, random access memory, disk operating system, central processing unit, beginning of message segment;*
- neologisation in which clearly non-vernacular terms are derived, typically through Greek and Latin borrowings: (science) *cytoplasm, halophile, isotope, neutrino, to plasmolyse;* (technology) *telephone, television;*
- nominal groups where the Head is of vernacular origin but where premodification includes some clearly non-vernacular element: (science) *deoxyribonucleic acid, catabolic pathway;* (technology) *digital fibre-optic data links, cathode ray tube, pseudorandom binary sequence generators;*
- nominal groups where both the head and some element of the premodification are clearly of non-vernacular origin: (science) *low density lipoprotein cholesterol, colloidal gold-low-density lipoprotein conjugates;* (technology) no examples as yet identified;
- acronymisation where the abbreviated, word-like form replaces the longer, full form as the primary mode of reference: (science) *AIDS, DNA;* (technology) *laser, scuba, CD-Rom, DOS, RAM, modem.*

For the sake of simplicity of presentation, the above examples all involved concrete, inter-stratally congruent categories. However, much specialist, non-vernacular terminology relies on what Halliday has termed 'virtual entities', the inter-statally incongruent entities derived when semantic categories such as process, quality and relator are mapped on to the lexico-grammatical category of nominal group. (See Halliday, Chapter 8, this volume.) As Halliday demonstrates, these virtual entities are central to scientific discourse. Examples include *apoptosis, osmolarity*, etc.

Specialist lexis in science and technology: textual exemplification

While the discourses of science and technology access the same set of lexical resources for their specialist terminology, they display different preferences in their use of these resources. Key elements of these differences will be illustrated by means of a detailed comparison between a text extract which exemplifies many of the features of scientific discourse and a representative technological text. The scientific text, from the field of microbiology, was identified by Halliday (Chapter 8, this volume) as typical of scientific discourse and analysed by him in some detail. The analysis here will be supported by reference to additional texts ranging from expert to more generalist or popular texts. These popular texts (for example, mass-circulation computer magazines) are relevant because they enable us to explore the interface between the specialist and the vernacular – the lexico-grammatical reflexes which occur when a non-vernacular discourse comes up against vernacular construals of reality and acts either to infiltrate some of its specialist categories into the vernacular domain or to draw the non-specialist reader into its own uncommonsense reality. It is in the computer magazines, for example, that the general public is introduced to the new devices and processes brought into being by a key area of technological innovation and acquires a particular set of lexico-grammatical resources to talk about these devices. It is in such a context that we can expect to see the underlying semantic functionality of the various specialist vocabularies revealed as they come up against and interact with the vernacular.

The analysis of the texts' specialist terminologies, set out in Tables 10.1 and 10.2, notes the following features:

- whether the term is 'basic' (single-word form) or 'non-basic' (expanded group, typically a nominal with sub-classificatory pre-modification);
- whether the term involves word forms derived from the vernacular lexis or whether it involves new word forms derived via borrowings from non-native sources (typically Greek and Latin);
- whether the term includes acronymisation;

Table 10.1 Text analysis, scientific text, 'Effects of Solutes on Growth and Metabolism' (Stanier 1937)

Borrowed versus independent acronym	Basic: vernacular	Basic: non-vernacular	Non-basic: vernacular head and premodification	Non-basic: vernacular head; non-vernacular premodification	Non-basic: non-vernacular head; vernacular or non vernacular premodification	Virtual (Y/N)
Borrowed			transport mechanisms			Y
Borrowed				cellular function		Y
Borrowed				intracellular concentrations		Y
Borrowed		metabolites				N
Borrowed				catabolic pathways		N
Borrowed				biosynthetic pathways		N
Borrowed				nutrient concentrations		Y
Borrowed				microbial populations		N
Borrowed		nutrient				N
Borrowed		medium				N
Borrowed				limiting nutrient concentrations		Y
Borrowed		osmoregulation				Y
Borrowed		solutes				N
Borrowed		molecules				N
Borrowed		ions				N
Borrowed				metabolic activity		Y
Borrowed		osmolarity				Y
Borrowed		bacteria				N
Borrowed					internal osmolarity	Y
			cell wall			N

Table 10.1 (continued)

Borrowed versus independent acronym	Basic: vernacular	Basic: non-vernacular	Non-basic: vernacular head and premodification	Non-basic: vernacular head; non-vernacular premodification	Non-basic: non-vernacular head; vernacular or non-vernacular premodification	Virtual (Y/N)
Borrowed				internal osmotic pressure		Y
Borrowed				external osmotic pressure		Y
Borrowed		cytoplasm				N
Borrowed					gram-positive bacteria	N
Borrowed					cell membrane	N
Borrowed		plasmoyzed				N
Borrowed					gram-negative bacteria	N
Borrowed				osmotic requirements		Y
Borrowed					sodium chloride	N
Borrowed		micro-organisms				N
Borrowed		osmophiles				N
Borrowed		halophiles				N
Borrowed			salt tolerance			Y
Borrowed		nonhalophiles				N
Borrowed			marine organisms			N
Borrowed					moderate halophiles	N
Borrowed					extreme halophiles	N
Borrowed					Pediococcus halophilus	N
Borrowed					growth medium	N
Acro	NaCl					N
Borrowed					high osmolarity	Y
Borrowed				biochemical basis		Y

Table 10.2 Text analysis, technological extract, 'B-ISDN interworking' (Sutherland and Burgin 1993)

Borrowed versus independent acronym	Basic: vernacular	Basic: non-vernacular	Non-basic: vernacular head and premodification	Non-basic: vernacular head; non-vernacular premodification	Non-basic: non-vernacular head; vernacular or non-vernacular premodification	Virtual (Y/N)
	networks					N
			packet switched public data network (PSPDN)			N
			packet switched public telephone network (PSTN)			N
Acro					64kb/s ISDN	N
			frame mode bearer service (FMBS)			N
			metropolitan area network (MAN)			N
Acro	interworking (? possibly non-vernacular)				B-ISDN	Y
			local area network (LAN)			N
Acro, borrowed					Ethernet LAN	Y
Acro			end-to-end communications			N
Acro					IEEE 802.6 MAN	N
Acro		ISDN				N
	traffic					N
Acro				Australian FASTPAC network		N
			high speed transmission facilities			Y

Table 10.2 (continued)

Borrowed versus independent acronym	Basic: vernacular	Basic: non-vernacular	Non-basic: vernacular head and premodification	Non-basic: vernacular head; non-vernacular premodification	Non-basic: non-vernacular head; vernacular or non-vernacular premodification	Virtual (Y/N)
Acro				national LAN interconnect service		N
Borrowed				switched multimegabit data service (SMDS)		N
Acro					B-ISDN/MAN interworking	N
			connectionless server function			N
			protocol translation			Y
	bridge					N
Borrowed		interface (possibly now entered vernacular usage)				N
			cell header			N
Acro				IEEE 802.6 segments		N
Acro		ATM		ATM cells		N
Acro				ATM virtual path (VP)		N
			virtual channel (VC)			N
			beginning of message segments (BOM)			N
Acro				E.164 addresses		N
	packet					N
			message identification field (MID)			N
			connectionless server			N

- whether the terms are what Halliday labels virtual entities (nominal groups with nominalised Heads) or inter-stratally congruent terms (concrete nominals, verbals, etc).

Individual terms are placed in a column according to which combination of these features they represent. Thus column 2 of Tables 10.1 and 10.2 contains all specialist terms which are both 'basic' and derived from the vernacular lexicon. Whether the term includes acronymisation and/or borrowing from non-native sources is indicated by an entry in column 1. ('Borrowed' = Greek/Latin borrowing; 'Acro' = acronym. 'Borrowed' forms are also marked in **bold** type face while acronym forms are marked with *italics*.) For reasons which will be set out below, our primary concern here is not with standard abbreviatory acronyms (where a full form is first presented and then the single-word form as an abbreviation). We are more interested in those which display some lexical independence from the underlying full form. Accordingly, only 'independent' acronyms (those without a full-form explication anywhere in the text or which enter productively into processes such as nominal group expansion) will be treated as individual lexical items. Thus a term such as *frame mode bearer service (FMBS)* will not receive an entry in column 1 as an independent acronym.

Text 1 – science

Readers are directed to the Appendix of Halliday's chapter (Chapter 8, this volume) for the text of 'Effects of Solutes on Growth and Metabolism', a text drawn from the domain of microbiology. The analysis of its specialist terminology is presented below in Table 10.1.

Text 2 – technology

The technological example is extracted from an article published in the specialist telecommunications journal, *IEEE Communications Magazine*. It was authored by senior researchers from Australia's primary telecommunications provider, Telstra (then known as Telecom Australia). (See the Appendix for the full text.) The following paragraph is provided by way of a taste of typical technological style. Analysis follows in Table 10.2.

> The Australian FASTPAC network is a hierarchy of MANs interconnected by high speed transmission facilities to provide a national LAN interconnect service. The B-ISDN will need to interwork with networks based on IEEE 802.6 MAN technology and networks offering switched multimegabit data service (SMDS) [3]. A suitable reference configuration for B-ISDN/MAN interworking has been identified in CCITT Recommendation 1.327 [4].

LEXICAL EXTENSION VERSUS RE-VALEURISATION

Overview of lexical differences

The two texts reveal clear differences in the lexical preferences of the two specialist lexicons. We notice marked differences in the 'basic' terms (simple nominal forms without pre-modificatory classification) – a point of obvious interest since such items represent an ideational domain's more stable, salient and more widely referenced categories. In the scientific extract, basic terms are almost exclusively non-vernacular, Latin/Greek borrowings: for example, *metabolites osmoregulation, solutes.* In contrast, the basic terms of the technological text are primarily vernacularly derived terms as well as acronyms – thus *traffic, bridge, packet and B-ISDN, ATM.* The same preferences are reflected in the expanded nominal forms. The science text prefers forms where either the Head or some element of the pre-modification is of non-vernacular origin – *moderate* **halophile, catabolic** *pathway.* In contrast, the technological text prefers elaborated nominals where all elements are of vernacular derivation (packet switched public telephone network) or where either the Head or some element of the premodification is an acronym (**ATM** *cells, Broadband* **ISDN**).

Redeployed vernacular lexis

Technology

The vernacular origin of terms such as *traffic* and *packet* may at first obscure their specialist nature. But the categories referenced by such terms are, of course, not the same as those referenced by the terms in vernacular contexts. In everyday language, *traffic*, for example, refers to the movement of vehicles while in the specialist domain of telecommunications it refers to the movement of signals through the telecommunications network. There is, of course, an obvious connection between the vernacular and the technological application of the term – they are related by an analogy turning on the notion of directed movement towards a fixed destination. A similar relationship exists between the vernacular *packet* and its technological counterpart – a 'unit of data'. The connection involves a shared notion of 'bundling up' or 'packing together'. The same semantics can be observed operating generally within vernacularly derived basic technological terms. For example, the technological use of the term *memory* – a component of electronic computing machines – involves a metaphor of storing and retrieving information.

In all such cases, technology redeploys a vernacular lexical item but does not replace or displace the original everyday sense of the term, acting rather to extend it. It does this by broadening the polysemous range of the vernacular vocabulary item, essentially through lexical metaphor. This is possible because the polysemous nature of much vernacular lexis means that different phenomena may be referenced by the same lexical item when there is some salient point of similarity. (For a discussion of polysemy in general see Allan 1986. For a discussion of the role of polysemy in generating new terms in vernacular botanical taxonomies see Berlin 1995.) Thus the polysemous range of the term *mouth* extends to include the *mouth* of animals, the *mouth* of a bottle and the *mouth* of a river. The relationship between the technological *packet* and the vernacular *packet* or technological *memory* and the vernacular *memory* is therefore of the same order as that between the *mouth* of a river and the *mouth* of an animal.

Similar polysemous extension can be observed across the technological lexicon in, for example, the *read* in *read only memory* (reading extended to include the electronic accessing of information), *scanner* (to scan, extended to name a device which rapidly produces a copy of a document), the *Web* (an interconnected network of sometimes bewildering complexity), *speaker* (a device which emits noise), *to mirror* (one Web site is said to mirror another when it contains a regularly updated copy of the other site's data) and so on.

The 'non-basic' specialist terms in the technological text (those in which a Head is sub-classified through premodification) have a similar lexical constitution and are directed towards the same communicative objective. We note that they too are typically derived from items drawn from the vernacular lexicon both in their Head and in their premodification. In some instances the Head is an element which redeploys vernacular lexis in the manner outlined above, with the premodification mobilising additional vernacular elements. Consider, for example, *message identification field connectionless server*. The Head, the term *server*, involves only a trivial extension of the vernacular sense of the word – within the technological lexicon, a *server* is a device which acts to assist other devices in carrying out some function. This Head is then sub-classified (a sub-type of *server* is indicated) by means of pre-modification through categories drawn from the vernacular lexicon – *message identification field connectionless*.

A related sub-type of elaborated term uses common, vernacular terms to establish reference to the specific technological category. Thus *local area network, beginning of message segment, disk operating system*, etc. The Head of such terms often has highly generalised reference to, for example, some location (*field* as in *data count field* or *segment* as in *beginning of message segment*) or to some abstraction of functionality or means – thus *facility* (*high speed transmission facility*), *service* (*national local area network interconnect service*), *system* (*disk operating system*), etc.

Such terms take categories which are part of vernacular experience (*system, service, unit*, etc.) or which are connected to vernacular experience through polysemous extension (*server, packet,* etc.) and then enlist further vernacular terms to specify some sub-type of that category. Thus a *disk operating system* is unproblematically a mechanism or means for operating a disk. Specialised reference is thereby achieved by the combination of non-specialised categories. While the categories thereby referenced may not typically be encountered in the course of everyday experience, their lexis indicates that they are ontologically of the same order as categories of vernacular experience.

Redeployment of vernacular lexis in scientific discourse

Although there are no examples in the microbiology text cited above, a minority of specialist scientific terms do involve a redeployment of vernacular lexical forms. Although not the norm in science, such terms will be examined here because they provide general insights into the semantics of scientific terminology.

Vernacular lexis redeployed by the specialist scientific vocabulary includes, for example, the botanical term *fruit* and the geographical term *desert*. Thus under scientific terminology, *desert* refers to an ecosystem in which there is insufficient surface water to support permanent plant growth. The *Encyclopaedia Britannica*, for example, defines *desert* as an area where 'the level of aridity . . . is a mean annual precipitation value equal to 250 mm (10 inches) or less'. The online *BioTech Life Science Dictionary* (Indiana University: HTTP) defines *fruit* as 'the seed-bearing structure in angiosperms (a major division of the plant kingdom, commonly called flowering plants) formed from the ovary after flowering'.

In both instances, the redeployment does not extend the vernacular sense by metaphorical extension, as was the case with technological terms. Rather the scientific categorisation challenges the vernacular sense of the term. *Deserts* in commonsense terms are dry, hot places with scant vegetation, typically featuring sand hills and the occasional oasis. The vernacular meaning is at odds with the scientific in that it excludes the cold deserts of, for example, the Arctic which the scientific categorisation explicitly encompasses. Similarly, the scientific sense of the term excludes the notion of *desert* associated with the *desert island* so beloved by popular-cultural cartoonists – an ecosystem where the obligatory well-developed palm tree testifies to the presence of sufficient ground water to support permanent plant growth.

A similar semantics operates with the term *fruit*. Under the vernacular system of valeur, the term is defined prototypically by reference to items such as *apple* and *orange* and is loosely held to encompass edible parts of plants which are sweet to the taste and are typically not eaten with main courses in western culinary traditions, at least within the version of vernacular reality with which I operate. The vernacular *fruit* is thus clearly at odds with the scientific. It excludes items encompassed by the scientific categorisation such as *pumpkin* and *tomato* and is unclear about *avocado* (avocados are similar in shape to stone fruit and yet are not sweet and are not eaten as dessert). As well, the vernacular *fruit* includes at least one item which is excluded by the scientific categorisation, that of *rhubarb* (an item formerly popular as dessert in Australia).

In both instances, the vernacular and the scientific categories entail a different system of valeur relationships. The vernacular *desert* enters into an immediate paradigmatic relationship with categories such as *jungle, forest* and *ocean* while the scientific desert enters into a valeur relationship with other scientifically defined ecosystems such as *tundra* and *rainforest.* Similarly, the vernacular fruit enters into a valeur relationship with *vegetable, meat, seafood,* etc. while the botanical *fruit* enters into a meronymic relationship with other systematically defined parts of plants.

Technological versus scientific redeployment of the vernacular

Two key observations follow. First, technology favours vernacularly derived lexical items, both in its 'basic' and 'non-basic' specialist technology, while science only makes minimal use of such lexis. Second, even when science does use such items, it puts them to a markedly different use. Science takes the terms but redefines them. The scientific terms challenge vernacular experience, insisting on a semantic breach with vernacular meanings. In technology, however, such lexis provides for a direct connection between the specialist ideational domain and that of vernacular experience. Such items acknowledge and encompass the meanings these terms take in the vernacular lexicon and act only to extend their scope.

Acronymisation and specialist terminology

The technological preference for the acronym

The second primary lexical resource utilised by the technological text was the acronym. The short extract analysed above contained numerous examples of what will be termed 'abbreviatory' acronyms (forms where an elaborated nominal group is presented first and the acronym immediately after as an abbreviation) as well as two examples of independent acronyms (forms where the underlying full-form nominal is not provided anywhere in the text). In contrast, the scientific extract is free of acronyms, with the exception of the acronym-like chemical term *NaCl*, not an acronym in the strict sense of the term. In this, the two texts are illustrative of a general trend found across a significant selection of scientific and technological texts – the author's initial investigations of texts from the technological domains of telecommunications, computing and electronics, and scientific texts from the domains of biology, zoology, astronomy and geology indicate a significantly higher occurrence of acronyms in the technological domain. Acronyms, however, do occur not only in both scientific and technological texts but broadly across the language. As well, their frequency varies across individual texts within a given ideational domain as it does across the sub-domains which make up the general category of science. (Medical research texts, for example, appear to feature a higher number of acronyms than some other domains.) Thus while the tendency illustrated by the texts analysed above may be suggestive, and may point to underlying differences in communicative purpose, we cannot draw strong conclusions from a simple count of acronyms within texts, unless our sample is significantly larger than that covered in my initial investigations.

We can, however, draw stronger conclusions when we identify clear patterns of difference between scientific and technological discourse in the way acronyms occur and in the way they are used. The following discussion will outline a number of such differences and argue that these ultimately reflect an underlying distinction between the lexicon extension of technology and the lexical revaleurisation of science.

The linguistic properties of the acronym: a general overview

Acronyms are typically formed by combining the first letters of the words of a complex nominal group and using all upper case for the letters of the newly derived word-like form – thus *CD* from *compact disk*, and *RAM* from *random access memory*. Acronyms are of two types: what might be called proper noun acronyms which reference the names of single human institutions or social entities – *NATO, the CIA, the USA*, etc. – and common noun acronyms which reference general entities such as *RAM, CPU*, etc. Proper noun acronyms behave in the same manner across discourse types and will therefore be excluded from the analysis.

Common noun acronymisation is associated with two separate but related lexico-grammatical outcomes. All acronyms, whether in technological texts or otherwise, begin their lives, so to speak, as abbreviations, as a mechanism for speeding up the expression plane. As Martin states,

> It is important to note here that acronyms such as PLF are not technical terms, but abbreviations. Unlike technical terms, items such as PLF do not have the function of accumulating a number of less specialized meanings in a single lexical item (thus while they may be 'spelled out' through an elaborating structure at group or word rank, they are never defined). Rather, acronyms function as reductions on the expression plane; they make it quicker to write or say a wording – writing or saying P-L-F is faster than pronouncing or spelling the nominal group for which it stands.
>
> (Halliday and Martin 1993: 229)

This 'speeding up' of the expression plane is not, however, the only possible lexicogrammatical outcome of acronymisation. Once the complex nominal group has been reduced to a single word-like form, it is possible for that reduced form to lose its status as abbreviation and to become a word in its own right, replacing the original complex form as the name of the item in question. That is, the derived form acquires the status of a fully fledged, independent member of the lexicon and supplants the original complex form. This potential for full lexicalisation has been realised in terms such as *laser*, originally derived from **l**ight **a**mplification by **s**timulated **e**mission of **r**adiation, and scuba from **s**elf-**c**ontained **u**nderwater **b**reathing **a**pparatus. Although dictionaries may list the complex nominal term in definitions of these words, the original complex nominal is no longer a functional part of the word's everyday usage and the use of lower, rather than upper case indicates that for all practical semantic purposes, these terms are words, not abbreviations.

Only a small minority of acronyms achieve the full lexicalisation of terms such as *laser* and *scuba*. A larger proportion, however, achieve what might be termed partial lexicalisation, a state in which the acronym form is used as the preferred name without any reference to the original complex nominal. Terms such as *CD-ROM, DOS* and *BASIC* (the most widely used computer language), for example, have achieved this partial lexicalisation. Speakers unproblematically use *CD-ROM* or *DOS* without knowing or needing to know that they are derived from *compact disk read-only memory* and *disk operating system*. Such terms have a 'valeur' within the lexicon which the speaker can access without a knowledge of the original complex nominals from which they have been derived.

The tendency for at least some of the most widely used acronymic terms to move towards full lexicalisation is reflected in the following definition of *DOS* (a key software component of the many millions of personal computers in use around the world today) from *PC Home* (Australian Edition), a computing magazine designed explicitly for those without technological expertise.

> Dos was produced as a result of a business venture between IBM and Microsoft in the early 80s and, in a nutshell, is the link between you and your PC. Probably the best analogy is to describe Dos as a bi-lingual interpreter. In other words, it translates what you ask your PC to do, via a series of basic commands, into what the PC understands.
>
> (*PC Home*, March 1994: 23)

Even though the intention here is to provide a basic definition for computing novices, there is no spelling out of the complex nominal form, and lower rather than upper case is used, evidence that *Dos*, at least for *PC Home*'s editors, is now a lexical item rather than an abbreviation.

Instances where acronyms occur within a text independently of the full form they originally acted to abbreviate may in some cases, of course, be explained inter-textually. That is, the full form is not provided because the writer assumes the reader can supply the full form by recalling other texts where the elaborated form is provided. The nature of the definition of *Dos*, however, indicates that as lexicalisation proceeds, the connection with the full form becomes increasingly weaker. In instances of the type exemplified by *Dos*, no connection with a full form, whether intra-textually or inter-textually, is required for the term to function as referencing item.

Technology and acronym lexicalisation

There is a significantly stronger tendency for acronymisation in techno-logical discourse to move toward lexicalisation than in the scientific texts analysed by the author. This tendency is reflected within the lexico-grammar in a number of ways.

Within technological texts, a much higher proportion of acronyms achieve independence of the full form they initially acted to abbreviate. That is, they freely occur without the full form present at any point in the text. Two such independent, lexicalised acronyms occurred within the space of the few paragraphs of the telecommunications article cited above. Such lexicalised acronyms occur with a significantly lower fre-quency in scientific texts. Here, acronyms are almost always presented as abbreviatory rather than as lexicalisations – the complex nominal will be presented at first mention in the text, with the reduced form supplied afterwards. The following is typical of both expert and popular scientific texts:

> There is now substantial evidence that the events occurring in the brain in response to stress, specifically at the *hypothalamic-pituitary-adrenal (HPA)* axis, are similar to those occurring in response to an activated immune system. In both instances, the *HPA* axis is stimu-lated by . . .
>
> (*Scientific American*: Science and Medicine, November/December 1995: 16)

Perhaps the best context for demonstrating abbreviation versus lexicalisation is provided by popular texts of the sort found in mass-circulation science and technology magazines or in the science and technology sections of mass circulation newspapers. Within highly specialist, narrowly targeted expert texts, instances of independent acro-nyms may be explained inter-textually – the expert reader may be assumed to have the inter-textual knowledge required to provide the full form of the term. But no such assumptions can be made of the inexpert reader of popular magazines. It is in the commercial interests of such publications to make their texts as accessible as possible to the inexpert reader and therefore to assume as little expert knowledge as possible of their readers. It is in their interest, therefore, to avoid jargon, to keep unfamiliar specialist terminology to a minimum and to provide explication of that specialist terminology which is central to the domain and therefore cannot be avoided. Given these objectives, we would expect the preferred mode of acronym presentation in popular magazines to be that of the style described above – full form first-mention presentation of the complex nominal followed immediately by the acronym as abbreviation. Tellingly, this expectation is met by popular science magazines such as *New Scientist* and *Scientific American* but not by popular technological magazines such as *PC Magazine*, *PC World*, *Electronics Australia* and the computing and telecommunications sections of the daily newspapers. Perhaps the most notable feature of such texts is their very high number of independent, unexplicated, 'lexicalised' acronyms. The following extract from the opening of an article in the mass-circulation *Windows Sources Australia* is typical of this feature (independent common-noun acronyms italicised).

> WResMon II Stops Crashes
> It's just plain silly to have to worry about running out of a measly 64K block of *GDI* resources when you're sitting in front of a *PC* with 4M, 8M, or 16M of *RAM*. Now there's a solution – WResMon II provides you with your own private *INI* file and mastery of the Windows *API* functions.
>
> (*Windows Sources Australia*, July 1994: 89)

Such terms pose obvious problems of comprehension to inexpert readers, precisely the readers the publications must attract if they are to maintain and increase circulation. The fact that these terms remain in such high numbers, despite the problems, strongly suggests that they are in some way unavoidable, or at least that they provide communicative positives which significantly outweigh the negatives. Their presence can be explained in terms of communicative functionality. The independent acronym forms are preferred because within technological discourse it is the acronym itself, rather than the underlying complex nominal, which is the primary lexical item, the primary form operating within the lexicon to reference the category in question. The acronym has been at least partially lexicalised and thus acquired some of the qualities of fully fledged members of the lexicon. Since it represents the preferred name for the category in question, the acronym rather than the underlying elaborated form will be used within the text.

The lexicalised nature of technological acronyms is reflected at a number of additional points in the grammar, which once again show up most clearly in popular texts. When first mention of the acronym is accompanied by the full, expanded form of the term, the preferred mode is what I will term 'reverse acronym presentation'. The acronym is presented first with the full form following afterwards, typically in brackets. For example,

> VRML (virtual reality modeling language) has already become the standard development environment on the Net and there are a number of VRML authoring tools and browsers for exploring these Web environments.
>
> (*Sydney Morning Herald*, Computer and Communications Section, 12 December 1995: 4)

This structure reflects the lexical primacy of the lexicalised acronym over the complex nominal term. Rather than suggesting a process of abbreviation, such 'reverse presentation' forms construct the acronym as the primary term and the expanded form as its meaning – the structure is one of term plus dictionary definition.

Additionally acronyms behave as nouns, or at least as 'proto-nouns' rather than as abbreviations when they enter into noun-like processes within the nominal group. Thus acronyms can act as Classifiers in expanded nominal groups – *ATM network*. They can act as the Heads of premodified nominal groups – *General MIDI*, and they can act as Heads of nominal groups which enter into further recursive processes of acronymisation – *B-ISDN* from *Broadband ISDN* and *GM* from *General MIDI*.

Finally there is the phenomenon of pseudo-acronyms such as *TWAIN* and indeterminate acronyms such as *DVD*. Pseudo-acronyms are new terms which mimic acronyms but which, in fact, have no actual underlying complex nominal form. A new software standard, for example, for programs which communicate between scanners and computers has been named *TWAIN*. Software will be described as *TWAIN-compliant* or as supporting *TWAIN*. Glossaries of computing terms reveal, however, that *TWAIN* stands for 'Tool Without An Interesting Name', with the entry typically adding a comment to reassure the reader that this is not a joke, that this is the 'real' meaning of *TWAIN*. (It would appear that whoever coined the term had a humorous outcome in mind. For many years scanners and computers were notoriously difficult to connect. There appears here to be a word play on the quotation 'never the twain shall meet'.) With such pseudo-forms, the new term achieves legitimacy by mimicking the canonical form for new terms in technological discourse – the independent, lexicalised acronym. The term *DVD* is indeterminate in that it is variously held to stand for *Digital Video Disk* and *Digital Versatile Disk*. The term functions unproblematically, however, because as a proto-noun it acts to reference a new large-format digital storage mechanism irrespective of the extended form which might underlie it.

Acronyms in science and technology compared

This is not to argue, of course, that acronymisation in science is exclusively associated with abbreviation and in technology with lexicalisation. The abbreviatory acronym and its associated set of lexico-grammatical phenomena are found in virtually all social contexts – certainly within scientific, social scientific, bureaucratic and journalistic discourses – as well as within technology. Additionally, some acronyms within scientific discourse display features associated with lexicalisation. The terms *DNA* and *AIDS* for example occur typically as independent, lexicalised terms. The point, however, is that there are pronounced patterns of preference – the lexico-grammar of acronymisation within science (or at least within the sub-domains of science examined for this chapter) is predominantly abbreviatory while within technology it is overwhelmingly lexicalising. (The acronyms of certain domains within medicine appear to be more lexicalising than abbreviatory. A reason for this will be proposed in a later section.) Thus within both expert and popular scientific texts, independent first-mention acronyms occur only rarely and almost all acronym presentation adopts the full-form plus acronym structure. In contrast, independent first-mention acronyms are common in both expert and popular technological texts and the reverse dictionary definition structure is the preferred mode of full-form explication within popular texts. There was, for example, only one instance of an abbreviatory acronym structure in the twenty-six articles which made up the computer section of the *Sydney Morning Herald* of 18 November 1995. Tellingly, this instance involved a device which was very new at the time and over which there was still uncertainty as to name – the previously mentioned *DVD* device, then also referred to as the *Super Density Disk (SD)*.

The technological acronym explained

The association, therefore, between the lexicalising acronym and technological language is a close and highly salient one and provides one compelling criterion for distinguishing the technological from the scientific. The reason why modern technology favours neologisation by acronymisation may be linked to the nature of the reality that these terms are called upon to map. That nature has two aspects. First, it is constantly expanding as technological innovation comes up with ever more devices, processes and modes of interaction. Second, it is inherently unstable as new devices and processes are trialled, some successfully, others not so, as some devices, processes and relationships become obsolete or go out of fashion, or alternatively, achieve widespread use and acceptance and become part of vernacular experience.

The creator of new technological terms can choose, of course, from an array of lexical resources – they can redeploy vernacular lexis, borrow forms from Latin and Greek (and any other language for that matter), invent entirely new word forms or use acronymisation. In the past, Greek/Latin coinings were popular (thus *telephone, television*, etc.). But the acronym seems particularly well suited today to reflect the twin features of contemporary technological reality identified above.

Acronymisation well serves technology's innovativeness because it is a highly efficient and relatively unproblematic source of a virtually limitless supply of new terms. The would-be neologiser need simply formulate a descriptive nominal group of the type described in the previous section – *read only memory, disk operating system* for example – and then mechanically apply the rules of abbreviation. Such a process is obviously less demanding than one in which entirely new word-forms must be invented or where foreign vocabularies must be accessed. (The fact that classical scholarship is no longer so widespread may offer a part explanation as to why Greek/Latin coinings have declined. They remain the norm, however, in science for reasons which will be explained below, despite the decline in classical scholarship, suggesting that this does not provide a complete explanation for the emergence of the acronym in technology.) Acronymisation is thus eminently well equipped to meet the constant need for new lexis to map the ever-unfolding reality of technological development.

Of equal importance is the unstable, provisional nature of technological reality. Here we need to consider the semantics of basic terms – names constituted of single-word forms without pre- or post-modification – and what is entailed when acronymisation provides a term with at least some of the qualities of the basic term. The existence of a lexically minimal term – a single-word form – to reference a given category is generally seen as evidence that the category is stable and salient within its ideational domain. (See for example Bulmer 1970 and Berlin *et al.* 1993.) That is, the more permanent and salient the entity as an item of valeur, then the greater the likelihood that it will be denoted by a single word rather than by a descriptive nominal group with pre- or post-modification.

The shift, therefore, under lexicalising acronymisation from an extended nominal group to a single word can be expected to have semogenetic consequences. The single-word form will more strongly suggest ideational stability and salience than the complex, expanded nominal from which it is derived. This process has its parallel in the derivation of vernacular terms such as *blackbird* and *gum-tree*. As both items became established, salient items of valeur they acquired their own single-word names which were derived, in this case, simply by fusing what were originally independent elements of a complex nominal group. Thus the term *blackbird* no longer refers to any bird which is black but directly to a particular species of bird. Similarly, we no longer think of a *gum-tree* as a tree with gum. The single-word form now refers directly to a stable item of valeur with the presence of gum now entirely coincidental.

Thus by using the single-word acronym form, we are indicating that the category has at least some of the stability and functional saliency of entities which have their own unique, permanent name – their own dictionary entry. At least at the graphological level, and sometimes phonologically as well, we are dealing with what amounts to a new morpheme or at least a construct which shares some of the properties of a morpheme. As a consequence, the meaning of even the newest, most abbreviatory acronym goes beyond that of the longer form it abbreviates to include some suggestion of stability and salience. That stability may be limited to the text in which the acronym occurs, but it is nevertheless a genuine, if circumscribed, semantic outcome. When the acronym operates inter-textually and begins to achieve lexical independence, then the sense of stability and saliency attached to the item it references is enhanced.

We must note, however, by way of counter tendency, that there is always some restriction on lexicalisation, some falling short by the acronym of fully fledged membership in the lexicon, except for those rare cases where full lexicalisation is achieved. The acronym, in fact, explicitly signals its non-standard status, its non-membership in the lexicon through its all upper-case orthography, a graphological symbolism which also acts to signal a connection with the original process of abbreviation. From this perspective, then, the acronym must be seen as a provisional or proto-noun, a linguistic entity which, while more than just an abbreviation of the expression plane, is always less than a fully formed item of the lexicon.

This is not, however, to imply that the acronym is in someway semantically immature or inchoate – language does not allow for such a condition. Rather the provisionality of the acronym, its status as proto-form has direct semantic functionality. It enables the acronym to reflect the nature of the reality it has been called upon to represent. As stated above, technological reality is characterised by its instability and transience. Many of the new categories it throws up are provisional and never achieve permanence. Only a subset achieve stability and any sort of persistent salience and thereby require fully fledged nouns as names. For many of the categories it is appropriate that there should be referring terms which signal this instability and provisionality. This is exactly the semantics provided in technological discourse by the acronym as a proto-nominal form.

The upper-case form also acts to signal a connection with the complex nominal form from which the single-word form was derived. As discussed above, that complex nominal term typically involves categories drawn from the vernacular system of valeur. Technological acronyms, in this sense, are specialist terms which are self-defining – the reader simply references the underlying full form and the term's sense and application becomes clear. The meaning of the term *Dos*, for example, may be obscure but that of *disk operating system* is much more transparent. The lexicalising acronyms of technology therefore can be said to 'have it both ways' – they provide for new, unfamiliar single-word forms with some of the qualities of basic terms and yet simultaneously provide for a connection through the underlying full form to established, familiar vernacular categories. They are thus well suited to the task of extending vernacular reality.

Specialised terminology in science: 'classical' categories

The preference of science for Greek/Latin borrowings

The previous analysis of the microbiological text revealed a preference for terms of non-vernacular origin, derived primarily through borrowings from Greek and Latin. This preference can be observed widely throughout the scientific discourse. It is compellingly demonstrated by an example from another microbiological text, an extract from an article in *Scientific American* from December 1996. Many of the categories of the life sciences have both a non-native Greek/Latin derived name and a vernacularly derived name. In this case the term *programmed cell death* and its equivalent, *apoptosis*, both refer to the process by which cells die as a natural part of an organism's life cycle. As generalist, semi-popular journal rather than strictly specialist journal, *Scientific American* makes some concessions to vernacular discourse and consequently the opening paragraphs (as the reader is introduced to a new ideational domain) use both the vernacular and non-vernacular terms to reference the category, as well as a strictly vernacular, non-specialist equivalent, *cell suicide*. However, after this initial orientation, the Greek/Latin derived term *apoptosis* takes precedence and is the only name used for the remainder of the article. Tellingly, therefore, the non-native form is preferred despite the availability of a vernacularly derived, self-explanatory equivalent. (We note as well that the acronym option, *PCD* for *programmed cell death*, was not taken up.)

The 'classical' categorisations of science

In this preference for coinings of Greek/Latin origin, scientific discourse stands apart from the technological. In order to uncover the key semantic principles which underlie this difference it is necessary to explore the function of scientific terminology and the categories it references in greater depth.

In many of its endeavours, science enters domains not usually accessed as a part of vernacular experience. It uses its specialist devices to view, for example, distant galaxies or microscopic objects which are usually not accessible to unassisted human perception. The phenomena thereby identified will typically be non-commonsense categories and the names which label them will be specialist or non-vernacular, regardless of whether they were formed by the redeployment of vernacular lexis, by foreign borrowings or through acronymisation. But the same can be said of the lexis of other specialist domains in the sense that their categories likewise are not part of vernacular valeur systems. The vocabularies of, for example, sports or of music are full of unfamiliar, specialist terms which construe categories unique to those domains. The earlier section on the redeployment of vernacular lexis in scientific terminology has argued, following Martin, that the categorisations of science act to displace vernacular systems of valeur relationships. But the key point here is that scientific taxonomies do not simply act to replace one system of valeur relationships with another. Rather, they are different in kind from the vernacular – they are informed by principles of categorisation which render them qualitatively different from those of vernacular discourse.

In principle, science seeks to construe the world in terms of a system of valeur where category membership is determined by systematic, stable, explicit, verifiable and theoretically motivated criteria. These categories or items of valeur can be said, at least in the ideal, to be 'classical' in that they conform to Aristotle's ontological theories as set out in the *Metaphysics,* namely that reality is constructed from clearly bounded categories, the membership of which can be determined absolutely by the conjunction of necessary and sufficient features (Aristotle, trans. Tredennick, 1933). They are what Kempton has labelled 'devised classification systems' (Kempton 1981) and Taylor as 'expert categories' (Taylor 1989). Thus the revaleuristic scientific definition of *fruit* as the part of a plant formed from the ovary after flowering provides the necessary and sufficient criteria by which an absolute, clearly bounded category can be established. Thus tomatoes, pumpkins, capsicums, avocados and a range of inedible seed containers have an absolute membership in the category which is the equal of the membership of categories such as *banana* and *orange.* Similarly, a term from the analysed microbiology text, *extreme halophile* for example, references a category which is defined in absolute terms as 'an organism which requires for growth a medium in which there is a greater than 10 percent concentration of sodium chloride' (Indiana University: HTTP).

In contrast, vernacular language is much more catholic in its modes of categorisation, including some categories which are systematic, absolute and hence 'classical' in this sense (the vernacular term *bachelor,* for example), but more typically operating with flexible categories determined by reference to function or to social practice rather than by any set of necessary and sufficient features. As Wittgenstein, Labov and Rosch, for example, have demonstrated, vernacular categories are frequently unsystematic, contingent and *ad hoc*, may be determined by family resemblance and prototypal exemplars and often possess fuzzy boundaries. (Wittgenstein, trans. Auscombe, 1978; Labov *et al.* 1973; Rosch 1973; Rosch 1975; Taylor 1989).

The difference between scientific and vernacular systems of valeur is reflected at a number of points in the lexico-grammar, with one notable illustration provided by structures frequently labelled 'hedges' (Taylor 1989: 75–80). In vernacular discourse, for example, the phrase *'par excellence'* can act to indicate that an item represents an archetypal or core member of one of vernacular reality's fuzzy, prototype-determined categories. Thus in everyday speech we can say, 'The Sahara is a desert, *par excellence.*' Within the valeur system of science, however, such a statement would be incongruous – it would be meaningless to say, for example, 'The apple is the part of the plant which carries the ovaries after flowering, *par excellence.*'

This commitment to establishing absolute, clearly bounded categories defined by necessary and sufficient features is reflected in scientific definitions. These are typically concerned to specify both the superordinate category to which the term in question belongs and the necessary and sufficient criteria through which it enters into taxonomic relationships with its co-hyponyms. Thus we find the following typical definition in a chemistry textbook.

Mixtures are substances that can easily be separated without making any new chemicals.

Solutions are mixtures that have the same properties throughout.

Suspensions are mixtures containing fine grains of one element of the mixture which can be filtered out.

Colloids are mixtures containing tiny grains that do not settle out but which do not pass through filter paper.

(Heffernan and Learmonth 1981, cited in Halliday and Martin 1993)

It is also reflected in the preference of the life sciences for word forms exemplified by terms such as *gymnosperm, angiosperm*. Such terms manage to combine features of the basic term (graphologically they are single-word forms) with features of the expanded nominal group. For those with at least a basic knowledge of the Greek/Latin sources from which they are derived, they can be read as combining a Head (*sperm* = 'seed bearing plant') with sub-classificatory premodification (*angio* = 'contained', 'enclosed'; *gymno* = 'exposed, uncontained, naked' – thus 'exposed seed plant' versus 'contained seed plant'). Both elements, Head and premodification, act to make explicit the systematic criteria which organise the underlying taxonomy. Thus, *sperm* indicates that the two terms are co-hyponyms of a superordinate category of plants which depends on the presence of seeds for category membership. The pre-modificatory elements, *angio* and *gymno*, make explicit the necessary and sufficient criteria for distinguishing absolutely between the co-hyponymic members of the superordinate category.

The lexis of 'classical' classification – icons of un-commonsense

The original reasons for science's preference for Greek/Latin borrow-ings are, of course, historical. They relate to the social conditions which obtained at the time modern experimental science emerged, specifically the high status of Greek and Latin scholarship in western culture. Although the status of the classical languages may have declined in the twentieth century, a cultural habit, once established, may well continue to influence cultural practices, even when the social conditions which originally gave rise to that tradition no longer prevail. It is unlikely, however, that the practice would remain so dominant were it not com-municatively functional. We have already noted how Greek/Latin coin-ings have been replaced with redeployed vernacular lexis and acronyms in technological discourse.

We need, therefore, to consider the communicative functionality of the Latin and Greek derived terms. We need to explain why, for example, the generalist *Scientific American* (with its interest in attracting non-expert readers) should prefer *apoptosis* to *programmed cell death*. The most obvious feature of these terms is their morphological and phonological 'strange-ness'. Such terms typically strike the speaker as non-native and hence as in some way 'alien'. Such a feature serves an obvious purpose in the context of lexicon revaleurisation, in the context of a discourse com-mitted not only to replacing individual vernacular categories but also to establishing a system of categorisation which challenges that of the vernacular. The strangeness is thus iconic. It serves as a signal that the version of reality which these terms construe is 'alien' to the version of reality construed by the familiar, typically native or nativised forms of vernacular discourse. The foreignness of the term's form acts to mark the discourse as construing an alternative reality where categorisations are not only different from the vernacular but organised according to different principles of category formation.

Technological modes of classification and the 'classical'

The categorisations which underlie scientific specialist terminology are therefore distinctive and clearly demarked from those of everyday, com-monsense reality. Mode of categorisation provides another ground for distinguishing the technological from the scientific since the categorisa-tions of technological discourse, as a generalised system, have more in common with those of the vernacular than the scientific. That is to say, while some technological valeur relationships may be informed by 'classical' principles of category formation, the pursuit of absolute, clearly bounded categories is not the informing principle of technological valeur. Technological categories are not typically defined by necessary and sufficient features but focus, rather, upon functionality and social context. They may have fuzzy boundaries and be determined by prototypes or exemplars.

These features are reflected in the modes of specialist term definition found in technological discourse. Technological definition is not nearly so strongly oriented to the systematic mapping out of taxonomic space as that of science. Often the only form of definition offered is that provided by the 'reverse acronym presentation' discussed above. For example, *DOS (Disk Operating System)* and *RAM (Random Access Memory)*. Such definition assumes that all the explication needed for the unfamiliar single-word acronym form is the presentation of its underlying expanded nominal group. There is no articulating of any systematic membership in a superordinate category nor of any set of systematic co-hyponym relationships. More extended definitions – where, for example, some gloss on the meaning of the expanded nominal group is provided – have a similar orientation. They typically do not map out taxonomic relationships but are directed towards the category's functionality, its social purpose. For example:

ADPCM Adaptive Differential Pulse Code Modulation is a popular method for encoding and compressing digital audio.

Synthesiser   This is a computer chip or peripheral device that produces sound from digital instructions, instead of from recorded audio or physical equipment. Most synthesisers attach to PCs using MIDI.
(Windows Sources Australia, 1994: 71)

When technical terms are explicitly oriented towards articulating taxonomic relationships – for example, the set *LAN (Local Area Network), WAN (Wide Area Network), MAN (Metropolitan Area Network)* – that taxonomy is frequently not informed by 'classical' principles. The co-hyponym categories of *LAN* and *WAN*, for example, are prototypally determined and have fuzzy boundaries. Consider the following sets of definitions from two technological dictionaries.

Local Area Network: Short-distance networks, such as Ethernet networks and Token Ring networks. LANs are data networks that are restricted in space. Typical distances are less than 500 meters. LANs are usually low-cost, high-bandwidth networks that connect many nodes in a limited geographic area such as an office or a building.
(Gemini Consulting: HTTP)

Local Area Network: A data communications network which is geographically limited (typically to a 1 km radius) allowing easy interconnection of terminals, microprocessors and computers within adjacent buildings. Ethernet and FDDI are examples of standard LANs.

(Howe: HTTP)

Wide Area Network: Data network that is not restricted in terms of distance. Typical distances are larger than 100 kilometres. Telecommunication network that covers a large geographic area. Typically links cities, and may be owned by a private corporation or by a public telecom operator.

(Gemini Consulting: HTTP)

Wide Area Network: A network, usually constructed with serial lines, extending over distances greater than one kilometre.

(Howe: HTTP)

The definitions are clearly vernacular rather than 'classical' in their orientation to articulating valeur relationships. They provide prototypal exemplars, focus repeatedly on what is 'typical' or 'usual' and, perhaps most tellingly, provide no criteria for making an absolute distinction between the co-hyponym categories. The categorisation turns on the distinction between 'short distance' and 'extended distance', archetypally 'fuzzy' and context-dependent values. We note tellingly that *LANs* are variously specified as operating over distances less than 500 metres or less than one kilometre while *WANs* are variously specified to operate at more than 1 kilometre and more than 100 kilometres.

As a consequence, it would seem that categories such as *LAN* and *WAN* are prime candidates for the type of hedges discussed above. We might well say, 'Our department's network is a LAN *par excellence* because it's located in just the one room and only has one server.'

CONCLUSION

The lexis of the scientific and technological texts analysed in the course of this chapter reveals, therefore, a marked pattern of difference. These patterns of preferences have been shown to reflect an underlying distinction between lexicon revaleurisation and lexicon extension. The Greek/Latin-derived terms of the scientific texts stand as icons of the breach between the 'classical' scientific systems of valeur and those of commonsense reality. In contrast, the vernacularly derived terminology of the technological texts provides a bridge between the novel but potentially everyday categories thrown up by modern technological innovation and those of general vernacular experience. I propose therefore the label, 'techno-cality' for the lexicon-extending specialist terminology of technology as a counterpart to Martin's 'technicality', his label for the revaleuristic specialist terminology of science. The lexico-grammar of this 'technocality' reflects the fact that there is no difference in kind between the reality constituted by *RAM chips, CD-ROMs* and *Broadband ISDN* and that of *spades, motorbikes* and *claw hammers*.

One important qualification remains, however, to be noted. The chapter's analysis has been based on the examination of scientific texts which were all directed to the core concern of western experimental science – theorising about the fundamental relationships of cause and effect and of category formation by which the natural world is consti-tuted. But we cannot assume that all texts which receive the label 'scientific' will necessarily be so exclusively focused. The field of medi-cine, for example, combines an interest in such theory with an interest in the development of devices and techniques for acting upon the human body in the course of disease prevention and cure. This second focus is instrumental, therefore, rather than 'theoretical' in the sense outlined above. It is, in fact, 'technological' in that it is concerned with the development of tools by which humans can act upon each other and the physical world. We would predict therefore that the specialist lexis of such a domain would be multi-modal – would combine revaleurising technicality with lexicon extending technocality. More generally, we would predict that the nature of the specialist lexis of any given domain would reflect the degree to which it is devoted, on the one hand, to scientific theorising and on the other to the development of instrumental technologies. Preliminary investigations into medical texts suggest that the prediction of multi-modality may be justified. The area remains in need of further investigation.

REFERENCES

Allan, K. 1986. *Linguistic Meaning*, London, Routledge and Kegan Paul.

Aristotle 1933. *Metaphysics*, translated by Tredennick, H., London, Heinemann.

Bazermann, C. 1988 *Shaping Written Knowledge: The Genre and Activity of the Experimental Article in Science*, Madison, Wisconsin, University of Wisconsin Press.

Berlin, B. 1995. 'Speculations on the Growth of Ethnobotanical Nomenclature' in *Language, Culture, and Society* Blount, B.G. (ed.), Prospect Heights, Illinois, Waveland Press.

Berlin, B., Breedlove, D.E. and Raven, P.H. 1993. 'Folk taxonomies and biological classification', *Science, 154*: 273–85.

Bulmer, R. 1970. 'Which Came First, the Chicken or the Egghead?' in *Échanges et communications. Mélanges offerts à Claude Lévi-Strauss à l'occasion de son 60ème anniversaire* Pouillon, J. and Marand, P. (eds), The Hague, Mouton and Co.

Gemini Consulting Inc. *C4 Lab online glossary of technological terms*, available HTTP: http://www.digital.gemconsult.com/glossary/index.html

Halliday, M.A.K. 1967. *Grammar, Society and the Noun*, London, H.K. Lewis for University College London.

Halliday, M.A.K. and Martin, J.R. 1993. *Writing Science: Literacy and Discursive Power*, London, The Falmer Press.

Heffernan, D.A. and Learmonth, M.S. 1981. *The World of Science – Book 2*, Melbourne, Longman Cheshire.

Howe, D. *Online Dictionary of Computing*, London, Imperial College London, available HTTP: http://www.wombat.doc.ic.ac.uk

Indiana University, *BioTech Life Science Dictionary*, available HTTP: http://www.biotech.chem.indiana.edu/pages/dictionary.html

Kempton, W. 1981. *The Folk Classification of Ceramics: A Study of Cognitive Prototypes*, New York, Academic Press.

Labov, William, Bailey, C.-J.N. and Shuy, R.W. 1973. *The Boundaries of Words and Their Meanings*, Washington DC, Georgetown University Press.

Lemke, J.L. 1990. 'Technical Discourse and Technocratic Ideology' in *Learning, Keeping and Using Language: Selected Papers From the 8th World Congress of Applied Linguistics*, second edition Halliday, M.A.K., Gibbons, J. and Nicholas, H. (eds), Amsterdam, Benjamin: 435–60.

Martin, J.R. 1985. *Factual Writing: Exploring and Challenging Social Reality*, Geelong, Deakin University Press.

Rosch, E. 1973. 'Natural Categoriser', *Cognitive Psychology* 4: 328–50.

Rosch, E. 1975. 'Cognitive Representations of Semantic Categorisations', *Journal of Experimental Psychology: General* 104: 192–233.

Rose, D., McInnes, D. and Korner, H. 1992. *Stage1: Scientific Literacy – Literacy in Industry Research Project*, Sydney, The Write It Right Project, Metropolitan East Disadvantaged Schools' Program, NSW Department of School Education.

Stanier, R.Y., Ingraham, J.L., Wheelis, M.L. and Painter, P.R. 1937. *General Microbiology*, fifth edition, Basingstoke and London, Macmillan Education.

Sutherland, S.L. and Burgin, J. 1993. 'B-ISDN Interworking', *IEEE Communications Magazine*: 60–3.

Taylor, J.R. (1989) *Linguistic Categorisation*, Oxford, Clarendon Press.

Windows Sources Australia, 1994 *Glossary of Terms*, Sydney: Windows Sources Australia.

Wittgenstein, L. 1978. *Philosophical Investigations*, translated by Anscombe, G.E.M., Oxford, Basil Blackwell.

APPENDIX

B-ISDN Interworking:

B-ISDN can be used to establish communications between networks based on different technologies (extract)

Economic considerations place finite limits on the rate at which new technology can be deployed and the rate at which existing technologies can be depreciated. This means that networks exist simultaneously, e.g., packet switched public data network (PSPDN), packet switched telephone network (PSTN), 64 kb/s ISDN, frame-mode bearer service (FMBS), metropolitan area network (MAN) and B-ISDN. In general terms, the purpose of interworking is to enable a network user to establish communication with a user of another network and vice versa, but there are other scenarios which may require interworking:

● A network may have global coverage by design (e.g. Local area network

– LAN). In this case user of networks using a common technology (e.g., Ethernet LAN) may establish end-to-end communications using another network (e.g., IEEE 802.6 MAN).

- A new network (e.g., B-ISDN) may have limited service support capabilities and/or limited coverage in early stages. In this case, a B-ISDN user may establish end-to-end communication using another network (e.g., ISDN).
- A particular network (e.g., PSTN) may be better suited to supporting a type of traffic (e.g., voice) generated by a user of another network (e.g., early B-ISDN).

This article will focus on interworking existing networks with B-ISDN. Interworking is certainly not a new problem and so the status of some current International Consultative Committee for Telephone and Telegraph (CCITT) recommendations are reviewed in the next section. Then the remaining sections examine specific examples of interworking with B-ISDN (names, MAN, LAN, 64 kb/s ISDN and FMBS).

Status of Interworking Recommendations

CCITT has been actively studying interworking scenarios and a number of recommendations have been developed. CCITT Recommendation I.510 discusses definitions and general principles for ISDN interworking [1]. Many of the same principles apply when considering interworking with B-ISDN. Table 1 shows the draft CCITT Recommendations pertinent to interworking existing networks with B-ISDN.

MAN/B-ISDN interworking

The Australian FASTPAC network is a hierarchy of MANs interconnected by high-speed transmission facilities to provide a national LAN interconnect service. The B-ISDN will need to interwork with networks based on IEEE 802.6 MAN technology and networks offering switched multimegabit data service (SMDS) [3]. A suitable reference configuration for B-ISDN/MAN interworking has been identified in CCITT Recommendation 1.327 [4] (Fig. 1).

In Figure 1 interworking between the B-ISDN and IEEE 802.6 MAN takes place across the M reference point. The P reference point [5] is an internal network reference point used to access a specialized network resource such as a connectionless server function (CLSF).

A relatively simple protocol translation exists between the IEEE 802.6 segments and ATM cells.

This protocol translation would take place within the bridge at the interface between networks.

One of the key issues to resolve in determining the appropriate cell header is the establishment and use of ATM virtual path (VP) and virtual channel (VC) connections within the B-ISDN to transfer the MAN segments [6]. Three scenarios appear worthy of further consideration:

1   Each bridge attached to the B-ISDN maintains a semi-permanent VP connection to every likely destination bridge, in this case, beginning of message (BOM) segments enter the bridge where E.164 addresses are analysed to determine the approximate VP connection to forward the segments on. Subsequent segments of the same packet are identified via the message identification (MID) field.
2   The establishment of VC connections is triggered by the arrival of BOM segments at the bridge. In this case, the bridge uses E.164 address information contained in the BOM segment to establish a connection across the B-ISDN.
3   Each bridge attached to the B-ISDN maintains a single semi-permanent connection to a connectionless server in the B-ISDN. The connectionless server analyses the E.164 address information contained in the BOM segment.

(S.L. Sutherland and J. Burgin, *IEEE Communications Magazine*, August 1993)

11 Technicality and abstraction in social science

Peter Wignell

INTRODUCTION

This chapter discusses what will be referred to as the discourse of social science both in terms of its phylogenesis and in terms of how it is currently presented to initiates through undergraduate textbooks. The discussion is based on five 'canonical' texts from the archive of social science and on one 'standard' undergraduate textbook from the discipline of sociology. The key points in the discussion are the emergence of and the nature of technicality in social science.

A sizable body of research into the construction of knowledge in specialised disciplines has been conducted within the paradigm of systemic functional linguistics. That research has been concentrated on what have been referred to as the discourses of science and humanities, either treating each separately (Wignell, Martin and Eggins 1987; Eggins, Wignell and Martin 1987; Shea 1988; Halliday 1987, 1988, 1989a; Martin 1990a, 1990b) or comparatively (Martin, Wignell, Eggins and Rothery 1988; Martin 1989, 1993; Wignell 1994).

One strand of that work, beginning with Wignell, Martin and Eggins (1987) and Eggins, Wignell and Martin (1987), has concentrated on how these two discourses present their respective construals of the 'world' to initiates in the context of secondary education. In summary, the authors argued that science and humanities each utilise different selections of resources from lexicogrammar, discourse semantics, register and genre in the creation of specialised knowledge. Science is characterised as primarily using what is referred to as technicality. That is, it reconstrues its domains of experience technically by establishing an array of technical terms which are ordered taxonomically. This technicality is then used to explain how things happen or come to be. The humanities, on the other hand, use what is referred to as abstraction. In history, for instance, shifting from a *story* to an interpretation of a number of *stories* involves a number of progressive shifts in abstraction from context dependence to context independence as history moves from events to the interpretation of events.

Halliday's work represents a different, but complementary, strand and concentrates both on the genesis of scientific discourse and on the role of grammatical metaphor in science. Halliday and Martin (1993) contains a representative selection of both of these strands. See the next section for a brief summary of the characteristics of science and humanities.

This chapter represents an extension of that body of research into a new area, social science. The chapter examines how the discourse of social science constructs specialised knowledge. In particular, the roles of both technicality and abstraction in social science are considered.

The term *discourse* is used here with a wider meaning than that implied in Wignell, Martin and Eggins 1987, where *discourse* can be read to correspond with *the language of. Discourse* is used here in a wider sense, more aligned with Foucault (1972). *Discourse* or *discourses* will be regarded as organised bodies of knowledge and practice which are both enabling and constraining. That is, they are assumed to include both semiotic and material practice: disciplinary knowledge and disciplinary practice. *Discourse* is used, however, to refer to such bodies of knowledge and practice in a wider sense than *discipline.* The discourses of science, humanities and social science each include a number of disciplines. These disciplines differ in their objects of study but, it is argued, they construe their fields of study in similar enough ways for them to be characterised as belonging to the same discourse.

The hypothesis of this chapter is that the discourse of social science involves a kind of synthesis of the discourses of science and the humanities: that it is, as its name suggests, a combination of the social and science. The hypothesis presented here predicts that the discourse of social science will be shown to contain features of both science and the humanities, leading to tensions within the discourse, particularly between field and mode at the level of register with this in turn leading to particular kinds of complexity at the level of lexicogrammar. It will be argued that what social science does, in essence, is make the abstract technical: that social science takes as its starting point an abstract construal of experience and then reconstrues that initial abstraction technically. It will be argued that this, at least in part, is a result of the history of the discourse, which originated in the humanities and later had the science added. This hypothesis will be explored by considering the origins and history of social science and how social science is presented to initiates in undergraduate university textbooks.

SUMMARY OF THE DISTINCTIVE CHARACTERISTICS OF THE DISCOURSE OF SCIENCE

Put simply, science involves trying to understand the 'world' by looking at it through a technical framework: turning commonsense understandings into technical understandings. It does this by creating a technical language through setting up technical terms, arranging those terms taxonomically and then using that framework to explain how the world came to be as it is. This process is recursive: the technicality, once established, can be used to create further technicality, which can then be used to explain and can then be used to set up further technicality and so on.

In general technicality is used to distil: to create and develop field through defining, classifying and explaining. But, in the sciences, if we look at where the technicality originates, we can almost always find a more or less congruent logogenetic or phylogenetic beginning, either by backtracking in the text or going to other texts. In terms of register, field is foregrounded.

DEFINING, CLASSIFYING AND EXPLAINING IN SCIENCE

Defining

Defining, in the sense that this word applies to creating technical terms, is a process analogous to naming. Saying *we call animals that eat plants herbivores* is much the same as saying *Marge and Homer called their son Bart*. In each case a specific name (*herbivores* and *Bart*) identifies something (*animals that eat plants* and *Marge and Homer's son*).

Just as a name identifies a person, a technical name identifies some phenomenon. This is realised in the grammar through the roles of Token and Value (see Halliday 1985a). A name (a Token) is being assigned to some phenomenon (a Value): phenomena are given a name which gives it a specific identity in that particular Field. Halliday (1985a) discusses Token and Value in relation to their functions as participant roles in relational identifying clauses. Wignell, Martin and Eggins (1987) interpreted them more broadly as a kind of elaboration and regarded a number of elaborating lexicogrammatical structures as assigning Tokens to Values.

The following resources are typically used for defining (from Wignell, Martin and Eggins 1987: 40–55). (Technical terms shown in **bold**.)

Relational identifying processes:

(1) **water vapour**   is   the invisible gas [which ends up in the air when water evaporates]
  (Token)   (Value)

(2) an **embryo**   is   an organism [in a very early stage of development]
  (Token)   (Value)

Nominal group apposition:

(3) animals [that eat plants],   **herbivores** . . .
     (Value)   (Token)

Embedded clauses:

(4) an invisible gas   [called **water vapour**]
     (Value)   (Token)

Elaborating clauses:

(5) **prevailing winds**,   that is winds [that blow from one
                                 direction for most of the year]
     (Token)   (Value)

Here the principal resource used is elaboration, with the technical term, realised by the Token, standing for a more 'commonsense' Value. The movement is either from 'commonsense' to technical, and/or from technical to more technical.

Classifying

As well as naming things, science reorganises things. Classification is typically done through relational attributive, and occasionally existential, processes. These serve to arrange the technical terms into taxonomies. Two types of taxonomic relationships are constructed: part/whole and class/sub-class.

Part/whole (relational attributive; possessive and circumstantial):

(6) the **ecosystem**   has   two parts, the **physical environment**
                              and the **biome**
     (Carrier)   (Attribute)

(from Wignell, Martin and Eggins, 1987: 40–55)

(7) **carbohydrates** contain **atoms** of **carbon**, **oxygen** and
                                hydrogen
     (Carrier)   (Attribute)

Class/sub-class (relational attributive [intensive]; existential):

(8) **enzymes**   are   **catalysts**
     (Carrier)   (Attribute)

(9) there   are   three groups of **saccharides**: **mono-
                  saccharides**, **disaccharides** and
                  polysaccharides
                  (Existent)

(from Mudie and Brotherton 1985: 32 and 36)

Explaining

Explaining how things happen is typically done through implication sequences (Wignell, Martin and Eggins 1987: 40–55). A sequence of events is outlined typically using material processes and enhancement (sequence in time, cause and effect, condition). Implication sequences are also sources of new technical terms.

For example (from Wignell, Martin and Eggins 1987: 40–55):

(10) α   **frontal uplift** occurs
         (Token)
   ˣβ   when cold air meets warm air
   ˣγ   forcing the warm air to rise
         (second and third clauses = Value)

In this example a technical term, *frontal uplift*, is defined by an implication sequence. That is, the clause complex constituting the implication sequence functions as Value.

(11) (Grammatical metaphors shown in **bold**, abstractions shown in *italic*)

As air is moved upward away from the land-water surface or downward toward it, very important **changes** occur in the air *temperature*. Air moving upward away from the surface comes under lower **pressures** because there is less *weight* of atmosphere upon it, so it stretches or expands. Air moving downward toward the surface from higher *elevations* encounters higher **pressures** and shrinks in *volume*. Even if there is no **addition** or **withdrawal** of *heat* from surrounding *sources*, the *temperature* of the upward or downward-moving air changes because of its **expansion** or **contraction**. This type of *temperature* **change** [which **results** from internal *processes* alone] is called **adiabatic change**.

In the second example above there is a general pattern in which the amount of grammatical metaphors and abstractions (see Martin 1996) accumulates and is finally distilled into one technical term (*adiabatic change*) which functions as Token for the whole implication sequence.

SUMMARY OF THE DISTINCTIVE CHARACTERISTICS OF THE DISCOURSE OF THE HUMANITIES

Whereas science uses technicality the humanities use abstraction to understand and interpret the world (Eggins, Wignell and Martin 1987). Put simply, abstraction involves moving from an instance or collection of instances, through generalisation to abstract interpretation. That is, we shift from the 'story' to what the 'story' means. (Wignell [forthcoming] treats abstraction [as a mass noun] as a general resource for realising semiotic distance from context. This interpretation corresponds with the interpretation taken by Eggins, Wignell and Martin

[1987] and by Martin [1989]. Martin [1996] uses the term abstractions (as a count noun) in opposition to grammatical metaphors. The interpretation taken here is to treat both abstractions and grammatical metaphors as means of realising abstraction in text.)

For example, in history initially we might find individual people doing things in time and space (using tense and temporal conjunctions to order events), then a move to generic classes of people participating in general classes of activities set in time (using circumstances of location), then a shift away from the people to a focus on the events (nominalised as participants) and finally an interpretation of what the events mean (nominalisation of events and reasoning realised metaphorically).

This movement involves shifts in mode; the more interpretive a text is the more abstract it is in terms of mode. The resource most involved in these shifts in mode is grammatical metaphor.

A BRIEF HISTORY OF SOCIAL SCIENCE

It will be argued here that what is referred to as social science can be seen to have its roots in the humanities, particularly in the humanities discipline of moral philosophy, and in the discourse of the physical sciences. That is, in the mid seventeenth century, in England, the science of the social began through the importation of the discourse of the physical sciences into discussions of the social. This argument will be pursued by examining a number of archival social science texts and attempting to relate their emerging features to changes in the social context of the times.

In English, this process began with Thomas Hobbes in the mid seventeenth century. The key text here is Hobbes' *Leviathan* (1651). In *Leviathan*, Hobbes presented a long and complex argument about why people need sovereign government. Hobbes' method of arguing is different from that of more or less contemporary theorists of government, such as John Locke. Locke's (1690) *Second Treatise of Government* deals with similar issues to Hobbes but deals with them differently. Locke's text is abstract but not technical (see Wignell forthcoming).

Where Hobbes differs from Locke is in his method of argumentation. Hobbes introduced a style of reasoning drawn directly from the physical sciences of his time, principally from Galileo. He introduced an analogy from the physical sciences: that human beings are bodies in motion, and deduced from this his original premises on which he based his arguments on why humans need sovereign government.

The following short passage from Hobbes' *Leviathan* (1651/1986: 85) illustrates the initial importation of the discourse of the physical sciences into discussions of the social. (Technical terms are shown in **bold**, grammatical metaphors are shown in ***bold italic*** and generic abstractions are shown in *italic*. Abbreviations used in analysis are: rel = relational

Table 11.1. Adopting science to the social

(paragraph 4)
(1) The **cause** [of **sense**], is
(Token)   (rel: id)

the External Body, or Object, [which presseth the organ (proper to each **sense**),
either immediately, as in the Tast and Touch, or mediately, as in Seeing,
Hearing, and Smelling]:

(Value)

which **pressure**,   by the **mediation** [of Nerves, and other strings,
                             and membranes of the body],
(Initiator)   (circ: manner)

<<continued   inwards to the Brain, and Heart>>,
(material)   (circ: location)

causeth   there   a **resistance**, or counter **pressure**, or
                             endeavour
(mat-)   (circ: location)   (Actor)

[of the heart],   to deliver   it self:
                  (-erial)   (Goal)

which **endeavour** <<because Outward>>,   seemeth to be some *matter*
         (Carrier)   (rel: att)   (Attribute)
[without].

(2) And this **seeming**, or **fancy**, is [that (which men call   **sense**)];
         (Value)   (Token)

and consisteth, as to the Eye, in a *light*, or *Colour* figured; To the Eare, in a
    (rel: att: poss) (Attributes) →

sound; To the Nostrill, in an *Odour*; To the Tongue and Palat, in a *Savour*;
And to the rest of the body, in **Heat**, **Cold**, **Hardnesse**, **Softnesse**, and such
other *qualities*, [as we discern by feeling].

(3) All of which *qualities* [called Sensible],   are
(Token)   (rel: id)

in the object [that *causeth* them], but so many several *motions* of the
(circ: location)   (Value)

matter, [by which it presseth the organs directly].

---

process, id = identifying, circ = circumstance, att = attributive, poss =
possessive.)

In the passage above, Hobbes introduces the analogy of bodies in
motion to human behaviour. This analogy sets up the premise for a
long chain of reasoning. The extract shows a number of the features that
Halliday (1988) identifies in his analysis of Newton's science writing (note
that Hobbes was writing before Newton.) In fact, taken out of context,
the passage could easily be mistaken for an early medical text. A technical term 'sense' is established, linked anaphorically to an implication

sequence. The explanation of 'sense' is a 'scientific' one. Within the implication sequence (*the first sentence*) we find metaphorical reasoning (*the cause of sense, causeth*); grammatical metaphor is used textually to summarise information (*which presseth on the organ proper to each sense* → *which pressure*); this is in conjunction with other metaphors (*resistance, counter pressure, endeavour*) and the final sentence uses grammatical metaphor and generic abstractions to summarise the preceding text.

Why Hobbes might have done this needs to be considered in the light of the social context of his time. Hobbes was writing at a time of both social and intellectual upheaval. These upheavals were both interconnected. In political terms, Hobbes was writing at the time of the English Civil Wars; in social terms this was the time of the emergence of the bourgeoisie, in conflict with the aristocracy, as the dominant social class. Intellectually, it was the time of what is referred to as the 'scientific revolution'. Existing dominant ideas about the nature of the cosmos and the place of humans in it, based mainly on a combination of revelation and ideas derived from Classical Greece, were being challenged by ideas derived from observation and mathematical calculation (Copernicus, Kepler, Galileo). (See Harman 1983; Kearney 1971; Swingewood 1984; Zeitlin 1994 for an analysis of the *scientific revolution* and concurrent social changes. See Wignell forthcoming for a discussion of the above in relation to social science.) The discourse of the physical sciences, particularly physics (including geometry and mathematics) was emerging as the dominant paradigm for interpreting the physical world. It was also the paradigm most aligned with the emerging dominant social class.

It was from this context that Hobbes drew the physical sciences into discussions of the social. Hobbes, however, did not begin in a textual vacuum. Moral philosophers, for example Thomas Aquinas in the thirteenth century and Bacon in the late sixteenth and early seventeenth, had been discussing social issues for a long time, and continued to do so after Hobbes (for example Locke, Hume, John Stuart Mill). Hobbes imported the discourse of the physical sciences into a pre-existing discipline and in doing so laid the groundwork for a new discourse to evolve. Hobbes called what he was doing *Civil Philosophy*.

Civil Philosophy as a discipline appears to have begun and ended with Hobbes, but his legacy re-emerged in what was known as political economy. It will be argued here that political economy is the direct ancestor of all the modern disciplines of social science, except perhaps psychology. Disciplines such as economics, sociology and political science can all be traced back to this common ancestor. It is in the archival political science texts discussed in this chapter that the linguistic patterns which characterise modern social science can be seen to emerge.

Political economy appears to have been the only social science discipline for almost a century, from the late eighteenth century to the late nineteenth: a period which more or less corresponds with the industrial revolution and the emergence of industrial capitalism as the dominant mode of production, distribution and exchange in England. Key political economists such as Adam Smith (1776), David Ricardo (1817) and Karl Marx (1867) all analysed capitalism at different stages of its evolution.

Following Marx, political economy appears to have ended, or rather fragmented, as a discipline and the modern disciplines of social science began to emerge. Economics (capitalist economics) appears to have bypassed Marx and evolved from the political economy of Smith and Ricardo. Economics, coming out of the 'economy' side of political economy, is the social science most 'true' to its direct ancestry. The patterns which were evolving through Smith, and Ricardo and Marx reach their fruition in economics, although Marx appears to have been bypassed in modern capitalist economics. Political science appears to have come from the 'political' half of political economy and continued to evolve in a different direction from economics.

Sociology appears to have a more complex lineage. Sociology had its origins in France, after the French Revolution (see Swingewood 1984). The earliest French practitioners (Saint-Simon, 1760–1825; Comte, 1798–1857) of what became sociology adopted a more biological science analogy in their analysis of society. Society was regarded as akin to an organism with its own anatomy and physiology. This represented a contrast with the mechanistic, physical models of human behaviour prevalent in England at the time.

English sociology (Spencer, 1820–1903) also adopted a biological, organic analogy. Spencer, while adopting an organic and evolutionary approach which pre-dated Darwin, still preserved the notion of society being made up of an aggregation of individuals. The emerging French sociology viewed society more as a macro-organism. Along with this analogy from the biological sciences we also find in sociology ideas from political economy, such as the *division of labour*, picked up and extended to the whole of society rather than just restricted to economic activity (Durkheim 1893).

Sociology, then, appears to have emerged from a second importation from science: that of an analogy from the biological sciences instead of from the physical sciences. According to Foucault (1970), such an importation from the biological sciences would not have been possible in the seventeenth or eighteenth centuries, since the biological sciences of those times were concerned only with taxonomic relationships: ordering things. In addition to the influence of the biological sciences we also find a link with political economy.

In summary, then, the lineage of social science can be traced intially to a synthesis of the physical sciences and moral philosophy, leading to Hobbes' civil philosophy. This lineage re-emerges in political economy. Economics and political science emerge directly from political economy. Sociology involves a further synthesis of ideas from the biological sciences with some aspects of political economy, and, considering the moral aspect of much early sociology, a continuing influence from moral philosophy.

The following sections of this chapter summarise the principal features of science and the humanities, then consider briefly the phylogenesis of social science before looking at examples from current economics and sociology undergraduate textbooks. (For a more detailed discussion of the phylogenesis of social science see Wignell forthcoming.)

THE PHYLOGENESIS OF TECHNICALITY IN SOCIAL SCIENCE

The discussion below briefly outlines the phylogenesis of social science. Wignell (forthcoming) notes a number of semiotic drifts in the evolution of social science. These 'drifts' are discussed with reference to a number of key archival social science texts: Thomas Hobbes' *Leviathan* (1651), Adam Smith's *The Wealth of Nations* (1776), David Ricardo's *The Principles of Political Economy and Taxation* (1817), Karl Marx's *Capital (Volume One)* (1867) and Emile Durkheim's *The Division of Labour in Society* (1893).

SEMIOTIC DRIFTS WITHIN SOCIAL SCIENCE

Logical and experiential

A semiotic drift in the macro scale logical organisation of texts can be noted. This involves a drift away from macro scale consequential relations to macro scale relations of manner. This drift occurs in conjunction with two factors. First, as a field is built, much of the arguing is done through the field and is realised in the body of texts in external, field-based logical relations. That is, the field does the job of explaining 'this is how'. Second, there is a shift away from a more hortatory type of text to a more analytical type: a shift away from what people *should* do to what people *do* do.

For example, Hobbes, in constructing a macro argument foregrounds the logical. On the macro scale, Hobbes' text is an elaborate chain of deductive reasoning based primarily on conjunctive relations of implicit internal consequence. In the service of the argument Hobbes both builds a field, through analogy to the physical sciences, and draws on a number of fields, defining and classifying. In building a field Hobbes draws directly from the physical sciences of his time. Through adopting the analogy of bodies in motion from the physical sciences and applying it to man (sic), Hobbes gives a technical account of human behaviour: he names, classifies and explains. This initial introduction of technicality functions logically as the premise for a long chain of consequential reasoning. The overall pattern of the text is driven by the argument, by the chain of logic. The purpose of this chain of reasoning is largely to 'prove' that people need sovereign government.

As a field builds, in Smith, Ricardo and Marx, the role of the logical as the driving force of the text declines. Patterns of conjunctive relations change, with much less emphasis on internal consequential relations and more emphasis on internal relations of manner: the emphasis shifts from 'this is why' to 'this is how'. As technicality accrues, a field builds and becomes a tool for theorising with. Argument, increasingly, is confined to the arrangement and organisation of the field. Once the field is settled to the satisfaction of the builder, it is then used to reconstrue the 'world' or that aspect of human affairs which is in contention. The field is periodically argued about, then, once the argument is temporarily resolved and the field is temporarily settled it is used to explain. That is, argument becomes increasingly about the nature of the tools rather than about their application. Thus, metafunctionally, the balance between the logical and experiential shifts in favour of the experiential, with the principal macro scale logical relations being relations of manner, with the field explaining 'how'.

Experiential and textual

Two logogenetic and phylogenetic semiotic drifts are noted here. One is an experiential drift from abstraction to technicality and, in economic reasoning, from abstraction to mathematics (arithmetic). The other is a textual drift. As the logical declines in importance the textual metafunction increases in prominence in text organisation. It does this through interplay with the experiential component of the ideational metafunction. As the text(s) become increasingly technical in their construal of experience, the technicality not only increases in quantity but also becomes more textually prominent.

Textual drift

Logogenetically, at the macro and hyper scales technicality becomes increasingly prominent in Macro and Hyper Themes and News (see Martin 1990b). Technicality, in conjunction with abstractions and metaphors, becomes part of a condensation of information which is used as a point of departure thematically and part of a condensation of information which is used to summarise. At the hyper scale, this is noted more in Hyper Themes than it is in Hyper News. As well as a tool for interpreting technicality is also a means of distilling information into a smaller grammatical space, typically a nominal group. That is, as technicality distils experientially, it is made prominent textually. Once established, technicality becomes the point of departure.

Phylogenetically, in the emergence of disciplines, and logogenetically in texts upon which disciplines are built, with Smith in political economy and Durkheim in sociology, technicality emerges in Macro News as a distillation of a large quantity of preceding text. The main feature of the text which is reconstrued technically is that it is abstract text. That is, the text features long and persistent lexical strings of abstractions (typically generic) and more localised metaphors. An already abstract construal of experience is reconstrued technically.

For example, the short extract below marks the point where techni-

Table 11.2 The introduction of technicality in *The Wealth of Nations*

(paragraph 12)

1) [What are the **rules** (which men naturally observe [in exchanging them either for money or for one another]), I shall now proceed to examine.]

2) These *rules* determine [what may be called the relative or **exchangeable value** of goods].

(This is the first appearance of a technical term which is defined in the text.)

(paragraph 13)

1) The word ***value***, <<it is to be observed>>, has two different ***meanings***, and sometimes expresses the ***utility*** of some particular object, and sometimes the ***power*** [of purchasing other goods (which the ***possession*** of that object conveys)].

2) The one may be called '**value [in use]** '; the other, '**value [in exchange]** '.

3) The things [which have the greatest **value (in use)**] have frequently little or no **value [in exchange]**; and, on the contrary, those [which have the greatest ***value (in exchange)***] have frequently little or no **value [in use]**.

4) Nothing is more useful than water: but it will purchase scarce anything; scarce anything can be had in ***exchange*** for it.

5) A diamond, on the contrary, has scarce any **value [in use]**; but a great *quantity* of other goods may frequently be had in ***exchange*** for it.

(paragraph 14)

1) In order to investigate the **principles** [which regulate the **exchangeable value** of *commodities*], I shall endeavour to show, First, [what is the real *measure* of this **exchangeable value**]; or wherein consists the **real price** of all *commodities*. Second, [what are the different *parts* of which this ***real price*** is composed or made up]. And, lastly, [what are the different *circumstances* (which sometimes raise some or all of these different parts of **price** above, and sometimes sink them below their **natural or ordinary rate**)]; or, [what are the **causes** (which sometimes hinder the **market price**, that is, the **actual price** of *commodities*, from coinciding exactly with [what may be called **their natural price**])].

cality is introduced into *The Wealth of Nations*. The extract appears as a
Macro New (see Martin 1993) at the end of chapter four. The extract
introduces a technical analysis of 'value' (what things are worth). (Technical terms are shown in **bold**, grammatical metaphors are shown in
bold italics, and abstractions in *italic*.

Here the beginnings of a technical framework are introduced. Technical terms, *exchangeable value*, *value in use*, *natural price* and *real price* are
introduced as the forerunner to an analysis of economic behaviour. From
this point in the text technicality is used as the principal means of
analysis and tends to be located in the text at points of information
prominence: in Macro and Hyper Themes in particular.

Once established, technicality becomes the point of departure, both
logogenetically and phylogenetically, for further analysis and contestation. Ricardo (1817), for instance, takes Smith's analysis of *value* as his
point of departure and presents a counter-analysis. Ricardo's analysis is
also technical, both using existing technicality and building on it.

This is illustrated in the Table 11.3 in which existing technicality is
taken up phylogenetically as thematic (from Ricardo 1817: 9–10).
Here we find abstractions (*quantity*) used to refer to amounts, metaphors (*variation*) used to show change, metaphors of Modality (*probability*, *certainty*) used to show likelihood and logical metaphors (*cause*) are used to
show cause and effect.

Similarly Marx (1867) uses the same technical framework in his analysis of *value*. The trends of a progressive increase over time in the
amount of technicality, the use of technicality to argue with and the
textual prominence of technicality are fully realised in Marx. Marx's

Table 11.3 The phylogenesis of technicality

Two *commodities* vary in **relative value**, and we wish to know [in which the
variation has really taken place].

If we compare the present **value** of one with shoes, stockings, hats, iron, sugar,
and all other *commodities* we find that it will exchange for precisely the same
quantity of all these things as before.

If we compare the other with the same *commodities*, we find it has varied with
respect to them all: we may then with great ***probability*** infer that the
variation has been in this *commodity*, and not in the *commodities* [with which we
have compared it].

If on examining still more particularly into all the *circumstances* [connected with
the ***production*** (of these various *commodities*)], we find that precisely the same
quantity of *labour* and *capital* are necessary to the ***production*** of the shoes,
stockings, hats, iron, sugar, etc.; but that the same **quantity** [as before] is not
necessary to produce the single **commodity** [whose **relative value** is
altered], ***probability*** is changed into ***certainty***, and we are sure [that the
variation is in the single *commodity*]: we then discover also the ***cause*** of its
variation.

---

analysis is both technical and abstract: it is a technical analysis of a generically abstract world.

Marx takes as his point of departure Smith's and Ricardo's analyses. In order to develop his own analysis of *value*, Marx makes technical terms out of two things which were treated as abstractions but not defined and made technical previously, *commodities* and *labour*:

Commodities (Marx 1867: 47):

(12) as **values**, all **commodities**   are   only definite masses of
                                                       congealed
                                                       labour-time.
    (circ: role)   (Token)   (rel: id) (Value)

This involves a distillation of the preceding pages into a redefinition of commodities. A distinction between products and commodities is then introduced. Things produced for one's own use are not regarded as commodities because these things do not enter into any relationship with other things; they are not exchanged. Taking this addition into account a final definition of commodities concludes this section of the chapter. This definition is accomplished by enhancement in a clause complex (1867: 48):

(13) 'To become   a **commodity**
                  (Token)
    a ***product***   must be transferred   to another,
    (Goal)   (Material)   (Beneficiary)
    <<whom it will serve as a **use-value**>>
    by ***means*** of an *exchange*.'
    (circ: manner: means)
                                        (Marx 1867: 48)

Labour:

(14) 'In the **use-value** [of each **commodity**] there is contained **useful labour**,
    (Token)

    i.e. productive ***activity*** [of a definite ***kind***] and [exercised with a definite ***aim***].
                        (Value)

    Use values cannot confront each other as **commodities** unless the **useful labour** [embodied in them] is qualitatively different in each of them.'
                                                                    (49)

Useful labour is then excluded:

(15) 'Productive ***activity***,
     (Value)

if we leave out of sight its special *form*, viz., the useful character of **labour**,

is nothing but the expenditure [of human **labour-power**].
                                              (Token)

Tailoring and weaving, though qualitatively different productive ***activities***, are in each a productive ***expenditure*** of human brains, nerves, and muscles, and in this sense are human **labour**.

They are but two different modes of expending human **labour-power**. . . .

It is the expenditure of **simple labour-power**,
                        (Token)

i.e., of the **labour power** [which, on an ***average***, apart from any special ***development***, exists in the organism of
every ordinary individual].
                    (Value)

. . . **Skilled labour** counts only as **simple labour** [intensified],
    (Token)   (Value)

or rather, as multiplied **simple labour**,
                          (Value)

a given quantity of **skilled** being considered equal to a greater quantity of **simple labour**. A **commodity** may be the product [of the most **skilled labour**], but its **value**, by equating it to the product of **simple unskilled labour**, represents a definite quantity of the latter **labour** alone.'

                                                          (1867: 51).

These small additions to the technical framework are crucial to Marx's analysis of *value* and, in turn, of capitalism. In making *labour* technical, Marx has also made it more abstract. He does this through technicality: by establishing a taxonomic distinction between *useful labour* and *simple labour power*, where *useful labour* refers to different kinds of 'work' while *simple labour power* refers to *labour* in an aggregated, averaged, homogeneous and generic sense. In doing this Marx has used technicality to solve a problem with previous analyses: how to separate *use value* from *exchange value*. By equating *use value* with *useful labour* Marx has also equated *exchange value* (or simply *value*) with *simple labour*.

Phylogenetically, existing technicality becomes thematic at the macro scale both logogenetically in the text and phylogenetically in succeeding texts. The last person's theory becomes the point of departure for the next person's critique and reworking of the theory. Typically each reworking of the theory both redefines and rearranges existing technicality and adds some new technicality. Over time, as the theory gets 'bigger', an increasing amount of technicality is pushed to the foreground textually. The beginning chapters of Smith's text and Marx's, for instance, are scarcely similar in any way but they are clearly from the same field. In a direct phylogenetic lineage, Smith begins the field (as a Macro New with considerable preceding text), Ricardo reworks the field (field as Macro Theme) and Marx reworks the field (field also as Macro Theme). Thus, on a phylogenetic scale, what started as New information (in a Macro New) becomes Given information (in Macro Themes) and comes to represent the point of departure.

Experiential drift: technicality, abstractions and metaphors

Related to the interplay between the textual and experiential is the relationship between abstraction and technicality. In addition to being increasingly technical, the texts are also abstract. There are two complementary explanations for this. One is in the origins of the discourse, in its genesis, the other is in the role of the textual metafunction in its logogenesis and phylogenesis.

One source of abstraction can be seen in the origins of the discourse, both in its subject matter and in how that subject matter was treated. First the subject matter itself is far from tangible, unlike much of the subject matter of the physical sciences. For example, even the most abstract and mathematical of physical sciences, physics, has its base in the tangible, observable and measurable. In the science first used as an analogy by Hobbes, (physics/geometry/cosmology), while the theorisation is abstract, the abstraction is from a tangible base. This base is, however, generalised: what applies to one body in motion applies to them all under the same conditions.

Hobbes treats humans in exactly this way. He theorises from the ground up but still using a level of generalisation: *man* refers to all *men*, or rather, to *man* in the abstract: a hypothetical, idealised, generic *man*. In drawing his analogy from the physical sciences, Hobbes treats all *men* as being moved by the same set of principles: the same principles that apply to physical objects.

However, taking a top down approach, such as that adopted by Smith, requires an initial degree of abstraction greater than that found in Hobbes' text. Smith's, and subsequent texts, begin to theorise at a high level of abstraction. For example, the abstract use of *labour* (a motif that extends through Smith, Ricardo and Marx) does not move through stages of, say, this man working → these men working → work (verb form but realised nominally) → labour (abstraction). Instead its use begins at the most abstract (*labour*) and shunts back and forth depending on whether it is used to refer to an individual instance, a collective instance, *work* in general or *labour* in the abstract and, finally, with Marx, *labour* as a technical term. Even when using a hypothetical example, the text does not go below generic classes.

This abstract construal of experience precedes the introduction of technicality. Those things made technical have, logogenetically and phylogenetically, most often, been initially realised and developed abstractly, principally through generic abstraction. This often happens across texts and time. For example, Marx makes technical two things treated as abstractions by Smith, and which continued as abstractions in Ricardo: *labour* and *commodities*. This intervening level of abstraction is one feature that appears to distinguish the discourse of social science from that of science. That is, through its initial construal of an abstract 'world' and a subsequent shift into a technical construal, social science makes the abstract technical.

In social science, while individual people can be regarded as tangible objects, the 'objects' being theorised, if looked at congruently, in general are relations (or processes) rather than things. One instance can be treated congruently, but generalisation from more than one instance often requires the intervention of abstraction. For example, even a relatively simple concept such as an *exchange* is an abstraction via grammatical metaphor. In Smith's text, for instance, *exchange* undergoes a number of transitions before becoming relatively fixed as a nominalisation. Instantially it is realised congruently as a Process; in shifting into generic abstraction it is realised in nominal groups but morphologically still a verb; in being used technically it undergoes a double shift. First it is realised as a Qualifier (*value [in exchange]*: the location of the *value*). Then it shifts to being realised as a Classifier (*exchangeable value*: a kind of *value*). In this case the conversion becomes more or less permanent and fixed in a technical term, *exchangeable value*.

In all of the archival texts analysed Wignell (forthcoming) found that technicality and theory are built around a hypothetical, idealised and generic base. This in itself requires a degree of distancing and can be traced back to the origins of the discourse.

Critical in this is Hobbes' deduction of a hypothetical *state of nature* from his analysis of 'human nature'. It needs to be pointed out again that Hobbes does not suggest that his *state of nature* actually ever existed. He deduces it from the internal logic of his argument and uses it as a hypothetical account of what would happen if there were no sovereign government. It is an idealised, although hardly ideal, state, constructed by logical deduction to serve a larger argument.

The notion of the *state of nature*, conceived of differently by different people, is, however, taken up by others as if it were a historical original state, a sort of entrepreneur's Eden. Typically scanty knowledge of newly *discovered* indigenous people and *savages* serve as examples of people in a state of nature. John Locke (1690) also cites the books of Genesis and Psalms as evidence. Smith (1776) appears to proceed from the assumption that the *state of nature* is 'real'. Even Durkheim's *mechanical solidarity* has echoes of the *state of nature*. This originally hypothetical state is then used as a base for future theorising. For example, Smith uses the *state of nature* as a base for naturalising capitalist economic behaviour. The assumptions from which the theory is derived are, therefore, hypothetical and abstract.

Just as the *state of nature* is treated ideally, so is the current (for the times) state of society. Theory begins at the level of generic abstraction, with society, or some aspect of society, in total. This is then theorised from the top down into types. In looking, for example, at the origins of a technical theory of economic behaviour in Smith, the technicality begins at the top of the taxonomy and then moves down. In Ricardo's text, the technical theory is reworked from the top first and then extended downwards. The same pattern is found in Marx and Durkheim. Rather than being built from the ground up, theory builds from the top down. That is, it starts off at the most abstract and reaches down.

This initial level of experiential abstraction then works in conjunction with the textual metafunction. Initially abstract construals of aspects of human behaviour are reconstrued technically. The technicality is pushed into positions of textual prominence. Since the technicality is derived from abstraction, the abstraction is also pushed into prominence, eventually producing a discourse where abstraction precedes technicality (phylogenetically) and where theory precedes application (logogenetically and phylogenetically).

A small number of examples from a small number of key texts only are shown to illustrate the emergence and phylogenesis of technicality. What is perhaps more important for this chapter is the original premises about 'human nature' from which the technicality emerges.

Hobbes imported the discourse of the physical sciences to analyse *man* (sic). Hobbes begins generically: his *man* is a hypothetical 'standard average man'. He (sic) is also an individual man, not a social man. From his analysis of man Hobbes deduces that man, living in a *state of nature*, without government, with total freedom. Hobbes argues that in such a state '*the life of man (would be), solitary, poore, nasty, brutish and short*' (Hobbes 1651/1986: 186) and that people would be living '*in that condition which is called Warre; and such a warre, as is of every man, against every man*' (Hobbes 1651/1986: 185). Hobbes uses this vision of a state of nature to argue the need for sovereign government.

Similarly, in political economy Adam Smith (1776) derived his economic theory from a hypothetical generic man living in a state of nature. Smith's vision of the state of nature is, however, something of an entrepreneur's Eden rather than Hobbes' Hell on earth. The moral philospopher John Locke (1690) likewise argues from the same base. Where Hobbes, state of nature is hypothetical (what would happen if), Smith and Locke treat such a state as historically real (Locke cites the Bible as a source). Following Smith, Ricardo (1817) also argues from man in a state of nature. What these texts all have in common is that they begin at the generic, the hypothetical and the abstracted. That is, a world already construed abstractly (hypothetically) is made technical.

Summary

The point of the section above was to outline briefly the phylogenesis of technicality in social science. The discipline of political economy evolved into, in around one hundred years, a technical discipline. Over time, experientially, technicality was introduced, accrued and was increasingly used as the principal means of analysis. In conjunction with this experiential dimension, the textual phylogenesis of technicality shows a progressive push of technicality into points of textual prominence, beginning (with Smith) as a Macro New and progressing until it becomes the unmarked Theme on both the macro and hyper scales. In addition, technicality, once introduced, progressively became, logically, the prime location of argument within the field.

The culmination of these progressions represents the point of departure for the texts used in the synchronic discussion of social science below. The discussion below uses undergraduate textbooks from two social science disciplines, economics and sociology, as sources of data.

TECHNICALITY AND ABSTRACTION IN CONTEMPORARY SOCIAL SCIENCE

This section considers technicality in one social science discipline, sociology. The discussion is based on one contemporary undergraduate textbook: M. Waters and R. Crook (1993), *Sociology One* (third edition), Melbourne: Longman Cheshire. The discussion is intended to be read in the light of the preceding discussion of the phylogenesis of social science.

In terms of its textual organisation, both at the scales of book and chapter, the textbook analysed takes technicality as its point of departure. A whole chapter (Chapter 2) is devoted to outlining a technical framework, which is then applied in subsequent chapters. The pattern that is found in Marx as a result of over one hundred years of the phylogenesis of the discourse is replicated at a point which marks the early stages of the ontogenesis of the discourse for initiates. This in itself has pedagogic implications. What is phylogenetically a kind of Macro Given is ontogenically a kind of Macro New. That is, the discourse is at its most technical and abstract at a point where it is most new to initiates.

In conjunction with this textual positioning, the experiential nature of the technicality needs to be considered. This is done through examining both what is being made technical and how it is being made technical through analysing the transitivity and nominal group structure of examples of text where technicality is established.

Defining and classifying in sociology

As with the archival texts, technicality begins at the most superordinate end of the taxonomy and proceeds downwards. Waters and Crook (1993), in Chapter 2, establish field by setting up an array of technical terms through transitivity, exploiting the potential of the relationship between Token and Value. These terms are then progressively arranged taxonomically through lexical relations of hyponymy and meronymy. This is done progressively throughout the chapter, starting at the highest-order taxonomic level and working down. The first distinction is into two types of terms, *analytic* and *descriptive*. These two terms are defined by elaboration:

(16) α '. . . many of the terms [which are used in **sociology**] are
      analytic terms
          (Token)
  =β which are used to decompose, dissect, and discover **structure** in
      the **social world**.'
          (Value)

(1993: 25)

To make the Token/Value relationship more explicit in a 'naming' structure, this could be rewritten as:

(17) **terms** [which are used to decompose, are called **analytic terms**
     dissect and discover *structure* in the
     social world]
     (Value)   (rel: id)   (Token)

likewise:

(18) α 'These may be contrasted with **descriptive terms**,
                        (Token)
  =β which identify real *events* and *processes* [which can actually be
     experienced].'
                     (Value)

These terms represent the beginnings of a taxonomy:

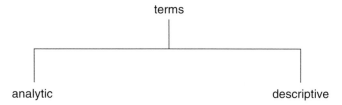

Figure 11.1 Taxonomy of types of terms

The rest of the chapter develops first under the sub-heading 'Analytic terms' and then under the sub-heading 'Descriptive terms'. Terms under these headings are defined and classified in taxonomic order. Examples of definitions are shown here. The examples are presented as they occur logogenetically in the text.

The first three analytic terms defined are *culture, social structure* and *personality*. *Culture* is defined as follows (1993: 25):

(19) . . . more or less shared *prescriptions* [of (what people ought or ought not to do) and of the *way* (things are)]

this	is referred to	by sociologists	as **culture**
(Value)	(Behavioural)	(Assigner)	(Token)

Culture is then redefined under the sub-heading 'Culture' (1993: 26):

(20) Formally defined:

a **culture** is   a *complex* [of more or less shared *ideas* (about [what is known], [how things ought to be], and [how things ought to be done], [which can be transmitted from one *generation* to the next)].

(Token)   (rel: id)   (Value)

Social structure is defined as follows:

(21) there are *arrangements* [by which human beings interact with one another]

this	is called	**social structure**
(Value)	(rel: id)	(Token)

Personality is defined as follows (1993: 25):

(22) there is the *way* [in which individual people relate to and respond to **culture** and **social structure**]

this	is called	**personality**
(Value)	(rel: id)	(Token)

In each of the three cases the Value is linked by anaphoric retrieval through '*this*'. In the final example, previously defined terms are as part of the Value, indicating use of field already built to build more field. In addition, in each case, the Value consists of a nominal group with a Thing which is a generic abstraction, to which is attached a more congruent, and, in the final, case a more technical, Qualifier.

The terms above are then used as the basis for further taxonomising. Culture (non-material, 1993: 26) is broken down into three 'categories': *knowledge, values* and *norms*. These are defined by apposition (1993: 26):

(23) *ideas* [about the *way* (the world is)]   (**knowledge**)
    (Value)   (Token)

    ideas [about (the *way* [it ought to be])]   (**values**)
    (Value)   (Token)

    and   *rules* or expectations [about   (**norms**)
            (how things should be done)]
            (Token)   (Value)

In the first two of these examples, semiotic abstractions are reconstrued as technical terms. In the third example a combination of an institutional and a semiotic abstraction are reconstrued as technical terms.

This pattern is also noted when these terms are later redefined under their respective sub-headings:

(24) **Knowledge**   may be defined   as stored and transmissible
                                        information
    (Token)   (behavioural)   (circ: manner)
                                        (Value)

    Values   are   ***preferential beliefs*** [about
                                        (the *way* [things ought to be])]
    (Token)   (rel: id)   (Value)

Preferences [about (the *way* [things generally ought to be (**values**)])] are translated into ***expectations*** [about (the *way* [specific things actually ought to be done])].

    These *rules* or ***expectations***   are called   **norms**.
    (Value)   (rel: id)   (Token)

Of these terms *norms* is subclassified. Table 11.4 summarises this classification and exemplifies the logogenesis of technicality.

The Values which all of these terms encode (with the exception of *prescriptive norms*) all contain abstractions, indicating a reconstrual of a 'world' already construed abstractly into one construed technically.

As well as defining, the passage above builds a cross-classifying taxonomy (hyponymy) of norms. That is norms are either formal or informal and either prescriptive or proscriptive.

Having moved down a layer in the taxonomy, a Classifier^Thing structure is used in the nominal groups realising the technical term (Token). The Classifier indicates a 'kind of'. Using the cross-classification above it would be possible to have, for example, an informal proscriptive norm, using two Classifiers.

Moving back up in the taxonomy, 'social structure' is redefined by shifting the same Token and Value into a relational identifying clause (1993: 29):

Table 11.4 Logogenesis of technicality: classification of 'norms'

These **rules** or **expectations** (Value)	are called (rel: id)	**norms**. (Token)
Formal norms (Token)	are (rel: id)	those [which are written down and objectified]. (Value)
By contrast, informal norms (Carrier)	have (rel: att)	the *character* [of **expectations** rather than of **rules**]. (Attribute)

The second **distinction** [[we need to make]] is between **prescriptive** and **proscriptive norms**.

Prescriptive norms (Token)	specify (rel: id)	[[what must be done]] . . . (Value)
Proscriptive norms (Token)	identify (rel: id)	*practices* [which are disallowed or disapproved]. (Value)

Source: Summarised from Waters and Crook 1993: 27–29

(25) **Social structure**   refers to   the *arrangements* [by which human
        beings interact with one
        another].
    (Token)   (Value)

This redefinition then becomes the starting point for taxonomic decomposition of social structure. This is summarised in Table 11.5. (Sub-
headings from the original text shown in parentheses.)

   This table demonstrates an extension of the building of technicality. A
new technical term, *roles* is introduced using existing technicality (as a
part of *social structure* and then defined using existing technicality (in
relation to *norms*). The Value in both clauses also introduces a part/
whole (composition) taxonomy; *social structure* consists of *roles*, *roles* consist
of bundles of *norms*. The technicality builds as the taxonomy is built.

   The examples in Table 11.5 show technicality accumulating through
existing technicality being used to both create and arrange more technicality. For example, in *the incumbent of a series of roles*, *roles* in the Qualifier
shifts to Classifier in *role incumbent*. This also happens in the case of *role set*.
In *role set*, *role* classifies a type of *set*. This shift from Thing to Classifier is
extended into *role conflict*. The combination of a technical Classifier with a
generic abstraction as Thing and the subsequent use of this to build
taxonomic relations has not been noted in any of the SFL literature on
the discourse of science. It was noted by Wignell (1990) in relation to
sociology and referred to as 'ambiguous taxonomies'.

Table 11.5 The logogenesis of technicality: social structure and roles

---

(Social Structure)

Social structure (Token)	refers to	

the *arrangements* [by which human beings interact with one another].
(Value)

The component *parts* of **social structure** are called (Value)		**roles** (rel: id)	(Token)

(Multiple roles)

Roles are (Token) (rel: id)	*positions* [made up of ***performances*** (which respond to a bundle of **norms**)] (Value)	

Each individual person (Carrier)	is (rel: att)	the incumbent of a *series* of **roles**. (Attribute)
These (Value)	are said to be (vbl/rel: id)	a person's **multiple roles**. (Token)

(Role set)

The **role** or group of **roles** [which is complementary to any given **role**]
(Value)

is (rel: id)	the **role set**. (Token)

The **role set** (Token)	provides (rel: id)	

the *reference point* [for the **role incumbent**], (Value)	←(circ: beh) (Token)→	the person [[occupying the **role**]]. (Value)

(Role conflict)

There are (P: exist)	several *types* of **role conflict** . . . (Existent)

Simple role conflict
As its name suggests, this is the most basic *form* of **role conflict**. It occurs when the *performances* [carried out by a **role incumbent**] do not match the *expectations* [of the **role set**].

Multiple role conflict
In figure 2.1 the most apparent ***possibility*** [for **multiple role conflict**] occurs between the **kinship based roles** [of wife and mother] and the educational **role** [of student].

Role set conflict
This *type* of *conflict* occurs when different members of a **role set** have different *expectations* [of the complementary **role**]

The most common *way* [in which **role set conflict** is resolved] is by the ***exercise*** [of ***authority*** (of the most powerful member of the **role set**)].

Source: Summarised from Waters and Crook 1993: 29–33

In addition to existing technicality being used to build more, the use of abstractions and metaphors is also noted, particularly in the Nominal Groups realising Values. There appears to be a general shift from Qualifiers which are either relatively congruent or contain already established technical terms (congruent for the field) to Things which are realised either as abstractions or metaphors. For example in:

26) **Roles** are   *positions* [made up of ***performances*** (which respond to a bundle of **norms**)]

a left-to-right shift is noted from a congruent Qualifier (containing existing technicality with a metaphor as Thing, which is itself a Qualifier with a generic abstraction as Thing. All this realises Value to a new technical term, *roles*, as Token.

Table 11.5 also shows part/whole taxonomic relations being built and introduces another method of defining common in the physical sciences: definition by an enhancing beta clause when the Process in the alpha clause is basically free of experiential content. Processes like *occurs* and *happens* used in this way are akin to relational identifying process. It would be possible to say 'This type of conflict **is** [when . . .]', with the enhancing beta clause embedded into the structure of one clause. This type of structure is used both to define and to begin to explain.

The *role* taxonomy concludes by introducing the terms *collective institutions* and *role differentiation* (*role* as Classifier again). This is summarised in Table 11.6.

The examples in Table 11.6 further emphasise the interplay between abstractions and metaphors in creating the technical framework of sociology. Various instances and combinations of abstractions, metaphors and existing technicality are distilled into new technicality. For example, the logogenesis of the technical term *social stratification* can be traced back to the initial introduction of *roles*.

The taxonomic arrangement of some terms is problematic. This occurs in the shift of *role* from Thing to Classifier. Classification is no longer in terms of types of *role* but by *role* as being a type of something else:, a type of *set* or a type of *conflict*. This signals a shift from statics to dynamics, these terms are arranged not so much according to what they are but according to what causes them to be. That is, for example, *role set conflict* is a type of conflict caused by (or located in) the *role set*. The *role set*, itself a technical term is the Agent responsible for causing a type of *conflict*. In terms of establishing technicality, these terms represent a shift in focus, some technical terms, already established, act as Agents in creating new technical terms. As well as just 'being there' some technical terms 'act', they are Agents which act on other things. The results of these actions lead to new technicality. Initial, or steady, states are acted on, leading to new final states, which are also given technical names. These appear to be nominalisations of the consequence of activity sequences and are

Table 11.6 Further logogenesis of technicality in sociology

(**Collective institutions**)

Groups of **roles** are organised into specific ***configurations*** or *networks* [which are focused upon different *aspects* of *social life*] . . .

These *networks*	are called	**institutions**
(Value)	(rel: id) (Token)	

and include **kinship, religion, politics, sport, social control** and so on.

An **institution**, then,	is	a regular *network* of **roles** [which has ***continuity*** through *time*].
(Token)	(rel: id)	(Value)

(**Role differentiation**)

The **roles** [that go to make up these **collective institutions**] are differentiated from one another in two *dimensions*: laterally and hierarchically.

Lateral role differentiation	is	**differentiation** by function . . .
(Token)	(rel: id)	(Value)

A common *way* [of talking about **lateral role differentiation**] is to refer to it as the **division of labour** the *way* [[in which human *effort* is divided and distributed in *society*]].

The second *way* [in which roles are differentiated from one another] is hierarchically. They are ranked above and below one another on a *scale* or *dimension*.

Three *dimensions* are often mentioned here:

class,	economic ***rewards*** and ***deprivation***;
(Token)	(Value)

status,	the ***prestige*** or ***esteem*** [[that a **role** receives]];
(Token)	(Value)

and **power,**	the *extent* [to which the **role incumbent** is able to make ***decisions*** (which are binding on others)]
(Token)	(Value)

A *process* [by which **roles** are organized hierarchically on one or more of these three *dimensions*]	
	(Value)

is called a *system* of **social stratification**.	
	(Token)

Source: Summarised from Waters and Crook 1993: 32–33

perhaps better modelled using the implication sequences used by Wignell, Martin and Eggins (1987).

TECHNICALITY IN SOCIOLOGY – SUMMARY

Sociology uses more or less the same set of resources in establishing technical terms and in classifying. So far the way the technicality has been presented to students is similar in grammatical form to how it is presented in the physical sciences and, like in the physical sciences, definitions at least have been presented as being unproblematic. That is, they have been presented simply as the way things are in sociology.

Unlike in science there appears to be little translation directly from the commonsense to the technical. Abstractions and metaphors intervene in the translation. This is evident in the structure of the Nominal Groups realising the Values where technical terms are being established. The typical pattern is (moving from left to right across the Groups): Qualifiers (often multiple Qualifiers) which are in their structure generally either congruent or contain a mixture of congruence and already established technicality; the Things to which those Qualifiers are attached are typically either abstractions or metaphors (most generally abstractions); the Tokens realising these Values are technical terms, which are themselves for the most part generically abstract (that is, if they have appeared in the text prior to being made technical they were realised typically as generic abstractions). Thus we find, typically, a two step translation: in establishing new technical terms we find relative congruence (Qualifiers) → abstraction (Things) → technicality; in building technicality from existing technicality the first step involves existing technicality appearing in otherwise relatively congruent Qualifiers.

The technical framework is used as a means of interpreting the 'world' but does not seem to be derived from the 'world'. The theoretical model appears to precede its application to the 'world'.

CONCLUSION

This work suggests that the hypothesis that the discourse of social science can be seen to have evolved from a synthesis of the discourses of the humanities and science is supportable given the evidence from the phylogenesis of the discourse and how the discourse is presented to initiates. Social science is a technical discourse, with technicality shown to have evolved over time to the point where it is the principal means of construing experience. In addition, technicality has also, over time, been pushed to points of textual prominence so that it becomes the unmarked point of departure phylogenetically, logogenetically and ontogenetically.

Social science uses much the same resources as scientific discourse in establishing a technical framework which is then used for interpretation. Social science differs from science, however, in what it makes technical. An analysis of the phylogenesis of the discourse shows an original abstract (and generic) construal of experience which was then reconstrued technically. That is, technicality interceded after abstraction: it is the abstract, idealised, hypothetical and generic which is being reconstrued technically.

REFERENCES

Bacon, F. 1625. (1966 reprinting). *The Essayes or Counsels, Civill and Morall*. Oxford: Oxford University Press.

Durkheim, E. 1893. *The Division of Labour in Society (De la division du travail social)*. (1964 reprinting). New York: The Free Press.

Eggins, S., P. Wignell and J. Martin 1987. The Discourse of History. *Working Papers in Linguistics 5*. Department of Linguistics, University of Sydney. [Republished in M. Ghadessy [ed.] (1993). *Register Analysis: Theory and practice* London: Pinter pp. 75–109].

Foucault, M. 1970. *The Order of Things: An archaeology of the human sciences*. New York: Pantheon.

Foucault, M. 1972. *The Archaeology of Knowledge*. London: Tavistock.

Halliday, M.A.K. 1985a. *Introduction to Functional Grammar*. London: Edward Arnold.

Halliday, M.A.K. 1985b. *Spoken and Written Language*. Geelong: Deakin University Press.

Halliday, M.A.K. 1987. Language and the Order of Nature. In M.A.K. Halliday and J.R. Martin (eds) 1993. *Writing Science: Literacy and discursive power*. London: Falmer. pp. 106–23.

Halliday, M.A.K. 1988. On the Language of Physical Science. In M.A.K. Halliday and J.R. Martin (eds) (1993). *Writing Science: Literacy and discursive power*. London: Falmer. pp. 54–68.

Halliday, M.A.K. 1989a. Some Grammatical Problems in Scientific English. In M.A.K. Halliday and J.R. Martin (eds) (1993). *Writing Science: Literacy and discursive power*. London: Falmer. pp. 69–85.

Halliday, M.A.K. 1989b. The Analysis of Scientific texts in English and Chinese. In M.A.K. Halliday and J.R. Martin (eds) (1993). *Writing Science: Literacy and discursive power*. London: Falmer. pp. 124–132.

Halliday, M.A.K. and J.R. Martin (eds) 1993. *Writing Science: Literacy and discursive power*. London: Falmer.

Harman, P.M. 1983. The Scientific Revolution. In *Lancaster Pamphlets*. London: Methuen.

Hobbes, T. 1651. *Leviathan*. (1986 reprinting). Harmondsworth: Penguin.

Hume, D. 1748. Enquiry into Human Understanding. In D. Hume (1777 edition, 1988 reprinting). *Enquiries Concerning Human Understanding and Concerning the Principles of Morals*. Oxford: Clarendon Press.

Kearney, H. 1971. *Science and Change: 1500–1700*. London: Weidenfeld and Nicolson.

Locke, J. 1690. On Property. In C.B. Macpherson (ed.) (1980). *John Locke Second Treatise of Government*. Indianapolis, IN: Hackett.

Martin, J.R. 1985. *Factual Writing: Exploring and challenging social reality.* Deakin University Press.

Martin, J.R. 1989. Technicality and Abstraction: language for the creation of specialized texts. In M.A.K. Halliday and J.R. Martin (eds) (1993). In *Writing Science: Literacy and discursive power.* London: Falmer. pp. 203–220.

Martin, J.R. 1990a. Literacy in Science: Learning to handle text as technology. In M.A.K. Halliday and J.R. Martin (eds) (1993). *Writing Science: Literacy and discursive power.* London: Falmer. pp. 166–202.

Martin, J.R. 1990b. Life as a Noun: Arresting the universe in science and the humanities. In M.A.K. Halliday and J.R. Martin (eds) (1993). *Writing Science: Literacy and discursive power.* London: Falmer. pp. 221–267.

Martin, J.R. 1992. *English Text: System and Structure.* Amsterdam: Benjamins.

Martin, J.R. 1996. Analysing Genre: Functional parameters. In F. Christie and J.R. Martin (eds) *Genres and Institutions: Social processes in the workplace and school.* London: Cassell. pp. 3–39.

Martin, J.R., P. Wignell, S. Eggins and J. Rothery 1988. Secret English: Discourse technology in the junior secondary school. In L. Gerot, J. Oldenburg and T. Van Leeuwen (eds) *Language and Socialisation, Home and School: Proceedings from the Working Conference on Language in Education,* Maquarie University, 17–21 November 1986, Macquarie University. pp. 143–73.

Marx, K. 1867. *Capital, Volume One.* (1974 reprinting). Moscow: Progress Publishers.

Mill, J.S. 1861. Utilitarianism. In H.B. Acton (ed.) (1972). *J.S. Mill, Utilitarianism, On Liberty and Considerations on Representative Government.* London: Dent.

Mudie, K. and J. Brotherton (1985). *Core Biology.* Richmond: Heinemann.

Ravelli, L. 1985. *Metaphor, Mode and Complexity: An exploration of co-varying patterns.* BA (Hons) Thesis. Department of Linguistics, University of Sydney.

Ricardo, D. 1817. *Principles of Political Economy and Taxation.* (1973 reprinting). London: Dent.

Shea, N. 1988. *The Language of Junior Secondary Science Textbooks.* BA (Hons) Thesis. Department of Linguistics, University of Sydney.

Smith, A. 1776. *The Wealth of Nations.* (1964 reprinting). London: Dent.

Swingewood, A. (1984). *A Short History of Sociological Thought.* London: Macmillan.

Waters, M. and R. Crook 1993. *Sociology One (Third Edition).* Melbourne: Longman Cheshire.

Wignell, P. 1987. *In Your Own Words.* Working Papers in Linguistics, vol. 5. Department of Linguistics, University of Sydney.

Wignell, P. 1988. The Language of Social Literacy: A linguistic approach to the materials in action in Years 7 and 8. *Social Literacy Monograph, No. 41.* Sydney: Common Ground.

Wignell, P. 1990. *Flowers in the Sentence: A look at the discourse of the sociology of medicine.* MA (Applied Linguistics) Special Topic. Department of English and Linguistics, Macquarie University.

Wignell, P. 1992. Abstraction and Technicality in Sociology. Paper presented to the *International Systemic Functional Conference,* July 1992, Macquarie University.

Wignell, P. 1994. Genre Across the Curriculum. *Linguistics and Education,* vol. 6, no. 4. Norwood, NJ: Ablex.

Wignell, P. forthcoming. *Making the Abstract Technical: On the evolution of social science.* PhD Thesis, Department of Linguistics, University of Sydney.

Wignell, P., J.R. Martin and S. Eggins 1987. The Discourse of Geography: Ordering and Explaining the Experiential World. In M.A.K. Halliday and

J.R. Martin (eds) (1993). *Writing Science: Literacy and discursive power.* London: Falmer. pp. 136–165.

Zeitlin, I.M. 1994. *Ideology and the Development of Social Theory.* (fifth edition). New Jersey: Prentice Hall.

12 Construing processes of consciousness

From the commonsense model to the uncommonsense model of cognitive science[1]

C.M.I.M. Matthiessen

One of the late twentieth-century movements in the academic world is cognitive science. It was initiated in the 1950s (1956 has been suggested as the year of birth) in the American research context by scholars such as Herbert A. Simon, George A. Miller and Jerome Bruner, partly as a response to the increasing disciplinary fragmentation of knowledge about human thinking, human knowledge and other aspects of the 'mind' and partly a reaction against behaviourism within psychology in the US. It was influenced by certain aspects of the cybernetics of the 1940s and took the computer model of processing symbolically represented information as central; Simon and Kaplan (1989: 3) speak of the 'information-processing revolution of the fifties and sixties, which viewed thinking as a symbol-manipulation process and used computer simulation as a way to build theories of thinking' (for a critical discussion, see Varela, Thompson and Rosch 1991). In taking the computer as a model, cognitive science follows a long tradition in western thinking where the current technology has served as a way of thinking about humans – in terms of clockworks, automata, machines, switchboards (e.g. in H.G. Wells' popular science writings of the late 1920s/early 1930s, the body is presented as a machine): the computer is merely the current candidate.

But what is 'the mind' – or more explicitly, what kind of experience is construed as 'the mind' and how is it located relative to related categories of experience? The most general answer is that 'the mind' is a linguistic construct – a category of our experience that we construe for ourselves by means of our everyday lexicogrammar. In other words, it is not a phenomenon that is given to us; it is one that is actively created by the resources of language. The construct of 'the mind' is thus part of our cultural-linguistic complex; but, according to Olson (1994), it is not one that is necessarily part of all cultural–linguistic complexes. He suggests that 'the mind' was construed in ancient Greece sometime after the Homeric period:

> Thus while it appears that the ability to recognize oneself and others as intentional is a fundamental part of being human, the attempts to

conceptualize these relations between action and intention, beliefs and desire are more complex and do appear to have a cultural history. A fascinating part of this history comes from the study of the Greek invention of the concept of mind, an invention that is thought to have occurred between the time of the oral poet Homer, 'author' of *The Iliad* and *The Odyssey*, and the time of the Greek philosophers Socrates, Plato and Aristotle.

(Olson 1994: 236)

The understanding of deception is usually taken as criterial in ascribing a 'theory of mind' to children and non-human primates and to that extent at least, the Homeric Greeks had an understanding of mind.

But, that understanding was seriously limited it seems by their limited understanding of subjectivity. We get a better picture of their psychology by an examination of their ways of referring to knowledge and speech. The most striking feature of the Homeric conception of mind is that they had none. There is no evidence of a concept of mind as distinguished from body and there is an absence of such terms as 'decided,' 'thought,' 'believed,' 'doubted,' or 'equivocated.' Homer's characters, of course, do all of these things (at least we feel comfortable in ascribing such states and activities to them) but Homer reports them in quite a different way. . . . Making a decision was represented, and hence experienced, as hearing voices dictate what one was to do.

(Olson 1994: 238)

One central issue has been the question of the relationship between the mind and the body, or more specifically, the brain. Various positions have been developed over the centuries. Descartes postulated the mind and the body as separate orders of phenomena (with a strange account of where they were related in the brain). Descartes' dualism has been very influential in the west; it has often been taken as the thesis to be accepted and supported (as in modern Cartesian approaches) or else rejected. Dualism has been rejected on the grounds that only the mind exists (idealism) or on the grounds that the mind and the brain are the same and that only the brain needs to be postulated ('identity theory', first proposed by U.T. Place 1956, with the contemporary further development of 'eliminative materialism' by Patricia and Paul Churchland).

In this chapter I would like to explore and problematise the question of how conscious processes are construed in our everyday discourses and 'mind' is construed in the discourses of cognitive science. I will begin by examining examples from casual conversation and the lexico-grammatical systems they instantiate to determine what the folk model of people sensing is like. I will then discuss how the folk model is reconstrued theories of 'mind' within cognitive science using the strategy of lexico-grammatical metaphor. After exploring how cognitive science construes 'mind' in relation to the folk model, I problematise this construal.

THE CONGRUENT FOLK MODEL OF PEOPLE SENSING

Commonsense or folk models of our experience of the world are unselfconscious ones construed and negotiated in myriads of everyday conversations across many generations.[2] The greatest generalisations embodied in these models are accumulated in the content systems of language as patterns of meaning – that is, they get embodied in the organisation of the system of meaning ('semantics') and the system of wording (grammar and vocabulary or 'lexico-grammar'); and they evolve over time as part of these systems. These generalisations also tend to be located in the most covert part of the overall system, the part least accessible to conscious reflection – what we may call, following Whorf (1956), the cryptogrammar (cf. Halliday and Matthiessen in press: Section 14.1). Consequently, the generalisations have to be brought out by 'deep analysis' of the crypto-grammar. Commonsense models tend to be construed in the congruent mode rather than in the metaphorical mode; that is, our experience is construed in terms of categories of meaning without the distance created by metaphor whereby domains of meanings are reconstrued as if they were other domains of meaning. Part of what we experience of the world is the domain of our own consciousness – our processes of seeing, thinking, wanting and feeling. This domain of experience is construed in the semantic and lexico-grammatical systems of English as one of a small number of distinct domains; it is constituted as a commonsense or folk model of our experience of consciousness (often known as 'folk psychology'; see e.g. Churchland 1981, D'Andrade 1987, Pylyshyn 1980, von Eckardt 1995). Our commonsense model of consciousness is construed in the congruent mode and it seems to construe *personal experience* of consciousness – something we can apprehend in daily life. The model is construed by the resources of transitivity in the clause and projection in the clause complex, instantiated in innumerable *texts* and distilled in the lexico-grammatical *system*.

THE FOLK MODEL CONSTRUED BY THE GRAMMAR IN TEXT

I will present the folk model by considering a few examples from text instances to illustrate some central aspects of the folk model of sensing embodied in the lexico-grammatical system of English. When we are concerned with texts where the folk model is being instantiated, the natural starting point is casual conversation since it is here that language is being used most unselfconsciously to construe our experience of the world. Eggins and Slade (1997) provide a recent insightful discussion of casual conversation and I have taken the first example, Text 1, from their book. The text is displayed vertically, as it unfolds; but I have separated out clauses construing processes of consciousness as the semantic domain of sensing – mental clauses – from other clause types horizontally in columns; and I have also set up four separate columns under 'mental' to distinguish the primary subtypes of 'perceptive' (seeing, hearing, feeling, etc.), 'cognitive' (thinking, knowing, believing, guessing, etc.), 'desiderative' (wanting, wishing, planning, etc.), and 'emotive' (liking, loving, disliking, hating, fearing, etc.).

The extract is an anecdote; it serves to amuse and is not a vehicle for developing a model of sensing. However, as in casual conversation in general, the interactants model conscious processes as part of developing the text deploying the resources of *mental clauses*. The model being manifested here involves the very simple but powerful generalisation that conscious processes can be construed as quanta of experience – *quantum of sensing* – involving a *Process of sensing* and a conscious participant involved in that process, the *Senser*. These constitute a complementarity of the conscious as change (the process unfolding through time) and the conscious as permanence (the participant persisting through time); this is the fundamental complementarity between the verbal and the nominal that we find in all English clauses:

I	hate	cockroaches
I	don't like	cockroaches
I	remember	. . .
I	thought	. . .
I	can feel	something . . .
I	looked	down
I	'm trying to think	
[you]	don't worry	about it
Senser	Process	(other)
nominal group	verbal group	

The Senser is the whole person, construed as a conscious being. All the instances above happen to be interactants – mostly the speaker; and this pattern is in fact typical of casual conversation. As speakers, we are all the time construing our own processes of consciousness. Ontogenetically

Text 1 Extract from casual conversation (Eggins and Slade 1997)

	mental perceptive	cognitive	desiderative	emotive	other (material, behavioural, verbal, relational, existential)
Pat:				**I hate** cockroaches more than rats.	
Pauline:				**I don't like** cockroaches either.	
Gary:					But cockroaches are just the thing – you just get them anywhere. Yeach but when you tread on them they crunch. A rat just squelches.
Pat:		I remember →			→ we were sitting for our analytical chemistry exam, and it was the final exams and they have sort of like bench desks where there's three to a bench normally and they had the middle seat empty and two sat either side and I was sitting there,
	→ geez I can **feel** something on my foot	and **thought** →			
		and **I thought** →		no, no don't **worry** about it, you know	'What on earth is this chemical equation?'
		And **I'm trying** to think,			but there's something on my foot
	and I **looked** down				and there was this cockroach like this [gesture] and I just screamed, jumped up on the chair and as I did that I knocked the bench and it went up and all Geoff's exam stuff went into the bin next to him, and I was standing on this chair screaming and the exam supervisor came running over 'What's going on there!'; and I said 'there's a cockroach down there!'. Cause you're not allowed to speak, sneeze, cough, anything in those final exams and there's me screaming on the chair.

bold type = item construing process, thing or quality of sensing this is surely also significant: Painter (1993) shows how one child began by construing himself as Senser and then later generalised to other people. Non-interactants are of course readily construed as Sensers – as long as they can be construed as conscious beings, which prototypically means humans. The Senser is represented by a nominal group that denotes the whole person; the interactants above are referred to by personal pronouns. The Process of sensing is realised by a verbal group which includes as the event itself a lexical verb denoting the mental change: *hate, like, think, feel, look,* and *worry* in the examples above. It is located in time by means of the verbal system of tense (past: *thought* or present: *hate, don't like,* etc. in the examples above; it may be modal instead of temporal (*can feel*) and it may be phased (the cognative *am trying to think*). In these respects, mental events are construed on the same model as all other types of event.

In addition to the Senser – the participant through which the process of sensing is actualised, there may be another participant, as in *I hate cockroaches, I don't like cockroaches, I can feel something.* The sensing is construed as involving the Phenomenon of sensing – the participant that is the domain of the Senser's processing, enters into the Senser's consciousness or is created by it. The things serving as phenomena above are ordinary things; but the Phenomenon of a mental clause can in principle be any type of phenomenon of experience.

One further central feature of mental clauses is also illustrated by the extract above: the content of somebody's sensing may be construed as a separate clause. This is known as *projection.* For example, Pat construes her experience of the world inside her at the beginning of her anecdote as *I remember,* and then she construes the content of what she remembers by means of a second clause, *we were sitting for our analytical chemistry exam.* These two clauses together form a clause complex where the mental clause projects the mental content clause; that is, it sets it up as being of a different order of reality – the reality created by processes of consciousness. The projected clause is called an *idea* clause.

The grammar thus construes a domain of sensing from the totality of the experience of the world it construes for us, treating this domain as a distinct clause type, that of mental clauses, contrasting it with material, relational and verbal clauses; and it maps this domain into a small number of related but distinct subdomains – those of perception, cognition, desideration and emotion. We can recognise these as topic areas within psychology (cf. Matthiessen 1993: 212); and when Guttenplan (1995: 24) presents a 'map of the mind' as part of an introduction to the philosophy of mind, we find interesting similarities to the map construed by our everyday grammar.

The grammar's contribution to the construal of sensing is thus both rich and varied. This picture is further enriched through lexis. Since lexis is the most delicate grammar (see Halliday 1961, Hasan 1996: Chapter

4), the different subtypes of sensing that are construed in the grammar give rise to more delicately differentiated lexical sets: see Matthiessen 1995: 270–81 for further subtypes and lists of lexical items. Such sets of mental lexis can be identified taxonomically in *Roget's Thesaurus* in several steps in delicacy (as in class IV [intellectual faculties], division (I.) [formation of ideas], section I [operations of intellect in general, thought: subsection 451: *think, reflect, reason, cogitate, consider*]) or in Levin's (1993) verb classes (e.g. verbs of perception, psych-verbs, verbs of desire). When we focus on such lexical sets, we find considerable further elaboration of the folk model of sensing in the form of 'local' distinctions and patterns. Such patterns emerge very clearly when a lexis is approached from the instance end of the cline of instantiation, i.e., when a corpus is examined. For example, a small sample of undergraduate essays by second-year students of as little as 11,000 words[3] reveals interesting patterns in the use of mental lexis – patterns that are local to the register. Thus when I performed a check for concordance on the string *beli** (to cover both nominal and verbal forms of the same lexeme), I found 16 occurrences, 11 of these found in clauses and 5 in nominal groups; 10 of the clauses with the verb *believe* were of the projecting type and in 9 of these psychologists were construed as the Sensers (as in *Smith (1973) believed* → *that there was a crucial flaw in Maslow . . .*). That is, in this sample, Sensers of believing are predominantly construed as psychologists, rather than as people in general. This picture is reinforced by the nominal groups; they all construe beliefs held by psychologists (e.g. *Maslow's belief that our human potential is innate*).

One other aspect of mental lexis is important to note in the present context: the lexical resources for construing our experience of consciousness are expanded through lexical metaphors relating to space, with the mind as a container, as Figure 12.1 suggests (cf. Lakoff and Kövecses 1987 on the construal of anger):

> – as space: (container:) *cross one's mind, escape / slip one's mind, an open mind, a closed mind, broaden the mind, keep in mind, be out of one's mind / senses, to be driven out of one's mind, to come to one's senses, to have in mind, to have something on one's mind, get something out of one's mind, search one's mind, at the back of one's mind, to put at the back of one's mind, at the top of one's mind, out of humour, in love, in mourning,*
> – as physical organ: *break one's heart, blow one's mind, to boggle the mind,*
> – as liquid / gas (contained in body): *explode, vent one's anger, blow one's top, to boil over, to smoulder, to cool down, too keep the lid on,*
> – as wild animal: *prey on one's mind,*

It is interesting to note that in these various lexical metaphors the Sensers are still very much present; they are not effaced.

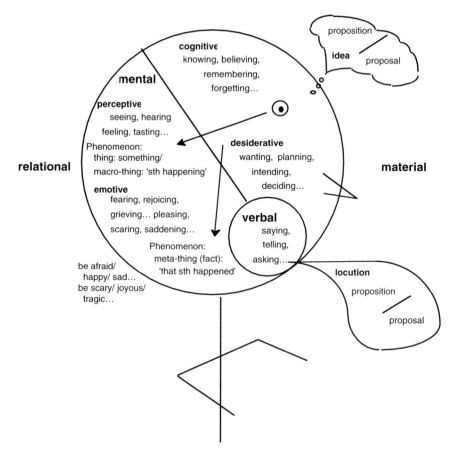

Figure 12.1 The container model of the mind of lexical metaphors

RECONSTRUING SENSING AS 'THE MIND' IN COGNITIVE SCIENCE

When cognitive science concerns itself with 'theories of the mind', there is a fundamental shift away from the folk model construed in everyday discourse. Before considering this shift in cognitive science, let me first examine an intermediate type – discourses that draw on the folk model but display certain features that are 'magnified' in cognitive science.

Interleaving clausal and nominal construals of sensing

As we have seen, emotions are construed in the folk model as one subtype of sensing, similar to, but also distinct from, perceiving, thinking and wanting: these are clauses of feeling, with emotive processes. One of the distinctive features of this area of the mental grammar is that emotions may also be construed by relational clauses as attributes of mind. Thus we have both *people fear bears, people envy their neighbours* and *people are afraid of bears, people are jealous of their neighbours*. However, these processes and attributes may also be reconstrued as participants, classified not as verbs or adjectives but as nouns. In many contexts, we see very clearly how this complementarity in the grammar is deployed, with the two alternatives existing side by side. Let me just give one text example. Jeffrey Masson and Susan McCarthy have written an interesting book exploring how and what animals feel; a central theme is that we have to construe animals as emotive Sensers and not reserve this role for humans – to put it in grammatical terms. In their discourse, clausal constructions of people or animals feeling and nominal constructions of their emotions alternate; for example (italics = mental clauses; bold = 'mental' nominal groups):

Text 2: Extract from popular book on what animals feel

> The error into which anthropomorphism can lead us is to see bears through our own emotions: *we fear them*, so we perceive them as angry and hostile. The equal and opposite error into which **the fear of anthropomorphism** can lead us is to refuse to recognise that *bears can feel **their own emotions***. Rogers learned to observe bears in terms of **those emotions**, discovering that *the bears themselves were often fearful*. He *learned what frightened them* and *how not to frighten them*: 'Once I started looking at bears in terms of **their fear**, and interpreted all the things *that used to scare me* and interpreted those in terms of **the bear's fear**, it was easy to **gain their trust** and begin walking with them very closely, sleeping with them – doing all the things that you have to do to see how an animal really lives in its world.
>
> (Masson and McCarthy 1994: 56–7)

Clausal constructions such as *we fear them, the bears are fearful, things scare me* are interleaved with nominal constructions such as *the bear's fear, their trust*. The nominal constructions can serve as elements of clauses. Experientially, they can serve as participants or circumstances; textually they can serve as Theme (vs. Rheme) and as New (vs. Given) and they can be determined and thus tracked in the discourse (as with *those emotions*, referring back in the discourse). For example:

Rogers	learned to observe	bears	in terms of those emotions
Senser	Process	Phenomenon	Manner
Theme	Rheme		
Given			New

When emotions are construed nominally as participants or circumstances, there is thus a textual payoff in the discourse; and they can be built up in the course of the discourse as experientially complex things. What is significant here is that the clausal and nominal models occur side by side complementing one another – or rather, they alternate as the discourse unfolds.

The move to the metaphorical mode of construal in cognitive science

The text discussed in the preceding subsection illustrates some of the central features of the move from our everyday construal of our experience of the world of consciousness – our folk theory of sensers sensing phenomena or projecting ideas – to the way cognitive scientistss construe that experience; the features are 'latent' in the every day grammar:

(i) First of all, clauses are *nominalised* as nominal groups: *the bear fear is reconstrued* as *the bear's fear.* This is one salient feature of *grammatical metaphor* within the ideational metafunction, explored in Halliday (1994: Chapter 10) and discussed elsewhere in this book (see also Halliday and Martin 1993, Halliday and Matthiessen in press: Chapter 6). The clause *the bear fears* constitutes the congruent mode of construing how the bear feels, with the feeling as a process unfolding in time; the nominal group *the bear's fear* constitutes the metaphorical model of construing how the bear feels. The Process of sensing is reconstrued as the Head/Thing of the nominal group and the participants as Modifiers (in this case, the Senser is reconstrued as the Deictic; in the nominal group *the fear of anthropomorphism*, the Phenomenon is reconstrued as the Qualifier).

(ii) Second, in the metaphorical version, the participants in the reified process (the nominalised verb) may be present or around in the discourse – as they are in the 'mildly' metaphorical passages in Text 2; but because modifiers in the nominal group are optional, the participants reconstrued as modifiers may be left out, as they are in much more metaphorical discourses of cognitive science to be discussed below.

(iii) Third, the metaphorical nominal groups are themselves construed in participant or circumstance roles, typically in clauses that have metaphorical features in addition to the nominal groups with nominalised processes of sensing. For example, in the clause *fear would confer no survival benefit*, the nominal group *fear* serves as the Token of an identifying relational clause and it is configured with a Value that is itself a nominalisation. The relationship between them is a metaphorical construal of cause; a more congruent variant would be the clause *complex animals would not survive any better because they are afraid.*

The move from the congruent mode of construing our experience of the world of consciousness to the metaphorical mode can often be found in introductions to accounts of how people sense the phenomena of their experience, as in the following passage from Restak (1988: 242), a popular introductory book on 'the mind':

Text 3: Introductory passage

> to explain the mind's operation in thinking. Here, for example, is an everyday situation: two people meet on a beach. Michelle **recognizes** that she's encountered Michael before, but can't *come up with* his name. But she does **recall** that he's a doctor, specializes in paediatrics, and lives in New York City.
>
> Michael **remembers** Michelle's name but can't *dredge up from* **his memory** any biographical details about her. He recalls they met previously at a party given by a friend to celebrate the completion of his residency. Michael can *bring* vividly *to* **mind** what Michelle was wearing and how attractive he found her.
>
> Ordinary **experiences** like this raise important questions about how **thinking** is organized. Why is it that Michelle can **recognize** Michael's face, **remember** significant facts about him, but can't *come up with* his name? In Michael's case, the organisation would seem to be different: he can remember names but specific life details are only a blur. What kind of mental organisation in Michael might account for these differences?
>
> The most popular metaphor for the human mind is that of a huge and intricate filing system. When Michelle and Michael encounter each other, facial **recognition** sets off an elaborate *search* through 'files' *stored* within billions of neurons . . .
>
> (Restak 1988: 242)

Restak begins by giving a commonsense account using the congruent grammar of mental clauses with projected ideas: *Michelle recognizes* → *that . . . she does* **recall** → *that* . . . . He also uses a lexical metaphor for remembering that is part of our everyday lexico-grammar – *dredge up from memory, bring to mind*. Here the 'mind' is construed as an object with extension in space – a container; and it can be construed as a circumstance (*from memory, to mind*) in a mental clause that is partially constructed on a material model of manipulating an object, but which is still mental since it is configured with a conscious participant (the Senser) and since it can project (*bring to mind* → *what Michelle was wearing*; cf. *bring to mind* → *that she was intelligent, dredge up from memory* → *that she was a physician*). When he has finished this account, he raises general issues for an uncommonsense, scientific account by using the metaphorical mode: *experiences like this* (rather than *people experience similar situations* or the like), *thinking* (rather than *how people think*), *facial recognition* (rather than *people recognize faces*), and so on. (When he harks back to the illustrative account of a particular situation of everyday experience, he returns to the congruent mode.)

Restak also deploys the lexical metaphor of a mental space that we find in the commonsense model – a space in which 'objects' can be stored, which can be searched, and so on: *facial recognition sets off an elaborate search through 'files' stored within billions of neurons.*

The metaphorical mode of construing in cognitive science

The shift in the passage from Restak is quite representative of what I think happens in mainstream cognitive science with respect to how cognitive scientists construe their object of study. We can see the essential nature of this move when the folk theory is reconstrued as if it was a scientific one by Dennett, a philosopher who has written extensively on consciousness, when he tries to characterise folk psychology.

Text 4: Folk psychology reconstrued

> What are beliefs? Very roughly folk psychology has it that *beliefs* are information-bearing states of people that arise from *perceptions* and that, together with appropriately related *desires*, lead to intelligent *action*. That much is relatively uncontroversial, but does folk psychology also have it that nonhuman animals have beliefs? If so, what is the role of language in belief? Are *beliefs* constructed of parts? If so, what are the parts? Ideas? Concepts? Words? Pictures? Are *beliefs* like speech acts or maps or instruction manuals or sentences? Is it implicit in folk psychology that beliefs enter into causal relations, or that they don't? How do *decisions* and *intentions* intervene between *belief–desire* complexes and actions? Are *beliefs* introspectible, and if so, what authority do the believer's *pronouncements* have?
>
> (Dennett 1990: 91 [my highlighting])

Dennett has in fact already made the move to the model within cognitive science: instead of saying *people believe that . . . people want others to . . .* etc., as people do in everyday discourse, he writes *beliefs, desires,* etc. Here mental clauses with a Senser, a Process of sensing (believing, wanting, desiring, etc.) and a Phenomenon entering into, or being created by, the Senser's consciousness – or a separate projected idea clause – have been reconstrued as nominal groups with a nominalised mental process as Thing/Head and (typically) no participants (Senser, Phenomenon) or projected ideas. If Dennett had tried to *constitute* the folk theory instead of *reconstruing* it as if it was a scientific theory, he might have written:

> Very roughly, when people believe something, they believe that something has happened because they have seen or heard it happen and if

they believe that something has happened and if they want something else to happen, they do something about it.

The two modes of construing our experience of consciousness are compared in grammatical terms in Figure 12.2. The scientific model is metaphorical; and it stands as a metaphor for the congruent folk model. As the figure makes explicit, there is a considerable *loss* of ideational information in the move from the congruent mode to the metaphorical mode: grammatically, a clause complex is compressed into a clause and the clauses that are combined in the clause complex are compressed into nominal groups. As a result, the subtle distinction between the cognitive projection of ideas (somebody believing that . . . .) and the perceptive sensing of acts (somebody seeing something happen) is lost, and participants can be left implicit. (The mental clause's capacity for projection is echoed in Dennett's definition of *belief: beliefs are information-bearing states . . .*)

Let us now turn to a chapter of cognitive psychology from a fairly recent textbook in cognitive science. We find passages that are like the introductory text on remembering quoted above (Text 3) in that the authors make a connection between the construal of our everyday experience and the cognitive science model; for example in Text 5 the authors introduce a distinction between two ways of knowing (or two kinds of knowledge!), declarative knowledge (in the congruent grammar, *know that* . . .) and procedural knowledge (in the congruent grammar, *know how to* . . .); they then relate declarative knowledge to the reader's experience.

Text 5: Extract from cognitive science text book

The notion of cognitive architecture

A basic point from computer science is *that an **information-processing** system can be understood in terms of its **data structures**, or **representations**, and the **processes** that operate on those **representations***. We will ask what the general properties **human cognitive representations** and **processes** have. The **representation** problem is often called the problem of **declarative knowledge**. The word declarative is simply a way of referring to the static, fact-like nature of **representations**: they are inert **structures** that are operated on by **processes**. For example, *if you know the fact that the weather advisory telephone number is 936-1234*, you can apply many **processes** to it, such as dialing it, telling it to someone else, or adding it to your own phone number. We will characterize two kinds of **declarative knowledge that** human beings have been hypothesized to possess: **propositions**, which are language-like **representations**, and **images**, which are perception-like **representations**.

(Stillings *et al.* 1987: 18)

(1) Folk model (congruent construal):

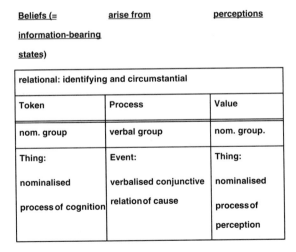

| they | believe | that something has happened | be- cause | they | have seen or heard | it happen |

$\alpha\alpha$:		$\longrightarrow$	$\alpha'\beta$:	$\longrightarrow$	$^{\mathsf{x}}\beta$:			
mental: cognitive and meta-phenomenal: idea			clause: projection (idea)		mental: perceptive and macrophenomenal			
Senser	Process					Senser	Process	Phenome-non
nom. group: consc.	verbal group					nom. group: consc.	verbal group	clause: act

(2) Scientific model (metaphorical reconstrual):

| Beliefs (= information-bearing states) | arise from | perceptions |

relational: identifying and circumstantial		
Token	Process	Value
nom. group	verbal group	nom. group.
Thing: nominalised process of cognition	Event: verbalised conjunctive relation of cause	Thing: nominalised process of perception

Figure 12.2 Congruent folk model reconstrued metaphorically as scientific model

Most of the phenomena of sensing are construed nominally (in bold: *structures, representations, knowledge, processes*, and so on). There are two congruent mental clauses (in italics): the first one refers to how cognitive scientists understands things, and the second one construes a familiar everyday experience for the reader. In the second one, the Senser is present as a participant. What has happened in the cognitive science model is that 'somebody knows that . . .' has been split into two aspects by means of grammatical metaphor, as schematised in Figure 12.3: 'knowing' as a process and 'knowing that' as content. The former is in turn often nominalised as *process* – or as specific forms corresponding to types of cognitive processes such as *retrieval, storage, activation*. The latter is construed as *knowledge, representation, information, (data) structure* and the like. The Senser recedes into the background: reified processes rather than sensers can 'operate on' knowledge: *the processes that operate on those representations . . . inert structures that are operated on by processes*. Examples such as *you can apply many processes to it* serve as a kind of bridge between the folk model and the cognitive science one.

Now consider a later passage from the same chapter on cognitive psychology. The cognitive modelling has now 'taken off' and the authors are construing one aspect of how people remember entirely in the metaphorical mode: Text 6 (names of representations in **bold**, terms for processes in *italics*; congruent mental clauses underlined).

Text 6: Extract from cognitive science text book

Working memory

The sharply limited **information**-*processing* capacity of controlled *processing* arises from the tendency of active information to either rapidly lose **its** *activation* or be replaced by newly *activated* **information**.

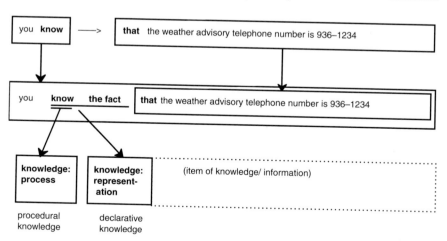

Figure 12.3 From knowing to knowledge

This limitation is often referred to as the limitation on **working memory**. It is important to distinguish between what is potentially part **of working memory** and what is effectively part of **working memory**, during any brief time period. Because of the parallel *processing* going on in sensory systems and in the spreading *activation process* in **declarative memory**, a great deal of **information** is *active* at any moment and therefore is potentially part of **working memory**. However, the *activation* of a particular item of **information** fades rapidly or is replaced if it is not picked up by some controlled *process*. Thus, the effective size of **working memory** is the small number of items that can actually *be processed* in the controlled system. In the phone dialing example **working memory** contained two goals of getting the coin into the slot and remembering the number as well as the number itself. The load imposed by a long-distance number depends on whether it is encoded as ten discrete items (which is probably rare) or as a few larger chunks. For example, people undoubtedly encode familiar three-digit area codes as single items of **information**. The best estimate is that controlled *processes* can handle only about three or four chunks of **information** at a time (Broadbent 1975). It is thought, however, that a chunk can be a well-integrated, fairly complex structure, such as a *script* stored in **declarative memory**.

Automatic Processes

Researchers hypothesize that automatic *processes* make very small, or possibly no, demands on **working memory**, so their capacity is very large relative to the controlled *processes*. They do not operate by interpreting **declarative information**. Rather, they are like compiled programs in computers. That is, they specify **information** *processes* directly, rather than having to be interpreted by some other *process*.

(Stillings *et al.* 1987: 52)

The tendencies we found illustrated in the previous extract are amplified here. Sensers are now virtually absent from the discourse (except as cognitive scientists: *researchers hypothesize that* . . .). Processes of sensing are reified as *memory, information* on the one hand, representing the content of sensing, and as *process(ing), activation* on the other hand, representing the process aspect of sensing. The potential of the nominal group grammar for classifying is taken up by the writers: there are examples from the taxonomy of kinds of memory – *declarative memory, working memory* (and elsewhere in the book: *long-term memory, short-term memory, semantic memory*).

When remembering is reconstrued as a thing, *memory*, it is construed as having extension in (abstract) space – *the size of working memory, part of working memory, working memory contained*; it can serve as a participant (*working memory contained two goals; what is potentially part of working memory.*) or a circumstance of location (*stored in declarative memory*; and reconstrued as a Qualifier within a nominalisation: *the spreading activation process in declarative memory*). Such patterns reflect the lexical metaphors of the folk model where mind, memory, etc. are construed as containers/locations as exemplified in the first section above.

When the process aspect of sensing is referred to by nominalisations (*process(ing)*, *activation*), these can be construed in participant roles: *processing going on . . . lose its activation, controlled processes can handle . . . the activation of a particular item of information fades rapidly, [activation] is replaced, automatic processes make very small, or possibly no, demands on working memory.* By a further step, modalities or phases of these processes may be reified and be construed in participant roles, as in the first clause, which illustrates one of the favourite clause types of scientific writing (see Halliday and Martin 1993): see Figure 12.4. Here a tendency is represented as causing a capacity; a somewhat more congruent version would be: *Controlled processing can only process information to a limited extent because active information tends rapidly to lose its activation or to be replaced by newly activated.*

As a final step in this exploration of the effects of deploying the metaphorical mode of construing sensing, let's consider Newell, Rosenblom and Laird's discussion of the 'architecture of cognition' as modelled in the Soar system. Just before the place where the extract starts, they have discussed the architecture of another system. ('Productions' are a kind of automatic procedures.)

The sharply limited **information-**processing capacity [of controlled processing]	arises from	the tendency [of active **information**] 'to either rapidly lose **its** activation or be replaced by newly activated **information**'

Token	Process	Value
Theme	Rheme	
Given		New
nominal group: nominalised ability	verbal group: verbalised conjunction	nominal group: nominalised usuality

Figure 12.4 Metaphorical causal relational clause

Text 7: Description of 'cognitive architecture'

Figure [A] <u>provides</u> a corresponding overview of Soar. There <u>is</u> a **single long-term memory – production memory** – that <u>is used</u> for both **declarative and procedural knowledge**. There <u>is</u> a **working memory** that <u>contains</u> a **goal hierarchy, information** <u>associated</u> with **the goal hierarchy, preferences** about what <u>should be done</u>, **perceptual information**, and motor commands. Interaction with the outside world <u>occurs</u> via interfaces between **working memory** and one or more **perceptual** and motor systems. All tasks are <u>formulated</u> as *searches* in **problem spaces**, that is, as <u>starting</u> from some initial state in a **space** and <u>finding</u> a desired state by the *application* of the operators that <u>comprise</u> the **space**. Instead of <u>making</u> **decisions** about what *productions* to *execute* – all

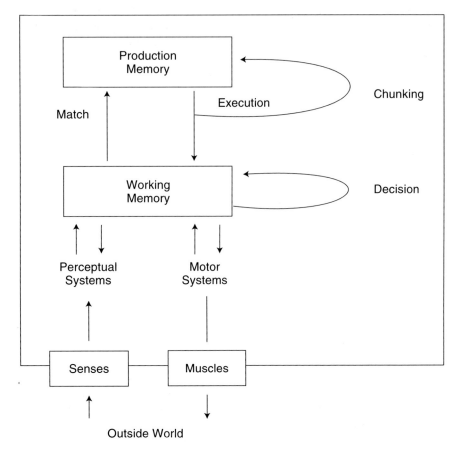

Figure A Overview of the Soar cognitive architecture
Source: Newell, Rosenblom and Laird 1989: 110–111

productions that successfully <u>match</u> are <u>fired</u> in parallel – **decisions** <u>are</u> <u>made</u> about what **problem spaces**, states, and operators to utilise. These **decisions** are based on **preferences** <u>retrieved</u> from **pro-duction memory** into **working memory**. When a **decision** <u>proves</u> problematic (because of **incomplete or inconsistent knowledge**), a **subgoal** <u>is</u> automatically <u>created</u> by the architecture and problem solving <u>recurses</u> on the task of <u>resolving</u> the impasse in **decision making**. This <u>generates</u> a **hierarchy of goals** and thus **problem spaces**. New *productions* <u>are created</u> continuously from the traces of Soar's experience in goal-based problem solving (a process <u>called</u> chunking).

(Newell, Rosenblom and Laird 1989: 110–1)

Like the previous one, this extract illustrates how cognitive science models are couched in terms of the computational metaphor. It also provides more examples of the way in which 'mind' and 'memory' is construed as an abstract space: *is a working memory that contains a goal hierarchy . . . formulated as searches in problem spaces . . . preferences retrieved from production memory into working memory.* This spatial construal is rein-forced by Newell *et al.*'s visual representation (Figure A), where e.g. 'working memory' is represented as a space with arrows pointing 'into' and 'away from' it; in general, the metaphor of abstract space enables us to 'cross over' from language to a visual semiotic (cf. Halliday and Matthiessen in press: 276–7).

The Processes in the passage are shown with underlining. They are all either 'material' or 'relational' (including 'existential'), with the possible exception of the two occurrences of *make + decision*, which can be seen as a metaphorical version of the behavioural process *decide*. Thus in terms of the clause system of PROCESS TYPE, the 'architecture of cognition' is built up by clauses construing our experience of the material world (*on preferences retrieved from production memory into working memory . . . productions that . . . are fired in parallel, problem solving recurses on the task . . . New productions are created continuously . . . is a single long-term memory – production memory – that is used for both declarative and procedural knowledge, starting from some initial state in a space, this generates a hierarchy of goals*) and the world of abstract relations (classification, constituency, identity: *the application of the operators that comprise the space, a decision proves problematic . . . all tasks are formulated as searches in problem spaces, is a working memory that contains a goal hierarchy . . . a process called chunking*).

One aspect of the reconstrual of the folk model of sensing that I have not commented on yet is the range of types of sensing construed in the congruent grammar: the four different domains of experience of con-sciousness that the grammar treats as distinct. The 'cognitive architec-ture' covers three out of these four domains of sensing construed by the congruent grammar. It represents the cognitive domains by means of the memories and processes of searching, etc. that operate on them, it represents the perceptive domain in terms of 'perceptual systems' and it represents the desiderative domain in terms of 'decisions' and goals However, the account does not cover the emotive domain. This is in fact a general feature of cognitive science. Thus Gardner notes that there has been

> the deliberate decision to de-emphasize certain factors which may be important for cognitive functioning but whose inclusion at this point would unnecessarily complicate the cognitive-science enterprise. These factors include the influence of affective factors or emotions, the contribution of historical and cultural factors, and the role of background context in which particular actions or thoughts occur.
>
> (Gardner 1987: 6)

CONSTRUING OUR EXPERIENCE OF CONSCIOUSNESS

Comparison of the two theories of 'the mind'

In the previous section I described various features of the theory of 'the mind' in mainstream cognitive science, basing this description on grammatical analysis of representative passages of text. Let me try to summarise the most salient features:

(i)   In commonsense theories, the congruent lexico-grammar construes our experience of the world around us and inside us into a small number of domains or process types. One of these is the domain of sensing – of a conscious senser involved in processes of consciousness, with the subtypes of perceiving, cogitating, desiring and emoting. This domain of conscious processing construed in the congruent system is taken over in cognitive science – sensing is the object of study.

(ii) In commonsense theories, the congruent lexico-grammar construes consciousness as process – or, more specifically, as a complementarity of change and permanence in the form of the configuration of Process + Senser. Here the experience of consciousness is construed as *personal*, i.e., as pertaining to the person construed in the role of Senser. In cognitive science, consciousness as process is reconstrued metaphorically as consciousness as thing (reifications such as *perception, vision, cognition, learning, memory . . . .*). As part of this metaphorical reconstrual, the conscious participants, the sensers, are effaced, and the things of consciousness become participants or circumstances in material or relational clauses. As a result, cognitive scientists can shift their model from our lived experience of consciousness to the realm of phenomena below consciousness: mental processes are in fact excluded from this model (except as an introductory transition) and consciousness is reconstrued on a *subpersonal* scale.

(iii) In commonsense theories, consciousness may be construed as a mental space (e.g. the mind as a container in which memories can be located, from which memories may escape, etc., consciousness as a level below which reside phenomena we are not aware of, etc.). In cognitive science, this spatial metaphor is retained and elaborated: *storage, retrieval, memory locations, memory networks.*

(iv) In commonsense theories, taxonomies of sensing are construes within the domain of processes; but these taxonomies are (like folk taxonomies in general) fluid and not institutionalised. In cognitive science, the reification of conscious processes facilitates the taxonomic interpretation of sensing within the domain of things – in scientific taxonomy: *memory – long-term/short-term memory, sensory memory, episodic/semantic memory; recall – free recall; learning – associative learning/cognitive learning/classical conditioning.*

The central metaphor here is grammatical in the first instance, which means that its effect is quite global; clauses of sensing are reified as nominal groups, which can then take on roles in various types of clause: see Figure 12.5.

I have approached the folk theory and the scientific one of cognitive science through lexico-grammar because this is where the work of construing our experience of the world gets done without design in microevents that accumulate to form a general model. This approach enables us to explore 'cryptic' aspects of theories (cf. Matthiessen 1993: 190–3). However, the two theories also differ at the strata above lexico-grammar; they differ at the stratum of discourse semantics and at the stratum of context. As far as discourse semantics is concerned, we have seen that the folk theory is constituted in an ongoing manner as part of the varied generic concerns of casual conversation. In contrast, the scientific theory is developed as a theory in the very specific genres of science. As far as context is concerned, they differ with respect to their institutional settings and in relation to the general context of culture. The folk theory is weakly framed, being constituted wherever and whenever we engage in casual conversation – in the myriad of everyday encounters from early childhood onwards. In contrast, the scientific theory is strongly framed, being developed and taught within institutions of higher learning and research.

The status of cognitive science theory

Writing from the standpoint of neuroscience, Sejnowski and Smith Churchland (1989: 302) emphasise that two levels of investigation have to be distinguished – the 'levels of analysis' and the 'levels of organisa-

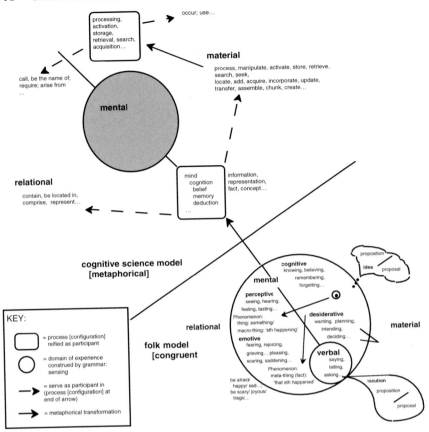

Figure 12.5 Scientific reconstrual of the mental domain

tion'. I think these two kinds of level can be interpreted in systemic functional terms as strata and ranks. Figure 12.6 represents two strata of abstraction. The 'lower' one is that of biological systems, with the neural system in focus. Within the neural system, there is a rank scale (1989: 305, Figure 8.1). The highest rank is that of the central nervous system – the whole biological organism from a neural point of view. The lowest rank is that of molecules.[4] These ranks are 'material' in nature: they can be observed (although not with discrete boundaries), measured, and so on.

What about the higher stratum of abstraction? Its status depends on one's philosophical position; in a material frame of reference, it might be entirely eliminated. In mainstream cognitive science, this stratum would be that of the mental system – often supported by the position of functionalism, originally proposed by the philospher Hilary Putnam (but see Putnam 1988 for a review of this position). According to functionalism, the relationship between mind and brain is analogous to that between software and hardware; that is, the two 'levels of analysis' would correspond to software and hardware respectively with the mind 'running on' the brain. However, my stratal interpretation of these two 'levels' constitutes an alternative way of construing the relationship. While functionalists will speak of the mind being realised by the brain, the implications are rather different if we understand this realisational relationship in semiotic rather than computational terms as a relationship holding between two strata of abstraction. One important implication is that we have to problematise the nature of the realisational relationship in the way realisation has been problematised in those linguistic traditions where the concepts of stratification and realisation play an important role (all drawing on the European structuralist tradition: Hjelmslev's glossematics, Firthian theory, systemic functional theory, stratificational theory). Thus we have to ask whether the strata of abstraction are like the strata within a denotative semiotic or like the relationship between a denotative semiotic and a connotative one (see Hjelmslev 1943 for the original principle, and see Martin 1992 for its development and application in current semiotic theory); we have to ask whether the strata stand in a natural or a conventional relationship to one another – whether the relationship is a natural one like that between semantics and lexico-grammar or a conventional one like that between content (semantics, lexico-grammar) and expression (phonology, graphology or sign); we have to ask whether the strata are based on the same fundamental intra-stratal principles of organisation (as they are in language) or on different ones; we have to ask whether and how the ranks within the lower stratum relate to those of the higher one. Questions such as these have not tended to be asked in mainstream cognitive science; but they are precisely the types of question that have been raised by a number of neuroscientists (cf. Sejnowski and Smith Churchland 1989: 303–4; Edelman 1992, in particular his critical postscript *Mind without biology*).

If we assume that there is a higher stratum of abstraction, would this then necessarily be that of the mental system as assumed in mainstream cognitive science? I don't think so. There is a semiotic alternative to the mentalist/cognitivist position: instead of construing this higher stratum of organisation in the terms of mainstream cognitive science, we can explore it in social–semiotic terms. Instead of modelling the higher stratum as a mental system, we model it as a social–semiotic system, with language as the prototypical human semiotic. A social–semiotic system is a system by which we make meanings; and unlike a 'mental system' it is an inherently stratified system (cf. Halliday 1995b). Language is stratified into content [meaning realised in wording] realised in expression (sounding, writing or sign, in a sign language). At the highest stratum we construe our experience into meaning; at the lowest stratum we operate with patterns of expression that are realised in our bodily

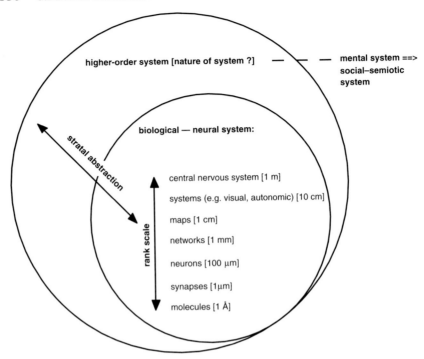

Figure 12.6 Stratal abstraction and rank scale

potential as articulatory movements, etc. If we adopt this perspective on the higher stratum of abstraction in Figure 12.6, the metaphor of 'knowledge' is replaced by that of 'meaning': see Halliday and Matthiessen (in press); for the characterisation of meaning in relation to the conscious, see Halliday (1992: 20–1).

What is the significance to this shift in perspective? I'll briefly list some points in relation to language relevant to our exploration of the position adopted by cognitive science.

(i) As a stratified system, language is inherently 'embodied' (cf. Varela *et al.* 1991): the expression stratum is realised in the human bodily potential; but the content strata are not confined to the mind as a container. In current thinking, the inter-stratal relation of realisation is a 'dialogic' one: patterns at a higher stratum are expressed by patterns at a lower one; but the lower patterns actively construe the high-order patterns (cf. Lemke's 1984 notion of meta-redundancy; see also Halliday 1992; Martin 1992: 496).

(ii) With this conception of stratification and realisation, we can begin to see that language and the brain must have evolved together in the history of the human species. According to Deacon (1992), neural processes for sequencing a choice may have facilitated the emergence of 'archaic' language in the first place; but once language had begun to evolve it began to 'drive' the evolution of the brain.

(iii) In this co-evolution of language and the brain, the nature of consciousness was critical. Edelman (1992) interprets consciousness in neural terms as a property of the brain as a system (rather than as a localised phenomenon), differentiating between primary ('being mentally aware of things in the world', 'having mental images in the present') and higher-order consciousness ('recognition by a thinking subject of his or her own acts or affections', 'a model of the personal, and of the past and future as well as the present'). He sees language as dependent on the existence of primary consciousness and suggests that language and higher-order consciousness evolved together (see Halliday 1995a for discussion).

(iv) Language is a social system. It evolved in social interaction among persons (or 'social subjects'); and it is learned in the course of social interaction. Unlike a 'mental system', it is not confined to the individual 'mind'; it is a collective resource. Unlike knowledge, meaning is inherently interactional in character: we construe the world jointly, by exchanging meanings and negotiating (see Painter 1993 for the ontogenetic perspective). Meaning is thus the foundation of inter-subjectivity (cf. Trevarthen 1987).

(v) There are different modes of meaning. We construe our experience of the world as meaning (ideational); but at the same time we also enact our social roles and relationships. These two modes are part of the same process of 'languaging'; any model we operate with is thus construed as a model of our experience, but we construe it interactively, negotiating the model as well developing it and assessing it according to consensus. Such a 'semiotic model' is thus quite a different construct from a 'mental model'.

(vi) Finally, by focusing on language, we can begin to see that the individuality constituted in the concept of 'mind' can be replaced by a more complex but more powerful conception (see Halliday and Matthiessen in press: Chapter 15, Lemke 1995 and Cranny-Francis 1995, for a discussion of socio-semiotically constructed 'polymorphous' bodies): biological individuals take on multiple roles (personalities) as social subjects (persons); and social subjects are constituted as semiotic subjects – meaners. Like a social subject, a meaner is a repertoire of roles, developed, maintained and negotiated in relation to other meaners; and a meaner is somebody who both construes and enacts.

These are some observations about the theoretical significance of the shift in perspective, from a mind-based perspective to a language-based perspective. One area where we are already beginning to see the benefits of adopting the language-based perspective is that of learning: see e.g. Halliday (1993), Hasan (1992), Painter (1993), Christie and Martin (in press) and contributions to the present volume.

CONCLUSION: A LANGUAGE-BASED CONSTRUAL

In this chapter, I have adopted a language-based approach in order to explore how the construction of 'mind' in mainstream cognitive science derives from our everyday folk model of people sensing. A language-based approach entails a focus on both text (discourse) and system: I have illustrated how the systems embodied in the models are construed in the discourses of everyday talk and in the discourses of cognitive science. Part of what I wanted to do was to explore the situation – to arrive at a fair description of how the object of study in cognitive science is construed. But I also wanted to problematise this object of study – to suggest problems with taking over 'the mind' as given domain from the folk model and then reifying this domain of conscious processes as a space populated by mental objects and constituting a separate level of representation. As the sensers of our everyday experience of processes of consciousness are effaced as part of this reification, there is also a shift from the conscious experience of persons to a subconscious, subpersonal level. I am not, of course, trying to suggest that such a level should not be posited as we attempt to understand how people 'do, sense, say and be' together with one another, but as it stands, the scientific model of the subconscious, subpersonal mind does not relate to, or even less explain, what our everyday lexico-grammar construes as processes of consciousness – our own personal experience of being sensers. A number of recent titles challenge the mainstream conception of 'mind': for example, Varela *et al.* (1991) *The Embodied Mind* and Gee (1992) *The Social Mind*. These all point to aspects that a language-based approach invites: embodiment, social interaction, semiotic constitution. But in the course of such reappraisals, it is not at all clear that 'mind' is still a useful construct – certainly not one that can be taken for granted as an object of study. If we adopt a language-based approach not only to exploring how people, both folks and scientists, have construed our experience of consciousness, but also to developing theoretical models in their own right, new productive alternatives are likely to become available.

In closing, let me quote Krishnamurti:

> And to examine our mind is to examine our common mind, because the content of our consciousness is the same as that of all human beings, who, wherever they live, go through the same process of fear, agony, torture, anxiety and endless conflict inwardly and outwardly. That's the common consciousness of mankind. So when you examine

your own consciousness, you are looking into the consciousness of man, and therefore it's not a personal, individualistic examination.

(1991: 194)

Perhaps his point can be reinterpreted in the light of the last section along the following lines. As members of the human species, we all have the same brains, so we all experience the same primary and higher-order consciousness. As members of different social and socio-semiotic systems, we construe our experiences in different ways, drawing on different lexico-grammatical resources. However, within the various groups we belong to, we construe our experiences interactively, developing nego- tiated and collective models; our language thus constitutes our collective consciousness – shared also across innumerable generations. And across various groups, there is a limit to the degree of variation in how we construe our experience of consciousness; it is likely that all languages embody folk models of conscious processes that are congruent with one another in general outlines although they may differ considerably in detail (see e.g. Viberg 1984 for a typological study of verbs of perception).

NOTES

1 This chapter draws on two earlier related presentations – Matthiessen (1993) and Halliday and Matthiessen (in press, especially Chapter 14). I am deeply indebted to M.A.K. Halliday for his input and for the joint construction of the discourse about cognitive science. I am also very grateful to David Butt for many insightful comments on cognitive science and to Jim Martin for suggesting 'meaning' as an alternative to 'thinking' to me many years ago.
2 For a general discussion of the linguistic status of commonsense models, see Halliday and Matthiessen, in press: Section 14.1.
3 This sample is from a research project into undergraduate essay writing directed by Chris Candlin and Guenter Plum at Macquarie University in collaboration with Curtin University, Edith Cowan University and University of Western Australia (see e.g. Candlin *et al.* 1996). I am indebted to them for access to their corpus.
4 Alternatively, we might re-interpret the relationship between synapses and molecules in terms of strata of abstraction – as a relationship between elements of a biological system and elements of a physical system. This type of modelling issue is very familiar from linguistics; for example, it took time within the context of American linguistics to realise that phonemes are not constituents of morphemes but rather units of phonological constituency.

REFERENCES

Candlin, C.N., G.A. Plum, R. Busbridge, M. Cayley, S. Gollin, E. Johansen, S. Spinks and V. Stuart-Smith 1996. *Becoming a psychologist: Contesting orders of discourse in academic writing.* Paper presented at Knowledge and Discourse Conference, University of Hong Kong, 18–21 June 1996.

Christie, F. and J.R. Martin (eds) in press. *Genre and Institutions: Social processes in the workplace and school.* London: Cassell.

Churchland, P. 1981. Eliminative materialism and the propositional attitudes. *The Journal of Philosophy* 78. (Reprinted in Lyons (ed.) pp. 214–40).

Cranny-Francis, A. 1995. *The Body in the Text.* Melbourne: Melbourne University Press.

D'Andrade, R. 1987. A folk model of the mind. In Holland and Quinn (eds) *Cultural Models in Language and Thought.* Cambridge: Cambridge University Press.

Deacon, T. 1992. Brain-language coevolution. In J.A. Hawkins and M. Gell-Mann (eds), *The Evolution of Human Languages.* Redwood City, CA: Addison-Wesley. (*Proceedings Volume XI*, Santa Fe Institute Studies in the Sciences of Complexity.) pp. 49–85.

Dennett, D. 1981. Three kinds of intentional psychology. In Healy (ed.), *Reduction, Time and Reality.* Cambridge: Cambridge University Press. pp. 37–61. Reprinted in Garfield (ed.) 1990. *Foundations of Cognitive Science: The essential readings.* New York: Paragon. pp. 88–110.

Edelman, G. 1992. *Bright Air, Brilliant Fire: On the matter of the mind.* New York: Basic Books.

Eggins, S. and D. Slade 1997. *Analysing Casual Conversation.* London: Cassell.

Gardner, H. 1987. *The Mind's New Science: A history of the cognitive revolution.* New York: Basic Books. (Paperback edition, with a new epilogue by the author: *Cognitive Science after 1984.*)

Garfield, J.L. (ed.) 1990. *Foundations of Cognitive Science: The essential readings.* New York: Paragon.

Gee, J.P. 1992. *The Social Mind: Language, ideology and social practice.* New York: Bergin & Garvey. (Series in language and ideology.)

Guttenplan, S. 1995. An essay on mind. In Guttenplan (ed.) *A Companion to the Philosophy of Mind.* Oxford: Blackwell. pp. 1–111.

Guttenplan, S. (ed.) 1995. *A Companion to the Philosophy of Mind.* Oxford: Blackwell.

Halliday, M.A.K. 1961. Categories of the theory of grammar. *Word* 17.3: 241–92.

Halliday, M.A.K. 1992. How do you mean? In M. Davies and L. Ravelli (eds) *Advances in Systemic Linguistics: Recent theory and practice.* London: Pinter.

Halliday, M.A.K. 1993. Towards a language-based theory of learning. *Linguistics and Education* 5.

Halliday, M.A.K. 1994. *An Introduction to Functional Grammar.* London: Edward Arnold. Second, revised edition.

Halliday, M.A.K. 1995a. On language in relation to the evolution of human consciousness. In S. Allén (ed.) *Of Thoughts and Words: Proceedings of Nobel Symposium 92 'The relation between language and mind', Stockholm 8–12 August 1994.* London: Imperial College Press; Singapore: World Scientific Publishing Co.

Halliday, M.A.K. 1995b. Computing meaning: Some reflections on past experience and present prospects. Paper presented to PACLING 95, Brisbane, April 1995.

Halliday, M.A.K. and J.R. Martin 1993. *Writing Science: Literacy and discursive power.* London: Falmer Press.

Halliday, M.A.K. and C.M.I.M. Matthiessen in press. *Construing Experience Through Meaning: A language-based approach to cognition.*

Hasan, R. 1996. *Ways of Saying: Ways of meaning*, ed. C. Cloran, D. Butt and G. Williams. London: Cassell. (Open Linguistics Series.)

Hjelmslev, L. 1943. *Omkring sprogteoriens grundlaeggelse.* Copenhagen: Akademisk

Forlag. (English translation: L. Hjelmslev 1961. *Prolegomena to a Theory of Language*. Madison, WI: University of Wisconsin Press.)

Holland, C. and N. Quinn (eds). 1987. *Cultural Models in Language and Thought*. Cambridge: Cambridge University Press.

Krishnamurti, J. 1991. *Meeting Life*. San Francisco: Harper.

Lakoff, G. and Z. Kövecses. 1987. The cognitive model of anger in American English. In C. Holland and N. Quinn (eds) *Cultural Models in Language and Thought*. Cambridge: Cambridge University Press.

Lemke, J. 1984. *Semiotics and Education*. Toronto Semiotic Circle Monographs, Working Papers and Prepublications 1984.2, Toronto: Victoria University.

Lemke, J. 1995. *Textual Politics: Discourse and social dynamics*. London: Taylor & Francis.

Levin, B. 1993. *English Verb Classes and Alternations: A preliminary investigation*. Chicago and London: The University of Chicago Press.

Lyons, W. (ed.) 1995. *Modern Philosophy of Mind: Seminal essays on the 'problem of mind'*. London: Everyman.

Martin, J.R. 1992. *English Text: System and structure*. Amsterdam: Benjamins.

Martin, J.R. in press. Beyond exchange: Appraisal systems in English. In S. Hunston and G. Thompson (eds) *Evaluation in Text*. London: Oxford University Press.

Masson, J. and S. McCarthy. 1994. *When Elephants Weep: The emotional lives of animals*. London: Vintage.

Matthiessen, C.M.I.M. 1993. The object study in cognitive science in relation to its construal and enactment in language. *Language as Cultural Dynamic. Cultural Dynamics* 6.1–2.

Matthiessen, C.M.I.M. 1995. *Lexicogrammatical Cartography: English systems*. Tokyo: International Language Sciences Publishers.

Newell, A., P.S. Rosenblom and J.E. Laird. 1989. Symbolic architectures for cognition. In Posner (ed.) *Foundations of Cognitive Science*. Cambridge, MA: MIT Press. pp. 93–133.

Painter, C. 1993. *Learning Through Language: A case study in the development of language as a resource for learning from 2 1/2 to 5 years*. PhD thesis, University of Sydney.

Place, U.T. 1956. Is consciousness a brain process? *British Journal of Psychology* 47. Reprinted in Lyons (ed.) 1995. *Modern Philosophy of Mind: Seminal essays on the 'problem of mind'*. London: Everyman.

Posner, M.I. (ed.) 1989. *Foundations of Cognitive Science*. Cambridge, MA: MIT Press.

Putnam, H. 1988. *Representation and Reality*. Cambridge, MA: MIT Press.

Pylyshyn, Z. 1980. Computation and cognition: Issues in the foundations of cognitive science. *Behaviorial and Brain Sciences* 3.1: 154–69.

Restak, R.M. 1988. *The Mind*. (The official companion volume to the landmark PBS television series.) Toronto, New York, London, Sydney, Auckland: Bantam Books.

Sejnowski, T.J. and P. Smith Churchland. 1989. Brain and cognition. In Posner (ed.) *Foundations of Cognitive Science*. Cambridge, MA: MIT Press. pp. 301–59.

Stillings, N.A. *et al.* 1987. *Cognitive Science: An introduction*. Cambridge, MA: MIT Press.

Trevarthen, C. 1987. Sharing making sense: Intersubjectivity and the making of an infant's meaning. In R. Steele and T. Threadgold (eds) *Language Topics: Essays in honour of Michael Halliday*. Volume 1. Amsterdam: Benjamins.

Varela, F., E. Thompson and E. Rosch. 1991. *The Embodied Mind: Cognitive science and human experience*. Cambridge, MA: MIT Press.

Viberg, Å. 1984. The verbs of perception: A typological study. In B. Butterworth,

B. Comrie and Ö. Dahl (eds) *Explanations for Language Universals*. New York and Amsterdam: Mouton. pp. 123–63.

von Eckardt, B. 1995. Folk psychology. In Guttenplan (ed.) *A Companion to the Philosophy of Mind*. Oxford: Blackwell. pp. 300–8.

Whorf, B.L. 1956. *Language Thought and Reality: Selected writing of Benjamin Lee Whorf*, ed. J.B. Carroll. Cambridge, MA: MIT Press.

Index